WITHDRAWN
UTSA LIBRARIES

RENEWALS 458-4574

DATE DUE

JAN 2 9			
DEC 17			
MAR 0 5 OCT 1 6 2008			
GAYLORD			PRINTED IN U.S.A.

D1025180

BODY & SOUL

ALSO BY ROBERT M. CRUNDEN

A Brief History of American Culture (1990, 1994)

American Salons: Encounters with European Modernism,
1885–1917 (1993)

Ministers of Reform: The Progressives' Achievement in American Civilization,
1889–1920 (1982)

BODY & SOUL

THE MAKING OF

AMERICAN MODERNISM

Library
University of Florida
of San Antonio

ROBERT M. CRUNDEN

BASIC
BOOKS

A MEMBER OF THE PERSEUS BOOKS GROUP

Library
University of Texas
at San Antonio

Copyright © 2000 by Robert M. Crunden

Published by Basic Books,
A Member of the Perseus Books Group

All rights reserved. Printed in the United States of America. No
part of this book may be reproduced in any manner whatsoever
without written permission except in the case of brief quotations
embodied in critical articles and reviews. For information, address
Basic Books, 10 East 53rd Street, New York, NY 10022-5299.

Library of Congress Cataloging-in-Publication Data

Crunden, Robert Morse.
Body and soul : the making of American modernism / Robert M.
Crunden.
p. cm.
Includes index.
ISBN 0-465-01484-4
1. Arts, American. 2. Arts, Modern—20th century—United States.
3. Modernism (Art)—United States. I. Title.
NX504 .C78 1999
700'.973'09041—dc21
99-048435

Book design by Victoria Kuskowski

00 01 02 03 04 / 10 9 8 7 6 5 4 3 2 1

FOR JOAN LEWIS, WITH AFFECTION

CONTENTS

INTRODUCTION

Body and Soul is the third book in my ongoing examination of American culture as it struggled to deal with the forces of modernity. In the first book, *Ministers of Reform: The Progressives' Achievement in American Civilization, 1889–1920,* I portrayed the dominant climate of progressivism, which elected three successive presidents, numerous governors, senators, and mayors, reformed public education, consolidated the professions as we now know them, granted women political equality, changed the nature of philosophy and many of the social sciences, and offered a lengthy series of specific reforms in an effort to remoralize and modernize a basically Protestant, capitalist nation. In the second, *American Salons: Encounters with European Modernism, 1885–1917,* I portrayed the progressives' most talented opponents. Modernists disliked the whole idea of a Protestant, scientific, moral culture. To them, the country seemed hopelessly provincial and philistine, offering no satisfactory training for artists, no meaningful jobs, no constructive criticism, no adequate journals, museums, schools, performing venues, and certainly no acceptable social status. They were a seemingly random grouping in terms of national origin, yet unified in their hostility to progressivism and its interminable meddling busyness, which often seemed more actively hostile to artistic creativity than any inert conservatism. Modernists were intellectuals in a philistine society, Catholics in a Protestant society, Jews in a Christian society, women in a male society, blacks in a white society, southerners in a northern society, homosexuals in a heterosexual society. They often identified with oppressed colleagues in comparable marginal circumstances: with the Irish, such as William Butler Yeats and James Joyce; with exiles from the European periphery, such as Wassily Kandinsky from Russia and Pablo Picasso from Spain; or with exotics, such as Bengali poet Rabindranath Tagore, or the performers of Japanese No theater. They sought sustenance in cultures existing as far from progressivism and its repressive Protestantism as possible: in ancient China, Greece, or India; in medieval Italy, Provence, or Japan.

Body and Soul is a sequel to both of these works but is not really comprehensible without persistent references to the progressive debacle: the flatulent rhetoric of war, which under the guise of patriotism repressed civil liberties, humiliated ethnic minorities, imposed a Red Scare, and killed soldiers to secure the profits of bankers; the viciousness of the peace, which made the very word "Versailles" synonymous with hypocrisy, vengeance, imperialism, and unpayable reparations; the absurdities of morality, which lingered in the farce of Prohibition, with its obscene profits, gangland violence, and corrupting effects on social behavior; and the impotence of politics, which granted women the right to vote only to see them support such ciphers as Warren G. Harding and Calvin Coolidge. American modernists refused to speak the language of such vacuous fanatics. They developed their own dialects, which they called "jazz," neoclassicism, dada, synchronism, the mythical method, the stream of consciousness, the physics of the fourth dimension, Gurdjieffism, or any number of other neologisms or adaptations from various European languages. Taken separately, such dialects did not seem to communicate with each other; within a few years, however, they began to fuse into the language of modernism: a language expressive of a climate of creativity hostile to politics, to traditional art, to institutional demands regardless of source, even to conventional notions of time and space.

Two major problems emerge when trying to conceptualize and organize the material during this period. The first comes from the calendar and involves the way most people think of units of time. Centuries and millenia are concepts that provide useful shorthand tools for the discussion of long blocks of time. When catastrophic events mark off somewhat uneven temporal hunks, the narrative mind often refuses to adapt, whimsically indulging in the chronological sport of, say, a "long nineteenth century" stretching from 1789 to 1914, or a "short twentieth century" from 1914 to 1991. Politics more often than not takes center stage as an organizing principle.

The "twenties" in America provide an example of this. These years have long been little more than an assumption, viewable in any textbook and all journalism. They were a jazz age, they roared, they were anxious or nervous or lost, they allowed a perilous prosperity, they focused narcissistically on the self. They began when women began voting and ended with a well-timed stock market crash. A new rubric, "the thirties," the Depression Decade, then arrived on cue. Publishers might extend dates back to 1914 to integrate the war, or forward to 1941 to contrast the two decades between the world wars. Few objected. It seemed plausible. The calendar was incapable of lying.[1]

The definitive work on the creative imagination in this context has long been Frederick J. Hoffman's *The Twenties: American Writing in the Postwar Decade* (1955, 1962). A great achievement for its time, it selected seven writers to exemplify significant emphases in cultural achievement: Ezra Pound, Ernest Hemingway, F. Scott Fitzgerald, Willa Cather, Hart Crane, T. S. Eliot, and Sinclair Lewis. In doing so, it largely severed literature from the other arts despite their constant interactions and cross-fertilizations; and it lumped the oddest people together in an arbitrary chronological space: What did Ezra Pound have even slightly in common with Sinclair Lewis? In what ways are the stories of Willa Cather like the poems of Hart Crane? And if this were really a "jazz age," why is F. Scott Fitzgerald the "musical" focus, while Louis Armstrong, Sidney Bechet, and Jelly Roll Morton have been segregated out of the index entirely?

All categories in cultural history, and the shapes and colors of all frames, remain arbitrary judgment calls. This book emphasizes the aural rather than the semantic and the visual. If the decade in fact roared, and jazz somehow was central to that roar, then perhaps music should be central to historical analysis. In approximately

1917, "jazz" crept out of the racial and linguistic underworld and began to appear in newspaper ads and common speech with an understood musical meaning. In that year the War department pressured New Orleans into closing Storyville as a patriotic moral necessity in the fight against the Central Powers, and the creative center of jazz soon moved to Chicago. The relatively integrated "black-and-tan" scene flourished there during the first jazz age, but the forces of moral reform cracked down and during 1926 and 1927 closed most of the viable musical venues. Duke Ellington opened at the Cotton Club in New York City on 4 December, 1927, heralding the city's new status as the creative center of a second jazz age. Jazz groups expanded, musicians who could read music slowly replaced those who could not, and improvisation gave way to "arrangements." Any jazz history will provide the details of this second jazz age—the swing era.

In art music, the most original creative force during the early 1920s was a European, Edgard Varèse, an émigré who organized the New Symphony Orchestra and the International Composers' Guild. He turned out six major works between 1918 and 1927, then ceased composition and returned to France in 1928. In 1926, Aaron Copland met Roger Sessions, during 1927 they made plans, and in April 1928 offered the first of the Copland-Sessions Concerts, which became the new center for innovative performance. Henry Cowell's New Music gave its first concert in Los Angeles in 1925 and in San Francisco in 1927; his *New Music Quarterly* began in 1927. After a lengthy gestation, *New Musical Resources* appeared in 1930. All these composers were Americans, a younger generation with lengthy careers ahead of them. The world of music had become definably different.

In criticism, the preeminent figure as the period began was Paul Rosenfeld. One of the circle around photographer Alfred Stieglitz, Rosenfeld was a man for whom music was central but all the arts worthy of his intelligent if mannered attention. By the late 1920s, Edmund Wilson had clearly eclipsed him. He soon had *Axel's Castle* (1931) behind him, and was on the tracks *To the Finland Station*

(1940), demonstrating political interests entirely foreign to Rosenfeld. Awe-inspiring in his literary interests, Wilson was lamentably ignorant of music, painting, ballet, architecture, and sculpture. American criticism too was changing in a definable way.

This sort of reclassification can go on indefinitely: In poetry, with the shift of William Carlos Williams to prose for a decade, or with T. S. Eliot's public pronouncement that, with *The Waste Land* (1922) behind him, he was "classicist in literature, royalist in politics, and anglo-catholic in religion." Or photography, where Paul Strand shifted from being an apolitical experimenter on chiefly American subjects to being a very political cosmopolitan forever on the move, and Charles Sheeler shifted from the cubism of country life to the realism of large-scale industrial sites. Or in painting, where an intense conservatism reasserted the importance of American places and their products. Or in prose, where all the eyes that had been admiring the progress of *Ulysses* as the signature work of the first jazz age suddenly blinked at the linguistic excesses of its successor, *Finnegans Wake*.

The second problem historians have to confront in dealing with modernism in America is the increasing chasm between what the larger public will buy and what academics in literature and the fine arts will write. While the public cannot seem to get enough biography, many academics and their less illustrious journalistic colleagues have swallowed whole a generation of postmodernist theory that has stripped art of context, killed off the artist, insisted on the instability of the art object, and "valorized" critical ingenuity. Somewhere between irrelevant detail and self-inflating generalization, history has disappeared.

It is the historian's job to steer a course between biography and theory in order to rediscover history. The twenties saw the fertilization, birth, or adolescence of many of the ideas that still dominate contemporary thought, whether today's thinkers like it or not. Building upon or rebelling against ideas from the preceding climate of Darwinism, modernists found aesthetic uses for pragmatism, replaced a biological view of the world with one adapted from physics, abandoned a world of stable values for one of relative values, shifted attention from the object to the subject, substituted Asian and African religious values for Western, hooted at conventional sexual norms, snorted at capitalism as base materialism, and tried, usually with limited success, to find a more congenial spot in which to practice art—all currently fashionable ways of thinking that today's theorists assume they have formulated for the first time.

Any solution to these two problems—too neat encapsulations of historical time and diverging popular and academic tastes—must present a text that uses accessible language to discuss issues of broad cultural significance across disciplinary borders. The most basic available terms, such as "modernist," "realist," "pragmatist," or "progressive" no longer mean the same thing from one discipline to the next, or from one time period to the next. Yet a book cannot retreat from confusion any more than a writer can both throw up his hands and write at the same time.

Modernists themselves have suggested the solution. For rarely did they apply themselves to only one discipline or idiom, confine their works' appeal to the high- or lowbrow only, or restrict their influences to those of one era only. Man Ray was a professional portrait photographer whose subjects still grace countless books. Virgil Thomson composed over one hundred and fifty musical portraits of friends, colleagues, and occasional commissioners. Gertrude Stein took the most theoretical approach to historical study, arguing that all portraits are a composite of jumbled images. Herself the author of portraits of Cézanne, Matisse, Mabel Dodge, and Picasso, who had himself already portrayed her in oil, she often theorized about the process. "After all the natural way to count is not that one and one make two but to go on counting by one and one. . . . One and one and one and one. That is the natural way to go on counting." That was the way the cinema worked. In the 1930s, she could no longer recall if she had even seen a cinema before writing her early works, but "any one is of one's period and this our period was undoubtedly the period of the cinema and series production." And out of such single images, "little by little in this way a whole portrait came into being." In her case, the portrait was of an entire family, standing in for all the country: *The Making of Americans. Body and Soul*, too, desires to create a composite portrait of the first jazz age, one that isn't rigidly and artificially confined to a certain time period or snobbily restrictive in its discussion of the arts of that age. The present book needs only the addition of one word to Stein's work: the making of modernist Americans.

Thus with Stein, the historian dwells not in the territory of the biographer, what "newspapers are full of," nor in the realms of theory, for the people and nation are real. In order to find out "by the intensity of movement that there was inside any one of them," Stein herself not only pillaged Victorian literature, she would when she could literally line up her own incoming correspondence and make a narrative out of it and her memories of its context. The historian gratefully follows her example, only desiring greater distance, detachment, and clarity. The sources of this book are chiefly letters, journals, and other contemporary primary materials. It uses works of art largely to illuminate the workings of the creative personality. It emphatically does not assume that historical or biographical detail explain any given work of art. This is history, after all, not criticism.

Any reframing of a musical period should begin with an overture. Paul Rosenfeld did not like jazz in this decade, although when he became familiar with works more sophisticated than *Livery Stable Blues* he changed his mind. No one in the Stieglitz circle cared for jazz; the experiments of Leo Ornstein were quite enough. But that is beside the point. Jazz here was a new modernist dialect, as were the Jewish photography of Stieglitz and the western feminism of Georgia O'Keeffe. Such dialects had to learn to understand each other, and by 1926 this was starting to happen. Rosenfeld is the place to start: He took the broadest view; he knew the most. You didn't have to be black to drum differently from the majority of Americans.

Part 1 tackles the assumption that most of what was important in American modernism happened abroad, chiefly in Paris. In fact that was far more true before 1917 than after. Few Americans really lingered more than a year or two in Europe, and those who did, such as Stein, Thomson, and Pound, usually found *themselves* abroad and recognized their essential Americanness. Most modernists followed the examples of Varèse and Duchamp and studied their country with freshened eyes. They came to terms with the city, including machinery, architecture, transportation systems, sounds, and the personality changes these all induced.

Part 2 synthesizes the early history of jazz as its focus shifts from New Orleans to Chicago to New York. It then shows jazz playing the role of an American folklore, an exotic artifact to be examined, much as Europeans had earlier studied gypsy music or African sculpture. Jazz became the expression of "primitivism," whites romanticizing blacks as they segregated and stole from them simultaneously. Many blacks themselves rejected both jazz and modernism and resented the condescension of white audiences and scholars even as they appreciated the attention—and the publishers. Culturally speaking, the whole concept of a "jazz age" does turn out to be a literary construct. Fitzgerald may have put the term in an early book title, but ironically enough he was also a man who disliked jazz and did not socialize with racial minorities.

Part 3 opens up the relatively new area of generational difference between modernists. Joyce, Stieglitz, Stein, Stravinsky, and others of the first generation were well established and sometimes intimidating role models to the young. Some of these trailblazers remain little known, however. Erik Satie has been emerging slowly since the 1950s, but few stress the seminal historical importance of Ferruccio Busoni, and almost everyone has missed Ernest Bloch in this context. Other important mentoring relationships, such as that between John Dos Passos and Fernand Léger, await definitive analysis. But whatever emerges, it seems clear that senses of priority and community were emerging as modernists learned to understand each other and their common tasks.

Part 4 supplied me with the most surprises. Analysts have long noticed the role that religion played in the career of T. S. Eliot, or the role that lack of one played in that of Wallace Stevens. They have also noted, sometimes with alarm, the wildly imaginative notions of William Butler Yeats. But even the most devoted and long-winded biographers have been known to neglect the role of spiritualism, the occult, hermeticism, Rosicrucianism, and the rest in writing up their subjects, or else passed by such things with scarcely a nod. This neglect misleads. The influence of G. I. Gurdjieff, P. D. Ouspensky, and A. R. Orage in America or among Americans abroad was substantial, touching many briefly, destroying promising careers, and energizing a few for life. Spiritual phrases permeated the language of nonbelievers, so that references to the fourth dimension, to the various planes of existence, and even to simple repetition take on larger contexts, often merging with ideas from the anthropology of James Frazer or the psychology of Carl Jung in ways that permanently changed the discourse of the intelligentsia.

The book ends, of course, with a coda. A second look at Malcolm Cowley and other memoirists offers chastening proof that a few artists and analysts knew what they were doing, and got many things right the first time.

OVERTURE

THE CRITICAL WORLD OF PAUL ROSENFELD

Insofar as American modernism had a representative person in the years around 1920, he was Paul Rosenfeld. By background, he was of recent immigrant stock. Both his father and his maternal grandfather had been émigrés, and as a boy in New York City Paul knew both the comforts and the insecurities of the Jewish merchant class and the German cultural values that pervaded it. Both his parents were mentally unstable and the marriage correspondingly explosive. Paul's mother, a competent pianist, died when he was ten, and life for several years thereafter was based at the Riverview Military Academy, up the Hudson River in Poughkeepsie. He found his classmates philistine and dull, and he took refuge in various religious, political, and sexual rebellions. When school was out, he lived with his maternal grandmother, the family brewery paying his expenses. His father died in 1908, leaving Paul largely on his own with a modest private income.

A bit of an aesthete, he went off to a Yale that accepted Jews, but none too warmly. He identified with Goethe's Werther, read Heine, Schiller, and Herder, found solace in the ideas of such more recent writers as Maeterlinck and Bergson, and made most of his friends in the Protestant community. He worked for the *Yale Literary Magazine*, and attended his share of football games and social events. But he found his Jewish heritage problematic. It gave him a rich background and elevated tastes in art and literature, but it also kept him out of a senior year secret society he wished to join, and made for trouble when he tried to use the Yale Club in the city. He went on to the Columbia School of Journalism, wrote several rather decadent and derivative plays, and had no clear idea of who he was or what he should do with his life.[1]

American modernism was essentially a language that outsiders developed as a way of expressing their inability to find psychologically satisfying places in the larger society. America as a whole was a Protestant business culture that had little respect for artistic or intellectual life. A young person who was Jewish, interested in music, art, and literature, and not inclined to long hours of work brewing beer had nothing attractive to look forward to. Educated, articulate, and a bit aimless, Rosenfeld was open to anything exciting that might come along in the world of the arts, and any older artist of distinction who might offer guidance and a sense of identity.

The exciting event came during a trip to Europe in 1914. For four months Rosenfeld sampled the major cities in England, Italy, Germany, and France. In June he was in London, where, apparently with no sense of what he was about to hear, he attended a concert in Bechstein Hall given by Alexander Scriabin, who was playing his own compositions. The pianist appeared overly elegant and even a bit prissy; he played with no hint of the theatrical, allowing his musical values to speak for themselves. He seemed detached from the highly original and oddly dissonant material he was presenting. Key signatures turned vague, and the major-minor system seemed to dissolve. Rosenfeld soon realized that out of an eclectic range of aesthetic and religious obsessions Scriabin had adopted a compositional system based on a "mystic chord" that he could not get out of his head, "built up in fourths from the tones c, d, e, f-sharp, b." Rosenfeld couldn't get it out of his head either, and it prepared his ears for many other varieties of modernist music.[2]

With World War I breaking out behind him, Rosenfeld returned to New York and used a Yale friendship to enter the worlds of journalism and music. Waldo Frank was a cellist who played regularly in an informal trio that also included Claire Raphael as pianist and Walter Kramer as violinist. One could scarcely ask for a better point of entry to the arts as America discovered European modernism. In addition to his cello playing, Frank was a novelist and social critic who was soon central to the short life of the *Seven Arts*, the most promising of the small journals of the arts during its brief year of life. Claire Raphael became Claire Reis upon her marriage in 1915, going on to a distinguished career to become a great organizer of both adult musical education and concerts of new music. Walter Kramer was on the staff of *Musical America*, and thus had access to the scores of controversial new compositions. Without visible effort, Rosenfeld found himself near the center of modernist activity.

He seized his opportunities. Attending performances of the trio, usually in the apartment of Raphael's mother, Rosenfeld soon met a Russian émigré pianist who was taking lessons from Bertha Tapper, Raphael's teacher. Leo Ornstein had begun giving concerts as a teenager in New York in 1911, playing both his own compositions and those of advanced Europeans. He had been back to Europe, then returned to New York, seeming like a displaced person in the face of both the war and persistent popular disapproval. By 1915, Ornstein and Rosenfeld were such close friends that Rosenfeld was hosting Ornstein at an inn in Blue Hill, Maine, a lovely summer colony near the Atlantic shore. They cheerfully plotted a series of concerts of new music, using Claire Reis as organizer. Unlike most such summer daydreams, this one came true. Ornstein gave four subscription concerts in the Reis apartment at 202 Madison Avenue in the winter and spring of 1916. About sixty people heard the works of Ornstein, Scriabin, Schoenberg, and others.

The chemistry of cultural transmission remains inexplicable to outsiders. Somehow this Russian Jewish immigrant and this aesthetically open Yale graduate communicated. Rosenfeld found Ornstein's works impressive and thought that he could see in them not only the impact of the modern city and the modern machine, but also the ways in which such contemporary elements were evocative of America as an "industrial landscape." Rosenfeld left Ornstein's first recital to walk the streets of his native city: "So strong, so promissory, New York had never lain. The modern music in the following weeks continued the establishment of communications between the interior and the exterior." Then, on an election night "amid the polytonal, polyrhythmic clangour of competing brass bands, I had a presentiment of a coming music of the American mind." He had already predicted as much in the *Seven Arts*, but now the "proof was the direct sounds of souls in contact with present existence: infinitely delicate and serious representations of the complex and nervous patterns of experience rising out of the relationship between the organism and the modern environment." He sensed the possibility of "an art of music democratically affirmative of the natural variety of attitudes and impulses." Music no longer needed a despotic grammar. "Music was free and composers were expressing hitherto voiceless groups and hitherto voiceless individual experience. The omens all but said 'YOUR TURN, AMERICA!'" He fell almost insensibly into the profession of music critic: His career would be in the writing of essays, chiefly on music, that would explain modernity to America and America to itself. In the process, Rosenfeld might find out who he was and where he really belonged.[3]

Rosenfeld mentioned Ornstein frequently in letters and essays over the next few years. To him, the pianist represented "youth," but specifically a Russian and Jewish youth. In rather odd imagery, Rosenfeld saw Ornstein as "the resurrection" of the "outlaw European Jew," a "Lazarus emerging in his grave clothes into the new world; the Jewish spirit come up into the day." His works were "full of the wailings and rockings of little old Ghetto mothers." He spoke "in accents that resemble nothing quite so much as the savage and woeful language of the Old Testament." Ornstein ignored normal musical procedures and developed a harmony different from that of any other composer. He used as many as five rhythms at a time, played off cacophonously against each other. He built in a recognizable way on the precedents of Claude Debussy, Modeste Moussorgsky, and Scriabin, but had made a music all his own. Critics and audiences may have been hostile and for awhile Ornstein seemed to subsist almost in a void. But the *Seven Arts* gave him a small platform; Rosenfeld touted his abilities, and no less a figure than the Swiss-American composer Ernest Bloch pronounced Ornstein "the single composer in America who displays positive signs of genius."[4]

In addition to his stints on the cello, Waldo Frank was a regular visitor to the 291 Gallery that Alfred Stieglitz had been running for a decade. A "restless and ruthless man, . . . with hair-tufts in his ears like a faun and a face like Socrates," Stieglitz exercised an increasingly dictatorial sway over his stable of painters. He showed their works, lectured them about eternal values, and doled out their money at whim. You were either for him or against him; Rosenfeld soon joined Frank as one of the devout, and this devotion persisted over numerous rough patches until Stieglitz died in 1946. At first "Mr. Stieglitz," in 1915 when Rosenfeld sent his earliest surviving note, Stieglitz had attained institutional status by 1918: he was "Dear 291" and remained that way. As erratic, despotic, and quarrelsome in his way as Rosenfeld's own father had been, Stieglitz soon became Rosenfeld's surrogate parent. Through him, Rosenfeld acquired an extended family chiefly of painters, enabling him to write sensible pioneering articles often based on the words of the artists themselves. Indeed, "family" as a word was not entirely metaphorical: Rosenfeld and Stieglitz were distantly related through Stieglitz's wife, and profits from breweries kept both afloat—secularized and acculturated German Jews who were making art their modern religion.[5]

While World War I did not cause anything like the disruptions to creative life in New York City that London and Paris experienced, it could wreak havoc on sensitive men who were normally unused to an atmosphere of discipline or violence. The least bellicose of men, Rosenfeld dutifully joined the army only to find himself in the insurance department; he felt infantilized, sleepy, and bored much of the time. He yearned after his new family, querying Stieglitz about the doings of Willard Huntington Wright, Waldo Frank and his wife, Margaret Naumburg, Marsden Hartley, and "Miss O'Keefe"—soon to be "Georgia," and definitely spelled "O'Keeffe." He dreamed at least once "of the Cézannes on the wall of your loft opposite the door."[6]

Demobilized, Rosenfeld devoted his time to establishing his career and settling into a cottage in nearby Westport, Connecticut. The *Seven Arts* was gone, but *Arts and Decoration*, the *New Republic*, and *Vanity Fair* were interested in his work, and the *Dial* passed through a complex reorganization that would make it Rosenfeld's chief outlet during the first half of the 1920s. In his spare time he wrote fiction, steadily if a bit futilely. He made a valiant effort to think of his creative writing as "fun" but feared he would never "be a creative writer." But he could see himself as the "sort of person who, when someone else does something good, comes to meet it." He could be a critic, "the artist's little brother." Should he do it well, his "might be a fine life." Meanwhile, Rosenfeld bought a John Marin picture from Stieglitz, professed to admire Hartley's work, and assured his friend "that you are the only great artist U.S.A. has produced since Walt Whitman, Henry Adams notwithstanding." It was the sort of behavior that won invitations to the Stieglitz summer home at Lake George.[7]

Nothing so clearly indicates the interdisciplinary quality of American modernism, and the kinship that outsider status could convey, than Rosenfeld's growing closeness to Stieglitz, O'Keeffe, and the 291 group as a whole. Frank aside, Rosenfeld was the only musically literate member of the group, a divergence of interest that seemed to concern no one. But whereas Stieglitz and the painters in his circle looked on Rosenfeld chiefly as a friend, patron, and critical cheerleader, paying no attention to the music that engaged his ears, he did pay close attention to their work. He bought it, he praised it to Stieglitz and O'Keeffe, and he wrote about it with increasing authority. As even the best in the group settled into their increasingly conservative and nationalistic styles and circled the wagons to repel any further modernist innovations, Rosenfeld grew. He grew from music into literature and painting, with occasional excursions into photography, sculpture, and dance; and he never abandoned the arts of Europe or of his contemporaries. He was not a perfect critic by any means, and his diffuse and metaphorical style can still obfuscate the hard intelligence behind his preferences. But he was the best and broadest critic of his generation.

I

Having been a part of the *Seven Arts* group, Rosenfeld seemed to belong among critics who on the whole had little appreciation for modernism. Sometimes known as "Young America," advocates of a "Beloved Community" of cultural aesthetes who believed that their work would encourage the formation of an American tradition of radical social democracy, these critics actually agreed on little beyond the religion of art that most of them practiced. Viewed together, they present not so much a spectrum from left to right as a collection of overlapping circles in orbit around the offices of the journal. Waldo Frank was about to enter a phase as an obsessive religious mystic, as expressed through unsuccessful novels and often perceptive cultural criticism. By the 1930s, he was a hard-core leftist, sympathetic to the Soviet Union abroad and collectivist experiments at home. Randolph Bourne focused most of his energies on educational experiments, passionately advocating the reforms of John Dewey. When Dewey supported American entry into World War I, Bourne broke savagely with him, criticized the pragmatism to which he was so indebted, and provoked the closing of the journal with his antiwar articles. Van Wyck Brooks had written several brief books that analyzed the aridity of the American past, the unfortunate disjunction between "highbrow" and "lowbrow" cultures, and the need to use the precedents of John Ruskin, William Morris, and the British Fabians to build an aesthetically sympathetic socialism as a basis for a nourishing American culture. In such a grouping, individualism was in constant tension with collectivism, aestheticism with pragmatism, European values with American ones, elite impulses with democratic ones.[8]

Paul Rosenfeld sympathized with certain aspects of his colleagues' obsessions: All felt themselves to be unwelcome men—the phrase taken from Frank's 1917 novel, *The Unwelcome Man*—in a culture dominated by capitalist and philistine values. All doubted that they could make acceptable livings doing the kind of journalism they wished to write. All now seem politically ineffectual, regardless of their frequent invocations of socialism. All wished to work in America, rather than in Paris or elsewhere in Europe, and tended to scorn the exile mentality. But these came close to exhausting the points of resemblance. None, Frank included, had much to say about modernist music, which was Rosenfeld's primary concern. Bourne died before his peculiar perspective could mature after the war, but Frank was such an egotist that he soon parted from most of his friends, including his wife, and showed little interest in anything more innovative than the work of Sherwood Anderson. Brooks rapidly lost interest in contemporary literature and openly loathed modernist writing. By 1926, the Beloved Community of Young America was a shambles, its effects visible chiefly in the work of such occasional new recruits as Lewis Mumford.

Rosenfeld lived near Brooks and kept in touch with Frank for awhile through the communications of the Stieglitz circle, but essentially he went his own way. Given his peculiar abilities and the few journals that were open to him, he focused on the music scene. As his reputation solidified, he thought of himself—at least when writing to Stieglitz—as a critic who was preparing "to 'photograph' musical America." By 1920 he had his eye on the newly reorganized *Dial*, and hoped "to do a musical chronicle" for it. With much rethinking and rephrasing, *Musical Chronicle 1917–1923* (1923) became the title of the resulting book. To a remarkable extent, it and its companion volume, *Musical Portraits* (1920), fulfilled his stated goal: "But there must be a criticism that is life-giving, and that is what I should like to learn to make." Unfortunately editors and readers didn't always agree, and he ran into particular trouble with *Vanity Fair*. "That insect [Frank] Crowninshield" only wanted pieces that were brief and superficial. Rosenfeld refused to compromise much, but admitted that he heard "on all sides that I am writing incomprehensibly; and the funny thing is," he mused to Stieglitz, "I feel that only in a few recent things have I gotten any where near the essence of the subject. One ends by wondering who is crazy."[9]

During this early phase of his career, Rosenfeld studied a narrow range of musical achievement, in part because of the need to write about concerts as they came chiefly to the New York City area. Concert taste in the early 1920s was neither broad nor sophisticated, and neither phonograph records nor radio broadcasts were factors of importance in educating public taste. Consequently, although Rosenfeld might allude to Mozart or Weber in writing on opera, and even go back to Palestrina when he had to, he in fact had little of significance to say before the work of Richard Wagner. Rearranged into something like a linear account, however, his work became a remarkably sensitive history of the end of romanticism and the rise of modernism.

Rosenfeld was ambivalent about the operas of Wagner. On the one hand, they were "the sign and symbol of the nineteenth century," bringing to ultimate form the "old conceptions of tonality" that the works of Mozart and Weber best embodied. Young persons of Rosenfeld's generation "were born Wagnerians." "For he was not only in the atmosphere, not only immanent in the lives led about us. His figure was vivid before us." But, on the other hand, he was as much a god in twilight as any character in *Die Götterdämmerung.* "Wagner's music is the century's paean of material triumph . . . forever seeking to form images of grandeur and empire." As autochthonous as the writings of their American admirer Walt Whitman, they were necessarily infected by many of the false values of their day. After Wagner, the world needed new departures whether it knew it or not.

Speaking technically, which he usually disliked doing, Rosenfeld explained that Wagner "discarded the old major-minor system" that had long been dominant in Europe. Most continental music had originally been for voice, and "the octave and the fifth, the bases of the system, are, of course, to be found only in the human voice." The "C-major scale and its twenty-three dependents" were based on these intervals. By use of a chromatic scale, Wagner eliminated "the monarchy of the C-major scale," especially in *Tristan und Isolde* and *Parsifal*. Critics who objected to the shattered precedents after each Wagner premiere were thus correct. They had presumably heard, figuratively speaking, "faintly piping in the distance, the pentatonic scales of Moussorgsky and Debussy, the scales of Scriabine and Strawinsky and Ornstein, the barbarous, exotic and African scales of the future, the one hundred and thirteen scales of which Busoni speaks." Today the rules are gone, as are the harmonies and consonances. "Siegfried has broken them along with Wotan's spear."[10]

The first major figure in Rosenfeld's modernist chronology was Modeste Moussorgsky. Writing chiefly of *Boris Godounow* and *Khovanchtchina* (to adopt his spellings), Rosenfeld always stressed the "marvelous originality of his art." Self-taught, indifferent to musical theory, "Moussorgsky composed as though he had been born into a world in which there was no musical tradition." Yet he did so with an acute sense of the Russian soil and all the centuries that had gone into producing one of the distinctive cultures of modern Europe. Rimsky-Korsakov and other editors might prettify the works and correct what looked like errors, but to Rosenfeld they were "castrators." Examined closely, Moussorgsky's music "has the grandeur of an essentially religious act," combining as it does the old and the new, the high and the low, the sacred and profane. "In Moussorgsky, music has given the new world its priest."[11]

In this essay, Rosenfeld noted that "Moussorgsky may have influenced Debussy artistically." Given the state of musicology at the time, this may have been an intuitive guess—Debussy certainly knew and admired Moussorgsky's work—although other composers, many writers, and some painters probably exercised greater influence. But Rosenfeld then moved quickly on to the far more complex reality of the way cultural history so often works. "Debussy's work," he said sensibly, "made for the recognition and popularization of Moussorgsky's." Debussy's early tone poems and

Pelléas et Mélisande were "the delicate and classical and voluptuous and aristocratic expression of the same consciousness of which Moussorgsky's is the severe, stark, barbaric; the caress as opposed to the pinch." In essence, Rosenfeld seemed to be saying, modernists were speaking dialects of the same tongue, and learning Debussy's language made it easier to understand Moussorgsky's: "once 'Pelléas' produced, the assumption of 'Boris' was inevitable."

Debussy was the recognizable father of modernity in Western music—his "music is our own, . . . proper to us, in our day, as is no other, and might stand before all time our symbol." Any truly great pioneer in any art seems unlike any other, and Debussy qualified: "He established a style irrefragably, made musical impressionism as legitimate a thing as any of the great styles." Rosenfeld emphasized the fragmentary quality of the compositions. "His style is an image of this our pointillistically feeling era." Structurally, it "is a fabric of exquisite and poignant moments, each full and complete in itself. His wholes exist entirely in their parts, in their atoms. . . . No chord, no theme, is subordinate." Harmonies became ends in themselves, appearing and dissolving as if having no boundaries, like bubbles in water.[12]

Before the arrival of Igor Stravinsky in Paris, Debussy reigned supreme over the avant-garde, breaking trail for Maurice Ravel and Erik Satie. Although an accomplished creative force, Ravel was not startlingly original. Satie, far less effective as a composer, was rather more original. Taking such innovations as the use of consecutive ninths and certain church modes from Debussy, Satie innovated chiefly by bringing in destructive ideas from popular culture. "The bladder he wielded struck double blows always, one to the theory of program music, the other to the practice of its votaries." Loving the idea of carrying a notion to extremes, he was in essence a nihilist, finding "perfect meaninglessness" in one composition after another. He mocked, he burlesqued, but he could not transcend his massive skepticism to create large-scale works of his own—something Ravel did repeatedly. The joking clearly amused Rosenfeld, but as a critic he preferred *Socrate*, Satie in a spare, serious, untypical mood.[13]

After Satie, truly creative work in Paris slackened. With Satie as their father, and poet Jean Cocteau as their advocate, Les Six seized the available headline space. The Group of Six were in reality three moderately gifted experimenters (Darius Milhaud, Francis Poulenc, and Arthur Honegger) and three who quietly sank from view (Germaine Tailleferre, Georges Auric, and Louis Durey). Writing in 1921, Rosenfeld found that the group as a whole had "authenticity" but little that was technically new. Often "simply diatonic," stuck in C-major, they sounded almost eighteenth century; at other times, "they are to be found playing two diatonic figures in totally unrelated keys contrapuntally off against each other." They loved taking clear, strong, and conventional melodies into a "meshwork of acid, piercing polyphony. But later, like prodigals, they return, and bask in the innocent sunshine of Mozart."

At this time in his life, Rosenfeld was no friend of popular culture. He noted the influences of jazz, the borrowings from military band music, the presence of black dance tunes from both North and South America, and the persistent presence of machines: "the canned and absurdly inhumanized expressions of gramophones, automatic pianos, orchestrelles, and steam-calliopes." The performing groups were small, the duration of the works brief, and such was all to the good. At times, making "the sign of the thumb and nose" was appropriate. But he was clearly squirming. "This music is at once charming and ill-mannered, gay and bitter, simple and scurrilous. There is much wit in it . . . and not a little sarcasm." He dismissed a good deal of it as being "watery, savorless, stale," in large part because it was not true enough to modernism. It quit before achieving originality.[14]

Even though French modernist music seemed to be in decline by the early 1920s, Paris remained central, largely through the presence of Igor Stravinsky. Here was a case of musical cousins meeting in adulthood: Stravinsky had studied with Rimsky-

Korsakov in Russia, the same man who had been the editor of Moussorgsky. Rosenfeld was a great if discriminating admirer of Stravinsky, pointing out that even given Rimsky-Korsakov's reputation as a master orchestrator, Stravinsky had in fact been a more adept handler of the Russian folk materials that both had inherited, and his orchestrations were better. In addition to this technical skill, Stravinsky was the modernist who introduced "the rhythms of machinery" into music. "Through him, music has become again cubical, lapidary, massive, mechanistic. Scintillation is gone out of it." As of 1920, his greatest achievement was *Le Sacre du printemps*, followed by *Petrushka*. In both he "makes the machine represent his own person." Rosenfeld remained less enamored of postwar work. After a performance of the *Concertino* by the Flonzaley Quartet, he wrote testily that the music was "a drab, rasping, tired shuffle and breakdown." It was "not so much part of a reaction from the musical past as it is a reaction from the war and the peace." Rosenfeld was mad at the audience for hissing, but he seemed at times to sympathize with the impulse. Nevertheless, Stravinsky remained for him the most important musical modernist, a role he was soon playing for young American composers.[15]

Rosenfeld made a commendable effort to discuss music elsewhere in Europe. Some of it he heard there, or studied if he could obtain the score. Usually, he had to wait for rare New York performances. He wrote in detail about Karol Szymanowski, the leading Polish innovator, and of such Italians as Alfredo Casella, Ildebrando Pizzetti, and Gian Francesco Malipiero, all names still moderately familiar to connoisseurs. But in the European modernist world, only Vienna challenged Paris as a center of importance, and only Arnold Schoenberg was worthy of as much detailed analysis as Stravinsky.

Even a half-century after his death, Schoenberg remains problematic for scholars, performers, and audiences. Rosenfeld handled him gingerly, as if he were an exotic parrot likely to bite if stroked. Rosenfeld began his first extended treatment of Schoenberg by labeling him "the great troubling presence of modern music, . . . for with him, with the famous cruel five orchestral pieces and the nine piano pieces, we seem to be entering the arctic zone of musical art." Adjectives, similes, and comparisons came forth in their usual profusion as he made clear his frustrations: When Stravinsky or Ornstein abandoned tonality, Rosenfeld felt "a certain sense of liberation." But he found Schoenberg baffling in his "wilful ugliness" and "geometric cruelty and coldness." The works struck him as displaying "form without significance," and were thus "head-music of the most unpromising sort." Such works as the *Five Orchestral Pieces* were neither the music of the past nor the music of the future. "They belong rather more to the sort of music that has no more relation with yesteryear than it has with this or next. They belong to the sort that never has youth and vigor, is old the moment it is produced."

Two years later, in a survey of new German music, Rosenfeld returned to Schoenberg. Referring now to both the *Five Orchestral Pieces* and *Pierrot lunaire,* he seemed obsessed by such words as "concentrated" and "compressed." But whereas these words could go either way, to a positive or a negative view, they seemed to want to do both simultaneously. The music remained head music, more impressive in the score than in the concert hall, but now Rosenfeld was trying, with palpable exertion, to view the experiments in a favorable light. The friend and even houseguest of Alfred Stieglitz and Georgia O'Keeffe, the flatterer of several of the artists of the 291 circle, he gave himself away when he wrote: "So intense is the denseness of the harmony; so intense the density of the color, that the paintings of Georgia O'Keeffe, with their terrific concentrations, their acid-sweet opposition of warms to warms, of scarlet to the violet-red of burning alcohol, seem the one form of expression to which this music can properly be compared." The remark had to be a compliment, not that either Stieglitz or O'Keeffe would have known the difference. Sure enough, by the last section of the survey: "There is no living German whose music we want more to hear than Schoenberg's; . . . the greater portion of them grow upon one."[16]

At the start of his critical career, Rosenfeld focused on European composers; he had little alternative. America had produced few classical composers of any note, and he did not care for their work. Charles Ives eventually surfaced as the most creative figure, but as of 1920 he was unknown and unheard, an insurance man in poor health who had few personal contacts with the younger generation of musicians until Henry Cowell and a few others began a sustained campaign to win him an audience. Edward MacDowell and Charles Martin Loeffler were patently derivative of European precedents; Charles Tomlinson Griffes died before attaining creative maturity. Certain academic composers occasionally turned out competent work, such as Horatio Parker's opera *Mona*, but to a critic of discernment the American prospect did not seem bright.[17]

Under the circumstances, Rosenfeld turned eagerly to Europeans who brought tradition and training with them when they came to America. Leo Ornstein was chronologically the first among these; he and Rosenfeld became good friends before America entered the war, and the critic regularly printed encouraging notices about the composer. But to Rosenfeld's great sadness, Ornstein did not seem to be fulfilling his promise. As early as February 1922, in reviewing Ornstein's sonata for two pianos, Rosenfeld noted tactfully that the brilliant early years were over and a new and less innovative adulthood underway. He still held great hopes for his friend, placing him in a long tradition from Chopin through Scriabin, but rather brutally noticed "a suspicion of a plebian flatfootedness, enough of a want of aristocratic distinction of line . . . to trouble even Leo Ornstein's most fervent enthusiasts." Privately, the relationship slowly petered out. Rosenfeld occasionally corresponded with his Russian friend, and they had a pleasant visit in 1923. But Ornstein never developed further. He was incapable of appreciating the work of such promising Americans as Roger Sessions, his own work disappeared from the concert halls, and he made a life for himself as a teacher rather than as a composer.[18]

As Ornstein disappeared from the creative horizon, Ernest Bloch took his place in Rosenfeld's pantheon of promising modernists. Fond of theories about the Orient and the Occident and their differing creative environments, Rosenfeld pounced on the Swiss Jew who fused the two. Out of place in Switzerland, Belgium, and France, Bloch was a Wandering Jew, "homeless" everywhere and not just in America. Rosenfeld sometimes went out of his way to say unpleasant things about Jews who attempted to assimilate into Christian culture, such as Mendelssohn and Mahler; he wanted his Jews to be proud and assertive in expressing their heritage. Just as Ornstein had been an unmistakable Russian Jew, so Bloch was a Swiss Jew, and neither was less an American for having emigrated. At times the logic of the argument approached the extreme: that somehow all really talented Jews were modernists at heart.

Bloch had tried to assimilate, musically speaking. He had composed a traditional symphony and even a Shakespearean opera—*Macbeth*, not *The Merchant of Venice*. But he soon discovered that Brussels and Paris were closed at the top to Jews, no matter how talented or assimilated, and the discovery led to the religious assertiveness of the *Three Jewish Poems*, *Israel*, and *Schelomo*. Here was a Semitic modernism, its themes often having "the subtle, far-flung, monotonous line of the synagogic chants," occasionally approximating "curiously to the inflections of the Hebrew tongue," or utilizing "terrible consecutive fourths and fifths," the impetuous rhythms being "savage and frenetic in their emphasis." Yet by composing with such skill, Bloch transcended his cultural origins: "He most surely is not" a "Jewish composer," Rosenfeld continued. "His art succeeds to that of Moussorgsky and Debussy quite as much as does that of Stravinsky and Ravel." He had only "to say yea to his own heredity before his genius could appear."[19]

In person, Bloch proved as impressive as his best works. In 1922, Rosenfeld attended a "Bloch afternoon" that recalled the occasion in 1920 when he had prepared the review that appeared in *Musical Portraits*. The experience was "marvellous," he wrote Stieglitz, "even more so perhaps than that first morning two years ago, though that was a top-notcher." He felt "something electrically leaping about. There was just Man." Everyone in the room felt "richer for the exchange. Bloch is immense, surcharged with truth, looking for the truth." And yet even with so impressive a figure and body of work, doubts began to creep in. Rosenfeld was irremediably prejudiced against the neoclassicism of the 1920s, which even his beloved Stravinsky exploited, and when Bloch burst forth unexpectedly with his *Concerto Grosso,* Rosenfeld reconsidered. The work was obviously not Jewish and was modernist; he found it "an excellent sign of the times, the humanistic, archaistic little work of a composer of romantic propensities," "noteworthy among its brothers for uniformity of coloring, popularity and homeliness of material, and archaism of form." That word "archaism" kept breaking in, implicitly denigrating a major achievement that still commands attention. It had to be Jewish but wasn't, and Rosenfeld grumbled that "the idiom is never arrestingly fresh. The counterpoint is amateurish too." Alas, however, Bloch soon did seem to be in decline, much like Ornstein. His work of the later 1920s and early 1930s, whether secular like *America* or Jewish like the *Sacred Service,* seemed a betrayal of promise. Bloch later recovered for a remarkable old age, but for Rosenfeld he was history.[20]

What proved ultimately of more importance, however, was the role Bloch took on as a teacher of native modernists. In 1923 he attended a concert at Smith College where he heard a preliminary version of *The Black Maskers,* the score Roger Sessions wrote to accompany a drama of 1908 by Leonid Andreyev. The story wallowed in decadent symbolism as it analyzed the disintegration of a man's soul, but the music had clearly transcended its sources of inspiration. Bloch arrived at Rosenfeld's house afterwards "in a state of tremendous excitement," declaring Sessions "a great genius, and the event the most important in American music," Rosenfeld wrote Stieglitz. "Bloch saw the score, but he had no idea how good it was until he heard it. On second hearing, it impressed him fifty times as much again." Rosenfeld wrote immediately to Sessions, and the composer happily agreed to come to Westport to play his work for the most perceptive critic in the country. He came in September and Rosenfeld was soon following his career in print.[21]

With Ornstein, Bloch, and Sessions, Rosenfeld had personal relationships that were so formative that they shaped the very words he wrote in criticism. He repeated Bloch's assessment of Sessions's first success almost verbatim, for example, in *Port of New York*. But with his third great immigrant enthusiasm, this was not the case. Edgard Varèse was slow to make his mark in New York, but when he did Rosenfeld was impressed.

The most illuminating essay that Rosenfeld wrote on Varèse is probably the one that focuses on *Intégrales* (1926) in a sustained comparison of that work to Schoenberg's *Serenade*, after a concert in which the International Composers' Guild performed both. "It was delicate lacework sound against brute shrilling jagged music," he wrote. "It was the latest ghostly flowering of the romantic tradition against a polyphony not of lines, but of metallic cubical volumes." He saw immediately that to move from the Schoenberg to the Varèse work was "like passing from the I-ness to the it-ness of things," from a postromantic individualism to a truly modern sense of objectivity and detachment. Varèse stemmed from Europe too, and showed as well a comparable "tendency to seize upon life in terms of the monstrous and the elemental." But Varèse had turned to the modern city for inspiration. He "never initiated the sounds of the city in his works, as he is frequently supposed to have done." Rather, he created a new polyphony in which he builds his music "vertically, moves more to solid masses of sound, and is very rigorously held in them. Even the climaxes do not break the cubism of form." With this music America finally said good-bye to the hegemony of Germany and found a form that was democratic and suited for the culture of the New World.[22]

Despite the freshness of his criticism and the frequency of his publication, Rosenfeld did not feel himself to be either happy or successful. Editors from Frank Crowninshield at *Vanity Fair* to Marianne Moore at the *Dial* questioned, reshaped, cut, or refused many of his efforts, even as they pressured him to stick to musical criticism and not to follow his broadening interests into painting, literature, and other arts. Like many of the Stieglitz circle, he was also shifting in a basic way from a focus on European works to a focus on American ones. "I know it is significant that the artists in whom I am most interested to-day are Amurkans," he wrote Stieglitz. They "seem like young men with the possibilities of careers while the Europeans seem pretty well cut out and defined."[23]

He wrote increasingly as if under great stress, and often projected his unhappiness onto New York both as a city and as a cultural scene. "The city is more than futile. There is less than nothing doing, as far as I or anyone with whom I have spoken can see." He felt that he and his fellow citizens "always seem to go deeper in a sort of Hades." He feared that "the world is breaking down, and there doesn't seem to be much of anything coming up." Europe seemed "really finished" to him: "This is certainly the time for the glacial age to redescend—wouldn't find much worth saving." Still, at least America retained a sense of possibility. "I still believe the fight against provincialism in America is the crucial one. We do all sorts of stupid things" in this country "because we have no respect for ourselves as Americans. I am sick and tired of foreign reputations and France-worship." He retained a sense of humor, but it wasn't easy. "The world is full of disintegration, or I have dyspepsia, I don't know which. Both, probably," he grumbled late in 1923. Meanwhile, he felt "homeless" and thought it "a homeless age."[24]

II

All things considered, Rosenfeld was correct to stress classical music as the art with the most modernist ferment; the choice was not solely a matter of personal capabilities. The most obvious competitor was poetry, not a subject of great concern to anyone in the Stieglitz circle. Jazz was coming up fast, but Rosenfeld had little interest in popular culture in the early 1920s. Instead he turned to painting and prose writing, although his musical interests never died and he would have published far more in the field if editors had been more supportive.

The bulk of Rosenfeld's best criticism of painting is included in *Port of New York* (1924). Four modernists of the 291 group especially attracted his attention. The one with whom he had the most intense relationship was Marsden Hartley. Rosenfeld's initial reaction to Hartley's paintings was strongly positive, and he delighted in creating a verbal penumbra about a work of art that appealed to him. After viewing one unnamed painting at Daniel's gallery in 1920, for example, he described it to Stieglitz as "a sort of plant with El Greco shadows, and looks like Marsden on the cross waiting for Djuna Barnes to drive the last nail." A few days later, Hartley himself dropped by with three canvases from a recent trip to New Mexico, although only one seemed complete. Rosenfeld's feelings were "violently discordant. I feel mixed wonder and loathing; wonder for the art, loathing for something I sense in it." He was full of admiration, knew the one unnamed painting that he had commissioned to be "superb and unique," but was not sure whether he could "manage to live with it. It is really a charnel-house; a bestial and over-refined appetite without pity, without love, without joy, without hope." Evelyn Scott had nicknamed Hartley "the monk of fear," and Rosenfeld dreaded the thought of having the work in his home. He had promised five hundred dollars for it, and Hartley needed the money.

Personal relationships continued amiable in spite of private doubts, and during the summer of 1921, Hartley showed Rosenfeld around London. When the time came for the sustained piece that appeared in 1924, Rosenfeld was as evenhanded as he could be. Although he felt the painter had not "immersed himself sufficiently deeply in his material," nor "been able to lose himself in his 'object,'" he nevertheless could begin his final paragraph: "Marvelous Hartley! There can be made no scrutiny of this body of work which cannot be summed up in this exclamation!" Still, he continued to be "uneasy" about both the article and the work, and assured Stieglitz that on second thought "the faults of Hartley don't seem to me as important, even though he had flat-looking periods in my eyes now and then."[25]

Hartley was rarely an exuberant companion, but he was positively sunny compared to Arthur Dove. Dove was a charming man who had run into a bad patch that was becoming lifelong. The victim of a bad marriage, acute poverty, and a style of painting that excited few purchasers, Dove lived for much of this period with a companion, Helen Torr, usually referred to as "Reds," on boats that he tied up near Manhattan or on the North Shore of Long Island, in Huntington Bay. Dove tried to make a living as an illustrator, and only had a limited amount of either spare time or space in which to paint seriously. But he and Reds were friendly with Stieglitz and O'Keeffe and others in the 291 circle such as Rosenfeld. The critic genuinely admired Dove's work and long contemplated an evaluative article on it, but delayed the writing because the editors he spoke to about it were not encouraging. He also admitted to a certain bewilderment. He confessed to Stieglitz in the summer of 1923, "Dove is a difficult problem for me for the reason that I have not a sufficient knowledge of his work, and also, that some of it seems slightly muffled to me, whether through his fault or my own I do not know." Their meetings proved fruitful, however, and Rosenfeld gradually came to understand what the painter was trying to accomplish. "I do indeed like Dove; he's like a whiff of something delicious—you can't very long perceive a sensation as subtle as that, but then you get it again, and it's quite thrilling," he continued to Stieglitz. "He spoke more articulately than I ever heard him, perhaps for the reason that I brought along a clue to what he had to say."[26]

In the resulting article, Rosenfeld rightly placed Dove directly into the nature that was clearly the inspiration for much of his art: "There is not a pastel or drawing or painting of Dove's that does not communicate some love and direct sensuous feeling of the earth." His compositions were "built up of abstract shapes that suggest the body's semi-consciousness of itself: of intestine-like shapes, shapes of fern-foetuses in May, animal udder-forms, forms

in nature which doubtlessly had a fascination for the mind unafraid of its own body." He then went on, presumably with the
tacit approval of all involved, to draw an illuminating parallel: "For
Dove is very directly the man in painting, precisely as Georgia
O'Keeffe is the female." Like Dove, O'Keeffe has the world
"within herself. Its elements are felt by her in terms of her own
person." But as a woman, the world she renders has "the sense of
woman's flesh in martyrdom, or in state of highness and glorifica-
tion through flooding unhemmed spirit." As a man, "Dove feels
otherwise." "He does not feel the world within himself. He feels
himself present out in its proper elements." Objects did not "bring
him consciousness of his own person." Instead, they made him
"lose it in the discovery of the qualities and identities of the object. The center of life comes to exist for him outside himself, in
the thing, tree or lamp or woman, opposite him." Dove, in short,
"has moved himself out into the subject."[27]

Rosenfeld had just as much trouble interesting editors in
O'Keeffe's work. Even as the words poured forth, as if to defy arbitrary limits, *Vanity Fair* was willing to accept a mere thousand
words; only special pleading got this doubled, but even so, Rosenfeld repeatedly voiced his frustrations. In the final version, he repeated his stress on sexual determinism, seeing in her work "an
American girl's utter belief . . . in womanhood." He had convinced
himself that "no man could feel as Georgia O'Keeffe and utter
himself in precisely such curves and colors." She rendered "in her
picture of things her body's subconscious knowledge of itself.
What men have always wanted to know, and women to hide, this
girl sets forth." He then took off into his own interdisciplinary
ozone layer and professed to see parallels between her work and
the "polyharmonies of Stravinsky and Ornstein," and proclaimed:
"It is as though O'Keeffe felt as great a width between minor sec-
onds as Leo Ornstein does."[28]

The fourth painter to attract extended attention was John
Marin. Rosenfeld bought a Marin work in 1919 that he found
"magnificent. It is almost too splendid for my room," he told

Stieglitz. He apparently had little or no personal contact with the painter, although he did note Marin's growing fame in a 1923 letter. In print, he placed the artist in the tradition of James McNeill Whistler, and clearly did not much admire the results. By 1915, the modernist Marin was beginning to emerge, and he was soon the great purveyor of the way the eye perceived movement. He gave his viewers "his impressions of three-dimensional movements of objects caught by the swiftly traveling eye. Because of this perception he stands among the great realistic discoverers."[29]

III

Rosenfeld had been writing fiction since his college days and continued to do so throughout the 1920s. He had only limited success and published only a small portion of the result. But the time expended was not wasted, for it helped shape his insights into the work of friends, and then of other writers, usually modernists. Such insight cut both ways, however, since it enabled him to see flaws in such work and thus to endanger relationships that meant a great deal to him.

The most persistent case was that of his college friend and musical buddy, Waldo Frank. Frank thought of himself as a profound novelist and turned out work steadily in the years after the war. But he had no more a novelistic gift than Rosenfeld had; he was at his best as a cultural critic. His wide reading in European psychological thinkers, and his obsession with mystical religious visions, vitiated what talent he had. He was also egotistical and humorless, filling his letters even to such close friends as Stieglitz with whining complaints about the lack of response to his work. He feared that such friends as Rosenfeld would turn on him, meaning that they would not assess his work or his wisdom at the unrealistic level he preferred. As far as Rosenfeld was concerned, he was right to worry.[30]

Rosenfeld often mentioned Frank and his wife, educational reformer Margaret Naumburg, in his letters. Margy, as he called her,

was the possessor of a mind cluttered with "the debris of intellec-
tualizations, Montisorrizations, Jungizations, Alexanderizations,"
and so on, and thus fully as contentious as her husband. Waldo
worried him more, however, for he was a close friend of long-
standing and common experience. Rosenfeld brooded about him
and his work, feeling obligated to write reviews yet skeptical in his
judgments. He procrastinated. "My mind is still chaotic with
Waldo. I haven't found my way out yet, although I am beginning
to hope," he wrote Stieglitz in the fall of 1920. "I am very sorry
things will become strained between us—I am very fond of him,
and want very much to see him. It is very bitter that I have to
speak my mind. And yet, anything else would be intolerable." A
few days later, he spent "a good, full day with them. I broke the
news of my review to Waldo by telling him we were enjoying the
last days of our friendship, in a joking manner." To give credit
where it was sometimes due, Frank responded well and "seemed
relieved that I was to do a review. I think that he feels anything is
better than being treated flippantly."[31]

Despite such mutual assurances, the friends drifted apart.
Rosenfeld estimated that only twenty minutes separated their
homes, but by 1922 they weren't making the trip. He decided in
that year that "the key to Waldo" was that he was "half the business man, and half the artist, and neither can develop himself
purely." Things festered into the late fall, when several chance
meetings, in which "matters have been thrashed out at great heat
at all times," cleared some of "the secretion of poison" out of the
air. But Frank kept writing and Rosenfeld kept reviewing, and in
the summer of 1923 the cycle was beginning again. By then
Rosenfeld was getting calloused. "I feel perfectly free to say almost anything. That is the reward, I suppose, of many things
which have happened." Brave words, for his private opinions remained far more contemptuous than anything he published. He
found several of the stories in *City Block* (1922) to be "dreadfully
bad. I was shocked." He told Stieglitz, "There is a vicious sentimentality in Waldo—and such ignorance of life!" And he con-

fessed: "I really hate these stories—I find them false." He did not find *Holiday* (1923) much better.[32]

With their mutual friend Sherwood Anderson, things seemed more promising. In a famous early notice in the *Seven Arts*, entitled "Emerging Greatness," Frank had greeted *Windy McPherson's Son* (1916) as a way out of a painful dilemma for American writers. Prior to Anderson, artists tended to fall into extremes: "Those who gained an almost unbelievable purity of expression by the very violence of their self-isolation, and those who, plunging into the American maëlstrom, were submerged in it, lost their vision altogether, and gave forth a gross chronicle and a blind cult of the American Fact." You could imitate either Henry James or Theodore Dreiser. Anderson escaped. In his pictures of small-town Ohio, "he suggests at last a presentation of life shot through with the searching color of truth, which is a signal for a native culture."[33]

Anderson had assumed the role of father figure to Young America in the years before America entered the war. He was the advertising man who had repressed his talent to make money for his family only to suffer a nervous breakdown under the strain. He had written his way out, with the stories in *Winesburg, Ohio* his great achievement to date, as they detailed in brilliant fragments the boredom and repression of American life. Beset by financial and marital problems, Anderson would appear and disappear in the world of 291. He was devoted to Stieglitz and O'Keeffe, friendly to Frank and Rosenfeld, and appeared eager to write critical articles on photography as well as fiction. In the summer of 1922, he arrived out of the West to visit Rosenfeld, full of new writing projects. "He has taken a small apartment, *secretly*, and is looking forward to the winter, the music, you, having occasional dinners with me, etc.," Rosenfeld wrote Stieglitz. "He is also giving up writing advertising, and counts on keeping himself an[d] his children on his writing." Anderson was having real trouble focusing on photography, however, and was abandoning his idea of writing a piece on Stieglitz's protégé, Paul Strand. "He has something against poor Paul, but what it is I cannot make out, and think it purely phantastical." He was at the same time full of praise for Marsden Hartley, whom he thought "the first American painter of the day."[34]

Anderson did not seem fully functional that fall. Rosenfeld at first thought him ill, and all but hanging on to his connections in the 291 circle to keep his psyche from collapsing. "He spoke very appreciatively of you in his own tones, and I was again struck by the curious manner in which you become for people not only a person but a symbol when you enter their lives," he wrote Stieglitz in mid-September. Rosenfeld himself was hardly thriving, and said he had "been about as inspired as a lamb-stew for several weeks." During the next week, Anderson worked on an article about Stieglitz, and no longer seemed unwell. Although thin, "he also looks hard and clear. He is merely going through a terrific event, and is pretty hysterical as a result of it sometimes." Anderson impressed Rosenfeld as "a queer man anyway; sometimes, he has what seems an almost compulsive need of getting at people, and until you understand, it is a little dreadful. It is like some gnarled root tortured and twisted trying to get up at the light," and unfortunately, "all sorts of bad stuff seems to drive up to the light along with the pure and vital juice." Rosenfeld feared that he was "a little dreadful talking about this man in this way. He is really infinitely pitiable, and also very wonderful."[35]

The winter proved emotionally downbeat but productive. Anderson finished his piece on Stieglitz and *A Story Teller's Story*, the most successful of his autobiographical writings, and left New York in January 1924, because he felt "shattered" by the stress of his private life. Rosenfeld buckled down to finish his essay on Anderson, and in it he dwelt as much on the man he knew as on the problematic prose he read. Rosenfeld's Anderson was a man who had suddenly discovered that "his own most special insanity, his own pariah marking," was "present everywhere." His loneliness, that he had thought "a desolation all his own," was sensed "in a million tight, apart bodies." "His boastfulness, lust, self-infatuation, his great weariness, promptings of the messianic delusion, despair," they too seemed ubiquitous.

Skeptical of the quality of some work, Rosenfeld admired *Winesburg, Ohio*. The style seemed "mature"; "even more than the subject matter," it seemed "impregnated with the inarticulate American, the man whose inner dance is as the dance of a bag of meal." Anderson was "not an intellectual critic of society" and his range was "fairly limited," but his characters were "protagonists in whom every American can feel himself." "We know ourselves in Anderson as we know ourselves in Whitman."[36]

The third prose writer in the Stieglitz circle came and went so quickly that he long remained absent from many accounts of 1920s writing. Subsequent critics have more than made up for this, for Jean Toomer profited enormously from the revolution in ethnic studies. Although he spent much of his life denying he was black, he had just enough black blood to qualify as the one black prose modernist in this decade.

Toomer was one of those artists for whom the language has a phrase: someone who can't get it together. His heritage, as he wrote in a public letter to the *Liberator* in 1922, included "seven blood mixtures: French, Dutch, Welsh, Negro, German, Jewish and Italian." He lived for years in both the white and black communities, his skin and that of most members of his family being white enough to pass. His grandfather was a well-known Louisiana politician, P. B. S. Pinchback; his mother had contracted an unwise marriage, and Toomer's father had deserted her. The boy grew up essentially under the guidance of his grandparents, and became what he always felt he was, an "orphan," when his mother died in 1909, when he was fifteen. Nothing seemed solid forever after. Toomer attended six different institutions in search of a college degree, yet never got one. He developed a habit of following fads of varying degrees of respectability: health enthusiasms of Bernarr Macfadden, the socialism of Bernard Shaw, Buddhism, and Theosophy, the religious mysticism of Georges I. Gurdjieff and P. D. Ouspensky, Quakerism, Jungian psychoanalysis, and eventually the Scientology of L. Ron Hubbard. He was also a reject of the army in the war, and of countless editors at journals and publishing houses. Indeed, his years in the 291 group now appear as his only productive ones; "happy" would be too strong a term for one so fragmented and depressed.[37]

Toomer arrived in New York City in the spring of 1919 and soon met Waldo Frank and several other writers. He read widely if miscellaneously and was soon a great fan of Sherwood Anderson. By 1922, he was writing Anderson about his admiration for *Winesburg, Ohio* and *The Triumph of the Egg*, and how they were "elements of my growing. It is hard to think of myself as maturing without them." He especially noted Anderson's "acute sense of the separateness of life," a skill that brought such psychological orphans together. Such art had for Toomer "a sort of religious function. It is a religion, a spiritualization of the immediate." The only other modern writer he publicly declared had influenced him was Waldo Frank. Small wonder that when Toomer finally met Rosenfeld, the critic thought that he talked "Waldoesquely, which means he is as yet unsure of his feelings and unable to see them clearly." He also appeared "attractive in many ways, independent, unsentimental, and strong."[38]

In 1921, Toomer served briefly as the substitute principal of the Sparta Agricultural and Industrial Institute. He had never before been in the deep South, but he took the opportunity to investigate the black roots that were a small part of his heritage. He delighted in the folk songs and spirituals and lamented what he sensed was the passing of the agricultural way of life. He stayed only two months, but could not forget what he had seen, and the sketches and poems of *Cane* (1923) began to take shape. He kept in contact with both Anderson and Frank, and in the fall of 1922 he and Frank took a second trip together. Frank wanted to see black life from inside, while Toomer wanted both to extend his personal impressions and to introduce his friend to an older generation of blacks. Since Toomer's skin had been darkening in the southern sun, they traveled at times in Jim Crow cars, and agreed that their best strategy was to "pass" as black professors.[39]

The book that resulted remains a mélange of poems, meditations, and sketches and is not a novel. It examined links between the individual and the community, between American blacks and their African heritage, and the parallels the black experience displayed with the Jewish. It looked unflinchingly at black male sexual exploitation. It evoked the importance of myth and religion. It contrasted the languages of North and South, and except for the fact that Toomer fled north rapidly each time he visited, seemed to prefer the indigenous South to the artificial North. It combined naturalism, realism, symbolism, and surrealism, something that would hardly have been permissible in a linear novel. It excited Toomer about his black heritage and made him feel black—at least until publisher Horace Liveright wanted to stress his "colored blood" in an ad.

Toomer blew up. "My racial composition and my position in the world are realities which I alone may determine," and he expected acceptance by others "on their basis," he told Liveright. I "do not expect to be told what I should consider myself to be." The business office could feature the word "Negro" in describing the book if it wished, just as Toomer himself had in *Cane,* but had no right to feature it in relation to the author. "Whatever statements I give will inevitably come from a synthetic human and art point of view, not from a racial one." Even as he was writing, something seemed to snap. He all but gave up creative work and never managed to write anything of importance again. He quarreled with Frank and apparently had an affair with Margy that contributed to the breakup of the Frank/Naumburg marriage. He began a restless search for religious solace that generated a well-documented mystical experience in 1926. His circle of literary friends rapidly shrank to three: Margy Naumburg, poet Hart Crane, and critic Gorham Munson, all of whom shared his religious passions. He denied, for the rest of his life, that he had any African ancestry. He was that new synthesis of all the races, an American. Rosenfeld gave his friend a sympathetic chapter in *Men Seen* (1925) and then scarcely a documented thought for the rest of his life.[40]

IV

By 1926, Rosenfeld's accumulated frustrations as critic were coming to a head. Tired of writing down to editors and readers, he tapered off as a critic to continue with his fiction and to plan a new yearbook of American writing. Working closely with Lewis Mumford and Alfred Kreymborg, he soon accumulated enough material for the first *American Caravan*. He then departed the East, to visit Sherwood Anderson in Virginia before heading for Santa Fe and the Southwest. One phase of his life was clearly ending, although the *Caravan* continued to spread the work of the remnants of the 291 circle. Its reception was good enough so that it continued into the mid-1930s, ceasing publication only because the Depression had made both its financing and its political detachment untenable. Rosenfeld himself felt the same pressures. His private income shrank, as did the market for his freelance work. Until his death in 1946, he lived precariously.[41]

But as critical influence went, Rosenfeld had done well indeed, his life providing not just publicity and judgment for modernist achievement, but something of a paradigmatic example of it. His sense of being unwelcome, of being abandoned in the world by parents who could cope neither with him nor even with each other, was crucial. Yet so was the relative financial security: if a spiritual orphan, he was also a well-educated and comfortable one. He shared his German-Jewish cultural roots with Stieglitz within the 291 circle and others outside it, such as Gertrude and Leo Stein. Allied to other marginalized souls, such as the homosexual Hartley or the Georgia O'Keeffe who insisted that she be treated as one of the boys, they constituted an extended family with a base in New York City, a watering hole at Lake George, and long distance refuges in the Southwest. Even those who were neither

German nor Jewish seemed to share the legacy of German-language postromanticism.

Given the inspiration of the Scriabin concert that had made such a deep impression, Rosenfeld was well prepared to interpret European musicians and their works to Americans. He stressed the achievements of Stravinsky and Schoenberg in Europe, and those of Leo Ornstein, Ernest Bloch, and Edgard Varèse in America. While they were evoking America as an "industrial landscape" and winning disciples like Roger Sessions, they were planting a first generation of securely trained American modernists. These figures took sustenance from Europe but lived at home, building the infrastructure of a secure American cultural life. As he mastered this musical scene, Rosenfeld branched out into painting and writing, giving artists in each discipline a common sense of purpose. He explained the goals of the group to a larger audience and vetted candidates for honorary admittance. Stieglitz hovered about, a paterfamilias increasingly eclipsed by his wife, but nevertheless a potent symbol.

Rosenfeld left his readers a number of lessons that helped them find their way in the welter of modernist achievements. He pointed to the city as increasingly the important focus of modern art, and to New York in particular. City life generated changes in language and conceptualization. The city was a new kind of organism that had a life of its own, a look of its own, a sound of its own, a speech of its own. It ingested or excreted people from foreign lands and rural areas. It invigorated artists yet accentuated their anomie. It permitted sexual gratification but often at the cost of great loneliness. In the long run, its publishers, museums, concert halls, and universities institutionalized modernist achievements.

The city also taught a paradoxical lesson about cosmopolitanism. It attracted not only Ornstein, Bloch, and Varèse, but also a group of painters, or antipainters, who brought dada, cubism, futurism, and other such European movements across the Atlantic. Before America entered the war, Marcel Duchamp had captivated the salon of Walter and Louise Arensberg much the way Francis

Picabia had the Stieglitz one. The years after the war sent many more, to reach a flood tide by the late 1930s. Many Americans going back to James Whistler and Henry James reversed the flow, and in the period between 1917 and 1926 at least a few modernists, Man Ray and Ernest Hemingway being perhaps the most visible, headed in the other direction. But despite this seeming openness and movement, core attitudes were in many ways closing themselves off both from Europe and from the wilder varieties of experimentation. Just as the 291 circle became more nationalistic and formally conservative, so did artists elsewhere, William Carlos Williams providing an example close to home. Much modernism would be "in the American grain," inspired more by Walt Whitman than Modeste Moussorgsky.

No one could visit the modern city without depending on the machine. You arrived on a train or in a car or on a bus. You crossed any number of bridges built by machines. You made "Manhattan transfers" on the subway before eyeing the skyscrapers or buying a mass-produced newspaper. You could observe industrial or residential slums that seemed like wastelands, the products of machines, neither the structures nor the scale of the poverty having been conceivable a century earlier. Food and sex seemed mechanized, automated, dissatisfying. People became about as varied as the ubiquitous black Model T Fords.

Human nature often responded badly to the stress involved. It sought ways out, often way out. It sampled fads from food to politics, but especially fads religious. Modernists in Europe had long been interested in Buddhism, Theosophy, pataphysics, and Satanism, often as way stations to more conventional and established faiths. Homeless orphans seemed willing to try anything, and at least a few found themselves fascists by the 1930s. Some sort of authoritarianism seemed vital in a world without obvious meaning.

Failing the attempt to find a meaningful faith, or as an adjunct to one, a modernist could escape to the Southwest. Mabel Dodge had led the way in 1918, the remnants of her New York salon occasionally joining her. D. H. Lawrence arrived from England to lend international distinction. The Southwest was a new spatial geography, the mountains, desert, and vegetation offering the greatest possible contrast to urban life. It was racially and spiritually diverse, with Native Americans offering the insights of a "primitivism" that had been appealing to European modernists for a generation by 1917. Anthropologists had long been on the scene, validating ideas of cultural relativism. Sexual experimentation was also possible, both interracial and homosexual, with Dodge once again becoming both experimenter and chronicler. Georgia O'Keeffe was the only one of the most eminent artists to join her, fight her, and in general to engage the new landscape on all levels.

What were largely absent from Rosenfeld's life and vision before 1926 were the two most important American contributions to modernism. He did not care for early jazz and popular culture generally, and had little exposure to the best of what was happening— that had long been based in the heartland, in New Orleans, Kansas City, Memphis, St. Louis, and especially for this period, Chicago. Later, after greater exposure to more gifted performers, he made amends. With film, and the new grammar of montage, fade-out, flashback, slow motion, and so on, Rosenfeld seemed uninvolved. The medium never spoke to him in any technical way. But then, everyone has quirks. He didn't want to live in Paris, either.

PART ONE

THE REDISCOVERY

OF AMERICA

ONE

EDGARD VARÈSE AND THE
SOUND OF THE CITY

When, toward the end of the 1920s, Paul Rosenfeld surveyed the American musical scene for a popular audience, he ranged swiftly over a large number of years and folk sources, but being a man of cultivated urban tastes, he preferred to dwell on art music. He personally knew, or knew of, many of those on whom he wrote. To end the book on the strongest possible note, he devoted his final chapter to Edgard Varèse. Lodged in his few pioneering works, Rosenfeld wrote, an attentive listener could discover "the greatest fullness of power and of prophecy yet come to music in America."

Like many European immigrants, Varèse had long held mythical, whimsical, and personal views about an America that existed chiefly in fantasy. Typically, as a boy he had absorbed the Leatherstocking tales of James Fenimore Cooper; untypically, as he had informed Rosenfeld, "the feeling of the prairies became associated in his mind with the sound of a piercing, bitter-high whistle," and the relationship "has persisted in his imagination, although he has never heard its actual replica anywhere in nature." But no more than other talented people do musicians create in sensible, logical, linear ways. That sound was America for Varèse: It could produce music inspired by the desert, as it eventually did, or it could more appropriately suggest something about urban life. In practice, Varèse was a totally urban animal. As his widow recalled him saying often enough, "the virtue of fresh air is very much exaggerated," and he insisted on following the wise example of birds who slept with their heads under their wings, protected from the insidious night air. His modernist language thus became the sound of the city, if in a special sense.

The easy assumption about a composer who evoked the sound of the city would be that he adapted urban sounds to instruments. Rosenfeld had the wit to hear that Varèse never did this. Instead, working with purely formal goals, he produced a musical experience that made the listener hear the city in a new way, as if common sounds were imitating the art. After one concert, Rosenfeld found the streets "full of jangly echoes. The taxi squeaking to a halt at the crossroads recalls a theme. Timbres and motives are sounded by police-whistles, bark and moan of motor-horns and fire-sirens, mooing of great sea-cows steering through harbour and river, chatter of drills in the garishly lit fifty-foot excavations." Walking the streets, you find "threatening machinery become strangely humanized and fraternal," and your mood improves. "A thousand insignificant sensations have suddenly become interesting, full of character and meaning; gathered in out of isolation and disharmony and remoteness; revealed integral parts of some homogeneous organism breathing, roaring and flowing about."

As numerous conservative critics noted in irritation, Varèse did not have conventional musical goals. He was, Rosenfeld wrote, "not so much interested in the creation of beautiful objects as in the penetration and registration of the extant." A composer who actually "philosophized in music," he was also "the poet of the tall New Yorks." He found a "fast-moving, high-pitched, nervous, excited reality surrounding us," and sensed "the vivacity and unconstraint, speed and daring of the pioneer-spirit of our best American life." This urban America was not just noise and confusion; it was rather "a new world not only of the new scientific and mathematical perspectives but of the latent, the immanent, free of prejudice and habit and dogma: the whole glittering region of the unrealized." Appropriately, the first piece he created in this cement soil was *Amériques*: a foreign name for a newly emerging modern environment. He intended the title, he recalled later, to be "symbolic of discoveries—of new worlds on earth, in the sky, or in the mind of men."[1]

I

Invalided out of the French army, Varèse had experienced a mixed welcome when he arrived in New York on 29 December, 1915. Long acquainted with Marcel Duchamp, he immediately entered something of a French cultural cocoon. He lived at the Brevoort, whose proprietors were French, and whose stationery described it as "anciennement," and located at "Coin de la 5me Avenue et de la 8me Rue." He accompanied Duchamp to the famous salon of Walter and Louise Arensberg, a home hung to the ceiling in French modernist art. One of the few who knew the composer personally, he could hear Lou Arensberg playing the work of Arnold Schönberg on the piano while the habitués played chess or satisfied their hunger while ignoring the music. Less welcome were the city itself and its inhabitants. He found it "banal" and "dirty," and them philistine, athletic types unable to converse on anything "except the question of the 'Dollar.'" He had trouble with the language, which he could not speak; and then he broke his foot when a car mounted the curb and struck him as he waited for a bus.[2]

The only significant modernist musician to emigrate to America during the war, Varèse had arrived in New York with two clear goals: to conduct music so effectively that he could earn a substantial living; and to use that money not only to support a daughter he had left behind, but also to experiment with new instruments that would in turn enable him to compose a new kind of music. His considerable European experience won him several opportunities to conduct, but as his widow noted later, "he was not a good judge of the Americans he met" and on the whole was "a failure at conciliation and compromise." He also experienced frustration when he tried to invent instruments or adapt the inventions of others. His imaginary America had contained the memorable figure of one

Thaddeus Cahill, the inventor of the "dynamophone," which reportedly could transform an electrical current into a mathematically precise number of vibrations. These in turn could determine the pitch of a sound with scientific precision and give a composer far more freedom than the conventional tempered scale. Varèse wanted to track Cahill down and encourage further experimentation, breaking away in the process from the sterile rebellions that constituted much of European musical modernism. "I dream of instruments obedient to thought," he wrote in Francis Picabia's short-lived journal *391*, "which, supported by a flowering of undreamed-of timbres, will lend themselves to any combination I choose to impose and will submit to the exigencies of my inner rhythm." Easier dreamt of than realized, for although Varèse worked seriously with the Thérémin and the Ondes Martinot over the years, he found sirens the most available producers of sound of the sort he wanted, and sirens excited both audiences and critics to unwelcome sarcasm about urban noise and compositional incompetence. Not until late in his life, with the developments of electronic sound, did Varèse come close to finding the instrument that he needed.[3]

Since a permanent conventional appointment did not materialize, Varèse decided to found his own orchestra. His first venture was the New Symphony Orchestra, which he put together in 1919. It failed ignominiously, both from organizational ineptitude and critical hostility: A performance of Béla Bartók's relatively innocuous *Deux Images*, op. 10, was found to be especially offensive. His reputation in tatters, he briefly sold pianos at Wanamaker's until mutual friends from the Arensberg circle brought him into contact with Juliana Force and her patron, Gertrude Vanderbilt Whitney. Mrs. Whitney put him on a dependable monthly stipend of two hundred dollars and offered to subsidize the International Composers' Guild (ICG), which Varèse wished to organize with harpist Carlos Salzedo. Through this organization he made his major contributions to American modernism.

The manifesto of the ICG appeared in *Musical America* for 23 July, 1921. It complained that contemporary composers had little opportunity to win a fair hearing for their works or to win even limited public approval. In other arts, a poet or a painter could present works directly through print or display. A musician could not do this: Interpreters and instruments, always quirky and fallible, intervened. Only "the most timid and anaemic" made it onstage, "leaving absolutely unheard the composers who represent the true spirit of our time." Refusing to die, the most adventurous were thus joining the ICG "to secure a fair and free presentation" of the best new work. The Guild claimed to disapprove of all "isms" and all schools, but of course it spoke for modernism—for all new experimental dialects that expressed themselves through the ear.[4]

With the intervention of Whitney and Force, American modernism found its most important outlets during the 1920s. While Paul Rosenfeld provided something of a cheering section through his well-known reviews, the painters, writers, and musicians of the Stieglitz circle, the Arensberg salon, and the Whitney Studio Club could intermingle and exchange ideas. Varèse entered the most creative phase of his life: *Amériques, Offrandes, Hyperprism, Octandre, Intégrales,* and *Arcana* followed in quick succession, all composed between 1918 and 1927, although not necessarily premiered in that order. One other important modernist American, Carl Ruggles, also received a subsidy and experienced a creative burst. No active musician remained unaware of what was happening. In the process, the composition of classical music transcended the European imitations of an Edward MacDowell and the eccentric experiments of a Charles Ives. Composers became a self-conscious group that could legitimately feel a kinship to developments in the other arts.[5]

Musically speaking, perhaps the most significant performance the ICG sponsored was that of Arnold Schönberg's *Pierrot lunaire* on 4 February, 1923, at the Klaw Theater, with Louis Gruenberg conducting. One of the seminal works of European modernism, it seemed to bring out the worst aspects of the characters of everyone involved. Schönberg himself, determined to be as difficult as anything he put onto paper, assaulted the sponsors with testy letters questioning their prejudices against German composers and their ability to exact proper performances from untested musicians. Something of a perfectionist, Gruenberg wanted an inordinate number of extensive, time-consuming rehearsals. Claire Reis, now a leading administrative force in the ICG, pushed him hard in the direction of scheduling reality and the need for the show to go on as planned. It did, and was a remarkable success in terms of its impact on a highly select audience, only to provoke yet more trouble. Reis, Gruenberg, and a number of others wanted to repeat the performance to take advantage of word-of-mouth publicity. Varèse, Salzedo, and Ruggles adamantly refused. They correctly pointed out that the policy of the Guild was to put on first performances only, and all scorned the very notion of popularity. Reis, Gruenberg, Leo Ornstein, and others thought otherwise and promptly seceded, to form the rival League of Composers (LC). Even thirty years later, Louise Varèse and Reis were still digging elbows into each other in their memoirs about the issues involved.[6]

Other issues also mattered, but not those that aging widows and bureaucrats liked to mention after World War II. Both Ruggles and Varèse were anti-Semitic. The animosity remained in an interview Varèse gave after returning to France in 1928. When asked about the influence of jazz, a subject of perennial interest to the French, he replied that jazz was not representative of American culture. It was rather "a negro product, exploited by the Jews. All of its composers from here are Jews." He was clearly referring not only to Gruenberg, but also to such Jewish students of the French composition instructor Nadia Boulanger as Aaron Copland and Marc Blitzstein, who learned in France the technical contributions that jazz had made to modernist language. Ruggles was profane on many subjects, but in one letter to Henry Cowell that has survived, he speaks of "that filthy bunch of Juilliard Jews" in a musical organization who were "cheap, without dignity, and with little or no talent," with special reference to Arthur Berger. These were apparently not isolated remarks and indicate that the anti-Semitism of Ezra Pound and T. S. Eliot was not an isolated or infrequent phenomenon among modernists in other disciplines.

With such prima donnas cultivating their prejudices and organizational ineptitudes, disintegration was not long in developing. By the 1925–26 season, the ICG was sinking deeply into debt, Varèse was not feeling well, and he and Ruggles were quarreling over the size of the orchestra that Ruggles could write for in his *Portals*. At the same time, Henry Cowell and his New Music Society were gathering strength in California and about to take over leadership of organized musical modernism in America. Varèse had for the moment explored the original ideas he had, and despite the fact that he had taken American citizenship he was determined to return to France. He and Ruggles settled their differences, but the ICG collapsed anyway, announcing its dissolution in November 1927.[7]

II

Varèse's career before he arrived in America has long been something of a mystery. In later life he grew ashamed of several of his musical ancestors and disowned his early works. What war did not destroy, he burned. "Moi, je suis l'ancêtre [I am the ancestor]," was a phrase he used about his musicological heredity. Common enough among creative people, such a wish often scatters leaves over a tangled bank of ancestors even more complex than most conventional genealogies. Varèse had a great many ancestors, some of them improbable, and all of them had consequences for his later role in American modernism.[8]

He was the offspring of an unhappy family. He hated his father, who tried to prevent his musical career and push him into engineering. Part of his heritage was Italian and for business reasons his father forced him to live in Italy, a country he disliked, in Turin, a city he regarded as culturally dead, in thrall to the past. Under such stress he became *un grand nerveux* with crippling depressions, subject to wild outbursts of temper. He once told Juliette Roche that he had long been tormented by a desire to strangle someone, "anyone, at random," and liked to show off what he called the hands of a strangler. But he also claimed that as a young adult in Vienna he had met Freud and that Freud had discovered the cause of his problem and cured him. True or merely anecdotally appropriate, the story highlighted many of the characteristics that both made him an American modernist and also the temperamentally self-destructive organizer and disorganizer of such groups as the ICG. He was always an outsider, a marginal in the opinion of Pierre Boulez, disaffected from his immediate environment, unable to communicate effectively for long with those in cultural authority. The very qualities that helped make him original also at times made him unbearable, his career problematic.[9]

Determined to make music his life, Varèse escaped to Paris. His cousin Alfred Cortot recommended the Schola Cantorum and arranged an interview with its director, Vincent d'Indy. Once admitted, Varèse soon found d'Indy a pedant only interested in producing disciples. He became friendly instead with Albert Roussel, and a passionate devotee of early, polyphonic church music under the tutelage of Charles Bourdes. After a year Varèse shifted to the Paris Conservatoire. There he worked well with Charles Widor, the great organist who taught him composition, but soon quarreled with Edgar Fauré, who "kicked me out." As impoverished as any young artist in the novels of the day, he picked up funds where he could. He modeled briefly for sculptor Auguste Rodin, only to get into a senseless argument. "He didn't know a damn thing about music," Varèse said, as if that explained the use of the vulgarism that got him tossed from that studio as well.

So he manufactured his own ancestors. In music these at first included Claude Debussy and Richard Strauss. Debussy was the more important, a personal friend. He was, Varèse recalled, "a man of great kindness, intelligence, fastidiousness and wide culture, . . . something of a sybarite and loved beautiful things and all the pleasures of the senses." He had the reputation of being "unapproachable, bearish and disagreeable," but never was with Varèse. Debussy appreciated the originality in the younger man's scores without especially liking them. "Rules do not make a work of art," he would say: "You have a right to compose what you want to, the way you want to if the music comes out and is your own." Strauss, on the other hand, seemed supreme at the time, but did not wear well. The master orchestrator of his generation, he and Varèse became acquainted in Berlin, but little came of it.[10]

Paris was far more than a musical environment. Varèse was close to several members of the group that called their house "L'Abbaye de Créteil," with reference to Rabelais and their own often libertarian attitudes toward life and art. The poet Henri-Martin Barzun and the painter Albert Gleizes later joined Varèse in New York during the war. He was always welcome at the salon of Cyprien Godebski, where every Sunday he might encounter not only Roussel, but also Maurice Ravel, Erik Satie, and Jean Cocteau. Ravel was soon experimenting with jazz rhythms and blue notes, while Satie became a great if neglected influence on American modernism. As for Cocteau, although he never made it to America in person, he traveled often enough in fantasy. Painters, poets, and musicians drew no distinctions between their arts.

Varèse had not suffered through his engineering training for nothing, and he long retained an extramusical attitude to the problems of composition. His chief technical memory of his years at the Conservatoire was the occasion when he came across "a definition of music that was the first to satisfy me completely." He took it from Hoëne Wronski, "physicist, chemist, musicologist, and philosopher of the first part of the 19th century," who defined music as "the corporealization of the intelligence that is in sounds." This was the meaning for his craft that stayed with him, for he was soon thinking of "organized sound instead of sanctified and regimented notes." As John D. Anderson has pointed out, Wronski was a mathematician who claimed to have a revelation in 1803—a combination of science and offbeat religion that will reappear often among modernists in both America and Europe. Varèse interpreted him to mean that sounds had an inherent intelligence or will independent of human perception. Sound was organic matter and could thus move freely in space.

Varèse next began "to resent the arbitrary limitations of the tempered system," doubts that were confirmed when he was reading around in the book by Hermann Ludwig Ferdinand von Helmholtz, *On the Sensations of Tone as a Physiological Basis for the Theory of Music* (1863). Varèse was especially taken with Helmholtz's experiments with sirens. He went to the *marché aux puces* to buy two small ones, and "with these I made my first experiments in what later I called spatial music. The beautiful parabolas and hyperbolas of sound the sirens gave me and the haunting quality of the tones made me aware for the first time of the wealth of music outside the narrow limits imposed by keyboard instruments." He used them to great effect in both *Amériques* and *Ionization*.[11]

The importance of this reading and thinking was more evident in retrospect than at the time. By all critical reports, Varèse's early works were not all that innovative, and his later memories more evidence of his desire to be his own ancestor than of any startling creativity. Whatever his evolving fascinations, he was not comfortable in Paris; he found the city "constipated," and by 1907 was in Berlin. The work of Hector Berlioz aside, he preferred German masterpieces to French, and soon found German composers more hospitable as well. He fell in with a talented group that included conductor Carl Muck, and the team of Richard Strauss and Hugo von Hofmannsthal, then the cutting edge of much that was new in music.

But his greatest friend turned out to be Ferruccio Busoni, a famous pianist and composer who already knew the work of the early American modernist Charles T. Griffes, and of Leo Ornstein. Busoni thus demands a closer look, for his role in these three careers was no accident. The assumptions of much musicological scholarship to the contrary notwithstanding, Busoni was the representative figure who stood at the head of a lost tradition of modernism, one that flowered in America between the world wars more luxuriantly than did the better known Austrian atonalism of Arnold Schönberg.

Something of a marginal like Varèse, Busoni too was more a Central European than a product of any single culture. His first language was German, which he had absorbed in Vienna, Leipzig, and Berlin, but he had spent much of his childhood in Trieste and Paris, and had married the daughter of a Swedish-speaking sculptor in Helsinki. He entered American cultural history in 1891, when he moved to Boston to teach at the New England Conservatory. The next year he moved to New York, where he spent two years before returning to Berlin in 1894. He later returned to America for four concert tours, all the while filling the mails with acidulous remarks on America's egalitarianism, and the bad taste he so frequently encountered.

Busoni, too, was never satisfied with teachers, role models, or traditions. He yearned instead for a universal music that transcended time and space to exist in a region where all melodies could exist at the same time. "Time," for a musician, was as crucial as "space" to a painter, and so, like Varèse, Busoni was insensibly moving toward a musical philosophy that in some ways owed more to modernist painting than to musical precedent. Just as painters in Paris experimented with cubism and its successors, Busoni was concerned with *die Allgegenwart der Zeit*. "I have almost found an explanation for the omnipresence of Time," he wrote his wife in 1911, "but I have not discovered why it is that we humans understand as a straight line from the past to the future, while it *must* be in all directions, like everything in the universe."

In 1906, Busoni completed the brief volume available in English as *Sketch for a New Esthetic of Music*, which Varèse and numerous other experimentalist composers took as the first trumpet call of a new music. Declaring that "Music was born free; and to win freedom is its destiny," he placed his emphasis from the start on a spiritual vision eerily reminiscent in its language of American transcendentalism. Sounding like a Theodore Parker informing his audiences of the distinctions between the transient and the permanent in Christianity, Busoni stressed: *"The spirit of an art-work, the measure of emotion, of humanity, that is in it—these remain unchanged in value through changing years,"* with italics his; *"the form, which these three assumed, the manner of their expression, and the flavor of the epoch which gave them birth, are transient, and age rapidly."* Demanding the freedom to experiment, which most artists wanted, he nevertheless insisted that such experiments only gave a superficial stamp of modernity to music. His music, like the music of the other modernists, aimed at *"the imitation of nature and the interpretation of human feelings."* He emphatically denied that he was advocating the "sounds" of nature—the slap at Richard Strauss perhaps adding an instrument to his orchestra—and decried the "debasement of Tone to Noise in imitating the sounds of Nature." Never precisely clear as to what he was advocating instead, he seemed to want composers to create as nature created, to behave as nature behaved: not to copy nature's results, but to function in a natural way. He seemed especially eager to dispose of, or else severely modify, the whole notion of the octave, either through the use of tripartite tones, or else an infinite range of tones.

Never much of a writer, Busoni nevertheless occasionally contributed short pieces to journals elaborating his ideas. In the most concise of his formulations, written in Chicago in January 1911 for publication in Berlin, he laid out the five possible paths that he saw for the development of modernism: 1) "The first new harmonic system rests upon chord formation according to customary scales," which he identified with Debussy; 2) "the symmetrical inversion of the harmonic order," which Bernhard Ziehn had suggested to him; 3) "keeping the voices independent of each other in polyphonic compositions," something he himself was already doing; 4) "anarchy, an arbitrary placing of intervals, next and over one another, according to mood and taste," which he said Arnold Schönberg was attempting; and 5) "the birth of a new key system which will include all the aforementioned ways." In theory, Busoni was ready to try anything.

In practice, he was never as radical as Varèse proved to be. Busoni did break down customary notions of tonality and rhythm, and he was also willing to employ dissonance whenever it suited him. He called for new instruments in music, and looked forward to the new sounds they would make, bells seeming to be a major priority. He did go quite a way toward polyphony, and experimented with new forms of notation that encompassed microtones, one-third tones, and the new scales that went along with them. By 1909 he was using a "free tonality," which he differentiated from the "atonality" of his friend Schönberg, creating polytonal effects, and even leaving out bar lines in order to have his music evoke the stream of consciousness. By common critical consent, he reached his experimentalist limit in the *Sonatina seconda*, op. 43, composed in 1912 and first played in 1913.[12]

Varèse's contacts with Busoni in Berlin had resonance for the history of musical modernism in America. For the next seven years, from 1907 to 1914, Varèse was essentially a cosmopolitan German, sampling the options available to any talented young person of that time and place. He accompanied Busoni to the first performance of *Pierrot lunaire*, and indeed the two were both outsiders, thrown together by similar characters and situations despite the difference in age and stature. Varèse especially recalled the "Florentine sarcasm" and "overpowering sense of the ridiculous" with which Busoni spoke of many of the people and events of the day. But despite his personal devotion to Busoni, and his later role as the inheritor of his ideas in an American context, Varèse was always his own person and never uncritical. Busoni, like Stravinsky after the war, advocated a classicism with which Varèse never felt comfortable, finding his friend's own compositions and tastes "orthodox." Varèse declared that "classicism, young or old, was just what I was bent on escaping." They could agree about "the strait jacket of the tempered system," yet disagree amicably about tonality: "I was through with tonality," Varèse recalled, but Busoni could never have said that, however much he might "free" it up. They also agreed that new instruments were necessary, and that machines would be among them. Their differences were essentially those between generations, when those generations have good personal relations. "It was as though his heart, loyal to the past, refused to follow his adventurous mind into so strange a future," Varèse wrote. "I owe a most tremendous debt of gratitude to this extraordinary man; . . . he crystallized my half-formed ideas, stimulated my imagination, and determined, I believe, the future development of my music."[13]

Despite spending so much time in Berlin, Varèse never severed his ties with Paris, and so was on the spot when the craze for *simultaneïsme* exploded in the pages of *Les Soirées de Paris*. Henri Bergson, the most famous philosopher in the city, had discussed "simultaneity" in *Essai sur les données immédiates de la conscience* (1889) and *Matière et Mémoire* (1896), leaning heavily as he did so on his exposure to the ideas of William James. As a person experienced the stream of consciousness, external things seemed to change, to succeed one another; but in fact they did not. External things coexisted, they were simultaneous with each other; a sentient being had somehow to keep them all in mind at once, an act of will counteracting the normal human wish to experience things one at a time. L'Abbaye de Créteil resounded with the subject, Barzun and Apollinaire speaking simultaneously at each other claiming credit for the idea when applied to poetry. Marius de Zayas told Alfred Stieglitz that it was "the last word" in the Parisian art wars, and the futurists debated its impact on painting in *Der Sturm*. Robert Delaunay promptly produced *Simultaneous Windows* and *Windows Open Simultaneously*.[14]

At this point, cubist painting complemented the ideas under discussion. The subject is easily oversimplified, but in their often-quoted book *Cubism* (1912), Albert Gleizes and Jean Metzinger saw as its essence the "moving around an object to seize it from several successive appearances, which, fused into a single image, reconstitute it in time." The resulting painting thus depicted these successive images into a simultaneous moment, freezing time and space in a manner congruent with what Bergson had had in mind. Varèse was fascinated. In the midst of the debates, always more aware of poets and painters than other musicians, he was personally friendly to Apollinaire and was accustomed to meeting him at the Delaunays' house. It all added up to an Orphist music. As Jonathan Bernard, the most thorough musicological scholar of this aspect of Varèse's music has written: "In Varèse's hands, simultaneity employed two techniques for presenting sound masses independently of one another: one, a high degree of timbral differentiation; the other, rhythmic patterns that resisted the listener's attempt to mesh them." By the time he was composing *Intégrales* in the mid-1920s, he would repeat sound elements as many as fourteen times without precisely replicating either the dynamics or the rhythms, thus achieving what he regarded as the musical equivalent of a cubist painter's movements around an object.[15]

Given all this trendy experimentalism, Varèse seems an unlikely candidate for a disciple of Richard Wagner, but as Olivia Mattis has pointed out in a remarkable insight, in a way he was. No one doubts that Wagner's influence was ubiquitous in Western Europe before World War I, but most modernists were fleeing it as fast as they could. Musicians fled it first, since they were closest to it; but in this context Varèse was more of a writer or painter. The key word here is *Gesamtkunstwerk*, the total work that unifies the arts in one all-enveloping aesthetic experience. That's what Wagner's operas were supposed to be, and while young rebels might scoff, they could not get the need for the total experience of time and space, of individual and nation, of eye and ear, out of their heads. Being jokers at heart, while simultaneously serious of course, they finally arrived at the perfect modernist solution: the circus as the total work of art for modern times. As improbable as it might seem, the circus worked perfectly. It was a self-contained world in which everything went on at once, sometimes three rings at a time. Clowns and lions and acrobats did their thing, presumably paying no attention each to the others. Masks, jokes, accidents, death-defying stunts, colors, sounds, and so on, all in a deflating yet invigorating spirit of play—just the thing to "play off" against the Wagnerian extravaganzas of their youth. The Cirque Médrano in Paris was a notorious lark for them all, from Gertrude Stein to Pablo Picasso, who indeed went together in 1911. In Schönberg's *Pierrot Lunaire* and Stravinsky's *Petrushka*, circus and clown, sane and mad, serious and comic come together, unifying composers who otherwise might seem to have little in common. Wagner would no doubt have been horrified.[16]

In this context, Varèse's connections to two of the more visible movements of modernism become relevant. Although the older he got, the more he tended to deny it, he was in fact involved with futurism over fully two decades on two continents. Through Apollinaire in Paris and Busoni in Berlin, he was familiar with the ideas that Filippo Marinetti and his associates were spreading and knew also several specific paintings, especially those of Umberto Boccioni. He was less enthusiastic about the musical innovations that were soon notorious. Balilla Pratella and Luigi Russolo were advocates of *bruiteurs,* to use the French term for what were *intonarumori* in Italian, *Geräuschtönern* in German, and noisemakers in English. In various interviews and articles, Varèse came down firmly in favor of new instruments and experiments in general, but was convinced that the futurists were making serious errors. "New instruments must be able to lend varied combinations and must not simply remind us of things heard time and time again," he told an interviewer. He refused to limit himself "to sounds that have already been heard. What I am looking for is new mechanical mediums which will lend themselves to every expression of thought and keep up with thought." He was himself headed in the direction of the Thérémin and the Ondes Martinot, and in time electronic sounds. He wanted to convey more precisely what was in his head, not what anyone could hear on the streets.[17]

Varèse also tended to play down his connections to dada, as if its anarchic tendencies did not befit his self-image. But he was close to Marcel Duchamp, Beatrice Wood, and Henri-Pierre Roché as they produced *The Blind Man* in New York and enjoyed the controversy over Duchamp's famous *Fountain,* the ready-made urinal submitted to a show. Such friends and such antics implied both a sense of humor and a sense of the aesthetic importance of everyday life, but the entire Arensberg salon was at that time also developing a serious interest in machine art, which Varèse shared. Both Francis Picabia and Duchamp produced work with a machine orientation, and the transition to a musical context was easy. Varèse had always wanted to eliminate interpretation in music: Violins and pianos separated composer and listener, and for someone committed to "organized sound" rather than beauty or tradition, machines that made consistent sounds seemed promising. In time, he was also fascinated by the machines that recorded and reproduced the sounds as well as those that generated them. Meanwhile, he indicated where his sympathies lay by possessing his own readymade, a weathervane that Duchamp had given to his wife Louise.[18]

III

The translation of Varèse's musical intentions into lay language that does not do violence to the niceties of linear development remains a daunting task. The sounds of the city could easily be noise to the uninitiated, and as befitted a man who wished to be his own ancestor, Varèse was forever obliterating the written record to rewrite his development to suit his current preoccupations. After 1927, without the structural support of the ICG, his rate of productivity declined, all but halting as he searched for instruments of sound generation that suited him. But like casual critics, he too tended to metaphor, leaving the technicalities to the graduate schools. Those metaphors all had their validity, and all evoked the city at least indirectly.

The first significant effort at self-definition came through a mask. Massimo Zanotti-Bianco was a friend as well as a journalist, and when he volunteered to explain Varèse to a larger audience in 1924, Varèse gave him accurate, evocative material to use. Zanotti began as so many were accustomed to begin, with the word "spatial." More than thirty years later, in recalling the piece, Varèse recalled the phrase, "masses in astral space" as an effective way of describing his atonal harmonies. He got the quote slightly garbled, but no matter, that much at least appears both in the original and in the memory of it.

Zanotti actually began with a discussion of rhythm and melody, and the way most musical discussions began with one or the other. He wished to go beyond these categories to have his readers "project an imaginary sound-mass into space," where they would "find that it appears as constantly changing volumes and combinations of planes, that these are animated by the rhythm, and that the substance of which they are composed is the sonority." He then suggested the possibility that a musical composition could be "a succession of geometric sound-figures," the result of "volumes and planes whose successive projections would give birth to architectures of sound whose logic would be given by the equilibrium of their sound vibrations and their forms." Such a conceptualization would merely be the logical step beyond where Busoni, who remained present but unmentioned in the essay, had left music in his essays of fifteen years earlier. It would make music independent and self-justifying.

In analyzing this "sound-geometry," Zanotti naturally stressed the percussion. "His musical body is divided into two parts: the sound-mass molded as though in space (the orchestra without the percussion); and its stimulus, its movement, its dynamics (the percussions)." The percussion section "penetrates the sound-masses, making them pulsate with a thousand varied and unexpected vibrations with an effect not unlike, in the field of vision, a ray of light striking through a crystal prism, giving it a multiple existence." Zanotti termed the results primitive at least in feeling because of the "primary, naked elements" that it involved. He thought that Varèse had managed to unify his emotional impulses with his abstract ideas. His first studies had been in mathematics, and he was now bringing geometry into music. The imagery then shifted abruptly, much like the music, and instead of geometry evoked Bergson: "his flux is continuous, and even when the play of the percussions stop one has the impression of a long syncopation." The description will do for a lay version of many Varèse works: "Sudden stops, sharply broken intensities, extremely rapid crescendi and dimenuendi give an effect of the pulsation of a very complex organism. . . . The atonal harmony, crudely coloring the sound groups, throws them into frigid relief, like great masses in astral space." And that was the phrase that stuck in the composer's mind, perhaps because it originated there. The rest of the article, and most other adjectival descriptions, were simply repetition. Varèse was the geometrician of space, and planes within space; his space was urban, and could have been Berlin, Paris, or New York. The head of the bird was under its wing listening to its internal intensities.[19]

Zanotti's passing imagery suggested the other metaphors in which Varèse habitually thought: the physics of crystallization and the architecture of stones. The discussions of crystallization apparently appeared first, possibly as a result of Varèse's long-term friendship with the architect, Charles-Édouard Jeanneret, known to history chiefly as Le Corbusier. Although the two did not actually collaborate until the composition of *Poème électronique* in the 1950s, they had long been aware of each other and in sympathy with each other's attitudes. In 1925, Jeanneret coauthored an essay, "Towards the Crystal," in which he talked about a "tendency towards the crystal" in later cubist art. Closely related to geometrical organization, crystallization was a way nature took to reveal to people "how its forms are built up by the interplay of internal and external forces. The crystal grows, and stops growing, in accordance with the theoretical forms of geometry; man takes delight in these forms because he finds in them what seems to be a confirmation for his abstract geometrical concepts." Nature could thus find common ground with the human mind because of a human need for logic and reason; the imagery supplied a need for explanation and order. Cubism thus had an organic logic, "which proceeds outward from within." Even the most austere-seeming structures of

European modernism, whether in paint, music, or architecture, partook of this biological, organic quality. Neither the cities of Le Corbusier's fertile mind, nor the compositions of Varèse's equally fertile intelligence, were as inhuman as they seemed to outsiders. Their sense of humanism simply included both buildings and cities as having organic qualities.

No less a student of Varèse than Jonathan Bernard has suggested that this essay, or conversations relating to its subject matter, lingered in Varèse's mind until he finally spoke his own version of its ideas. In interviews and essays of the 1950s, he repeatedly returned to crystallization to explain how he composed. His favorite source at that point was Nathaniel Arbiter, professor of mineralogy at Columbia University, who had defined the term this way: "The crystal is characterised by both a definite external form and a definite internal structure. The internal structure is based on the unit of crystal which is the smallest grouping of the atoms that has the order and composition of the substance. The extension of the unit into space forms the whole crystal. But in spite of the relatively limited variety of internal structures, the external forms of crystals are limitless." He then added words that Varèse said had long been effectively on his mind but that he'd never before encountered in print: "Crystal form is a *resultant* rather than a primary attribute. Crystal form is the consequence of the interaction of attractive and repulsive forces and the ordered packing of the atom." Those words, Varèse continued, suggested "better than any explanation I could give, the way my works are formed. There is an idea, the basis of an internal structure, expanded and split into different shapes or groups of sound constantly changing in shape, direction, and speed, attracted and repulsed by various forces." The form of his works would be "the consequence of this interaction. Possible musical forms are as limitless as the exterior forms of crystals." Or, as Le Corbusier might have added, the forms of the cities and of the buildings of which they consisted. In the modernist psyche, a physics of architecture was replacing the naturalistic biology that had dominated later nineteenth-century attitudes.

Varèse's works were the sounds the city produced as it functioned.[20]

Any mention of Le Corbusier almost automatically brings up the subject of architecture; this is legitimate in terms of structural imagery but stylistically misleading. Varèse in fact had long been interested in Romanesque architecture in ways that might well leave later students wondering at the complexities of creativity. The best source for his interest is an interview with Gunther Schuller, a composer and conductor with a great sympathy for modernist work. Schuller asked him about his lost early works and how they might have anticipated the works of the 1920s. Varèse replied that he would call his earlier works "more architectonic." He had been "working with blocks of sound, calculated and balanced against each other," and had been "preoccupied with volume in an architectural sense, and with projection." Schuller then asked him where such architectonic ideas might have come from, in view of the fact that such other pioneering modernists as Debussy and Stravinsky had been working along quite different lines.

Varèse replied by insisting that he had not been influenced so much by other composers as by "natural objects and physical phenomena." He had as a child been much impressed "by the qualities and character of the granite I had found in Burgundy, where I often visited my grandfather." Some of it was gray, some of it streaked with pink and yellow. "Then there was the old Romanesque architecture in that part of France." He said that he was used to playing in one of the oldest surviving churches in France, in Tournus, "one that was started in the sixth century and built in purest Romanesque style." He loved to watch the old stonecutters, "marvelling at the precision with which they worked. They didn't use cement, and every stone had to fit and balance with every other. So I was always in touch with things of stone and with this kind of pure structural architecture—without frills or unnecessary decoration." Clearly, poets were not the only modernists intent on leaving out connectives, or capable of choosing aspects of the distant and seemingly disconnected past for inspiration. Planes, crystals, blocks of stone, these were the metaphors in the mind of a musician. No wonder the music seemed difficult to access.[21]

The overall results remain controversial and difficult even to those who have made their peace with the work of Arnold Schönberg and Igor Stravinsky. But musicians and musicologists have been making Varèse into a legend, not to say a minor industry. Let Stravinsky have the last words: "Varèse's music will endure. We know this now because it has dated in the right way. The name is synonymous with a new intensity and a new concretion, and the best things in his music . . . are among the better things in contemporary music. More power to this musical Brancusi."[22]

TWO

PAUL STRAND AND THE
SIGHT OF THE CITY

In March 1917, Paul Strand submitted *Wall Street* (1915) to the Twelfth Annual Exhibition of Photography in Philadelphia, usually called the Wanamaker competition. A jury that included Alfred Stieglitz, Edward Steichen, and Arthur B. Carles awarded it first prize, singling it out from more than eleven hundred submissions. Concurrently, in New York City, the Modern Gallery showed the work of Strand, Charles Sheeler, and Morton Schamberg, thus bringing together the three most gifted of the younger generation and demonstrating that artists from Pennsylvania and New York shared a common fascination with both the city and the machines that enabled it to function. In June, *Camera Work* appeared with eleven gravures of Strand's work, eight of them dealing directly with New York City. In August, through friendships with Paul Rosenfeld and Waldo Frank, Strand placed an article in the *Seven Arts* in which, for the first time, he articulated an authentically American position on the role of photography in modernist art, tieing it as he did so to the work of Stieglitz and the 291 Gallery.

"Photography, which is the first and only important contribution thus far, of science to the arts, finds its *raison d'être*, like all media, in a complete uniqueness of means," Strand began. "This is an absolute unqualified objectivity." In the organization of this objectivity, the photographer's specific point of view became relevant, his intellect and emotions supplying "a formal conception" of the image under consideration. Earlier photographers had all made the crucial error of seeing photographs as if they were paintings, etchings, or charcoal drawings, in other words never letting this objective new machine function on its own terms. But Stieglitz had changed all that. In his most recent work, this "American in America" had evolved a "crystallization of the photographic principle, the unqualified subjugation of a machine to the single purpose of expression." Neither Stieglitz nor Strand had ever felt the least impulse to become painters; they were both "fascinated by the machine as a thing apart."[1]

Stieglitz felt an almost equal admiration for his newest disciple. Referring to a show several months earlier, he had written to a British photographer a letter that compared Strand to Alvin Langdon Coburn, the protégé of a few years earlier, who had gone to England and escaped from Stieglitz's direct influence. Strand is "without doubt the only important photographer developed in this country since Coburn," Stieglitz wrote to R. Child Bayley. By comparison, his prints were "more subtle" and had "greater lasting quality." Strand used no gumming trickery. What he saw was what you saw. "Straight all the way through, in vision, in work and in feeling. And original." Stieglitz always had trouble analyzing work he liked, resorting to vague adjectives and inexplicable decisions for or against a work of art or an artist. Strand was to be the photographic prince of the Stieglitz circle for a decade.[2]

Wall Street is a good place to start looking at the ambiguities as well as the originality of Strand's talent. The backdrop is the Morgan Bank, its tomblike windows supplying thick verticals in a gloomy series down the street. The effect is both distant and claustrophobic, for before these masses scurry buglike humans, mere undifferentiated shadows, all heading like lemmings off to the left, each casting a separate shadow in what seems to have been an early morning sun. In later interviews, Strand always insisted that he knew nothing of capitalism and had no political motivations, and on the conscious level at least no one need doubt him. Yet subconsciously, the suspicion of capitalism, of distant banks or governments or ordinary businesses, was never far from the modernist sensibility, even as such institutions sometimes paid the bills. And, of course, financiers always worked in the dark.[3]

I

Like Stieglitz and Rosenfeld, Strand had come out of a secularized Jewish environment. His grandparents had migrated from Bohemia to New York City in the 1840s; his father had Americanized their name from Stransky before Paul's birth. Circumstances were comfortable. Jacob Strand was a traveling salesman, selling French clocks and German enamelware, while his mother-in-law ran a home that seemed full of servants but devoid of male authority figures. Paul's mother Matilda wanted to become a singer, but increasing deafness limited her opportunities. She encouraged her son in his artistic aspirations, but otherwise remained a rather depressed and frustrated person with little to occupy her time. This combination of bourgeois success and blocked artistic impulse created an atmosphere in which a son could achieve a solid education and even occasional outlets for his skills, but never know much about joy, spontaneity, or wit. Early maturity did much to liberate Strand, but it could never quite overcome his humorless solemnity or his need to follow a male authority figure who seemed to understand the function of art.

In New York City, many children of the secularized Jewish bourgeoisie attended the Ethical Culture School (ECS) on 63rd and Central Park West, and Paul enrolled in 1904, shortly before his fourteenth birthday. In pursuing the goals of its famous founder, Felix Adler, Ethical Culture was essentially a rather genteel humanist religion dedicated to social betterment. In addition to the usual curriculum of languages, mathematics, and the sciences, it taught its children the sort of survival skills that Germans had long valued, from carpentry to printing. Almost by accident, the school had hired Lewis W. Hine to teach geography only to discover that his real skills lay in photography. He began to document normal school activities, and soon worked out a plan for integrating this new science into the practical course of studies. By 1906, he was in contact with Stieglitz about having the 291 Gallery put on a show at the school, an event that occurred in 1907. Both as a class and on their own, Hine's students in turn visited 291.[4]

Photography at the time was too new to have fully established boundaries or goals that would have been meaningful to a teenager. Even established figures such as Stieglitz and Steichen were still in the grip of a postromantic pictorialism that encouraged photographers to blur their focus, stylize subject matter, or use such natural devices as fog, snow, or steam to create an effect not unlike a painting. Lewis Hine was actually working on a different tack. During the 1890s, the Danish immigrant Jacob Riis had been encouraging a new type of photojournalism in the wake of his important investigations of poverty in *How the Other Half Lives* (1890), and improving technologies enabled the press to depict an increasing range of disturbing social conditions. At the same time that Hine was speaking to ECS students, he was also a photographer for the *Pittsburgh Survey,* a pioneering documentary investigation of largely immigrant and working-class life that would presumably inform politicians about the need for progressive social legislation. Already familiar with the painful scenes enacted daily at the immigration reception center on Ellis Island, Hine soon found his own evidence all but unbearable, and he left teaching for a life spent chiefly in creating a documentary basis for social reform.[5]

As a child of the bourgeoisie who knew the poor largely through the servants who attended his family, Strand assimilated only what he needed from Hine. Remaining unaware of what concerned his teacher outside of class, Strand fully absorbed Hine's published position that a photographer needed to have firm ideas about form and composition, and only with them in mind should he observe the real world with an eye for what was aesthetically satisfying. Merely making snapshots would not do. A photographer had to select, order, and compose the reality that he saw, and such an emphasis was inevitably formalist rather than reformist. Not only could the poor easily become more picturesque than pitiable; they could also become a matter of masses and shadows, of planes and angles, and not of reform legislation. Stieglitz had no more social conscience than one of the horses in his urban pictures; neither did Strand until the late 1920s. He apparently never even bothered to vote until the Depression caused a sharp reorientation in his perspective.[6]

Like so many young modernists, Strand did not know what to do when he graduated. He had no interest in university study, and a desultory year working with his father was more than enough to convince him that enamelware did not engage his imagination. He found some refuge at 291, familiarizing himself with the work of Stieglitz, Steichen, Coburn, Clarence White, and the rest of the Photo-Secession. He devoured *Camera Work*. Only in 1909 did he find a suitable substitute for Hine's classes in the Camera Club of New York, conveniently located nearby on West 68th Street. Although all but devoid of creative ideas about pictures, the club was a refuge for talented technicians eagerly mastering the complex details of processing negatives into positives, and trading the latest gossip about platinum paper or the use of prisms when attached to lenses. For fifty dollars a year, a young man could use the darkroom and other club facilities pretty much as he wished. Strand got his money's worth. He made heavy use of the library, which contained over a thousand books on both European and American photography as well as useful instruction manuals. He was soon exhibiting his work and sitting on committees that judged the work of others.

In June 1911, he spent two months touring Europe, taking a good many pictures but accomplishing little of cultural importance. He accomplished even less during a brief period of work for an insurance company. He then determined to make his way in photography, and went into business for himself selling pictures of college campuses to graduating seniors, and for five years he got by, branching out slowly from the Ivy League. By living mostly at home, he kept expenses down and earned enough to buy photographic materials. In 1915, he made an extensive trip through the Midwest, from Minnesota to Louisiana, and took a brief detour to attend exhibitions in San Francisco and San Diego. His surviving letters are all but devoid of professional detail. Yet the trip must have been something of an emotional catharsis, because when he returned to New York City, his work became significant for the first time. *Wall Street* was an early indication that something was happening.[7]

Never a man to make his own creative processes accessible in words, especially contemporary ones, Strand long posed scholars a problem. Why and how did his soft, mushy, postromantic eye become a hard, angular, cubist eye, producing work that seemed immediately distinctive then and remains so today? The most likely explanation is really an analytical guess, involving at least one predecessor and two other distinctive disciplines. Alvin Coburn had been the reigning star at 291 at the time, and for several years he had been experimenting with high vantage points that could provide new perspectives on city photography, with New York City as the subject of a major series. Although some of this work directly recalls that of his master Stieglitz, by 1909 Coburn was entering new avenues. In *The Stock Exchange* (1909), the people all but disappear in a distant blur as the sunlight stresses the relentless horizontals of the skyscrapers as they curve out of sight around the gloomy shadows of the buildings still ominously in shade, effectively squashing the diagonals of two pseudo-Greek pediments that rather plaintively recall the days when other values reigned. Sometimes, as in *The Park Row Building* (1909), steam or smoke recalled a postromantic mushiness even while the building still seemed clearly dominant; but by the time of *The House of a Thousand Windows* (1912), clear focus and plain geometry were winning, and the smoke was drifting harmlessly off to one side.

Although Coburn was saying several things in his work, one of them was that architecture had something important to communicate to modernism in America. This is an important point to make here, because architecture as a discipline contributed little to modernist discourse in America, in direct contrast to, say, the influence of the Bauhaus in Germany. But engineered structures as they appeared to viewers from heights were another matter. The sheer intimidating size, the new angles, the brutal effects of light and dark, the massing that could remind the anxious of their last nightmares, the endless sameness of bands of windows, the lack of any softening decoration—all these could help a photographer or painter express modernity. Add to these the side effects of the new technologies such as the suspension superstructures in Coburn's *Brooklyn Bridge* (1911), or the effect of shadow on parkland road construction, as in *The Octopus* (1912), and architecture sometimes seems to be present even when it isn't a conscious concern of the artist. It was a lesson that analytic cubism had already learned.[8]

As a young novitiate, Strand was especially eager to seek out and obey the father of 291. Stieglitz did not fail him. Having himself passed through several of the transitional states that were troubling Strand, he was capable of both technical and practical advice. On the technical level, he told Strand that one of his obvious problems was a soft-focused blurring; the cure was a camera with a smaller aperture to provide a sharper definition unless smoke, fog, steam, or snow blurred objects naturally. Strand soon reduced his aperture as low as f22, a firm step toward the even more demanding standards of the 1930s. On the practical side, Stieglitz deserved the major credit for introducing Strand to everything he had missed while on his own in Europe. Strand already knew the work of the synthetic cubists thanks to 291, and the telltale litter of fragmented lettering was already appearing in his work. More immediate as influences were Francis Picabia and Marcel Duchamp, whom he met late in 1915. Never an habitué of salons, even one so exciting as that of Walter and Louise Arensberg, Strand nevertheless attended enough meetings to sense the excitement in the air and to get ideas that popped up later in his mature work. His real problem, simply put, was his lack of any sense of humor or irony. No one could fully appreciate either Duchamp or Picabia without a well-nourished capacity for both. Strand was there, and he did learn, but he often missed what was going on. He lacked nuance.

The gifted children of the bourgeoisie nevertheless had to persevere, and Strand did. He joined 291 and all but abandoned the Camera Club. Stieglitz included him in the lunch bunch at the Prince George, gave him a March 1916 show, and put six of his photos into the October *Camera Work*. By then, to follow the revisionist dating of Naomi Rosenblum, he was at the height of his abstractionist creativity in such works as *Porch Shadows, Abstraction—Bowls* and *Abstraction—Cups and Orange*. Such works remain impressive. What they don't seem is French, witty, ironical, or distinctively American. They recall the work of Arthur Dove and perhaps Marsden Hartley and thus remain implicitly somehow "paintings," more urban than rural, more geometrical than organic, but still redolent of paint. They seem to have intimidated Stieglitz slightly; he was soon sharpening his aperture as low as f128 and muttering about delivering "just the straight goods."[9]

By the time of the Modern Gallery show of March 1917, which featured Schamberg and Sheeler in addition to Strand, a shift of momentous proportions was clearly underway. The focus was less on viewing architecture from a height than on viewing machinery from close up—often very close indeed. The result, especially in the famous *Wheel Organization* (1917), plugged Strand into what became one of the most fruitful of all modernist traditions—not cubism, not collage, but that aspect of New York Dada that a native could enjoy even when he had trouble laughing, let alone mocking—the readymade. Marcel Duchamp had started it all with his chocolate grinders, bicycle wheels, shovels, and the rest, first pictured, then the objects themselves unpictured, and soon the famous *Fountain*, the urinal doomed to exist only as a Stieglitz photo—a whole artistic tradition framed, as it were, like a criminal, cut off from society by the artistic police.

By thus rolling in, one wheel at a time, machinery came to replace architecture as the proper sign of the city. Even more than Duchamp and Picabia, in the American context Morton Schamberg and Charles Sheeler deserved first and second place. Schamberg was the most original, a savage irony enabling him to speak to the mind in ways usually only available to Frenchman like Duchamp. But he died young and little documented, his spirit so untypical of America that it rarely receives its due. Sheeler went on to become the Flaubert of industrial machinery, content to depict what was happening without feeling, called upon to comment at length on the moral implications of it all. Strand deserves a high place; several of his pictures are of permanent value. But he went on to other subjects, other styles, and other emphases, abandoning this original vein before it was truly played out.

The coexistence of the architectural photos and the machine ones also has an historical importance all but independent of aesthetic value. The first was a logical development from romanticism, almost measurable by the lessening degree of smoke, steam, and generic weather; as the air cleared, the focus sharpened, and precisionism could burst forth with a wail. The second was a logical development from realism, from a sustained attention to the minute details of common life, to the point of fragmentation, decontextualization, and disorientation. Modernism grew from both traditions, but they often mixed like oil and water, separating if left alone. For a brief time, Strand managed; over the long haul, he did not. He needed a Stieglitz to show the way; but such dependence also breeds resentment and rebellion. The process took about a decade.

II

American entry into World War I finished off an all-but-moribund 291. Both attendance and enthusiasm had long been declining at the gallery, and *Camera Work* had fewer subscribers for each succeeding issue. In July 1917, with Strand helping, Stieglitz cleaned out what remained and hunkered down at his Lake George summer retreat. Publicly silent, he was privately pro-German, as was Marsden Hartley. Too much German culture lay behind 291 and modernism generally for them to do more than acquiesce in the decisions of a government that had long been Anglophile. Young and vulnerable to the draft, Strand wanted none of that either, and when he personalized public affairs in his letters to Stieglitz, he knew he had a sympathetic ear. "It seems impossible to get away from the war—it touches everybody now and everyone finds the same resentment and lack of enthusiasm." Stieglitz agreed. For him the war had only brought to the fore all the weaknesses he had tried for years to overcome through his teachings.[10]

As befitted artists with narcissistic attitudes, both Stieglitz and Strand spent the next year pursuing private goals—actually, for a while, the same private goal, the intimate attentions of an exotically distant Georgia O'Keeffe. When she first met Strand, O'Keeffe was immediately impressed. She "fell for him," she informed her friend Anita Pollitzer in June 1917. "He showed me lots and lots of prints—photographs—And I almost lost my mind over them—Photographs that are as queer in shapes as Picasso drawings." She looked forward to the spread of his works about to appear in *Camera Work*, meanwhile hoping someday to introduce him to her friend: "He is great." The language is capable of several interpretations, from schoolgirl crush to detached professional admiration to mature infatuation, to name three that all seem operative. Strand, in turn, was seriously smitten. Both behaved as if they were doing something underhanded, as indeed they were. Despite his legal marriage, Stieglitz had long been estranged from his wife, and he and O'Keeffe had apparently consummated their relationship at some point in May. Everyone was playing with fire.[11]

Romance aside, most of O'Keeffe's passion for Strand was genuinely professional. "I've been wanting to tell you again and again how much I liked your work," she told him shortly after their first meeting. "I believe I've been looking at things and seeing them as I thought you might photograph them—Isn't that funny—making Strand photographs for myself in my head." She thanked him for helping her to see, "or should I say feel new colors." Three weeks later he sent her a set of prints, and she thanked him in a warm letter that clearly complimented both photographs and photographer, "the man I found in the big prints." Subsequent letters were teasing and provocative by turns, first poking fun at the man, then all but hugging him while she stared raptly at the works: "Why you know I love it all. The prints you sent me—the bowls—the shadows." She was clearly referring to his cubist photos.[12]

As letter after letter poured out of Canyon, Texas, the story became even more complicated; O'Keeffe was also emotionally involved with a local man, probably a former student, and a woman, Leah Harris, who eventually confessed her homosexuality. As passion and ink ebbed and flowed, O'Keeffe's health gave way, and so did the patience of both Stieglitz and Strand. Dreading tuberculosis, influenza, and female independence, the older lover dispatched the younger into the West to rescue the mutual favorite. Strand found her looking surprisingly robust in San Antonio, near where she had been staying with Harris. Happy, she showed little interest in returning to New York City, and was in fact planning to return to teach in Canyon. Strand entered into intricately detailed negotiations to get her to change her plans. He finally succeeded, taking a mass of photographs as he went, including numerous nudes of Harris. On 9 June, Strand presented O'Keeffe to her mentor in New York City, and one of the most remarkable monuments of American modernism could soon begin: Stieglitz's obsessive studies of O'Keeffe's body. As this project developed, their careers did so as well.[13]

While the family romance went on without him, Strand finally had to face the draft. He pulled every string he could to be assigned to a unit that would use him as a photographer rather than ignore his skills, but the best the army could do was to permit him to work as an X-ray technician at the famous Mayo Clinic in Rochester, Minnesota. The assignment turned out to be a blessing in disguise. After surviving extensive training he even informed his parents that he felt that art and science were closely related, and that he felt comfort in the impersonality of medical procedures. However, he made it clear that ideas were of more interest to him than restoring the sick to health. It was a shrewd bit of self-analysis, not only for an artist more interested in form than reform, but also for a frustrated lover trying subtextually to retain the body of work O'Keeffe had produced when he couldn't have the actual body of O'Keeffe herself. Strand was in fact simply maturing. Getting away from 291 and New York was good for him. He got to meet a broad range of people face-to-face without the intervention of a lens and took a number of photographs of doctors in the operating room. He sharpened his sense of the connections between art and science, and confirmed his preference for objectivity as a goal, rather than expression.[14]

For about four years, from about 1919 until well into 1923, Strand's work presents an oddly confusing aspect. On the one hand, he took a significant number of nudes of both sexes, but chiefly of Rebecca (Beck) Salsbury, whom he subsequently married. On the other, he continued to take pioneering shots of the city and of the machinery that made it possible, including the cameras that themselves made the photographs possible. The split actually derived from his two closest artistic friendships and the havoc they sometimes wrought on the neat categories of art history. Stieglitz was dwelling with fascination on the minute details of O'Keeffe's anatomy, fragmenting her in a paracubist mode. Ever the disciple, Strand promptly did the same to Beck, with marked lack of success. But a new member of the Stieglitz circle, Charles Sheeler, was coming at the city and its machinery from an entirely different direction, one that complemented and reinforced the more genuinely cubist tendencies that had already appeared in Strand's work by 1917.

Strand had missed New York during his military service and he returned at the first opportunity, in early August 1919. With 291 closed and Stieglitz at Lake George with O'Keeffe, he returned to his old haunt, the Camera Club, and looked around for paying jobs. Despite audible clucks from the countryside, he had little choice but to turn commercial. In a move that capitalized on both his prewar experiences shooting college campuses and on his wartime medical training, he developed a modest income making records of sporting events—horse racing, football, tennis, polo—where the study of motion appeared to be the artistic core of the assignments. He also became the regular photographer of official events at Princeton.

The growing closeness with Sheeler encouraged Strand to broaden his exposure to modernism in several ways. He became somewhat more involved with members of the Arensberg salon; long an admirer of Marcel Duchamp, he immersed himself in synthetic cubism and had at least a distant familiarity with New York Dada. Bits of lettering, pieces of buildings, parts of machines all appeared in his work on urban subjects, but he lacked the antic spirit that made Dada briefly appealing. He did, however, take these interests in unusual directions, doing some of his most enduring work on the rocky beach at Port Lorne, Nova Scotia, nature rather than the machine supplying formal structure. "I couldn't have done the rocks without having seen Braque, Picasso, Brancusi," he told Calvin Tomkins years later.[15]

The most famous fruit of this period was the experimental, seven-minute documentary film that Strand and Sheeler collaborated on during the first nine months or so of 1920. Sheeler had become fascinated with a French motion picture camera, the Debrie, which was light in weight and versatile by comparison to what photographers were used to. He wanted to use his new toy and *Manhatta* (sometimes *Mannahatta*) was the result. Some frames directly recalled Strand's earlier stills of the city; others evoked Stieglitz's puffing railway trains or passenger boats. The title alluded to Whitman, and a faintly romantic yearning seemed to underlie much of the material. Yet at the same time, modern architecture dictated angles and shadows, machines seized the eye, the cubist collage became cinematic, and the point of view became multiple. Several very high and low vantage points demonstrated a modernist vocabulary of self-reflexivity, and one or both artists were clearly familiar with Sergei Eisenstein's innovations in the use of montage.[16]

In several pictures of the years that immediately followed the film, most famously in the *Double Akeley* (1922) and the *Akeley Motion Picture Camera* (1923), Strand carried his precisionist analysis of the machine to its limits, a precisely focused fragmented view of the machine that enabled him to present fragmented views, precisely focused. He was not obsessive about it, presenting lathes, gears, drilling machines, and the rest along with the usual portraits and shots of nature. Morton Schamberg, rather than Duchamp or Picabia, was the most probable originator of such attitudes, with Sheeler the close collaborator of each man until a mildly critical review in 1923 alienated Stieglitz and he in effect read Sheeler out of his circle. Strand, still loyal, fell into line, although the issue seemed trivial enough. At heart, the problem was probably commercial more than artistic. Sheeler needed to make money and to Stieglitz such commercial intent was too tacky to tolerate. It also meant a certain independence from his authority. Stieglitz never liked to see anyone in his flock straying away from his lunch table.[17]

If 1923 was the artistic high point of Strand's precisionism, the Seven Americans show of "159 Paintings Photographs & Things Recent & Never Before Publicly Shown by Arthur G. Dove, Marsden Hartley, John Marin, Charles Demuth, Paul Strand, Georgia O'Keeffe, Alfred Stieglitz," which opened at the Anderson Galleries on 9 March, 1925, placed his mature work in a sometimes unexpected context. Not just fealty to Stieglitz was on display— these were seven Americans. An umbilical cord to Europe had been severed while all in attendance had been lost in admiration of the American-born baby.

Stieglitz had quietly given up on Europe. What inspiration Americans had needed, they had acquired. Three months earlier, Stieglitz had informed Sherwood Anderson of his intentions: "Only work that has never been shown anywhere to be in the exhibition. The stuff is ready—I think it would be the show of the year—and *American*." Two days after the opening, he noted with pride that even Paul Rosenfeld had seemed so bewildered on his first trip through that "he didn't know the difference between heads & tails." Stieglitz was all but on his knees: The gallery was breathing "a Cathedral feeling." As the show was ending he changed metaphors. He bragged about the number of visitors, and came close to bragging about the lack of sales. It was, after all, "a spiritual fight. . . . I feel I am still needed on the bridge. Never more needed."[18]

Well, yes and no. The fact was that Stieglitz was not all that needed anymore. Other galleries could easily take up the slack, and had they proved lacking in coterie enthusiasm they might have made up for it by actually selling a few works without subjecting prospective buyers to an inquisitorial monologue on the state of their souls. Strand was silently displeased by the way Stieglitz had hung his own work in a much more prominent position than his disciples', and gradually came to realize that he was uncomfortable in the still symbolist, still quasi-religious air. The bad taste that lingered from the tangled personal relationships did not help. O'Keeffe had cooled in her enthusiasm for Strand, for Stieglitz's family, and then for her husband himself, as he did more than just flirt with a string of women from Beck Strand to Dorothy Norman. Stieglitz grew increasingly querulous, picking fights with almost everyone close to him. The Strands grew apart and in time divorced. And while Stieglitz eyed the landscape for a series of "Equivalents," which he overvalued, Strand persisted in a sharp and sometimes gritty realism. He eventually began a lifelong series of travels, documenting the far corners of the world. Stieglitz saw it coming. "I realize more and more how far removed I am from what Strand is doing," he wrote their mutual friend Herbert Seligman in 1927.[19]

Much of that was still in the future. Appropriately enough, the Strands had wanted to spend their 1926 holidays in Europe, but had changed their plans. Although both were in ill health, they headed into the West, instead, for Colorado and New Mexico, lugging a large amount of photographic equipment. Strand's preferred style of fragmented close-ups proved as capable as his urban work of conveying an uncompromising and even embattled sense of nature. They proceeded to Taos, and an adobe cottage on the estate of Mabel Dodge Luhan. She proved as domineering as Stieglitz but far less of a professional threat. As the salons merged along with East and West, Strand grew out of any real need for either one. He was soon as free to be Paul Strand as he ever would be; his days as a self-conscious modernist were over.

THREE

JOHN DOS PASSOS AND THE
PHYSIOLOGY OF THE CITY

When America entered World War I, John Dos Passos was a bundle of energetic contradictions. He had supported President Woodrow Wilson during the 1916 elections because he had kept the country out of war. When the president abruptly reversed course and demanded that his supporters and all true patriots change their attitudes as he had, Dos Passos was outraged. The notion of conscription, which would compel young men like himself to fight and die for a cause they might not support, especially outraged him. Yet, aesthete and aspiring author that he was, Dos Passos was also fascinated by the sheer spectacle of a world at war. For months he remained in a tangle of mixed metaphors trying to decide what response he should make. He thought of his life as "a mad scramble after a bus that I never can catch, and juggling oranges all the while," as he wrote to his friend Walter Rumsey Marvin; yet only a few sentences later he confessed that "there is something frightfully paralyzing to me in the war." Everything he did seemed "so cheap and futile," in the face of the destruction of so much of the civilization he revered.

April 1917 was thus a cruel month of decisions. "I am trying to do three things at once—enlist in the mosquito fleet, be an ambulance attendant, and get a job as an interpreter or something of the sort with the first expeditionary force. Out of those something *must* pan out." He had changed none of his views on conscription or the military, he hastened to add. "I merely want to see a little of the war personally—and, then too, I rather believe that the deeper we Americans go into it, the harder we put our shoulders to the wheel and our breasts to the bayonets, the sooner the butchery will stop." As a painter, a man of the eye, he wanted to see for himself the most stirring events then occurring; as a writer, he wanted to take notes; as a political radical, he wanted his activity to be in some way a part of the larger good.[1]

As a Harvard graduate, Dos Passos was almost automatically interested in and qualified for the Norton-Harjes Ambulance Corps. Under the leadership of Richard Norton, the son of Harvard art historian Charles Eliot Norton, the corps had been operating on the western front since October, 1914, as a privately funded group of volunteers. Beginning officially as the American Volunteer Motor-Ambulance Corps, in 1916 it combined with the Morgan-Harjes section of volunteers which Henry Herman Harjes had organized on the spot. Harjes was the son of the chief European representative of the House of Morgan banking organization, a group that was both emotionally and financially devoted to the Allied cause. Usually referred to as "Norton-Harjes" from that point on, the unit's official name was "Sections Sanitaires de la Croix Rouge Américane aux Armées Françaises," and as the name implied, it was an affiliate of the American Red Cross. At the time Dos Passos joined, the organization was distinct from a much larger group, the American Ambulance Field Service, which was based in Paris and had no Harvard connections.[2]

Dos Passos began his career in the ambulance service on 20 June, 1917, when he boarded the *Chicago* for Europe. He found the war he expected. "The war is utter damn nonsense—a vast cancer fed by lies and self-seeking malignity on the part of those who don't do the fighting," he wrote Marvin two months later. "Of all the things in this world a government is the thing least worth fighting for." He invariably assimilated the point of view of the soldier in the trenches. "None of the poor devils whose mangled dirty bodies I take to the hospital in my ambulance really give a damn about any of the aims of this ridiculous affair—They fight because they are too cowardly & too unimaginative not to see which way they ought to turn their guns." He had spent his first night working under a poison gas attack that lasted five hours, and the danger continued to be a daily reality. "Our ambulance . . . is simply peppered with *holes*—how the old bus holds together is more than I can make out." Ever the aesthete taking his own pulse, however, he confessed to enjoying the reality of the experience. "It's queer how much happier I am here in the midst of it than in America, where the air was stinking with lies & hypocritical patriotic gibber."[3]

Dos Passos barely realized it at the time, but by belonging to the Norton-Harjes he was participating in the end of Victorian America. Like his famous father, Richard Norton believed in the redemptive value of Art, implicitly capitalized. Always critical of the commercial orientation of the democratic majority of Americans, he had faith that an elite with a proper grounding in Art could so guide the masses as to usher in a culture in which a gentleman could take pride and find comfort. His hospital unit consisted largely of Ivy Leaguers, with the Harvard presence the most conspicuous. The men not only volunteered, they paid their own way; some even brought their own ambulances, which family or business connections had donated. They were, in Norton's customary phrase, "gentlemen volunteers" whose chief motive was "service" to the highest of Victorian ideals. Even as the war groaned on and the quality of recruits declined, Norton persisted as best he could. His brother Eliot was raising funds in America ample enough to pay all the expenses of every volunteer, but Richard persisted; "We don't want the rough-neck type," he wrote Eliot in January 1916.

Early in that year, however, values, organizations, and troops had all been under stress. The American Red Cross, with Woodrow Wilson listed as its president, was growing and consolidating. Norton and Harjes found it tactically useful to combine their units and funds, with the Red Cross supplying almost automatic credentials when dealing with French or British military authorities. Facing a steady decline in elite volunteers, Norton nevertheless persisted in demanding the highest standards of dress and deportment, and by sheer force of character and ability usually got them. But by the middle of 1917, when writers and artists started appearing, things were looking ominous. The Red Cross was proving incapable of appointing leaders and staffers. The new arrivals were not gentlemen. They did not appear to have ideals or the ability to speak French. The last straw was the arrival of Col. Jefferson R. Kean to take charge, full of plans to reorganize. He informed Norton of his intentions and offered him a commission as a major in the new hierarchy. Norton resigned the next day, 24 August, 1917, as did all five of his assistants.[4]

Dos Passos was there. "Picture the scene," he wrote to his Harvard friend Arthur McComb, a slightly Americanized Britisher who was in the process of becoming an art historian. "An automobile full of gentlemen with large jowls and U.S. army uniforms— Richard Norton, courtly in a monocle—in front a large crowd of ambulance drivers." As an occasional shell screeched overhead, Norton spoke in front of "a much shrapnel-holed barn like structure, our cantonment—the section dog by name 'P2' wanders about uneasily." Norton closed his brief remarks with an entirely characteristic turn of phrase: "As gentlemen volunteers you enlisted in this service, and as gentlemen volunteers I bid you farewell." Dos Passos was convulsed at the "wonderful phrase," especially since as Norton said it a shell burst thirty feet away, "which made every one clap on their tin helmets and crouch like scared puppies under a shower of pebbles and dust." He solemnly swore "to remain for the rest of my days a gentleman volunteer."

Yet even as the generation gap was making Norton a walking anachronism, Dos Passos could not avoid appearing merely the next incarnation of Charles Eliot Norton's ideals. The next section of the letter went on in an odd direction: "Do you remember the Chinese court that in one of the Mongol invasions refused to fight, but went on, in the gardens of a walled town, carrying out its avocations, writing poems and painting pictures and deciding contests of singers until the invaders broke in and slaughtered them all?" he asked. "Theirs was the true courage, the courage to disregard all in life that did not suit their tastes, to prefer extinction to giving up what they considered worth while." As disgusted as Norton that the American vandals were breaching his garden wall, Dos Passos resigned as well and headed for Paris.[5]

And so, via the ambulance service, Dos Passos was able to sample the delights of a proper city. He became a "gentleman of leisure" rather than a "gentleman volunteer." "I'm amusing myself going to many concerts, eating many delightful meals in miscellaneous restaurants, snooping about bookshops—& being as unmilitary as possible," he wrote Marvin. "To a certain extent I'm eating the lotos—and a delightful lotos," sampling the Luxembourg gardens, the escargots and the patisseries, and the "concerts with lots of César Franck." With a Harvard friend, the poet Robert Hillyer, he was even making progress on a collaborative novel. Only occasional blots marred the landscape. "Paris is full of American uniforms and of Serbian generals."[6]

Too restless to enjoy the good things in life, however urbane, for long, Dos Passos joined Section 1 of the American Red Cross Ambulance Service and headed for Italy in November 1917. He meditated increasingly on the cities he experienced. Milan struck him as "cold and clammy" and "ponderously dull," "a city of bankers that might be Denver, Colo., for any charm or beauty." Genoa was better, aided by his visit being chiefly during a night when a burning oil ship provided a "pearly pink glow" of illumination. Venice moved him to think "Byronically, de Mussetly," and of course he could not get the paintings of Titian and Giorgione out of his head. His term of enlistment expired in Rome in June 1918. "Rome is a rather wonderful place," he wrote Marvin, noting especially "a feeling of endless age, a mellowness of disillusion in which all crude bright things have burned themselves away in a wonderful selfpossession of pale eternity." He was one with the sunlight "on the old walls of Roman brick and on the obelisks and the mosscovered fountains."[7]

By the time he left Italy, Dos Passos was under something of a cloud. He and several of his friends had rather too obviously enjoyed themselves, aired their views on American culture and Red Cross bureaucrats, and written letters indiscreet in their references to both information and opinion. Still hungry for experience, he went to Paris just in time for the last great German offensive on the line from Chateau-Thierry to the Argonne forest. As Big Bertha dropped random shots on the city itself, he volunteered to serve as a stretcher-bearer. Almost fifty years later, the attack was still etched in his memory. "The night I particularly remember it was my job to carry off buckets full of amputated arms and hands and legs from an operating room."[8]

Failing either to clear his name or to win acceptance in a new Red Cross post in Paris, Dos Passos sailed reluctantly for America to see if he could pull any strings and find something useful to do. He succeeded, more or less, his nearsighted eyes causing him more trouble than his caustic tongue. After memorizing the eye chart, he entered the Medical Corps in New York City and went immediately to Camp Crane in eastern Pennsylvania. Flunking a legitimate eye exam, he was assigned to a casuals company that seemed to be a holding pen for those volunteers that the army could not use. The time he spent there proved decisive for literary history.

Dos Passos spent only a month at Camp Crane, but he took his feeling of total boredom to the grave. It was the domain of "Queen Ennui," who provoked a sense of inanition so great, he informed John Howard Lawson, that it "approaches Nirvana." His elitist yearnings for the true experience of democracy had borne tasteless fruit. "You wanted to be in America—well here you are—drowned in it," he wrote in his journal. Everything he valued seemed elsewhere. "It's funny how American life is always pitched in the key comedy—low comedy—farce—sometimes for a moment exulted into the high comedy that makes the spheres laugh. Never tragic," he wrote Marvin. He sounded almost like a homesick teen lost in a new prep school. "Write lots to the Prisoner of Camp Crane."[9]

But Dos Passos processed these emotions in a way unlike anyone else. Where a common recruit might polish his poker game or an educated one catch up on his favorite author, Dos Passos ransacked the languages and religions of the world to make a philosophical point that he would never abandon: "Organization is death. Organization is death—as I sweep acres of floor space and wash windows many as the grains of sand in the Lybian Syrtes," he grumbled to McComb. "I repeat the words over and over in anagrams, in French, in Latin, in Greek, in Italian, in all the distortions that language can be put to. Like a mumbled Ave Maria, they give me comfort."

Even Queen Ennui had her lessons. "The redeeming feature is in the men I run into here," he confided to McComb. "It's like discovering a new country to be completely cut loose from ones class and their habits of thought." Even as the camp was quarantined because of the worldwide influenza epidemic, he was making notes for what became his first fictional success, *Three Soldiers* (1921). An Indiana soldier prone to jealousy and violence became the model for the character of Christfield; a tough-talking street kid from California named Fuselli went into the book without even a slight change of name. And the third soldier was already in place: Andrews would be something of a fusion of Robert Hillyer and of the author himself.[10]

Leaving Camp Crane on the last day of October, the soldiers boarded the *Cedric* just as the Armistice was proclaimed. The voyage was miserable but educational, as seasickness, homesickness, influenza, and other diseases made everyone miserable. He rose to the status of acting-quartermaster-sergeant, devoting his time to mess hall and hospital, largely, he thought, because he could type with two fingers and speak French fluently. Dosing his own influenza with rum, he survived to become the least effective drillmaster in France. His attitude, stutter, and eyesight having provoked more laughter than obedience from his men, he was busted back to private; he never rose higher.

If war got Dos Passos back to France, peace made the enjoyment of Paris possible. He bent every rule and procedure he could to get into the city while in uniform, and to win a discharge so he could please himself as soon as possible. Already familiar with prewar modernist painting, ballet, and literature, he labored hard to catch up to postwar standards. He enrolled for courses at the Sorbonne. He fell at least half in love with a French pianist, Germaine Lucas-Champlonnière, and together they explored the work of Erik Satie and Les Six, as well as the work of such better-known modernists as Claude Debussy and Maurice Ravel. At tea at the home of her mother, she would perform "Milhaud's songs on the piano," and then they might go out to their favorite opera: "Together we cultivated a mania for *Pelléas and Mélisande*. She'd sing and I'd mumble the words as we went up the stairs at 52 rue de Clichy: 'Toute ta chevelure, Mélisande, est tombée de la tour.'"[11]

I

John Dos Passos's war experiences might seem a bit far afield from the imaginative perception of New York City, but in fact they were not. The ambulance services and the army were institutions, and war a theater where those institutions played out their assigned roles. Cities too could be theaters, huge stages upon which institutions such as businesses, fire departments, transportation systems, and the like functioned systemically, like parts of an enormously complex body. In strictly chronological terms, by the end of 1919 Dos Passos had passed through five such institutional experiences, with his ambulance service counting as number four and the army as number five. He found all of them dehumanizing and in his mature work the dehumanization of modern American life became the obsessive central theme.

The first institution almost everyone has to deal with is the family, but in the common understanding of the term, Dos Passos never had one. He was an illegitimate child of privilege. His father, John Randolph Dos Passos, was a wealthy lawyer and speculator who had long since stopped speaking to his legal wife. When at home he slept in the library, with his pet black snake Socrates quietly keeping him company on a cushioned chair nearby. When he and his wife entertained, guests quickly discovered that they had to address each one separately. Yet the Dos Passoses did not divorce: He had no grounds to divorce her, and she refused to seek any against him. Even had this not been the case, the Roman Catholic Church would never have approved and neither wished to break church law. Instead, the author's father visited his mistress and son when he could, keeping them lonely but comfortable during his long absences.

The author's mother, Lucy Sprigg Madison, was a southerner who, in the tradition of the Victorian novel, chose the wrong man at an early age. Ryland Randolph Madison, as his name implied, could claim legitimate connections to two of Virginia's first families, but his true sympathies lay with hard liquor. Lucy married him at sixteen, had a son, but apparently never lived with her husband. She became an office worker in the District of Columbia, and in time met Dos Passos, one of her father's most impressive business associates. Although still legally married, she described herself as a widow, lived in a house for which her paramour paid, and in time bore him a child he doted on. She named their son Jack Madison.

Because of these complications, the author grew up in Europe, where his parents could appear as a family without provoking scandal. Living often in Brussels, he had French as his first language; even his father used the language—badly—when he wrote, in part to conceal the contents of the letters from the prurient, in part to encourage his son in all things academic. The boy thought of himself as a "hotel child," nowhere really at home. His mother and her female friends overprotected him, and he never learned to be friends or even play with other children. Giving in to his misery, his parents finally permitted his return to America. He enrolled in the Sidwell Friends School in Washington, then still austerely Quaker. He hated it; he could not play a single sport well; he could not even see properly. When he finally acquired thick glasses, they only seemed to make his awkwardness stand out clearly.[12]

As it turned out, Lucy spent her time in Washington as lonely as ever, in delicate health. The humidity oppressed her and she soon uprooted her son and removed him to England. His father approved; as an imperialist, he thought a solid British preparation ideal for his son. Sent off to Peterborough Lodge in the London suburbs, the boy found himself all but excluded from student activities by the caste rigidities of the system. Once again, he was an outsider, a student without a country, without even a father's name he could call his own. As an institution, his "family" clearly was dysfunctional.

The second institution was the Choate School in Wallingford, Connecticut, which he attended for four and a half years. This was probably the most stable period of his life before college, but he fitted in no better. "I hated boardingschool—being called Frenchy and Four-eyes and the class grind," he recalled half a century later. He arrived as the youngest and smallest boy at the school, and proved adept at nothing except his studies. "I do not know why it is but no one ever treats me as if I were one of them," he wrote forlornly in his diary. "Every one is very nice to me but—that is all I have no friends—there is no one who cares a rap about me. . . . How happy I could be if I could only have one true friend who did not treat me like a damned little fool." Years later he reduced his prep school experience to one sentence, a Camera Eye stream of consciousness in *The 42nd Parallel* (1930) that envisioned himself as the inept skater who couldn't remain vertical, doomed always to be overshadowed by the Anglo-Saxon types who seemed to embody all the positive myths of the country he wanted to call his own: "We clean young American Rover Boys handy with tools Deerslayers played hockey Boy Scouts and cut figure eights on the ice Achilles Ajax Agamemnon I couldn't learn to skate and kept falling down." Small wonder that, when stuck at Camp Crane, he felt his misery to be so great that it recalled his Choate experience before all others.[13]

Graduating too young to matriculate immediately, the teenager spent a year abroad before encountering his third institutional experience at Harvard. Always bookish, he kept literary diaries that record an astonishing amount of reading, both curricular and extracurricular. He made close friends, E. E. Cummings being the best known to posterity. He enjoyed a modest literary success and won the respect of his peers. Like T. S. Eliot and Conrad Aiken before him, he explored the streets of Boston, enjoying especially "the cheaper parts of the city—those are the only parts of any city that are ever alive." Much of the surviving evidence makes it hard to believe that he could have been too unhappy, but he seemed able to bring his own little cloud along to block off the possibility of too much sunshine. He derided the philistinism and materialism of the place, and muttered to himself that only socialists and Jews could be bothered with him. Even after the war, he could snort repeatedly to Rummy Marvin, of "the enervating air of college and correct clothing—Christ! the only thing those sons of bitches think of is whether their pants are pressed." And once again, in a Camera Eye, he could berate himself for not having "the nerve to break out of the bellglass / four years under the ethercone breathe deep gently now that's / the way be a good boy."[14]

The pattern persisted: Always somehow illegitimate, belonging nowhere, talking with both lisp and accent, too small and nearsighted to be properly American, and too intelligent not to register eleven insults for every ten intended, Dos Passos did not even have his own name until he went off to college. With him, as with his confreres, modernism was the language that expressed this outsider status. Not until he arrived in New York City to live did he realize that everyone was beginning to feel dehumanized, unable to find congenial places in the modern world. New York was another stage upon which institutions seemed to function, that in fact did not work to human advantage. But only someone able to profit from his disadvantages could put such a statement of the modern condition into words, and those words into a new form.

II

John Dos Passos may well have been the best-read American modernist, perhaps of all modernists. Such claims are not readily quantifiable, especially given the problem of how to count paintings and music and the "reading" of architecture. Ezra Pound and T. S. Eliot provide the closest competition in literature, Paul Rosenfeld and Edmund Wilson in criticism. Even professors in the audiovisual arts rarely seemed broadly informed, however wide their knowledge of their own fields. The record of Dos Passos's reading that survives in journals and letters makes him exceptional in this as in several other areas. He had haunted museums; he had sought out buildings far from the usual tourist track; he had listened to the newest music, often when played to accompany the newest ballets. He shortly began a series of travels that almost killed him, whether from rheumatic fever, typhoid, or Muslim bandits, it hardly mattered. The sheer inquisitive energy of the man can leave an outside observer feeling exhausted even while sitting safely in a library chair.

Dos Passos's growing awareness of modernist languages was thus only a small part of his cultural adventuring. With French as his first language, he took naturally to French symbolist poetry. Even at Harvard, far removed from the Brussels of the lonely years of living with his mother, he could still gleefully inform Rummy Marvin that he was "indulging in an orgy of two modern French poets—Verlaine & Verhaeren. The latter's a Belgian and very wonderful." All but unknown in the English-speaking world today, Emile Verhaeren served much the same function for Dos Passos that Jules Laforgue served for T. S. Eliot—showing how modern, urban, industrialized life could stimulate poetry, and especially the life of crowds, on trains, as they went about an existence that seemed increasingly dehumanized. Indeed, with an eerie appropriateness, Verhaeren died a few months later, crushed by a train he was about to board at the Rouen station. And Dos Passos's knowledge of modernist verse began at the beginning. He devoured the works of Arthur Rimbaud during a Paris visit in 1917, with such effect that even more than a decade later, the Camera Eye of *The 42nd Parallel* could cheerfully dismiss genteel Boston culture in general, and the Harvard faculty in particular, and suggest that they all "go take a flying / Rimbaud / at the moon." In all likelihood, not a single one would have known what he was talking about.[15]

French symbolist and early modernist writing was in general compatible with, and often influential upon, British aestheticism. Long before Frank S. Flint and T. E. Hulme introduced Ezra Pound's generation to French poetry and thought after Laforgue, British writers and painters were beginning a long and fertile flirtation with decadence and variations on the theme of art for the sake of art, rather than art for the sake of some larger moral lesson. Indeed, the line between France and England, poetry and prose, health and decay, was often nonexistent. "I'm awfully glad you like the Swinburne you've read so far," Dos Passos wrote Marvin in 1916. He particularly liked the sonnet to *Mlle. De Maupin*, "a strangely exotic book you must read someday, by Gautier—a combination of rather decadent beauty and real passion and smut of a very low order. I think the sonnet's one of the most beautiful in English." As he read further, he found the verse consistently more to his taste than the prose. He loathed Oscar Wilde's *The Picture of Dorian Gray*, but found Walter Pater's *Marius the Epicurean* oddly appealing. "It may be all sheer rot, but its a sort of rot that is at times beneficial."[16]

Dos Passos was not, on the whole, familiar with the achievements of American culture, finding them thin and moralistic compared with what was available elsewhere. But with an instinct that has proven historically valid, he managed to fasten on the three most important precursors for his own generation. He was familiar enough with the art and writings of that first defender of art for the sake of art, James A. McNeill Whistler, to inform Marvin in 1916: "If I ever enter another incarnation, and am consulted about my status, I shall be a combination between Whistler and Debussy!"

That same year, as he was rummaging about Spanish culture and doing nothing whatever that seemed likely to remind him of American ideas, he was recommending that Marvin read both the abridged version of William James's *Principles of Psychology* and his *Varieties of Religious Experience:* "I think you will have an awfully interesting time, as they are wonderfully fascinating books and not a bit dry."[17]

Unsurprisingly, however, first place went to Henry James. Even before Ezra Pound made his survey of James's work toward the end of the war, Dos Passos was plowing through the novels after his own fashion. James's skill in painting portraits in *The Europeans* reminded him of "the delicacy of the Angelico, or better, of some of the more refined Dutch portrait painters." The "minute, almost microscopic" descriptive skills evident in *Daisy Miller* impressed him, while "the dialogue in places almost reminds me of Oscar Wilde, although intensely more restrained and realistic." As James himself did, he sampled the work of Henrik Ibsen along the way, commenting especially on *The Enemy of the People*. Dismissing Turgenev's *Fathers and Sons*—which James would not have done—he moved on to perhaps the key work in the canon, *The Portrait of a Lady:* "a most remarkable miniature study of a fascinating character. H.J.'s women are marvellous!" James's dramatic novels, based in part on his assimilation of Ibsen's principles, were only a few short years away, and in time Dos Passos carried the notion of multiple voices far beyond anything in the work of James.[18]

He was thus ready for imagism. Active as a staff member of the *Harvard Monthly*, he was in a position to hear about and often review new writing. He praised Ezra Pound's anthology, *Des Imagistes* in May 1916, and noted as well Frank S. Flint's *Cadences* and Hilda Doolittle's early work. No poet in the Boston area could not have heard of Amy Lowell, often of her person as well as of her work, and Dos Passos took particular note of her chief English supporter, Richard Aldington, who was briefly Doolittle's husband. Aldington seemed in 1916 "the best of the Imagists." He was also the one who most clearly formulated the imagist platform: Great poetry should use "the language of common speech," using the "*exact* word, not the nearly exact, nor the merely decorative word." Great poetry needed to create "new rhythm—as the expression of new moods" and not "copy old rhythms, which merely echo old moods." It allowed "absolute freedom in the choice of subject," and especially insisted on the "artistic value of modern life." It presented "an image," not as any substitute for painting but in an effort to "render particulars exactly" and avoid "generalities, however magnificent and sonorous." Modern Imagists wanted a poetry that was "hard and clear, never blurred nor indefinite," and insisted that "concentration is of the very essence of poetry."[19]

As this progress toward the concrete noun and the precise image indicated, American modernism would display a blunt realism that often seemed in direct conflict with its predominantly romantic origins. Gertrude Stein, a favorite of Dos Passos's friend E. E. Cummings, had not yet instructed students to "forget grammar and think about potatoes," but the food was on the table. In Dos Passos's case, the feast was from two kitchens. The little-known Dutch writer Louis Couperus, in *Small Souls*, gave him a sense of how a writer could vivify ordinary life in all its sharp-tongued triviality. "Without a trace of didacticism, the novel is a tremendous satire, cold and unemotional, on the life of a small European capital." It also led directly to the experiments in Unanisme by Jules Romains, and the ultimate achievement of *U.S.A.* The larger feast came from Gustave Flaubert. Like Stein, Dos Passos was devoted to "Un Coeur Simple," and referred reverently to Flaubert as "one of my Olympian gods, even the Cloud-Compeller himself." He was, he recalled in his memoirs, "absorbed in the problem of how to write clearly." Flaubert helped the most. "I caught his obsession for the *mot juste.*"[20]

III

Like many modernists, Dos Passos took inspiration from arts far afield from writing, their very distance affecting every mature work that he wrote. The first of the fine arts to motivate his behavior, for example, was actually architecture. When he graduated from Harvard, his first choice was Belgian Relief, but they turned him down; the second was the ambulance corps, but his father vetoed that temporarily; his third was to go to Spain to study architecture. "I really am interested in architecture—and I think the grinding study necessary will be good for my lazy & undisciplined soul," he wrote Marvin; "unfortunately I'll have to take some Math too, since architecture is not possible without it—horrid thought."

Never was math less relevant; his interest was chiefly visual. Along the way, he noted the "charming old churches and . . . beautiful houses in High Renaissance style" in Bordeaux, and lamented that "Madrid's modern and not awfully interesting." What really seemed to get his juices flowing was the appearance of almost anything of great age. Sometimes this could be a custom, ritual, or dance of ancient origin, but most often it was a building or its ruin. "You can't imagine the wonderfulness of a little village we passed just at dawn," he wrote after walking all night along an old road to Toledo; "with a big buttressed church and a tall leaning church tower and everything pearl-blue and purple and lemon yellow." At times he seemed to be painting architecture in words. Subsequent trips to Sens, Rouen, or the Italian Riviera yielded similar responses throughout both the war and the peace.[21]

What Dos Passos needed instead of math were courses on the fourth dimensional physics of memory, then something of a fad in French artistic circles, for his manner of seeing buildings not only violated time, it evoked words about music. "We followed the quais along the Seine to Notre Dame," he recalled in his memoirs. "We peeked through the sandbags into the Sainte Chapelle. We came back through the courtyards of the Louvre and the flowerbeds of the Tuileries." In spite of the war, you could still watch Punch and Judy shows or buy sweets, "the thin wafflelike *galettes* I remembered from when I was a child." "The old gray buildings moved us like music. I caught my first glimpse of the slender dome that soared above the arches linking the pedimented wings of the Institut de France, which for years was to be my favorite building in the world."

The passage is a laboratory example of aesthetic physics. The author experiences time first as war, as he peers through sandbags; second, as childhood memory, his lonely days as a hotel child, visiting places most of his countrymen could never see. But then there is a third, less precise layer, that of the buildings themselves, chiefly the religious thirteenth century but with later, more secular additions. Two specific times would meld into Time, joining several centuries with the doubled present. They come realistically back to earth with the galettes, a nicely Proustian touch, and the Punch and Judy shows, evocative as they were to any modernist as musically aware as Dos Passos. The *pierrot* shaped such works as *Petrushka* and *Pierrot lunaire*, and thus the effect is carnivalesque, highest and lowest culture joining in the fourth dimension.[22]

The complexity of Dos Passos's response thus far transcended sensitive tourism. It became even more important when he settled in New York City to collect the impressions that went into *Manhattan Transfer*. There the architecture lacked the human and historical complexity of Paris. It seemed cold, inhuman, and present. A painter would have to be a precisionist, not an impressionist, to do it justice.

The evolution of Dos Passos's taste in painting followed a comparable course. At Harvard, he had studied medieval and Renaissance Italian art, so he was well prepared for his first on-the-spot immersion. "I've gone quite dippy about early Italian fresco painting," he enthused to Marvin in April 1918. "God, I've never seen such gorgeous, unimaginably interesting decoration as those people—even the rather poor ones could do—from Giotto to Botticelli." He had no problem, looking back fifty years later, in making the necessary disciplinary and chronological leaps. "I am sure that the great narrative painting of the thirteen and fourteen hundreds profoundly influenced my ideas of how to tell a story in words."

In fact, he was experiencing the medieval, the Renaissance, and the modern in art with a distinctly modernist simultaneity. While a student at Harvard, he had dropped into the Armory Show in its third incarnation after New York and Chicago. In New York it had included the work of many Americans, but by the time it came to Boston it was entirely European, thus presumably reinforcing his sense that whatever was happening in art was happening in Paris, Cologne, or Munich. Once stirred, he was especially open to futurist ideas when he encountered them later in Milan. Reading the words even before seeing most examples of the painting, he found Filippo Marinetti, Umberto Boccioni, and the rest dealing with many of the same problems as he: How to convey the feeling of urban life, of humanity in the mass, of rapidly shifting colors and planes as motion, especially speedy motion, dominated an artist's perception of the modern. His own paintings, shown at the Whitney Studio Club in 1923, showed "elements of Futurism and Cubism" according to their most thorough student. As it turned out, however, Italian futurism, like Spanish cubism, was happening largely in Paris, and so could merge with his interests in the other arts.[23]

Dos Passos's interest in modernist painting achieved a climax of sorts in his private life in his relationship with Gerald Murphy, the now legendary host to such other members of the "Lost Generation" as Ernest Hemingway and Scott Fitzgerald. Meeting first in 1923, they found their friendship ripening in the mid-1920s, as *Manhattan Transfer* took shape. Murphy was not only a painter of museum-quality modernist works, he was friendly as well with such French artists as Fernand Léger. Their lunches and long walks together made a permanent impression. "As we strolled along Fernand kept pointing out shapes and colors," while "Gerald's offhand comments would organize vistas of his own," Dos Passos recalled. "Instead of the hackneyed and pasteltinted Tuileries and bridges and barges and *bateaux mouches* on the Seine, we were walking through a freshly invented world." The three of them "picked out winches, the flukes of an anchor, coils of rope, the red funnel of a towboat, half a woman's face seen behind geraniums through the casement window of the cabin of a barge." He felt cleansed of visual cliché: "The banks of the Seine never looked banal again after that walk." Small wonder that Léger's works would make appropriate illustrations for *Manhattan Transfer.*

Indeed, the parallels between these two friends serve to connect European and American modernisms more closely than was customarily the case. Léger too had considered architecture as a career and had never lost an architect's sense of structure even when assimilating cubist stylistic innovations in painting. He too liked to paint with words, and to use them to analyze time and annul conventional assumptions about space. He too had realist ancestors, Gustave Courbet playing the role of Flaubert in the development of Dos Passos, using such a stylistic model to examine the minutiae of city stimuli, the chimneys, rooftops, and the rest providing him with "the maximum expressive effect" that he wished for his cityscapes. And for him, too, the war proved the ultimate reality. A painter "up to my ears in abstraction" before becoming a soldier, he was "suddenly stunned by the sight of the open breech of a .75 cannon in full sunlight. It needed nothing more than this for me to forget the abstract art of 1912–3. . . . Once I'd bitten into that reality the essence and meaning of objects never left me." The war created a new relation between man and machine, it speeded up the very rhythms of life, and it provided a raft of appropriate metaphors when as artist then turned his attention to the city as subject. As Léger produced *La Ville* (1919), so Dos Passos produced *Manhattan Transfer.* It comes as no surprise that Léger was a friend of Edgard Varèse, an enthusiastic follower of the purist architectural theories of Le Corbusier and Amédée Ozanfant, or a collaborator with the poet Blaise Cendrars, who completed the circle of artistic influence by being a good friend of Dos Passos. Poets, painters, architects, and musicians from both hemispheres were learning to understand each other's languages.[24]

Like many writers with symbolist tendencies, Dos Passos at times seemed to approve of the oft-repeated assumption that all art aspired to the condition of music. Most Harvard aesthetes apparently did. But Dos Passos was never one to harbor a passive enthusiasm. He was so passionately fond of the work of Debussy that he left the impression that he came close to marriage with his French pianist companion over their shared enthusiasm for *Pelléas et Mélisande*. He was as devoted to Diaghilev's Ballets Russes as his limited opportunities permitted, starting with its Boston tour performances in February 1916, which featured Stravinsky and Debussy, as well as more traditionalist composers such as Rimsky-Korsakov and Borodin. He could scarcely have avoided associating the music with futurist art and modernist choreography, of the Russian if not the Italian variety, given the influence of Nathalie Gontcharova, Michel Larionov, Michel Fokine, and Leonid Massine over those works that reached America.

By the time Dos Passos became a visitor to the Murphys, he was thus traveling in fast company. The Murphys had studied with Gontcharova and helped Diaghilev repair sets; they were personal friends of Picasso, Braque, and other painters who had contributed their talents to specific performances. In the entire American colony, only Cummings came close to sharing Dos Passos's knowledge and enthusiasm. And lest this description of Dos Passos's interests in music seem too narrow, he was a personal friend of Roger Sessions from Harvard days, and thus aware of the most avant-garde of all the American composers of the early 1920s. The idea of the total work of art took on added meaning here: Just as architecture could be totally organized space, so certain ballets could be completely integrated multiartistic syntheses, involving fiction, poetry, music, painting, dance, and drama, all reinforcing each other and all modernist discourse.[25]

All these arts contributed something to Dos Passos's vision of the city and to his sense of what new form could capture its essence most effectively. But all things considered, none were as formative to the way his imagination worked as the film, both as snapshot and as cinema. Film first impressed him at Camp Crane, where he noted that distraction was so difficult to find that a recruit would have welcomed almost anything. He personally enjoyed the sort of mindless entertainment that seemed appropriate to a mindless place. "The great indicator of the pathetic state into which I am fallen is that I gurgle and chortle with delight over them," he noted in his diary. But when he came to write up this experience in *Three Soldiers*, the chortling was gone and the malign influence of the new technology in the hands of an institutional bureaucracy remained. Fuselli, most obviously, can scarcely think on his own, passively substituting government clichés and stereotypes about Huns.[26]

This ambivalence soon pervaded his very sense of who he was as an artist. When his friend McComb protested that *Three Soldiers* was not an objective account of the American military experience, Dos Passos instantly took refuge in photographical analogy: His method was "photography from a point of view," and his point of view was that of an underdog. An artist, in other words, could profit from watching institutional misuse of a medium. But what remains fascinating over the next several years is the way ambivalence about the city went hand-in-camera with ambivalence about the cinema. The city attracted and repelled him: It offered cultural advantages while dehumanizing anyone who sought to take advantage of them. New York City was "marvellous" and "hideous" both, and required all the skill a documentary journalist could muster. Learning most from the D. W. Griffith of *The Birth of a Nation* and especially *Intolerance*, Dos Passos was familiar with fade-ins and fade-outs, with achronological usages of time, and the external portrayal of inner streams of consciousness. Above all he appreciated the montage effect, where up to four disparate but parallel plots could unfold, each silently commenting on the other, the entire work achieving in this manner an impact that was more than the sum of its parts. "I' started a rapportage on New York," he recalled almost half a century later; "there was more to the life of a great city than you could cram into any one hero's career. The narrative must stand up off the page. Fragmentation. Contrast. Montage. The result was *Manhattan Transfer.*[27]

It may seem appropriately inconceivable, but the novel in a sense is a fourth dimensional portrayal *both* as a snapshot and as documentary cinema. It is a snapshot from a vast distance of time and space, freeze-framing roughly a quarter of a century, dozens of characters, and a significant number of institutions as they move without progressing, as if they were trapped on a roller coaster that ran continuously into itself, up, down, and around, over and over again. Yet constituting the snapshot would be dozens of films, portraying the characters as they moved in what seem to be "normal" linear lives. Coincidentally or not, it arrived in the world hard on the heels of that other, now more studied exercise in fourth dimensional conceptualization, Duchamp's "The Bride Stripped Bare by her Bachelors, Even"—a work that in fact never was completed. Cinema helped give Dos Passos what chess gave to Duchamp: another plane upon which to imagine.

IV

Although he had been writing in both English and French from an early age, Dos Passos was slow to find a style he could call his own. At Harvard he sounded indistinguishable from many other aesthetes clearly in thrall to British decadence. Camp Crane and France ended that phase but did not really usher in a new one. He worked on a manuscript usually entitled "Seven Times Round the Walls of Jericho," at first with his Harvard friend Robert Hillyer, then on his own. Never published as written, its characters and themes pervaded *One Man's Initiation—1917* (1920, 1969), *Three Soldiers* and *Streets of Night*, published belatedly in 1923. Of these, only *Three Soldiers* had much success. If it did not make him "as famous as Wrigley's," as Jack Lawson suggested, it did make critics sit up and take notice. But its machine symbolism did not quite work, his original outline became a casualty of the war as surely as John Andrews, the character who ran off with the plot, and the style had not become truly his own. The war had tempered English prose; it hadn't yet hammered out a replacement. Nevertheless, *Three Soldiers* is clearly modernist: It shows the influence of both painting and film, with some effort at establishing the fragmentary nature of perception and the simultaneity of seemingly unrelated events.[28]

Dos Passos was in New York City, most of the time, from September 1920 into March 1921, and again from early May 1922 into early 1924, except for trips to North Carolina and France, with a brief side trip into Spain. His recorded responses to his visits cover an extended range of emotions. He liked seeing more of such friends as Cummings, and having access to two literary journals. At first glance the *Dial* seemed more appealing. It occupied "a charming house with paradise bushes in the backyard," had "a lovely dark stenog named Sophia and some beautiful tall ice-tea glasses. They speak only French during office hours and are genteel, though I admit, delightful." However, the *Freeman* proved more supportive, even speaking British as it often did. Dos Passos shared a number of political attitudes with its editor, Albert Jay Nock, and the journal printed numerous excerpts of Dos Passos's account of Spain, *Rosinante to the Road Again* (1922).[29]

Friends and publishers meant a lot, but they could not entirely compensate for the "grotesque, the farce—quality of American life," which he had noted in a 1918 diary entry. Both government and business had corrupted discourse, and the individual seemed equally swamped by goods and words. He mused about abolishing the idea of property but "did not have faith enough in human nature to be an anarchist." He was appalled by the adverse effects of Prohibition. The amount of alcohol available "will send the entire population of New York into D.T.s if it continues," he marveled to Lawson. He began to refer to the place as the "City of Destruction," the phrase from Bunyan that reappears in *Manhattan Transfer*. But like Cummings, Dos Passos really needed an enemy to fight against, a target to shoot at. Both were satirists, with oddly sentimental streaks. When writing in favor of something, they rarely functioned half so well as when they wrote out of loathing.[30]

When, in one of his last autobiographical efforts, Dos Passos tried to convey his intentions in writing *Manhattan Transfer*, he called on a source that must have confounded a good many casual readers; but the idea itself was admirably clear. "We have a small shrimp in these counties, which is taken in the Thames and in the sea, the whole of whose body is transparent," he quoted from William Harvey's *Circulation of the Blood;* "this creature, placed in a little water, has frequently afforded myself and particular friends an opportunity of observing the motions of the heart with the greatest distinctiveness, the extreme parts of the body presenting no obstacle to our view, but the heart being perceived as though it had been seen through a window." Dos Passos then went on, speaking for himself: "The aim, the never quite attainable aim of the novelist or historian, is to see men's private emotions and their movements in masses as clearly as William Harvey saw the heart of the shrimp and to express what they see as lucidly as Harvey did in the little paragraph I have just read."[31]

Manhattan Transfer is *the* American city novel. Any number of works take place in cities, but their focus is invariably a central character, like Dreiser's Frank Cowperwood or Farrell's Studs Lonigan; or a social milieu such as the upper class of Marquand's Boston or Wharton's New York; or an institutional environment, such as the newspaper world of Howells or the wheat market of Norris. These works never make the city itself the protagonist. Europeans, as usual, got there first. From Balzac to Biely, Europeans had come very close to such a focus, and by the early 1920s all American modernist writers were aware of Joyce's Dublin. But even in this elite context Dos Passos stood in the first rank. His work not only captured the most important city in the hemisphere, it did so in a new style that made use of cinematic grammar, cubist conceptions of planes and perspectives, jazz rhythms, the collage, and other such modernist innovations. Here were the words to go with the sounds of Edgard Varèse and the pictures of Paul Strand.

The novel is in essence physiological: It analyzes the functioning of an organic system, the macrocosmic version of Harvey's microcosmic shrimp. It begins with the act of ingesting, as the water washes in a ferry that disgorges people even as it wallows in garbage; it will end when the city excretes the only character to retain his humanity more or less intact. In-migration and detritus are diastole and systole, and the view of human nature appropriately sanitational. Having no real sense of perspective, the unwitting arrive wishing to get at "the center of things." They conceive of that center as a place of employment, sensory stimulation, and enlightenment. What they find is an urban environment that is literally heartless but functionally digestive. Manhattan Transfer is actually a station where train meets subway in New Jersey. That subway then becomes the blood vessels nourishing the bodily extremities, giving no thought to the individuality of those who enter the system. Once you get on the subway or off the ferry, you are fodder.

One key modernist device for portraying character was the stream of consciousness, that term invented by William James in *The Principles of Psychology* (1890) even as his brother Henry was doing something very close to it in *The Portrait of a Lady* (1881). Dos Passos played with this device in *Three Soldiers*, but that was a novel in which the leading characters retained a good measure of common humanity. In *Manhattan Transfer*, the closest character to a spokesman for the author is Jimmy Herf. He arrives on 4 July, 1904, possibly a broad hint about his representative nature, and lives as a hotel child with a mother who is always trying to make the poor kid into a gentleman. He likes to read, and seems both imaginative and romantic, but his life is much constricted by his mother's ill health. He is good at languages, goes to Hotchkiss (read: Choate) and Columbia (Harvard). Other parallels are there as well, at least implying that Herf had a consciousness that could stream. But those vestiges of the older modernist novel aside, the true consciousness that streams in *Manhattan Transfer* is the city's. The following is representative and clearly a combination of film and snapshot, an overview of several cinematic strands, not to evoke a character's mind, but the city's:

Noon on Union Square. Selling out. Must vacate. WE HAVE MADE A TERRIBLE MISTAKE. Kneeling on the dusty asphalt little boys shine shoes lowshoes tans buttonshoes oxfords. The sun shines like a dandelion on the toe of each new-shined shoe. Right this way buddy, mister miss maam at the back of the store our new line of fancy tweeds highest value lowest price ... Gents, misses, ladies, cutrate ... WE HAVE MADE A TERRIBLE MISTAKE. Must vacate.

Noon sunlight spirals dimly into the chopsuey joint. Muted music spirals Hindustan. He eats fooyong, she eats chowmein. They dance with their mouths full, slim blue jumper squeezed to black slick suit, peroxide curls against black slick hair.

Down Fourteenth Street, Glory glory comes the Army, striding lasses, Glory Glory four abreast, the rotund shining, navy blue, Salvation Army band.[32]

Yet too many critics focus on Herf because he reminds them of the author. The person to watch is really Ellen (or Elaine, or Helena) Thatcher, for she embodies the author's views about what the physiology of the city does to those who enter its orifices. Ellen is the baby born on the first page, squirming "like a knot of earthworms" (3). Appropriately enough for a future cog in the urban machinery, they oil her, then present her to a mother who denies that the child is hers. Her father Ed may want a "homey" (9) daughter, but Ellen would prefer to be a boy. Even as a child, she seems to reject reality and shows ominous signs of adaptation to a hostile environment: Her tongue clicks "like the ticking of the clock" (44) and her arms and neck keep growing stiff. She wants to be rich, a suitable desire for a child of a man obsessed with money. Although she doesn't like men, she keeps marrying them, her beauty attracting those whose values are as superficial as her own. Having married John Oglethorpe, her chief emotional response is nausea: "If she touched him she would die" (117) is merely one line indicative of many. When stressed out this way, she usually goes into a fetal position, brooding in uteral waters:

She drew her knees up to her chin and sat thinking. From the street she could hear the occasional rumble of a truck. In the kitchens below her room a sound of clattering had begun. From all around came a growing rumble of traffic beginning. She felt hungry and alone. The bed was a raft on which she was marooned alone, always alone, afloat on a growling ocean. A shudder went down her spine. She drew her knees up closer to her chin. (168)

Roughly halfway through the book, Ellen meets Jimmy Herf, and they interact occasionally as she goes through various promiscuous activities and is divorced from Oglethorpe. Emblematic of urban culture as well as its capitalist base, she attracts and then disappoints repeatedly. As an actress, she can put "the passion and terror" (212) into her performances, but it's all surface show and means nothing. As World War I starts, Ellen and Jimmy speak of the conflict in the spectatorial terms that were so common at Dos Passos's Harvard. They talk not of dying but of being a nurse or war correspondent, and then dance. Here the life seems animated—for what could be more animated than a dancer—but the imagery undercuts the appearance: He is becoming plaster, she a machine for taking him apart.

'Get up on your toes and walk in time to the music. . . . Move in straight lines that's the whole trick.' Her voice cut the quick coldly like a tiny flexible sharp metalsaw. Elbows joggling, faces set, gollywog eyes, fat men and thin women, thin women and fat men rotated densely around them. He was crumbling plaster with something that rattled achingly in his chest, she was an intricate machine of sawtooth steel whitebright bluebright copperbright in his arms. (228)

It is the diastole and systole of the city: you put it up, you tear it down, machines dictating the emotional level.

As the stress level rises, Ellen becomes much like any other urban structure, "a stiff castiron figure in her metalgreen evening dress" (261). This does not stop her from becoming pregnant, but her mate dies in a freakish fire, she has an abortion, and turns into a parody of the American way:

> She watches the tilt of her leather hat, the powder, the rosed cheeks, the crimson lips that are a mask on her face. All the buttons of her gloves are buttoned. She raises her hand. "Taxi!" A fire engine roars past, a hosewagon with sweatyfaced men pulling on rubber coats, a clanging hookandladder. All the feeling in her fades with the dizzy fade of the siren. A wooden Indian, painted, with a hand raised at the streetcorner. (268)

She marries Herf and they have a baby boy, Martin, but a child doesn't keep them from growing apart. She moves tropistically toward George Baldwin, an ambulance-chasing lawyer rising rapidly to the position of district attorney. The price is high:

> Through dinner she felt a gradual icy coldness stealing through her like novocaine. She had made up her mind. It seemed as if she had set the photograph of herself in her own place, forever frozen into a single gesture. An invisible silk band of bitterness was tightening round her throat, strangling. . . . Ellen felt herself sitting with her ankles crossed, rigid as a porcelain figure under her clothes, everything about her seemed to be growing hard and enameled, the air bluestreaked with cigarettesmoke, was turning to glass. (375)

In the end, she feels "like a busted mechanical toy." The imagery gets a bit mixed, but the city does that to people.

To anyone cognizant of Dos Passos's entire career, with its shifts from aesthete to modernist to political radical to right-wing conservative, *Manhattan Transfer* is fascinating in its ambiguities and oxymorons. On the surface—appropriately enough—the book is an indictment of capitalism. It repeatedly sees life as a gamble and finds the results intolerable. Like some obsessive follower of

Henry George, Dos Passos locates a vast amount of social evil in real estate, and the rise of land values under population pressures. As the popular song had it, "Everybody's Doing It" (218), speculating on land values and the profits to be made in construction. The industry remains imaginatively central, for it involves not just the city but the machine, all the cranes, bulldozers, and cement mixers that go into a modern structure. In combination, they hit this writer where he lived. Not only did building corrupt politics and thus disorient democratic men, it corrupted the language. No one could talk sensibly about the social costs involved; they merely mouthed clichés about "the forefront of progress" (15). Yet, as always in Dos Passos, drunks and dreamers were in the shadows with visions of how things might be different. Architect Phil Sandbourne has a colleague, Old Specker, who sounds like a slightly disconnected Mies van der Rohe: "'Man you ought to see his plans for allsteel buildins. He's got an idea the skyscraper of the future'll be built of steel and glass. . . . He says he's found New York of brick an that he's goin to leave it of steel . . . steel and glass'" (75). Stanwood Emery states the ultimate wish for a New York architect: "Kerist, I wish I was a skyscraper" (252). Instead he dies in a building fire that he himself started while drunk.

A reader leaves the book rightly feeling that the city is more animate than the dehumanized souls that feed its appetites; they merely flood and drain, as impersonal as water.

Glowworm trains shuttle in the gloaming through the foggy looms of spiderweb bridges, elevators soar and drop in their shafts, harbor lights wink.

Like sap at the first frost at five o'clock men and women begin to drain gradually out of the tall buildings downtown, grayfaced throngs flood subways and tubes, vanish underground.

All night the great buildings stand quiet and empty, their million windows dark. Drooling light the ferries chew tracks across the lacquered harbor. (305)

Paul Strand left photographs that prove that Dos Passos wasn't just making it all up. All that passage lacks is the sirens from a few fire engines, compliments of Edgard Varèse.

V

Manhattan Transfer had a political stance mostly by implication. Politics was corrupt and so were the businessmen, lawyers, and journalists who participated on its fringes. But the book was no sooner published in 1925 than the pressure of friendship and events pushed Dos Passos from apathy to commitment, and in making the move he was only the most obvious of the many artists for whom he seemed to speak. In finding and articulating a political stance Dos Passos retained his place in the modernist vanguard, and in the process helped show why the end of 1926 was a crucial watershed in cultural history.

As soon as *Manhattan Transfer* was safely in his publisher's hands, Dos Passos felt free to travel and did so. He headed for Europe and the Murphys, saw Ernest Hemingway frequently, was in and out of North Africa, and did not return to New York City until the spring of 1926. His expressionistic play *The Garbage Man* was due for a brief run, but even more important, it was pushing him closer to Lawson's pet project, the New Playwrights Theatre. With support from financier Otto Kahn, the group incorporated on 22 January, 1927, and immediately began putting on plays. Inspired almost as much by the Abbey Theatre in Dublin as by the Theatre of Revolution in Moscow, this new drama group in its three-year history always tried to marry Russian futurist means to politically leftist ends. This was something new in American modernism.[33]

John Howard Lawson rarely finds a place in histories of modernism. He appears rather as a Communist playwright and Hollywood scriptwriter, most renowned for being one of the more visible of the artists persecuted after World War II as an uncooperative witness before congressional investigators. But Lawson was an example of how members of one climate of creativity could profit happily from the innovations of an earlier one without sharing its essential spirit. A born collectivist, secular and humorless much of the time, he was nevertheless drawn to jazz, vaudeville, and other achievements of popular culture. Experimenting with the devices of expressionism in *Roger Bloomer* (1923), he reached a sudden maturity in *Processional* (1925). He claimed later that his chief inspiration came from "newspaper stories of labor strife in Mingo County, West Virginia," full as they were of "murders and pitched battles," and in a narrow sense this was no doubt true. But artistically speaking, Lawson was also drawing on many of the same ideas and experiences as his friend. Together, they had viewed the same war, and at least once had shared a hospitable haystack in trying to write it up. Lawson too found the experience of war disorienting and alienating and had sought relief in all the arts available in Paris. He even admitted to being a little in awe of Dos Passos's remarkable familiarity with all the arts—especially the Ballets Russes. Indeed, it seems clear that Erik Satie's *Parade*, with sets by Picasso and book by Cocteau, was a prime source for some of the scenes in *Processional*. Just as Dos Passos was a modernist who developed briefly into a collectivist, in other words, so Lawson was a collectivist who had early affinities to modernism. Accidents of friendship brought the two together at a fluid time in the life of each. *The Garbage Man* owed much to *Processional*, and Lawson's politics were perhaps all the push Dos Passos needed to move him to the left for the next decade.[34]

Whatever the personal dynamics involved, Dos Passos was clearly well along in a major period of transition. Eager to revive the pacifist radical tradition that he recalled from the old *Masses*, he was involved with and occasionally wrote for the *New Masses* when it became an important voice for the left in 1926—the first issue appeared in May, with Dos Passos listed on the board. Even more crucial was the growing opposition he felt toward the inflicting of the death penalty on the accused Italian anarchists, Nicola Sacco and Bartolomeo Vanzetti. Sentenced to die for murder, they had become a focus of worldwide attention as the case dragged on. He published a pamphlet and did what he could. In the end, they affected him more than the other way around. When they died on 23 August, 1927, he was committed to political radicalism for a decade. The evidence of his greatest work, *U.S.A.*, is conclusive that he brought all his urban modernism with him.[35]

FOUR

WILLIAM CARLOS WILLIAMS AND THE SUBURBAN DOCTOR'S EYE

In 1951, when he published his autobiography, William Carlos Williams noted in the foreword that "as both writer and physician" he had "served sixty-eight years of a more or less uneventful existence, not more than half a mile" from where he happened "to have been born." This decision to remain in place, clearly limiting to both his life and his art, mystified even his closest friends. They assumed that the suburbs were stultifying and that art could only thrive within the boundaries of New York City, or better, Paris. Could they but have read his mail, they would have been even more puzzled. "I was really an unhappy, disappointed child," he was writing his wife in 1927. "It was due to the mood of our home and to my eager desires, which no world, and certainly not the Rutherford of those days, could satisfy." Since he was unable fully to satisfy any of his oppressive drives, he was "gnawing" his "insides all day long."[1]

A man of images based on realities, he piled one unhappy fact upon another. Rutherford, New Jersey, although not far from New York, had no sewers, water, or gas, no electricity or telephone service, when he was young. Pavement was all but nonexistent, dust was everywhere, and sidewalks merely wooden crosspieces nailed to two-by-fours in a pattern that encouraged yellowjackets to nest. Most homes had outhouses and cesspools; water came chiefly from the accumulation of rain. Over the years, progress cured many problems, but important limitations were simply givens. "Here the world of art is nonexistent," he grumbled to his friend Kenneth Burke in 1921. A few years later, his home town became "this microscopic banality, this suburb, this vacancy," in a private journal.[2]

For a young physician finding a niche for himself, there could be no escape. Rutherford newspapers captured glimpses of Williams going through his medical day. He was a school medical inspector, a police surgeon, and a doctor for the children's home. He served on the county mosquito commission and the board of health; during World War I he was the borough food administrator. He took part in campaigns for the construction of hospitals, parks, playgrounds, and a new high school. All these tasks were in addition to a growing practice in obstetrics and pediatrics, which he opened on 19 September, 1910. Nor was there any compensating beauty in the area. Williams referred repeatedly to the Passaic River as "the vilest swillhole in christendom," "O river of my heart polluted," and not even the strongest boosters of nearby Paterson ever tried to make it seem worthy of poetry. Yet Williams managed, with results that still affect how writers and students think about poetry. The fact of the matter was, as Alfred Kreymborg pointed out: "You live in the suburbs, you even *like* it."[3]

The statement seems indisputable. Individuals vote with their feet far more clearly than they do marking ballots. Although Williams did wander to Germany, France, Italy, Austria, Switzerland, and England, and gave his choice of a permanent location a great deal of agitated thought over the years, he did stay; and all things considered, he did like it. He liked being a doctor, not only because he could earn a living by doing something useful, but because the job gave him inexhaustible material for poetry, new ways of perceiving it, and yet with the built-in distance from the world of art that his peculiar psychology seemed to demand. Much of his best work could not have been written in the city. It could only have come from some place nearby, from an author who in practice had to move about *his* domain. Williams needed a bit of space, between his houses as between his words, so that he could travel between them. His movement within his suburb became decisive for many of his best works: They offer versions of what a poet can see while on foot or on a bicycle, in a buggy or, in time, a car. He went after the subjects of his verse like a hungry bee checking out the local clover, and clover did not thrive in a real city. "In passing with my mind / on nothing in the world / but the right of way / I enjoy on the road by / virtue of the law— / I saw," one of the poems in *Spring and All* (1923) begins, to be followed by a straightforward list of the people and situations he could recall. "The supreme importance / of this nameless spectacle / sped me by them / without a word—," yet of course the words are sitting before the reader, their importance now taken for granted.[4]

I

Outsiders have at least as much trouble penetrating the world of medicine as they do the world of poetry. But when Williams says that "the city of the hospital is my final home," he is stating a truth that transcends his own often violent rejection of metaphor. He was eager to expand his sense of both life and its cure to argue that "the entire world today is a hospital," making that institution "a very normal environment," and one "only incidentally concerned with illness." Equally interested in medicine and poetry, he stated flatly that "they amount for me to nearly the same thing." He himself was almost indifferent to "cures" for pathological conditions; the whole idea of "a cure is absurd" anyway. "Cure to a physician is a pure accident, to the pathologist in his laboratory almost a disappointment. The real thing is the excitement of the chase," "discovery," and "the accumulation of wealth." Williams thus felt justified in ignoring customary medical attitudes. Since normal office and hospital procedures did little either for patient or doctor, he "came to find writing . . . a necessity"; "to treat a man as something to which surgery, drugs and hoodoo applied was an indifferent matter; to treat him as material for a work of art made him somehow come alive to me."[5]

Such a complex of views could not help but influence both the form and the content of the resulting verse. One of the best-known poems in *Spring and All* has as its observing "I" an implicit doctor in his car driving "By the road to the contagious hospital," thus as was so often the case taking a cubist view of nature, seeing it from a moving perspective; nature, in turn, remained a "nature morte," a still life. The wind might blow and the clouds move, but nature itself was a collection of "dead, brown leaves" and "leafless vines— / lifeless in appearance" even as spring approached. The imagery is appropriately obstetrical as "They enter the new world naked, / cold, uncertain of all / save that they enter." The objects in nature stir as new flesh "quickens," as a poem quickens in the peripatetic imagination of the obstetrician. The attentive reader realizes that the house of nature, the house of art, and the houses of the medically needy all evoke each other, babies, leaves, and poems bursting forth as the doctor scrawls down the relevent information on his prescription pad—large enough, after all, for the sort of poems Williams felt inclined to write.[6]

The effect on Williams's criticism was similar. He felt such a close affinity for Marianne Moore, for example, that he all but took her into his car as a fellow passenger. Her art, he was sure, accomplished its goals "by rapidity of movement. A poem such as 'Marriage' is an anthology of transit. It is a pleasure that can be held firm only by moving rapidly from one thing to the next." Like a distracted doctor at the wheel, "she despised connectives," taking each impression as it came and leaving all else to the reader. She worked as if she were in a diagnostic laboratory. "With Miss Moore a word is a word most often when it is separated out by science, treated with acid to remove the smudges, washed, dried and placed right side up on a clean surface." He then tied his own biological imagination to the more physics-oriented one of so seemingly distant a fellow modernist as composer Edgard Varèse: "And from this clarity, this acid cleansing, this unblinking willingness, her poems result, a true modern crystallization." Thus, as Kenneth Burke noted perceptively, Williams was both "an imaginative physician and a nosological poet."[7]

The normal round of the doctor, however, not only included the viewing of the world through a moving car window and the assumption that life in a hospital was normal reality, it also meant a new stress on voices. Whether in his office or in the home of a patient, a doctor was always subject to a barrage of complaints and descriptions in multiple accents, from multiple viewpoints, of what the problems were. No two parents or children necessarily agreed on anything, and all wished to convince the doctor of the correctness of their perceptions. An imaginative doctor could then turn the cacophony into a Greek chorus, a scene from Dante, or a wry sense of how Williams's Paterson might resemble Joyce's Dublin. Called upon to examine a woman who had been raped, for example, Williams managed to work his voice, her voice, and the rapist's all distinctively into the first ten brief lines, including the title, which was integrated into the text:

THE RAPER FROM PASSENACK

was very kind. When she regained
her wits, he said, It's all right, kid,
I took care of you.

What a mess she was in. Then he added,
You'll never forget me now.
And drove her home.

Only a man who is sick, she said,
would do a thing like that.
It must be so.

The reduction of such incidents to coherent art prepared him to understand much of what Joyce would be doing, and all but dominated the method of such parodistic prose as *The Great American Novel*. The irony here is considerable, since the giving of medical evidence to a doctor would seem on its surface about as far from a modernist language as it would be possible to get. But add to such voices a sense for the fragmentary nature of medical office discourse, and the need to lay out not only a diagnosis based on analysis of discrete slide specimens, but also a course of treatment based on discrete dosages, and you get poems where connectives really are lacking. As Kenneth Burke recalled him saying, "there is nothing that with a twist of the imagination cannot be something else."

The response of the doctor to the litany of complaints and miscellaneous trivia was not precisely what patients or readers would expect to hear from a physician. Health professionals always filtered what they heard through a perceptual apparatus trained in a technical rhetoric. They also developed a sense of the speaker: If one speaker complained of an obscure pain it usually meant a period of marital stress; in another, the same words might imply a peptic ulcer. One patient's period of hyperactive talk and nervous sweating might be a response to parental disapproval of a planned wedding; the same symptoms in someone else might be a prelude to a diabetic attack. In response to this barrage of words, a shrewd doctor might prescribe rest, a change of diet, a drug, or a placebo, each in a wide range of appropriate voices. In the process, he might become a voyeur of eye or ear, prying as much for artistic as for medical reasons. He might compose a case history, a prescription, or a poem—or indeed a poem that reduced a case history to the space available on a prescription pad. All separations between art and life could easily disappear, especially if the doctor usually composed late at night in a state of advanced fatigue:

> *O tongue*
> *licking*
> *the sore on*
> *her netherlip*
>
> *O toppled belly*

O passionate cotton
stuck with
matted hair

elsian slobber
upon
the folded handkerchief

I can't die

—moaned the old
jaundiced woman
rolling her
saffron eyeballs

I can't die
I can't die.[8]

Doctors also developed idiosyncratic relationships to machines and to technology generally. Overmedicated contemporary readers often remain unaware of how primitive medical science and its delivery were when Williams received his training. Knowledge of antisepsis had only recently become widespread. The causes, even the names, of many diseases remained obscure; cures were even harder to come by. Most drugs worked badly if at all. Derivatives from opium and alcohol could temporarily dull pain, but just as often addicted or confused patients while doing nothing to cure the disease. Influenza, tuberculosis, hepatitis, diabetes, polio, diphtheria, and a dozen other diseases were far more difficult to prevent or to cure than they have become since the introduction of wonder drugs in the 1940s. Not having decisive answers, doctors were often prisoners of the equipment of delivery: the bicycles, traps, and automobiles that took doctor to patient; the telephones that conveyed the bad news; the electricity that made sanitation easier; the increasingly sophisticated microscopes. It is thus somehow appropriate that when Williams set out to spoof *The Great American Novel* (1923), he claimed that the heroine was "a little Ford car—she was very passionate—a hot little baby." The information was of course misleading, but so was most "science" and "technology" of the period.[9]

The insistence on medicine being at the core of his being as well as his poetry intruded even on decisions and locations where Dr. Williams had no possibility of treating patients. When he chose to go to Europe for a year in 1909, he did not choose Paris, as Americans were doing in increasing numbers, even though he could manage the language and was familiar with French culture. He did not choose London, even though his friend from the University of Pennsylvania, Ezra Pound, was rising swiftly in the world of English verse there. "I chose Leipzig—to Pound's disgust." London had little to offer someone who already knew who he was. "I was a physician; that was to be my life, especially as I had no ability at all for literary intrigue. I knew I could not live as Pound lived, and had, besides, no inclination to experiment."

Even when he did visit Paris, as he did early in 1924 among other visits, and mingled with the literary bohemian set that revolved around James Joyce and Robert McAlmon, he could never find the words, or actually enter into the attitudes, that his numerous contacts seemed to require. Prone to extramarital dalliance, he nevertheless remained socially stiff and medically alert. One of the most illuminating of the anecdotes in his autobiography is his paragraph about a woman who was well known in literary circles, whose friends decided to honor with a dance. "She had T.B. and was being sent away for treatment somewhere in the country." Personally attractive and popular, she was nevertheless "coughing all over the place and showed that she had been going downhill fast." She had been having a final fling with an American sailor, but his furlough was ending as well. "Dancing, drunk, gay, through her tears she was saying a sorrowful farewell, a hat was being passed for her, while everyone in the place was exposed to her malady." This was a world more evocative of Edgar Allan Poe than of Ezra Pound; if Paris was a party for Williams, it was a party where at least one guest had served on his local board of health.[10]

II

Sometimes the poets and painters came to New Jersey. "Grantwood was the focus of all these events," Williams recalled later. "I was hugely excited by what was taking place there." Years earlier, persons unknown had put up summer cottages, and Alfred and Gertrude Kreymborg now occupied one of them. As editor of *Others*, Kreymborg attracted the sort of friends Williams found stimulating. Orrick Johns, Man Ray, Malcolm Cowley, and Alanson Hartpence were often in the neighborhood, usually with attractive spouses, and visitors might include Walter Arensberg, Marianne Moore, and Marcel Duchamp. Eager to participate in both magazine and conversation, "on every possible occasion" Williams drove over "to help with the magazine which had saved my life as a writer." He would arrive, Kreymborg recalled in *Troubadour,* "looking like Don Quixote de la Mancha driving the rusty Rosinante," with "enough of the Spaniard in his blood and the madman in his eye and profile to have warranted the comparison."[11]

Most often, however, the traffic went the other way. As a suburban doctor, Williams occasionally went to New York hospitals to consult or operate, and most Fridays during the major part of the year to visit Walter Arensberg in his famous salon, or Lola Ridge in her somewhat less well known and much less well financed one. Williams would check out the shows at 291 or the Modern Gallery, conduct editorial business with Kreymborg or Robert McAlmon, dine with friends, and then return on the ferry. This activity inevitably fused his mode of transportation, the seasons he experienced as he went, the ideas he experienced in paint and poetry, and the form of his own verse.

"I have discovered that most of / the beauties of travel are due to / the strange hours we keep to see them" he announced in "Jan-

uary Morning." People and buildings streamed through his consciousness, in all-but-random-seeming sections of unequal length
and unequal lines, at times evoking mythological musings. The
operation that provided the occasion for this particular trip was
postponed, but the poet took over without regret. "The young
doctor is dancing with happiness / in the sparkling wind, alone / at
the prow of the ferry!" He noted the Palisades, so naturally impressive and so near to Grantwood, "to bear a crest of / little peer-
ing houses that brighten / with dawn behind the moody /
water-loving giants of Manhattan." He wanted to write a poem
that even his mother could understand, but found his mood hard
to summarize because it kept shifting. Despite the sometimes
doleful aspects of medical life, he ended feeling a kinship with
"the young girls" who would sometimes "run giggling / on Park
Avenue after dark / when they ought to be home in bed." He
called the piece a suite, presumably a musical reference implying
that he has drawn representative items from a longer work: life—
the life of a poet, a doctor, a patient, and a people—as it sounds in
polyphony but appears to the eye in cubist fragments.[12]

Despite having left an impressive bibliography of works in a
wide variety of genres, Williams could be infuriatingly unclear
when it came to articulating his artistic values and intentions. Having never attended college, he never learned the history of literature or the customary ways of addressing an aesthetic problem. He
was an autodidact, with all the informational gaps and psychological insecurities that so often accompany that condition. A medical
degree was not a Harvard college degree, and time spent studying
in Switzerland, Germany, and France did not necessarily impart
linguistic fluency or social ease. He did not even have the inclination, let alone the time, to play chess, which was the real social cement of the Arensberg salon.

So Williams learned his aesthetics by guess and by golly, and by
having such friends as Charles Demuth. Fellow students in
Philadelphia, they met "over a dish of prunes at Mrs. Chain's
boarding house on Locust Street and formed a lifelong friendship

on the spot." Williams at the time was having thoughts about pursuing painting as his chief artistic outlet and Demuth was likewise pondering literature, his role model being James McNeill Whistler, the initiator of several important tendencies in the history of American modernism. But the two also shared an intuitive bond that most critics ignore: Demuth was chronicly ill. He was lame, seemed tubercular, and was definitely diabetic. Near death when several Canadian doctors developed the use of insulin for mitigating the worst effects of diabetes, he hung on for more than another decade of painful productivity. A domineering mother micromanaged what she could of his precarious life in Lancaster, Pennsylvania, and sheer medical necessity prevented anything like a productive exile in Paris. But like Williams, Demuth could commute, either to Rutherford or to New York, and he did so whenever circumstances permitted. And since he was also homosexual, he provided the vigorously heterosexual doctor with invaluable contacts to Marsden Hartley and the gay artistic community in the city, and to the overlapping group centered in Gertrude Stein's flat in Paris.[13]

Through these painters, Williams could internalize the meaning of paint for poetry. Demuth was apparently the first person to call his attention to the work of Cézanne, for example, and that remains the starting point for most internalist accounts of the development of modernism in French painting. Cézanne was the great simplifier, the man who could impose many different perspective angles on the same work and clarify his palette as he did so. Once he had digested such lessons, Williams was ready for cubism and the simultaneity of the early work of a favorite American artist, Stuart Davis. And from there: "It was the work of the painters following Cézanne and the Impressionists that, critically, opened up the age of Stein, Joyce and a good many others." In taking "that step over from feeling to the imaginative object, on the cloth, on the page, that defined the term, the modern term—a work of art, what it meant to them."[14]

From this original inspiration, Williams moved through the several directions that French modernist painting was taking. A painter might have found this taxing to the point of stylistic incoherence, but this was not necessarily the case with a poet. One obvious example was Henri Matisse. A friend of Leo and Sarah Stein, proprietor of a small school in Paris that attracted painters as able as Max Weber and Patrick Henry Bruce, Matisse was almost as well known and liked as a person as he was as a painter. Both Sarah Stein and Eduard Steichen brought small quantities of his work to America, and Williams apparently first saw "The Blue Nude" at a 1915 show at the Montross Gallery. Marius de Zayas featured Matisse again in a 1920 show, and Williams was moved to write "A Matisse" for the second issue of *Contact* (1921). His essay was evocative and descriptive rather than analytic, but it represents one of the few formal efforts he ever made to write about painting until he commented on the work of his friend Charles Sheeler in the late 1930s. He conveyed the essence of his response most clearly in a personal letter. "It is strange, nothing whips my blood like verse. . . . Verse lifts me up superbly," he wrote Marianne Moore in 1928. "Mostly it is something I have written myself that rouses me. Often, though, I get the same feeling from the work of others. The best of French painting does it. Matisse does it."[15]

No one with Williams's friends in New York City and contacts in Paris could remain ignorant of the work of Pablo Picasso, but during the 1920s Williams took little public notice, and his passing references sound unimpressed. He was a bit warmer toward Georges Braque, but his preferred cubist was Juan Gris. On record in several places about his admiration for a painter who was also a favorite of Gertrude Stein, Williams was especially impressed by the architectural sense he found in Gris's paintings. The references made clear that Williams knew a few of Gris's writings as well as his paintings, most likely "On the Possibilities of Painting" (1924). What he took from these few works was a sense that even an abstract work of art could make order out of a fragmented world. The creativity of a poet could work like that of an architect, using local stones to erect an orderly building, or like that of a synthetic cubist using collages of miscellaneous items to reconstruct a usable visual reality.[16]

In *Spring and All,* in the poem only later given the title "The Rose," Williams specifically introduces the work by recalling a reproduction of an unnamed work by Gris, and saying that it "is important as marking more clearly than any I have seen what the modern trend is: the attempt . . . to separate things of the imagination from life, and obviously, by using the forms common to experience so as not to frighten the onlooker away but to invite him":

> *The rose is obsolete*
> *but each petal ends in*
> *an edge, the double facet*
> *cementing the grooved*
> *columns of air—The edge*
> *cuts without cutting*
> *meets—nothing—renews*
> *itself in metal or porcelain—*
>
> *whither? It ends—*
>
> *But if it ends*
> *the start is begun*
> *so that to engage roses*
> *becomes a geometry—*
>
> *Sharper, neater, more cutting*
> *figured in majolica—*
> *the broken plate*
> *glazed with a rose*

The brother of an architect, the admirer of a painter, was attempting to build cubist poetry.[17]

Aside from Marcel Duchamp, who exercised his influence largely outside the use of paint on canvas, the only other European artist who conceivably could have had much impact on Williams was Wassily Kandinsky. Through his influence on Marsden Hartley and the sale of *Improvisation #27* to Stieglitz from the 1913 Armory Show, Kandinsky was a visible presence. But the spiritual emphases that gave him his appeal to Hartley made him temperamentally unappealing to Williams, and in practice the only real "influence" seems to have been in the use of the word "improvisation." Just as Hartley liked Kandinsky's use of the word "spiritual" but probably never paid much attention to Kandinsky's actual ideas, so Williams liked the idea of improvising poems on the spur of the moment, the better to convey the essence of his stream of consciousness. And even in the use of this word, first place probably should go to poet Arthur Rimbaud, whose *Illuminations* (1886) helped inspire *Kora in Hell*. Although not then available in English, they were accessible to Williams, and translators occasionally referred to them as "improvisations."[18]

In fact, for reasons of friendship, affinity, and proximity, American developments in painting during the early and middle 1920s were far more significant. In August of 1923, the writer and editor Matthew Josephson introduced Williams to Charles Sheeler, and one of the most important interdisciplinary friendships in American cultural history commenced. In and out of the Stieglitz circle depending largely on the whims of an increasingly irascible Stieglitz, Sheeler was the leading precisionist in the country. He was the most genuinely proficient of the group in both painting and photography. Georgia O'Keeffe and Charles Demuth were chiefly but not exclusively painters, while Stieglitz and Strand were photographers in practice, whatever their critical interests.

The most precise effort to systematize precisionist attitudes is now that of Peter Schmidt. Logically enough the first premise was that "images ought to be rendered as precisely as possible." A photograph should have a sharp focus and achieve its effects without the photographer retouching it. A painting should have "a 'photographic' rather than a 'painterly' surface," having as well an overall sharpness that a camera could not duplicate. Second, precisionists "revised the genres of still life and landscape" to treat new industrial architecture as mountains, expressing modern ideas of the sublime by means of steam and smoke. The two forms in effect became one, nicely complementing the insights that Cézanne pioneeered. Third, each picture should be what Stieglitz called an "equivalent," meaning that it should be chiefly a portrait of an emotional experience. A sharply detailed object could most effectively articulate the tangible. Fourth, an artist should remain impersonal; the subject should be from public experience and accessible to public comprehension. Fifth, in America, artists should seek out autochthonous materials. Americans had absorbed the lessons of European modernism and should now domesticate them. America too could be an Arcadia. Industrial machinery and its products were aesthetically basic, and evocatively American.[19]

Even before meeting Sheeler, and before he had more than cursory personal relationships to other members of the Stieglitz circle expecting Demuth, Williams was working out his ideas in *Contact*, a little magazine that struggled through five issues between 1920 and 1924 before expiring from lack of money and readers. The first paragraph called for an art that "is indigenous of experience and relations" and proclaimed the editors' "faith in the existence of native artists who are capable of having, comprehending and recording extraordinary experience." *Contact* would be "open-minded toward all experiment," and "American, because we are of America." The last page contained a "further announcement" to the effect that it would be insisting on "the essential contact between words and the locality that breeds them." Aware that many readers might see his ideas as merely a projection of his friend Ezra Pound's imagism and vorticism, by the third issue Williams had specifically separated his group from Pound's. In "Yours, O Youth," he was ready to insist that lengthy exile in Europe weakened art. For Americans, good art only came from contact with the local area and its characteristic products: "It has been by paying naked attention first to the thing itself that American plumbing, American shoes, American bridges, indexing systems, locomotives, printing presses, city buildings, farm implements and a thousand other things have become notable in the world," he insisted. "Yet we are timid in believing that in the arts discovery and invention will take the same course."[20]

III

These influences now seem all but overwhelming: fauvism, both analytic and synthetic cubism, improvisation, imagism, vorticism, precisionism, localism, and stream of consciousness hardly exhaust the list, not to mention topics such as architecture that are not really ideas. Under the stress of wanting to be "new" as a poet while remaining "good" as a physician, Williams all but floundered in confusion. What helped bring it all together for him, at least in poetry, was Marcel Duchamp and New York dada.

"Dada" remains a word that analysts at all levels invoke with little agreement as to what, if anything, it actually means, or even to which arts it applies. Whatever "it" might be in essence, in historical context it arose in Zürich among a group of anarchist and nihilist artists who were disgusted with Western art, thought, and behavior, especially as they manifested themselves in World War I. The group favored a small café, Cabaret Voltaire, that served as a geographical if not truly conceptual point of unity that soon gave its name to a journal. An Alsatian poet, Hugo Ball, and his companion Emmy Hemmings "ran" the place in what they assumed was the spirit of one of the great skeptics of Western history. Ignoring Voltaire's rationalism and indeed much of the spirit of the ideas for which he stood, habitués of the cabaret denied logic and reason and indeed philosophy as a whole, and focused obsessively on the arts. Such institutions can put on musical and theatrical events, host poetry readings with painted backdrops, and send patrons out to be critics; they are intrinsically interdisciplinary. But such potentialities can generate much confusion as well.

No narrator of anything relating to dada is reliable by conventional historical standards, so even basic definitions come across as ex post facto anecdotage. To combine them plausibly: Needing a name reflective of their mood, the artists thumbed through a French-German dictionary and Chance pointed its finger at an entry that translates: "DADA. Noun masculine. Linguistics. Funny or childish term, used to describe a horse. Plural: des dadas.—Figurative: obsessive idea, learning, project one endlessly toys with, and always comes back to." This was lovely. It implied a new birth and early childhood, a horse that could easily have "hobby" as its first name, humor, obsession, and a certain spontaneity. It seemed inherently self-reflexive and -destructive. Like the war, it meant nothing, and everything. To those who found it too tedious to make yet further critiques of most aspects of Western civilization, it thumbed its nose, it fingered its caca, it wailed and drooled, and in general giggled past the necessity of dealing with that with which no one should have to deal.[21]

The exigencies of a world war did not prevent word of the new stirrings from reaching New York. On 30 September, 1916, Tristan Tzara wrote Marius de Zayas about what was going on in Zurich, enclosing ten copies of what was probably *Cabaret Voltaire*, the only issue of which had appeared in June 1916. One of the most important links between American and European modernists, the Mexican de Zayas was a veteran confidant of Alfred Stieglitz and had already played a significant role in acquainting the 291 circle with European ideas before the outbreak of the war. On 16 November, 1916, he responded to Tzara, enclosing copies of *291*, his own journal, which was, in fact, rather more avant-garde than its Swiss counterpart. The fact, put simply, was that New York was already in something of a dada mode. Americans could never be quite as cynical or nihilistic as Europeans, but they had absorbed a number of European ideas, and were in the process of absorbing people as well.[22]

America had had its decadence. It has yet to find its historian, but especially in the atmosphere of Harvard and the coterie around George Santayana, and nearby in the circles of photographer F. Holland Day and architect Ralph Adams Cram, the ideas of art, homosexuality, the ego, irrationality, and the will to power circulated with disorganized abandon. Young men read Schopenhauer, Stirner, and Nietzsche and quietly detached themselves from those ideas that had formed the basis of Brahmin culture. An occasional critic such as Benjamin de Casseres brought such ideas to small but receptive groups of readers in *Camera Work*, while immigrants like de Zayas added a much-needed cosmopolitanism to such discussions. Something of an innocent in modernism when he first went to Paris, de Zayas had one inestimable advantage over even such a visitor as Marsden Hartley: As a Mexican he was both fluent in Spanish and a living example of Spanish culture. He proved especially attentive to the role of African art, and "primitivism" generally, in modernist painting. He was prepared to announce that: "Art is dead" by 1912. Understood to mean "art as we have known it," it looked forward in an eerie way to the Armory Show and the arrival of Francis Picabia and Marcel Duchamp in New York City.[23]

In the swirl of controversy surrounding the Armory Show, few observers noticed that the cutting edge of the avant-garde had shifted from the Stieglitz salon to that of Walter and Louise Arensberg. While Stieglitz personally bought a Kandinsky work at the show, and gave Picabia a welcome that was positively effusive by the slightly chilly standards of 291, Arensberg effectively captured the real lion of modernity by offering Duchamp temporary lodgings, a subsidy, steady sales, invaluable contacts, and vast amounts of approval between 1915 and 1923. Unlike Stieglitz, Arensberg was a true decadent, and in the long course of history, Duchamp has proven the most influential of all modernists in the visual arts.

Many scholars writing on Williams ignore dada, and most scholars of dada place Williams as at best on the fringes of the movement, but this is inaccurate. The problem is both one of context and one of the easiest surviving records to consult. Although an outsider to much of American culture because of his British, Spanish, and Jewish heritage, which lingered on in his middle name, Williams was by training a bourgeois professional, a middle-class American tied to his job and neighborhood. Even his exposure to Swiss education and Parisian art did not and could not make him party to the nihilism, anarchism, and despair that was so common among creative Europeans for whom a devastating war would be the core fact of their lives. Stiff, earnest, and often humorless, Williams was doomed for life to live on the edge of bohemia, a true suburbanite for whom a Sunday trip to Grantwood represented an act of cultural intrepidity. He could chat casually with Arensberg or watch Duchamp play netless tennis with Man Ray, and literally nibble his way into modernism, picnicking.

But actual participation, truly getting into the spirit of Nietzsche or dada was beyond him, across the Hudson and far across the Atlantic. Neither his suburban soul nor his imperfect French were up to the strain. He knew it, but he kept trying, and then he left a self-flagellating account of his efforts in his autobiography, written during a period of poor health and creative aridity. The suave Duchamp, so famous in art and so devastating in his effects on women, intimidated and even humiliated Williams, probably unintentionally. In Williams's account, he tried awkwardly to praise one of Duchamp's paintings that was hanging on the Arensberg walls. Duchamp responded noncommittally—How does one respond to remarks on one's art from a suburban physician in a language one is still studying in between flirtations and games of chess? But the effect was one of deflation. "I could have sunk through the floor, ground my teeth, turned my back on him and spat," he groused thirty years later. "I realized then and there that there wasn't a possibility of my ever saying anything to anyone in that gang from that moment to eternity." He kept hearing about the work of Duchamp, Albert Gleizes, Jean Crotti, and Picabia, but felt his own responses were inappropriate, which in the short term they doubtless were. "I bumped through these periods like a yokel, narrow-eyed, feeling my own inadequacies, but burning with the lust to write."[24]

Williams did himself an injustice; he was earnest about everything, and for a "Carlos" he sometimes seemed more Germanic than Spanish. He thought about the irrational; he worked at being spontaneous; he grammatically took apart grammar. Through Demuth, Hartley, and Gris he got more comfortable with current painting; by reading Gertrude Stein and paying attention to the mail from Ezra Pound, he realized that important innovations were emerging from the postwar chaos. A poet had to rethink grammar and logic just as a painter had to reimagine perspective. His suburban soul soon balked only at the medical frontier. When that very epitome of the dada psychology, the Baroness Elsa von Freytag-Loringhoven, offered to give him her syphilis to "free my mind for serious art," he declined the honor.[25]

By 1923 he had his wind up, and *Spring and All* remains the preeminent achievement of American dada in words. He took new looks at the city, seeing "Lights / speckle / El Greco / lakes / in renaissance / twilight / with triphammers / which pulverize / nitrogen / of old pastures / to dodge / motorcars / with arms and legs—",-although sometimes his medical vocabulary still intruded: "where bridge stanchions / rest / certainly / piercing / left ventricles / with long / sunburnt fingers." Perhaps most successful was the unforgettable image of J. P. Morgan as the rapist-capitalist art collector, the man who used his ill-gotten gains to pillage the old Italian and Dutch masters that were the core of European museums. Deliberately using a lyrical frame pockmarked with the damage done to the language by contemporary advertising, Williams adapted dada to local circumstances:

> *The sunlight in a*
> *yellow plaque upon the*
> *varnished floor*
>
> *is full of a song*
> *inflated to*
> *fifty pounds pressure*

at the faucet of
June that rings
the triangle of the air

pulling at the
anemones in
Persephone's cow pasture—

When from among
the steel rocks leaps
J.P.M.

who enjoyed
extraordinary privileges
among virginity

to solve the core
of whirling flywheels
by cutting

the Gordian knot
with a Veronese or
perhaps a Rubens—

whose cars are about
the finest on
the market today—

And so it comes
to motor cars—
which is the son

leaving off the g
of sunlight and grass—
Impossible

to say, impossible
to underestimate—
wind, earthquakes in

Manchuria, a
partridge
from dry leaves

Williams was soon associated with the journal *Broom*, picking up "found" objects for his poems that sometimes seem suspiciously similar to Duchamp's readymades, and even using detritus after the manner of Kurt Schwitters's *Merzkunst*.[26]

IV

The early 1920s, framed by *Kora in Hell* (1920) and *Spring and All* (1923) plus *The Great American Novel* (1923), were the high point of Williams's early creativity. He wrote incessantly when he could, producing several of the poems that have had the greatest impact on posterity. But he experienced a sense of burnout and exhaustion. Following a suggestion from Ezra Pound, he determined to give himself and his wife a year off from children and patients, abandon the suburbs, and live for awhile at the center of things. They spent the fall of 1923 in New York, chiefly researching American history, and then the first half of 1924 traveling in Europe. The flow of poetry slowed, coming almost to a halt in 1927, producing a hiatus of over a decade. Prose took its place—the prose of a suburban poet trying to locate himself first in America, then in Europe, and finally in a semifictional exploration of his wife's family.[27]

The governing figure of the fall of 1923 was that of an American "working against time." Williams had only a few months to read a collection of erratically selected documents in the American History room of the New York Public Library, with not even a college education let alone any professional training to get him started.

Like many autodidacts he scorned the professional; in few of his writings is his belligerent anti-intellectualism more apparent. But since he was not a historian nor did he want to be, no one need feel obligated to regard *In the American Grain* (1925) as a work of history, which it is not. Just as so many of his poems were directly subversive of "poetry" in his time, and *The Great American Novel* a deconstruction of the novel form, so *In the American Grain* is an antihistory. It worked against time, against linearity, against context, and against many of the conventions of the field. As chemistry it was alchemy; as medicine it was homeopathy.

Modernists did not believe in "history" as most historians and educated readers usually did. Modernists used historical data like stray objects they might have found in the family attic, Pound's *Cantos* being the best-known example. But Pound had a solid humanistic education and the equivalent of about two years of graduate study; other leading modernist poets, such as Eliot, Stevens, or Cummings, were equally well trained. On their territory, Williams was a parvenu and he knew it. But *his* territory was suburban medicine, and there he was secure in ways beyond them. What a suburban doctor saw was human and social pathology, the various sicknesses of the poor and the profligate, of the Passaic and Paterson.

So he fussed about in his chosen attic, sampling documents and pamphlets and old books eager to find puritans to blame for the narrowness of the American soul, or capitalists to blame for the blight that oppressed anyone living in his locality. He read not like Charles Beard but like Marcel Duchamp, seeking objects to name, readymades to put on display in a new context, appealing to the mind and not the eye. "In these studies I have sought to re-name the things seen," says the opening sentence, and as for certain historical conventions, he expressed himself most clearly elsewhere in an essay on Virginia that was roughly contemporaneous: "Unity is the shallowest, the cheapest deception of all composition . . . ability in an essay is multiplicity, infinite fracture, the intercrossing of opposed forces establishing any number of opposed centres of stillness." Like Duchamp, this connoisseur of readymades had once been a cubist.[28]

The resulting chaos was in part self-imposed. "The book is as much a study in styles of writing as anything else," he recalled in a 1939 letter to Horace Gregory. "I tried to write each chapter in the style most germane to its sources or at least the style which seemed to me appropriate to the material." He copied, openly in some cases and not in others, many paragraphs, and not a word in the sections on Cotton Mather, Benjamin Franklin, or John Paul Jones was his own. He thought the results seamless, but that was hardly the case. No one could stitch together objects found in a trunk.

Given his operating premises, what worked best for Williams was the spontaneous response he felt to a meeting with a man he had not known when he conceived the book. Knowing of their mutual interests, bookseller Adrienne Monnier arranged an introduction for Williams to Valéry-Nicolas Larbaud on 26 January, 1924 in Paris. Ill at ease and forced to speak French, Williams soon found his mind racing with new ideas and problems. Larbaud had read the sections Williams had been publishing in *Broom* as he went along, and made numerous suggestions about what was missing or needed further analysis. They talked most memorably of "Bolivar and the grand manner in which Spain undertook its new world colonization as contrasted with England's niggardliness," he informed Marianne Moore a few days later, and he was still elaborating on the same subject two months later. He made the meeting and the circumstances leading up to it the occasion for his chapter on Pere Sebastien Rasles—a chapter in which Rasles had to wait fifteen pages before he is allowed his ten pages of glory. A French Jesuit largely unknown even to historians, Rasles made contact with the Native Americans, "TOUCHING them every day." For this the British killed them. During a skirmish he drew their fire intentionally to allow Indian women and children to escape; "and they mangled him besides, leaving him disfigured and with his bones all crushed within him." The rest of the book is equally pro-French and pro-Spanish, even when the heroism is quixotic or destructive; and anti-British, for they brought chiefly puritanism, the source of much of what Williams disliked about contemporary America.[29]

History thus here becomes that modernist staple, yet another tale of tales: Williams writing of what he has heard, from a man telling tales of what he has read, which were in turn tales told by eighteenth-century chroniclers. The orality is thus central, but it is an orality about Williams's favorite word, "contact." Rasles had it, Red Eric had it, Samuel de Champlain and Daniel Boone had it, even Edgar Allan Poe had it: Each touched a tribe, a place, a locality, each planted a seed in the motherland of a doctor who wanted to deliver his own sensibility even as he delivered babies. Puritans like Cotton Mather, capitalists like Alexander Hamilton, did not have it. Balancing Carlos versus Williams, listening to a Latin question the Anglo-Saxon, the poet never hesitated. The book had unity.[30]

V

Unity or not, signs of authorial fatigue were everywhere in the book, as well as in *A Voyage to Pagany*, which followed—a 1928 volume based on a 1924 trip. Almost in anticipation of bad reviews, he became hypersensitive to light. Normally unpolitical, he was outraged at the execution of Sacco and Vanzetti. Hopelessly dependent on contact with his own family, he lost even that temporarily when his wife and boys spent the 1927/28 academic years in Europe, leaving the poet both depressed and barren of verse. He published an eighty-five line poem, "Paterson," that took on importance later, when he returned to the theme in his later epic poem *Paterson*, but that at the time looked more like the end than the beginning of his career. The Dublin of James Joyce was much on his mind; if Dublin, why not Paterson? To a poet who seemed determined to make verbal purses out of improbable ears, it certainly was a challenging question. The readymades, the Merz, had well over a decade to wait, but then such ideas in such things did not usually tarnish.[31]

FIVE

CHARLES SHEELER AND
THE CUBISM OF COUNTRY LIFE

In the course of one year, Charles Sheeler reached his first artistic maturity and achieved substantial public recognition as a photographer. In 1916 he had begun working as assistant to Marius de Zayas at the new Modern Gallery. Several intimates of Alfred Stieglitz, wishing as tactfully as possible to introduce a note of commercial reality into the business of selling modernist art, had pushed Stieglitz into at least passive acceptance of their perception of what sort of sponsorship their artists needed, and the Modern Gallery was the result. During the next year, de Zayas honored Sheeler, Morton Schamberg, and Paul Strand with a photographic show in March, and then in December gave Sheeler an exhibition of his own. The next year, Sheeler entered the thirteenth John Wanamaker photographic exhibition in Philadelphia, and walked off with both the first and the fourth prizes; Paul Strand won both second and fifth; and Schamberg won the third. Even as Stieglitz all but abandoned creativity due to a deep depression brought on by his unhappy marriage, his disaffection from a war fought against his cultural fatherland, and his inability to attract readers to *Camera Work* or buyers to 291, his disciples were clearly taking over, and in doing so were restoring photography to a place as an art equal in rank to painting.[1]

Almost pathologically shy, and self-effacing in ways that even affected his art, Sheeler stood out in the garrulous and histrionic Stieglitz set simply by not standing out. His work spoke for him. He apparently had had some contact with Stieglitz as early as

1911, but the first letter of any importance was written in 1915. Eager, almost desperate for approval, Sheeler knew intuitively that flattery could do no harm. In 1916, he saw a collection of Stieglitz' works for the first time, and assured him that "they are absolutely unparalleled." Always on the lookout for disciples, Stieglitz responded with increasing enthusiasm. He soon integrated Sheeler into the surviving 291 set, which by then included Strand, de Zayas, Marsden Hartley and, increasingly, Georgia O'Keeffe. When de Zayas formed his own gallery, Sheeler was a natural choice to be his assistant as well as an artist on display, and he was soon managing the place whenever de Zayas was away. And since Stieglitz often sat on competition juries, or had great influence on those who sat in his stead, Sheeler was assured of respectful attention for any work he might submit. He remained at the top of the photography profession until he willfully suppressed his work to focus on painting in the 1930s.[2]

II

Sheeler was born in 1883 to a prosaic Philadelphia family with no interest in the fine arts. Lacking any clear sense of what he should do, in 1900 he enrolled for three years in the School of Industrial Art. "The program there comprised, drawing from the antique, life class, and applied design," he recalled about thirty-five years later. The course was essentially an "introduction to the various orders of ornament, Greek, Egyptian, Romanesque and others, and the application of them as designs for carpets, wall-papers and other two-dimensional surfaces. That phase of design having to do with forms in the round was outside our province." Such unimaginative activity drove Sheeler to boredom rather than a job, and instead of entering the workforce and becoming a useful citizen, in 1903 he entered the Pennsylvania Academy of Fine Arts.[3]

The atmosphere was better there. He made friends with such talented fellow students as Schamberg and Walter Pach, and all of them profited, at least over the short term, from the teachings of William Merritt Chase. During the last half of the nineteenth century, academy students had received instruction from such talented artists as Thomas Eakins and Thomas Anshutz, but all things considered, the institution "had declined," and Chase was about all that was left. His enthusiasm was "infectious," but his painting style was lush, spontaneous, and superficial, aimed more at capturing the picturesque moment than at communicating worthwhile ideas. He could not build "the elements in a picture" nor was he given to "consideration of the forms as such." He was an improvement over the teachers at the School of Industrial Art, but irredeemably second-rate.

What Chase did do was take his classes to Europe; Sheeler and Schamberg spent the summers of 1904 in England and Holland, and of 1905 in Spain. Sheeler loved seeing the originals of many works in the National Gallery in London, and was impressed by the living standards of the leading British painters — he mentions visiting the studios of Sir Lawrence Alma-Tadema, Frank Brangwyn, and John Singer Sargent. In Holland, the work of Frans Hals and Rembrandt made the deepest impression, but the limits of his training caused him to filter the new perceptions in odd ways. Upon his return to Philadelphia, for example, he tried to do a work in the style of Hals, using the methods of Chase. No one will be surprised to learn that he could not do it in one flashy, spontaneous sitting. The next year he was into Velázquez, El Greco, and Goya.

By 1908, Sheeler and Schamberg were out on their own, sharing a Chestnut Street studio and soon a small house in rural Doylestown as well. But they missed Europe, and so in December they headed off for Italy, visiting galleries in Naples, Rome, Venice, Milan, and Florence: "We realized that a picture might be assembled arbitrarily, with a primary consideration of design, that would be outside of time, place or momentary conditions," he remembered. "With these observations our interest in representing the casual appearances of nature ceased. We were from then on to be interested in causes rather than effects." He was especially impressed with the work of Tommaso Masaccio and Piero della Francesca; he had no idea that he was, in an odd way, following in the path of Leo Stein, who had made an extended study of Andrea Mantegna before going on to Paris and the connoisseurship of modernism.

The Paris Sheeler found in 1909 was "seething." For the first time, he "saw the paintings of Picasso, Matisse, Braque, and Derain among those then working, and of Van Gogh and Cézanne among their immediate predecessors." In respectful bewilderment, he visited the salon of Michael and Sarah Stein, but the pictures put him into a state of "shock." Nothing from Philadelphia to Rome had prepared him for the experience of fauvism or cubism. The pictures "bore no relation to the nature, as I knew it, and in their deliberate deviations gave me no clue to their reasons." Philadelphia teaching from Eakins to Chase had always been tied to nature, and he could not quickly sever the connection between what he saw and what he painted. But he left in no doubt that something important was going on.

Circumstance then played a sly trick on Sheeler, his art, and those who have tried to analyze what happened. Even as world painting, Sheeler's included, was taking leave of nature as a direct inspiration of art, economic necessity was driving him back, not only to nature but to the common objects of everyday experience. Needing an income, he began selling his skills with a camera. His best customers proved to be architects who needed to document the homes they had designed; Sheeler became an accomplished documentarian. From exteriors he moved to interiors, documenting family paintings, decorative room schemes, porcelains, silverware, furniture, and statuary. He had little choice, and could just as easily take pictures of Chinese or Roman art as American, some examples of which he was apparently showing Stieglitz in 1915. It all presented a nice problem, parallel in a complex way to the artistic development of John Dos Passos in prose: the influence of architecture on another medium, especially when that medium was developing away from any direct representation of the object.[4]

One thing led to another. From buildings, to the interiors of buildings, to crafts, pottery, furniture, tools, machinery—soon not even the barn door was safe from the analytical eye. Sheeler discovered that his Doylestown house was within spying distance of Dr. Henry Chapman Mercer's Moravian Pottery and Tile Works, and he and Schamberg were soon friendly with Mercer, a man capable of collecting almost anything, so long as it was early American and had once been useful. Aspects of his collection were more appropriate for a flea market than a museum, but the twentieth century was moving away from "museums," and, well, what was so bad about flea markets? Mercer was Curator of American and Prehistoric Archaeology at the University of Pennsylvania and thought he knew what he was doing, in effect becoming a pioneer of material culture studies. Sheeler was fascinated. He loved the mundane, the practical, the useful; unlike Mercer, he really liked old things only when they *were* useful. Just as old poetry was speaking to Ezra Pound, old iron and wood began to speak to Sheeler. In short, while painting was driving Sheeler away from the delineation of the external, photography was returning him to it. No wonder he was confused for several years.

Architecture presented the problem, but it also supplied the solution. Obsessed by his Doylestown house, Sheeler snapped picture after picture of both inside and outside. It embodied his close relationship to Schamberg, it protected memories of Europe, it evoked the old America — it had been built by a Quaker in 1768— it played with light and shadow. It was thus architecture that provoked the photography that could in turn stimulate a modernist painting. Marius de Zayas knew what was going on. "It was Charles Sheeler who proved that cubism exists in nature and that photography can record it." Sheeler was soon finding it in barns as well as studios.[5]

II

This photography subsidized the painting of a man all but obsessed with the work of Cézanne. The surviving documentation suggests that Sheeler saw this work at the Druet Gallery in Paris as well as at the home of Sarah and Michael Stein, in 1909, and was soon attempting imitations back in Doylestown. He saw twenty Cézanne watercolors at 291 in 1911, and two years later several more in the collection that Dr. Albert C. Barnes was assembling— by 1915 Barnes owned fourteen, although no record indicates which ones Sheeler actually saw. A letter to Robert Henri has survived, however, in which he describes himself as "still reeling" from a May 1913 visit. The Armory Show, early in 1913, included fourteen Cézannes as well as six Sheelers. Even photographic evidence confirms the infatuation: A 1913 print of Sheeler's *Studio Interior* has a matted and framed print of Cézanne's *Smoker* hanging in a prominent place, the only picture visible by someone other than the photographer himself.[6]

"My attention in painting, at this time, was largely given to trying to realize a design composed of natural forms through a more or less arbitrary use of color," he summarized in the 1930s. "Sometimes with distortion of form to give direction or emphasis where needed. Subject matter was for the most part drawn from still-life and landscape." The Armory Show catalyzed his development away from Chase and toward Cézanne: "My work dealt with abstract forms. Sometimes with a clue to natural forms being evident, but quite as often without that evidence." Always, he recalled, it was derived directly from something seen in nature. "Color was entirely arbitrary with the intention of contributing to the organization of the forms comprising the design." His pictures in the years before America joined the war "represented an attempt to apply the principles found in the early Italians and the contemporaries of Paris." With the perspective of time, he came "to consider this period as having its chief value in clarifying my understanding of essentials and the necessity of an underlying structure." Abstract painters like himself wanted "to divorce the object from the dictionary and disintegrate its identity."

While experiencing this metamorphosis, he met Walter and Louise Arensberg, became a regular at their now famous salon, and even borrowed for awhile their small Cézanne, *Still Life with Apples* — Sheeler could only remark: "That picture was painted by one of the Angels. Incredible." For a shy man accustomed only to the company of Schamberg, the salon represented a rare social as well as an artistic opportunity. Not only did he meet the most adventurous painters and poets in America, in rooms where the walls were packed with examples of modernist art, he ate well: "About two in the morning large trays conveying rice pudding and compotes of fruit would appear and along about six the Arensbergs would have their place to themselves—for a few hours."

This relationship to the Arensbergs remains of vital importance not only for placing Sheeler within the avant-garde, but also for realizing how typical many of his concerns were. Not only did he thrive on rice pudding and compote as food, he also thrived on them as putative still lifes, as literal subject matter for a realistic imagination obsessed by Cézannist volumes and cubist planes. On their part, Walter and Louise Arensberg bought several of Sheeler's works, hanging them without a qualm among the Picassos and the Duchamps. They also commissioned Sheeler to be their official photographer, and the surviving pictures are now among the most important pieces of evidence scholars have for discussing the interests and achievements of the salon. The friendships proved lifelong, even surviving lengthy periods during which the Arensbergs lived in California. Sheeler framed and planed a salon of frames and planes; his realism was no aberration but an integral part of American modernism. His Bucks County barns belonged, a cubism of the countryside that was a legitimate relative of Edgard Varèse's music and William Carlos Williams's poetry. Marcel Duchamp was not the only connoisseur of staircases to visit New York.

Indeed, Duchamp became a special friend. "He was built with the precision and sensitiveness of an instrument for making scientific measurements, speaking cryptically out of a highly sophisticated mind frequently touched with a sly humor," Sheeler recalled. Where a touchy William Carlos Williams had never felt congenial with Duchamp, Sheeler did fine. Deadpan wit with a touch of dada rather appealed to Sheeler, and when he made his first *Self-Portrait* (1923) as a telephone, Duchamp liked it and said so. They shared a love of the common, ordinary, mass-produced items of everyday life, and in a sense Sheeler's barns are not only country cubism, they are ready-made architectures. Even in the 1930s, when they had scarcely seen each other for a decade, Sheeler and Duchamp could meet and share common interests with a warmth that might easily puzzle those who were sure neither man was capable of such an intimacy.

Given the excitements of the Armory Show and the Arensberg salon, no one could have blamed Sheeler for feeling increasingly restless where he was. "During the years following the Armory Show, life in Philadelphia seemed much like being shipwrecked on a deserted island. Whatever was happening that was stimulating and condusive to work was taking place in New York," he remembered. "With Philadelphia Modern Art, as it was then called, was of the same status as an illegitimate child born into one of the first families." The last straw was the death of Schamberg in the 1918 influenza epidemic. Devastated, Sheeler moved to New York in 1919, although he retained possession of the Doylestown house until 1926. He was soon assisting de Zayas at the Modern Gallery and serving as a freelance documentary photographer for other galleries as well.[7]

III

The rhythms and volumes of life changed accordingly. For awhile, Sheeler was one of the few Americans comfortable in both the Stieglitz and the Arensberg circles, indeed in *both* Stieglitz circles, for he got on well with de Zayas, as the Mexican modernist closed one gallery and then opened and closed another, to the growing disapproval of the belligerently anticommercial Stieglitz. Sheeler and Strand made their *Manhatta* film (1920) and all seemed serene, but Sheeler was too stable and understated for such company; worse, he was unashamed of having to make a living. Stieglitz was already down on Edward Steichen, Agnes Meyer, and de Zayas for actually encouraging sales, and when Sheeler showed signs of wanting to work for the advertising industry, Stieglitz picked a fight. In a review that would have been inoffensive to most well-disposed artists, Sheeler had criticized Stieglitz's continued use of platinum prints, as being rather aristocratic, precious, and needlessly diffuse in effect; better to use cheaper, more available, and harder-edged silver. He was right, which only made matters worse. So Stieglitz and Strand snarled privately, and Strand publicly as well; Sheeler moved on to the Whitney Studio Club and Galleries, where Juliana Force, who happened to be a native of Doylestown, treated him better; and to Condé Nast, which did not regard money as unmentionable. He also found a ready-made group of ex-Stieglitz associates who had useful contacts: Edward Steichen, Clarence White, Max Weber—it was quite an honor roll.[8]

With the advantages of hindsight, we can see now that the major strand uniting Sheeler's most important work between 1917 and 1927 was the cubist sense of the planar structure of found architecture. They were readymades for an American cubist who, like Duchamp, was passing beyond cubism toward chance, *blague*, dada, and the absent presence of an artist who was scarcely visible even in his own *Self-Portrait*. Sheeler photographed, he painted, and sometimes it is very hard indeed to be quite sure which was which, although he was later clear enough about the distinction: "Photography is nature seen from the eyes outward, painting from the eyes inward. Photography records unalterably the single image while painting records a plurality of images wilfully directed by the artist." For those who now experience these works chiefly through published books, the experience can get a bit eerie: seeing pictures in books, of pictures in living rooms, which may in turn be paintings based on photographs, or even vice versa. The Chinese box of modernism, the shifting from the fourth to the third to the second dimension, as befitted a friend of Marcel Duchamp, was merging into postmodernism even before it was a word.

But in barest outline the progression was: 1) Cézanne's sense of volume and plane replaced the applied ornament and the facile brushwork of the Philadelphia apprentice years. 2) Cubists, especially Picasso and Duchamp, contributed a style that was briefly liberating, which trained the eye to see architecture in a new way. 3) The Doylestown environment supplied random exteriors and one interior that proved that cubism existed in nature—"country cubism." 4) The move to New York supplied random large buildings that unified these interiors/exteriors by casting their own shadows, supplying streets or pillars or window frames that served as verticals, horizontals, and diagonals to evoke a cubist sense of multiple planarity. 5) The film *Manhatta* complicated things nicely, adding a new art form, a new paracubist sense of a moving eye that could then of course freeze for a still, to generate a painting based on that still. Thus an urban vision could complement a cubist vision, to double back within the mind of the artist to inform what may be the masterpiece of the whole process, *Interior* (1926), which seems to recall everyone from Cézanne and and Duchamp to Strand, not to mention the Dos Passos character in *Manhattan Transfer* who wanted to be a skyscraper. Here was the true meaning of the urban skyscraper, reduced to its formal elements and made back into a still life—the interior of the room becoming the objective correlative of the interior of the painter.

But in terms of earning a living, or even more than a coterie reputation, Sheeler was going nowhere as a painter in the mid-1920s and his productivity seemed to dry up. He preferred to paint, but he *had* to photograph, and the pressures of commerce drove him to the job that made him famous. He did a substantial amount of freelance work for N. W. Ayer and Son, a Philadelphia advertising firm. He took striking shots of Kodak cameras and L. C. Smith typewriters, and did what he could to popularize Champion sparkplugs and Firestone tires. Through Steichen's influence, he joined the staff of Condé Nast in April 1926 and his work appeared in gratifying quantities in *Vanity Fair* and *Vogue* over the next three years. He liked the money but hated the work. "I know little or nothing but my job which by this time has come to be like a daily trip to jail," he was moaning to Arensberg in January 1927. "It continues just as strenuous as ever, and more irksome." As a small token of his growing frustration, he and his wife left New York and moved forty miles north to South Salem, as if to balance the newer surfaces of urban life with the older ones of Bucks County memory.[9]

His big break came in October 1927. His advertising agency had recently taken on the account of the Ford Motor Company, and had suggested that Sheeler go to Detroit to make "an extensive collection of pictorial photographs of the plant." To a man who as a rule had no audible political opinions, who thus did not share the anticapitalist bias of many intellectuals, the invitation was stimulating on grounds of aesthetics. Usually called "River Rouge" or just "the Rouge," from its location near the Rouge River near Dearborn in Michigan, the Ford plant was above all "architecture," an external collection of volumes and planes that presented on a new scale the very problems that had long been his chief source of inspiration. The place simply "defied description," he wrote Arensberg. "The subject matter is incomparably the most thrilling I have to work with." A year later, like a painter infatuated by his most attractive model, he fell in love with the Lincoln cars he was shooting and bought one. "To sit at the wheel is a revelation," he glowed to Arensberg, sounding like the adman he had become. "My pleasure in it is akin to my pleasure in Bach or Greco and for the same reason—the parts work together so beautifully."[10]

This project, this positive attitude to industry and the machine, remains of crucial importance in the history of American modernism. Here is an artist who had assimilated much of what European art had to offer, from Cézanne to Duchamp, and integrated it firmly into the rural landscape, to the artifacts, to the very furniture of rural America. He had been at the center of the two most important modernist salons located in America and had seen his own work hanging on the walls in unblushing proximity to the works of those Europeans. He had not only documented these works with his own camera, he was a close friend of, and writing to, the man whose taste had been decisive in the field since shortly after the Armory Show.

The lessons are compelling: 1) The perception of an object in space, of what most analysts effectively mean by the words "structure" and "architecture," was at the core of the meaning of modernism as an aesthetic. From apples or tulips in space, through landscapes to barns to cityscapes, and finally to those temples of machine technology, the gigantic factories, the planes of continuity persist, giving a linear, two-dimensional look to problems that in essence were three- and even four-dimensional. 2) Once again, as with Strand, Dos Passos, and Williams, the timing coincides to indicate a significant shift within the modernist paradigm. A phase of individual artistic development was ending around 1926, and a new, collective phase was taking its place. This new view was not necessarily political, nor was it necessarily a result of a particular event, like the execution of Sacco and Vanzetti. It was rather a collective realization among many modernist artists that there was more to life than the individual consciousness, and more to art than planes and volumes. As Sheeler said in his "Autobiography," "Since industry predominantly concerns the greatest numbers, finding an expression for it concerns the artist." The photos and paintings that emerged from the Rouge were, for Sheeler, what *U.S.A.* became for Dos Passos: examples of a new modernist sense of the community, a coming to terms with the world outside.

PART TWO

DIFFERENT DRUMMERS

SIX

THE PULL OF CHICAGO

As early as 1936, the myth of the diaspora began to appear in print. "Up the Mississippi, from New Orleans to St. Paul, from the river on to Chicago, from Chicago west to San Francisco and from Chicago east to New York," Louis Armstrong wrote in his first autobiography. "That was the path jazz followed." Few serious historians questioned the assumption that jazz, however rural some of its roots, first took shape in the black musical community of New Orleans, or that somehow everything began to change in 1917. The heart of that community seemed to be Storyville, the fabled vice district where prostitution was legal and white money could end up in black pockets in exchange, among other things, for the excitements of a new and sometimes wildly disturbing music. When the forces of Christian morality, progressive reform, and the Navy department forced the closing of Storyville in November 1917, one phase of musical history seemed clearly over.

"It sure was a sad scene to watch the law run all those people out of Storyville. They reminded me of a gang of refugees. Some of them had spent the best part of their lives there. Others had never known any other kind of life," Armstrong continued in his second autobiography. "I have never seen such weeping and carrying-on." Prostitutes headed for the suburbs, pimps had to find more productive employment, and jazz musicians had far fewer places where they could earn a living. Some headed north or west, but most of the better ones spent a year or two on the river, playing on boats that paddled out on most pleasant winter evenings, and in the summers headed north as far as they could go. White folks in St. Louis or Davenport could thus hear the new music firsthand, and could be part of a relatively integrated musical milieu in Chicago when that city took over jazz leadership, as it soon did.

The myth had its truths. Certainly several important musicians worked in Storyville, then on boats, and then in Chicago. Certainly Chicago was the center of creative innovation in jazz, from 1917 to about 1926, while New Orleans went into a permanent eclipse. And just as certainly, and with more explanatory force, the Chicago atmosphere of illegal alcohol, gangster profiteering, and musical innovation replicated in eerie ways the New Orleans precedents of sexual exploitation and its musical backdrop. But as history, not to mention geography, the myth posed problems. The Mississippi River did not go anywhere near Chicago, for example, and no jazz musician arrived there by water. Everyone took trains, usually trains from major cities like New Orleans itself, or Kansas City or St. Louis. Even more mystifying was the assumption that jazzbands played in whorehouses. Such institutions employed pianists often enough, but never bands; ragtime piano could be appropriately atmospheric, but a hot Dixieland number with more than two hundred beats to the minute would definitely impede the serious business underway in the back rooms. Bands normally played in saloons, or honkytonks as they were often called, and those remained open, presumably as full of sailors as ever. Besides, any effort to watch the actual behavior of important musicians would show conclusively that they had been leaving since about 1907, mostly to go on the road, from date to date, as the caprice of the market dictated.

In the process, they sent creative ideas into the world that went far beyond Storyville, black life, and music. They created the myth of a jazz age, of a great party of frivolity, alcohol, and sexual indulgence that entertained people between the more serious problems of World War I and the Depression. Unfortunately for historical accuracy, "jazz" properly speaking had little to do with the creative lives of most people in the 1920s; white publicists bleached the blackness out of it and banked the profits, only to

lose them in 1929. And as the cultural history of Chicago unam-
biguously indicated, one jazz age was clearly over within a year or
so of 31 December, 1926.[1] Three black males illustrate the complexities of what actually happened: Jelly Roll Morton, Sidney
Bechet, and Louis Armstrong.

JELLY ROLL MORTON

Jelly Roll Morton claimed later that he had invented jazz, if not
single-handed at least with two very gifted ones. Because everyone knew him to be a gambler, a pimp, and a braggart, everyone
chuckled and turned the page. Certainly, he could verge on the unbearable. By the time of his Chicago prosperity, he literally glit-
tered as he walked. He wore a diamond ring, and sported a
diamond tie stud. He flashed a locket, a watch, and a belt, all with
diamonds. His very garters combined diamonds with gold. A diamond half a carat large flashed from his teeth, and of course his
mouth was open often enough anyway. He loved fancy suits, shirts,
and socks. He was vulgar beyond the dreams of white, Protestant,
proper Americans. But, as braggarts sometimes do, he had a point.
No single person "invented jazz." But if anyone were present at its
creation, he was. He was also the first real master of jazz form, and
he left a trail of recordings with which any skeptic could test his assertions. Insofar as such things are documentable, Morton was first.

In the fashion of all American modernists, Jelly Roll Morton
was an outsider to mainstream culture; but all such artists are outsiders in different ways. In his case, he was a Creole of color, black
by the aberrancies of American usage, but Mediterranean and
Caribbean by any application of common sense, and certainly in
his own opinion. He was born Ferdinand Lamott on 20 October,
1890, although he and a good many scholars have conferred a variety of misleading names and birthdates on him. "All my folks
came directly from the shores of France," he insisted to Alan Lomax in the 1930s, visual evidence to the contrary notwithstanding;
but he may well have been accurate in asserting that no family

member he could recall was "able to speak a word in American or English." Nothing was stable in his life. He was probably illegitimate; his very name was apparently a misspelling of "Lamothe" or "La Menthe," and he later changed it to "Mouton" in honor of a stepfather, and then "Morton," because he "didn't want to be called Frenchy."

His musical growth was hardly more stable than his name. He was a child of New Orleans, and his early musical experiences included a variety of string band and piano music. He recalled later that his "first instrument was made up of two chair rounds and a tin pan," but he soon moved on to the harmonica and the Jew's harp. "We always had some kind of musical instruments in the house, including guitar, drums, piano, trombone," and kids tried them all as the whim hit. For some years, the only type of music he heard was classical, and not until he attended a ragtime performance at a private party did he decide to specialize. Finances reenforced his preferences, for pianists could earn good money in "the District," which was the usual local name for Storyville. They were also well placed to sample the pleasures as well as the profits from gambling, drugs, alcohol, and prostitution.

But nothing was less stable than place, "New Orleans" becoming a word denoting a style of play more than a fixed city. Starting in 1907, Morton was on the road constantly, to Biloxi, St. Louis, Pensacola, Memphis, Washington, New York, and the West Coast. Ragtime, in the form of his piano and the rhythms of one accompanying drummer, was ubiquitous, both on its own and as part of a vaudeville routine or a silent film. On approximately 15 August, 1914, as the guns were sounding in Europe, he settled for about three years in Chicago, with regular forays to nearby cities like Detroit and St. Louis. In short, while Storyville shaped his mental and musical worlds, its closing was essentially irrelevant to his life. He spent the five years from 1917 to 1922 on the West Coast, and his "Chicago career" really only began when he returned to the city and began cutting his first discs in June 1923.[2]

Morton reentered Chicago in his usual tactful, understated way. A great composer after his fashion, he went to the Melrose Brothers Music Store to reclaim works he had tossed off so casually that their legal as well as their musical identity had been compromised. Overhead a large banner proclaimed "WOLVERINE BLUES SOLD HERE," and from inside came the sounds of an inept and unidiomatic rendition. No one forgot the scene. "A fellow walked into our store with a big red bandana on his head and hollored, 'Listen, everybody, I'm Jelly Roll Morton from New Orleans, the originator of Jazz!'" Lester Melrose remembered. In a manner doubtless adapted from silent cowboy films, Morton took over the space available, as if the music store were a saloon. "He talked for an hour without stopping about how good he was and then he sat down at the piano and proved he was every bit as good as he claimed and better."

The situation was ripe for mutual exploitation, and as always, white publishers, recording companies, and agents walked off with the bulk of the profits. Blacks on the whole lacked the legal knowledge and sophistication to protect themselves, and custom undercut any musician's claim to the profits of his creativity. Many simply sold the rights to their songs outright, and as Earl Hines recalled later: "Whenever he needed money, he'd write a tune and sell it to one of the downtown publishers like Melrose for fifty or seventy-five dollars." Instant money in hand seemed more useful than promises of long-term royalties from white businessmen. Besides, New Orleans musicians, cornet player Freddie Keppard being only the most paranoid, were long fearful that even seeing a musician play, let alone allowing his work to be written down, would mean a loss of control in the many cutting contests that musicians staged. Keppard placed a handkerchief over his fingers as he played, so no one could capture his fingering; Morton was behaving in a similar, secretive manner. "You may wonder why I didn't copyright my tunes in the old days. Well, it was not only me, but many others," he told Alan Lomax; "we kept our melodies for

our private material to use to battle each other in battles of music."
The winners of such battles could usually count on the best jobs.
Their secrecy in practice barely slowed the progress of creative
theft and exploitation: "They would steal our tunes and come out
with them anyhow." Certainly the Melroses had incomes far in excess of Morton and his fellow musicians.

Musically speaking, ragtime was something of a dead end, a
form that resisted further creative development. The innovation
that has earned Morton the title of "First Great Composer" of jazz
was his ability to fuse ragtime with blues. This implied the oxymoronic capacity to write down the improvised, to capture forever
in a score or on records the whims of the moment. On a piano, it
meant fusing the black keys, which Morton notoriously preferred,
with the white, the African pentatonic with the European diatonic.
"This was not just a matter of flatting thirds and sevenths," Gunther Schuller has pointed out in his definitive study of early jazz
recordings. "It meant re-thinking the music he played in terms of
a melodic-harmonic language that did not exist in Western music."
In this new language, "the blue notes, like the embellishing microtones of Indian and other Asian music, gave the music its expressive latitude, subject, nevertheless to relatively strict habits of
voice-leading, harmonic functions, and rhythmic associations."

Morton hit his creative peak in six solo sides that he recorded
for Gennett in Richmond, Indiana, and maintained it through the
legendary Red Hot Peppers ensemble recordings of 1926 for Victor in Chicago. After that things got sloppier by the year, and although recordings are available into late 1939, the creative edge is
gone. But at his best, Morton managed to be a pianist who could
accomplish something rare in jazz. "A jazz pianist who is going to
perform unaccompanied must in effect fulfill three functions simultaneously," Schuller has written: "He must play a melody or
some form of a leading line; he must provide an underlying harmony; and he must also be his own rhythm section and bass line."
Morton not only had the ego for three men, he played as if he were
his own bass and drum accompanists. In the process, he rivalled

Charles Ives in his explorations of complex polyrhythms. But no more than Ives could he fight the pressures of instrumentalists, bandleaders, and recording companies in their inability to assimilate real innovation, or their need to realize profits from compositions that invariably sold best when they most resembled popular dance tunes.[3]

SIDNEY BECHET

Early in his autobiography, Sidney Bechet made it clear that a special form of communication had long been central to the black experience. His grandfather, Omar, had been a slave who "could do anything. He could sing; he danced, he was a leader." On Sundays when slaves had a free day, "he beat out rhythms on drums at the Square—Congo Square they called it." Omar "made his own drums out of skins of a pig or a horse hide. He knew horns." In this manner blacks could exercise a psychic freedom even before their bodies won emancipation. "That was how the Negro communicated when he was back in Africa. He had no house, he had no telegram, no newspaper. But he had a drum." At first, perhaps the drumbeat was all they had, but still, it conveyed the troubles, the wrongs, the cruelties, the blues of slavery. But "little by little they began to sing it" too. Not enough time had passed by his day for anything sophisticated to emerge; perhaps legal freedom was a basic requirement. "But still, as an idea, the way he played his horns, the way he beat on his drums, he was still a background music. It was still a music that hadn't broken loose, it hadn't stopped being scared." This heritage "was an awful early beginning."

Bechet's father had been a boy at emancipation. He "fooled around with horns and the instruments they had, and he sang along with them—the spirituals and all the shouts—and he danced too." Although he was a shoemaker by trade, "where he really lived, where he really learned who he was inside himself—that was always where the music was being played. That was his real life." This heritage, this stress on music as communication among the marginal members of society, remained central to jazz, and to American modernism writ large. It would lead as well to habits of excess, to a tendency to resort to violence, especially when drinking, gambling, or otherwise under stress. Like many from his background, Sidney Bechet was fascinated by hoodlums and by violence. And he committed his share of acts, more than once facing imprisonment or deportation because of them. They were the dark side of the music of probably the best clarinet player in jazz during its first flowering. The violence and the beauty of tone were in essence saying the same things.[4]

Like Jelly Roll Morton, Bechet was a Creole of color. His name has proven as resistant to formula as Morton's. At the time, New Orleans folk all but universally called him "Bash-ay," and in his first autobiography Louis Armstrong even spells his name "Bachet." New Yorkers called him "Basha," and he even ran a Club Basha named in his honor. Parisians, wise in the ways of Anglo-Saxon barbarisms, always called him "Bash-ett," while later students, showing off their school French, now generally call him "Besh-ay." Such were the emblematic ways of jazz, as if he were hard to define in any specific way. The sound was never stable, and always moving. Nor, indeed, was his instrument. He had a party trick that in its subtle way brought together elements of what jazz musicians often did. As John Chilton has written, "he gradually took his clarinet to pieces, but continued to play a tune on the remnants, dramatically completing the act by playing on the mouthpiece only." Blacks seemed able to cope with any effort to keep them from communicating.

Bechet always denied that the closing of Storyville had much impact on jazz in general or him in particular. The dates might suggest otherwise, but he was probably correct; the real operating factors in 1917 were financial. New Orleans musicians commanded only minimal rates of pay, and numbers of them had been ranging far afield for years. Chicago simply paid more, and in most cases the union situation favored players from New Orleans. In most cities, unions controlled the rights to regular playing assignments, and required newcomers both to serve an apprenticeship period and to pass a sometimes stringent sight-reading test. Like most pioneers of early jazz, Bechet couldn't read. As a result of such fortuitous circumstances, such Louisiana players as Lawrence Duhé were already settled into bands, in this case at the De Luxe, and had been since April 1917. Bechet joined the group in 1918 and immediately became its "featured hot man."

Ever quarrelsome, Bechet lasted about a year, and then started looking for ways out. He found a suitable one early in 1919 when Will Marion Cook, one of the most gifted black musicians playing more conventional classical and popular orchestral material, offered to take him on a postwar European tour. They sailed in June as the Southern Syncopated Orchestra (SSO). While there, Bechet not only played at Buckingham Palace at the request of the trendy Prince of Wales, he attracted attention of more professional importance. Ernest Ansermet, conductor of L'Orchestre de la Suisse Romande and a long-time intimate of Igor Stravinsky, was in London with the Ballets Russes. He caught several performances of the SSO. Already aware of the technical aspects of ragtime and blue notes, Ansermet knew talent when he heard it. The assessment appeared in the *Revue Romande* for 19 October, 1919. The SSO had "an extraordinary clarinet virtuoso who is, so it seems, the first of his race to have composed perfectly formed blues on the clarinet." Two pieces especially impressed him. "Extremely difficult, they are equally admirable for their richness of invention, force of accent, and daring in novelty and the unexpected." They suggested to him a style and form that was "gripping, abrupt, harsh, with a brusque and pitiless ending like that of Bach's Second Brandenburg Concerto." Ansermet would "never forget" the name of Sidney Bechet. "What a moving thing it is to meet this very black, fat boy with white teeth and that narrow forehead . . . who can say nothing of his art, save that he follows his 'own way,' and then one thinks that this 'own way' is perhaps the highway the whole world will swing along to-morrow."[5]

Such glory was insufficient to carry Bechet for very long and his penchant for women and alcohol soon did him in. Bechet got into an altercation involving assault on a female companion, was found guilty, and sentenced to fourteen days of hard labor. He served his time, was promptly deported, and was thus back in New York on 13 November, 1922.

Both time and place were fortuitously appropriate. New York had most of the money in the entertainment business, loosely defined, and within five years would all but wipe Chicago off the map when it came to both creativity in jazz and the dissemination of all music by mechanical means. Bechet quickly found gigs with a society orchestra, and took the somewhat improbable role of a Chinese laundryman who played jazz in a show, *How Come*. One of his fellow cast members for a brief period was the equally temperamental singer Bessie Smith; one viewer who never forgot the experience was an unknown pianist named Edward Kennedy Ellington—he had never previously heard Dixieland. The engagement didn't last long—they rarely did—but such was the New Orleans presence in New York that Clarence Williams, another emigré from the late teens, grabbed the chance to introduce Bechet to his first recordings. Better established in business than most blacks, Williams arranged for Bechet to record *Wild Cat Blues* with the Clarence Williams's Blue Five for Okeh. Playing a soprano sax, Bechet confirmed his place as the best instrumentalist active at that time. "Everybody had that record. That was all you could hear," Barney Bigard recalled in his memoirs. "Every time you passed someone's house that had the door or windows open, they would be playing that song on their Victrola." Only later did he leave New Orleans, come to New York, and actually meet Sidney Bechet.

The next year, Louis Armstrong arrived to offer serious competition from a position with Fletcher Henderson's Orchestra. Bechet was the most competitive of players and could never have tolerated so talented a rival off the stage, even one so congenial as Armstrong. But sheer professionalism has compulsions of its own, and at least the two played different instruments. Clarence Williams brought them together for several sessions, beginning 17 October, 1924. *Texas Moaner Blues* is probably the pick of the litter, musically speaking, and Armstrong clearly dominates. But the fact of the record is perhaps more important than its obscure life as music: Here were two of the three greatest musicians to emerge from New Orleans musical culture; both had passed through Chicago, and both were recording in New York City. It was a long way from the Mississippi River and Storyville at best a distant memory. Bechet—along with his enormous German shepherd, Goola—was soon playing with Duke Ellington's Washingtonians, and had a famous cutting contest with a young rival named Coleman Hawkins. Bechet won, after a night so memorable it survives in Ellington's memoirs and several histories, but unfortunately neither the contest nor the music with the Washingtonians survives on records.[6]

Ever restless, Bechet soon tired of New York City, and when he had the opportunity to join the band of Claude Hopkins as it was departing for Paris to back performances of a show called *La Revue nègre*, Bechet took it. Everyone travels in his own way. On the boat, he spent most of his time with a singer named Josephine Baker. But his mind, at least in retrospect, was actually on more ancestral matters. "France, it's closer to Africa. I've wanted to be as close to it as I could," he wrote in his memoirs. "My grandfather, he was Africa." The experience of Paris provoked a strong atavism. "It's all so mixed up with the music," he continued. "In Paris it's like I can hear all what was happening to it when my grandfather was making it, back in those days when it had just been brought over from Africa and was still finding itself in the South." The matter needs stressing. Paris for Creoles of color was a cultural home, a cosmopolitan musical center with no traditions of slavery, segregation, or prejudice.

The show moved on to Belgium and Germany, only to fall apart when Baker accepted a position with the Folies Bergère. Bechet quickly joined a band headed for the Soviet Union and was playing in Moscow on 22 February, 1926. He wandered through the country for awhile, then headed back to Germany and a series of stints that took him swiftly across Europe from Sweden in the north to Turkey in the east to Spain in the west. He apparently even made it to Egypt. By 1928 he was back in Paris. But he could never stay out of trouble for long and a shooting incident on 20 December, 1928, landed him in jail for the better part of a year. He was then deported once again.[7]

LOUIS ARMSTRONG

Of these three great soloists, Louis Armstrong was the youngest, the most appealing, and the one whose personal experiences came the closest to embodying not only the myths surrounding the Storyville diaspora, but also larger white needs for a true primitive, the natural talent who could rise from the very bottom of the social ladder to a career in entertainment that brought both fame and fortune. Facts complicate his story, as they usually do, and of course the fame and fortune were not for high artistic achievement but for the meretricious film and entertainment appearances of the years after his "chops" failed him. But Armstrong had been great, the evidence survived, and only the churlish could begrudge him his rewards.

He was born on 4 August, 1901, to a prostitute working the District, and heard most of his early music listening at windows and doors as he ran errands or just hung out. Food was scarce and life was violent, and a boy had to cultivate survival skills as he could. Having only musicians and hustlers for role models, he scarcely knew what to do or to become. Chance sent him to the Colored Waifs' Home, and there he learned the rudiments of band music—tambourine, drum, alto horn, and cornet. By conventional standards he learned most things wrong. He also learned to think of himself as an entertainer more than a musician. Whatever the market rewarded, he learned to do, from dance and march cornet playing to informal singing.

The only real father figure Louis Armstrong ever seemed to recall was Joe "King" Oliver, the best cornetist in the city, who usually worked in the Edward "Kid" Ory band, a group that at times included Bechet as well. In the summer of 1918, Oliver got an offer to go to Chicago; although reluctant to go, he realized that New Orleans had already lost much of its talent and that many of the friends he had were already gone. He accepted, thus providing his protégé with a crucial personal link to Chicago; and incidentally opening up a place in the Ory band, which Armstrong promptly inherited. This was his "first big break," he recalled, and he was careful to pay psychological homage to his hero. "I was doing everything just exactly the way I'd heard Joe Oliver do it," he continued. "I even put a big towel around my neck when the band played a ball down at Economy Hall. That was the first thing Joe always did." The band broke up in 1919 and Armstrong had to look elsewhere.

He continued to play in local restaurants into 1919, and then for three years spent long summers playing on the riverboats that plied the Mississippi all the way up to St. Paul. Sometimes, according to the season, the trips were local only, based in New Orleans, or St. Louis, or Davenport, and sometimes days would go by as the boats paddled long hauls between music-loving ports. Musicians learned much from each other, and sometimes had the opportunity to play for, and with, local talent along the way. In this fashion New Orleans style jazz did indeed spread north, if not directly to Chicago. That required a train trip from St. Louis or Davenport.[8]

Life on the boats of the Streckfus family, under the direction of cocktail pianist Fate Marable, provided discipline that Armstrong needed. "A lot of guys who came on the boat didn't make it because they said it was too strict. You had to go to rehearsals on Tuesday and Friday mornings and you got fined more for missing a rehearsal than you did for missing a night's work," recalled bassist Pops Foster. "You also had to play the music you had and a lot of guys couldn't do it." Many players read badly if at all, and had to hang about memorizing tunes by ear. Working conditions were highly personalized and a bit arbitrary. As long as the Streckfuses were happy, the job was secure. They required fourteen numbers during an evening, often long ones, and the works changed every two weeks. What with obligatory encores and re-peated choruses, the level of boredom could rise. Many players quit, but the experience "made musicians out of a whole lot of guys that way. Louis Armstrong, Johnny St. Cyr, and I didn't know nothin' about readin' when we went on the boats, but we did when we came off."[9]

In the literal sense, the boats went nowhere, going up and down the river, or out and back from a port along the way. But fig-uratively, they did lead to Chicago, since the musicians used the experience not only to mature as artists but to make reputations that went not only to Chicago but to the distant coasts as well. For Armstrong, Chicago came first; in the summer of 1922, Joe Oliver sent for his protégé and Armstrong summoned up his courage and left the one city he had ever been able to call home. For about seven years, with time out for tours and a hiatus in New York, he remained the greatest example of the spirit of black New Orleans as it spoke the new, modernist language of jazz to the nation and to Western Europe.

Armstrong's provincial appearance as he began his Chicago ma-turity became the stuff of legend, the outward sign of the inner metamorphosis his talent required. "Everything he had on him was too small for him. His atrocious tie was dangling down over his protruding stomach and to top it off, he had a hairdo that called for bangs, and I do mean bangs," his second wife, Lil Hardin recalled. The bangs "jutted over his forehead like a frayed canopy. All the musicians called him Little Louis, and he weighed 226 pounds." Even the housing was a revelation. When Oliver took him to the shabby rooming house where he was to stay and told him he would have a "private bath," Armstrong didn't even know the phrase. In his neighborhood, after all, "we never heard of such a thing as a bathtub, let alone a *private bath*." They had always used a clothes washtub out in the yard, or a foot tub. But both the landlady and her food were pure New Orleans, and he was soon comfortable; and in a new tuxedo.[10]

No one should underestimate that tuxedo and its many successors. Any book on jazz in the period that has pictures at all, will generally feature both formal portraits of individuals and carefully staged ensemble shots. The situation seems odd to later eyes, for the external face of jazz contrasts so utterly with its implicit anarchy, its disreputable origins, and its traditions of improvisation, not to mention its continuing exploitation of such vaudeville effects as imitation animal noises. But even a brief thought about the nature of caste and class in America will suggest a rationale for it all. White musicians lived in a world that was essentially lower class, even when temporarily prosperous. Black musicians shared this world but faced the additional burdens of caste. Segregation, with all its attendant indignities, was custom where it was not law in most of the country. Yet many whites wanted black music even when they did not want black neighbors. They associated black male musicians especially with sexual promiscuity, the consumption of illegal alcohol, and the social use of various narcotics. Tuxedos sent a clear message that jazzbands publicly accepted the values of white America. The music might sound wild and crazy, but appearances could be deceiving in a number of ways. Dance floors could remain segregated from bandstands; teenagers could play the records in suburban homes. It only sounded as if the end of civilization were impending.

Yet black discontent with the degradation of "normal" living conditions ran deep in the musical community. Jazz, indeed, was one of the major ways of expressing that discontent, and rather noisily making the point that black culture had original things to say. Armstrong always presented a smiling and respectable face to the camera, but he was hardly unaware of the fact that music could be a major weapon in the long battle for integration. At the time, in fact, the entertainment industry in which music played a major role was far more important even than athletics in this effort, with the courts, the military, and the schools contributing little until the late 1940s and 1950s. "Fate Marable's Band deserves credit for breaking down a few barriers on the Mississippi—barriers set up by Jim Crow," Armstrong wrote later of his life before Chicago. "We were the first colored band to play most of the towns at which we stopped, particularly the smaller ones." Whites were simply "not used to seeing colored boys blowing horns and making fine music for them to dance by." Sometimes the group faced ugly experiences and overheard offensive remarks. "But most of us were from the South anyway," and they would just keep playing, in effect answering back through music. "Before the evening was over they *loved* us. We couldn't turn for them singing our praises and begging us to hurry back."[11]

Chicago offered several additional ways to get the essence of the message across. It was the most open urban environment in the country at that time. In many cities blacks could play for white audiences, and white musicians could thus learn things simply by becoming customers and paying attention. But apparently Chicago was the only place where "black and tan" nightclubs flourished. Such places might be chiefly black by public reputation, but open to whites who wished to enter; genuinely integrated; or chiefly white but open to political or economic pressures to be at least intermittently tolerant. Dempsey Travis, editor of a variety of sources on the history of Chicago jazz, insisted that even the best clubs would admit blacks, although seating tended to be segregated, whites near the stage and blacks "behind them at the outer edges, and in the rear near the entrance." At least some places seated customers more by the size of their tips than the color of their skin, definitely a step toward a capitalist egalitarianism. Certainly the city felt relatively relaxed on racial issues. "Somehow it seems, looking back on it now, that there was a lot more mixing of the races in Chicago at that time than there was in Harlem," recalled New York pianist Willie the Lion Smith. "I sure found the 'toddlin' town' to be real friendly."[12]

The artistic complexity of the Chicago jazz scene comes through most clearly in the reminiscences of white performers. "Chicago, not New Orleans, was the town that really cradled jazz." New Orleans may have spawned it, but it only developed "in Chicago through the genius of King Oliver and Louis Armstrong," Bud Freeman insisted. "Almost all the white musicians who played this music listened to King Oliver's Creole Jazz Band," he continued. Freeman was seventeen when he first went to Lincoln Gardens. "Aspiring white jazz musicians used to go there all the time, and the people there were wonderful. They paid no attention to us; they knew we were there to hear the music." The doorman, whose weight in memory seemed "about 350 pounds," always greeted Freeman and his friends with the same words: "I see you boys are here for your music lessons tonight." Indeed, and the larger message came through as well. These blacks "were not allowed to come into our shops and cinemas, but we whites were allowed to go out to their community, where they treated us beautifully. I found their way of life equally as important as their music."[13]

Recordings reinforced the "music lessons" and created numerous self-paced students in distant locations. In one of the most atmospheric of all the jazz autobiographies, Mezz Mezzrow returned repeatedly to the records he acquired in his quest for knowledge of the new black language. He heard Blind Lemon Jefferson's *Black Snake Moan* while walking around in a "Jewish ghetto," "bought that record right away" and spent the next day with a friend, "paddling around in the sun playing *Black Snake Moan* and a gang of other blues." Walking down another street on another day, he heard Bessie Smith "shouting the *Downhearted Blues* from a record in a music shop." He "flew in and bought up every record they had by the mother of the blues—*Cemetery Blues, Bleedin' Hearted*, and *Midnight Blues*—then I ran home and listened to them for hours on the victrola." He was fascinated by the ways in which words and music seemed to reinforce each other, and stopped and started the records over and over in an effort to transcribe them. And then Louis Armstrong recorded *Heebie Jeebies*, "one that almost washed me away," the first time "Old Gatemouth ever put his scatting on wax." The record "took all of Chicago by storm." Musicians shouted the lyrics to each other in lieu of more conventional greetings, "scatting in each other's face. Louis' recording almost drove the English language out of the Windy City for good."[14]

Louis Armstrong began to make recordings with King Oliver's Creole Jazz Band on 6 April, 1923, when the group cut a session for Gennett; they cut another for Okeh on 22–23 June; and then burst forth in October with additional sessions for both those companies and Columbia as well. A final session for Paramount in December completed the series, which historian James Lincoln Collier has termed "the first substantial body of real jazz." Relics of the pre-electrical recording methods, they had severe problems of balance and clarity, and the equipment often ran as much as 10 percent slow or fast, creating irritating pitch distortions. Nevertheless, this series of roughly forty sides "taught American musicians, and serious jazz fans, what the new music was all about."[15]

WHITE JAZZ

Black jazz from New Orleans came first and was the most original, but for a long time enthusiasts had trouble sorting out issues of race and quality. Even the word seemed obscure, its origins and meaning open to debate. It apparently began as black slang, "jass" being just another four-letter word describing what four-letter words usually describe, and as "jaz," "jass," and eventually "jazz" it still occasionally has that primal connotation. Applied to an improvisatory music that had its roots in ragtime, the blues, minstrelsy, military march music, and black spirituals, its first known appearance in print seems to have been in a San Francisco newspaper in 1913, and the term was more common in the North than in the South for a decade or so. It first appeared in the black press in Chicago on 30 September, 1916, referring to the trio that usually played at the Pekin Inn. Like so much in the first jazz age, it reflected what those who were relatively detached and distant thought of something essentially foreign to their normal lives and expectations.[16]

But the nation as a whole did not read the black press, or listen knowingly to black music in 1917. Insofar as jazz acquired an audience much beyond downtown nightclub areas in major cities, it did so first through the performances and then the recordings of the Original Dixieland Jazz Band (hereafter usually ODJB) in Chicago, New York, and on tour between 1917 and 1923. Nick La Rocca was its leader, a cornet player from a musical Italian immigrant family that did not want its children trapped in the musical underworld. He absorbed opera and marching music, and regularly heard a wide variety of popular materials echoing off the boats that came and went on the river. Refusing to study medicine, he pondered John Philip Sousa instead, playing the band records over and over. By 1905, when he was sixteen, he was part of a pickup group that also included a violin, a guitar, and a bass; by 1908 he had a real band, one that had abandoned the violin but added clarinet, trombone, and drums. The music was essentially ragtime march and no one called it jazz.

Late in 1915, a Chicago cabaret owner named Harry James, in town for a boxing match, heard a band playing that was one of several managed by Jack "Papa" Laine. He decided the music was much superior to that normally available in Chicago, and queried Laine about a possible move north. In February 1916 he wired a firm offer for ten weeks. Laine handed the job to La Rocca, and by 3 March, 1916, five very provincial white males were getting off the train. Their first task was to find a secondhand clothing store. "They had never seen overcoats before," James chuckled in an interview, "and when they walked out of the store in these long, black overcoats, they looked just like five undertakers!"

Opening at Schiller's Cafe as "Stein's Band from Dixie," they were soon a popular success, with occasional drunken old vaudevillians urging them to "jass it up." They were still playing rags, and at a slower pace than would soon be the norm. The cornet set the pace and, as commentators quickly noticed, the clarinet and brass then began having "conversations" that clearly echoed the opera of La Rocca's immigrant home. Nothing much was written down, the musicians working effects out by ear ahead of time. Fame did not bring any rise in salary, but it did bring unwanted attention from the antisaloon and law enforcement officials. A period of reorganization ensued, and the "Original Dixie Land Jass Band," with La Rocca still leader, opened on 2 June, 1916, at the Del 'Abe Cafe. It was the last word in sonic vulgarity more than the first of the jazz age. Drummer Tony Sbarbaro decorated his part of the bandstand with dolls and teddy bears and punctuated his work with sounds from cowbells and a kazoo. There was a large woodblock, clearly left over from old minstrel shows. And the most famous titles demonstrated an adolescent fixation on animal noises: *Livery Stable Blues*, *Tiger Rag*, and *Ostrich Walk* were sure crowdpleasers. Especially the first: Larry Shields had his clarinet crow like a rooster, La Rocca whinnied on his cornet, and Edwin Edwards did a donkey number on trombone.

Fame led to an offer of a two-week run at the Paradise, a ballroom in the Reisenweber Building at 8th Avenue and 58th Street, with the promise of a well-paid run if the group proved popular. On 15 January, 1917, the "Original Dixieland Jasz Band" opened, with no noticeable enthusiasm. New York was always more oriented to commercial pop and dance music than Chicago, and it took time to build anything like a respectable audience. But business slowly improved, "jass" became "jaz" and then on 2 February, 1917 the *New York Times* finally had it right. "Jazz" it was, at least most of the time. On 26 February, 1917, the group made it permanent, recording *Livery Stable Blues* and *Dixieland Jass Band One-Step* for Victor Talking Machine Company. It appeared on 7 March and sold over 1,000,000 copies. As Gunther Schuller has noted concisely, their performances "were an infuriating mixture of bad and good, of tasteless vulgarity and good musical intuitions."[17]

Both the originality of the music and its popularity rankled the truly gifted. "Those were all numbers they had learned from playing opposite us back in New Orleans," Sidney Bechet grumbled in his memoirs. The whites learned from the blacks but were able to add nothing new of their own; "they never had it to add. It was all arranged and you played it the way it was written and that was all." Not quite—the music was rehearsed, played, recorded, and then written. But the rest of the indictment stands.[18]

Several other white New Orleans groups brought the new music to Chicago, going back to one under Tom Brown in 1915 that seems to have been the first. None matched the ODJB in terms of impact, but the Friar's Society Orchestra, which metamorphosed into the New Orleans Rhythm Kings (hereafter usually NORK), had a more direct influence on the best young white players. Several drifting musicians in the area organized under the name in 1921, with a repertoire partially borrowed from ODJB, partially improvised from popular material in the air. In 1922 and 1923, they cut several records, the last session including Jelly Roll Morton, making those sides the first interracial recordings known to history: *Mr. Jelly Lord*, *London Blues*, and *Milenberg Joys*.

White youth in the suburbs were all ears. When he and his friends first heard *Farewell Blues*, Jimmy McPartland remembered, "we went out of our minds. Everybody flipped. It was wonderful." They tried several other titles at a local ice cream parlor that had a Victrola. "We stayed there from about three in the afternoon until eight at night," listening to the same records over and over. "Right then and there we decided we would get a band and try to play like these guys." They picked out their instruments and were soon writing down the music, bar by excruciating bar: "It was horrible on people's ears," so "we had to move around because the neighbors couldn't stand it too long." They finally got *Farewell Blues* and "nine or ten others" down well enough to play creditably.

As a case study of the transference of black cultural initiatives to the larger white community, McPartland and his friends have a small but secure place in history as "the Austin High Gang." The group consisted chiefly of McPartland on cornet, his brother Dick on guitar, Bud Freeman on sax, Frank Teschemacher on clarinet, Dave North on piano, Jim Lannigan on bass tuba, and Dave Tough on drums. Most of the players actually attended Austin High School, in a Chicago suburb, or else like Tough dated a girl who attended. But the friendship circle became wide indeed, and came to include such prized jamming participants as Bix Beiderbecke and Benny Goodman.

Many of those involved left autobiographies or extensive interview materials, and the consensus on artistic progress, if not on dates and spelling, is remarkable. Coming from respectable middle class families, they all felt estranged from the values of their homes. They instinctively liked music that represented a tonal challenge to nineteenth century Germanic norms. They were familiar by their midteens with the names of Igor Stravinsky, Claude Debussy, and Maurice Ravel, and sometimes with less well known and less predictable figures, such as Erik Satie, Jacques Ibert, or Gustav Holst. They were vaguely aware of Cézanne and other modernist painters. They discussed the *American Mercury* when it began publishing in 1924. Dave Tough was the aesthetic and intellectual sparkplug, and to see him often was to hear about modernism and know that one was not entirely alone.

Knowledge about jazz came first from white sources, usually ODJB records and NORK gigs. That derivative but instructive initiation accomplished, they were prepared for more serious stuff, almost always involving riverboats, Joe Oliver, Louis Armstrong, and the New Orleans musicians that dominated the Chicago scene by 1923. By rumor, and then through the presence of Pittsburgh pianist Earl Hines, they learned about Harlem stride piano and its development from James P. Johnson to Willie the Lion Smith and Fats Waller. No one had much formal education; several could not read music; all admired black culture and detested the barriers that segregation imposed.[19]

The two greatest performers to emerge from this milieu were only on its edges and fitted its profile only approximately. Bix Beiderbecke's German-American family in Davenport matched the Austin High norm, with their dislike of jazz and incomprehending rejection of everything their son loved or did. Like many examples of natural genius, he seemed a genetic sport, so gifted as to be scarcely able to communicate with anyone unless the subject were music. He was "dreamy" and his family thought him "good for nothing," according to the most detailed memoir, "born homeless," an "*exile*, raised as it were, to the third power." He seemed both unreachable and unteachable in school, and capable only of musical self-education. From a traditional, technical point of view, he learned everything incorrectly, from embouchure to fingering. But his ear was so acute he could play beautifully without being able to read a note. Such lack of traditional skills made for constant trouble with union officials, who often made life as difficult for white jazzmen as it did for blacks. The respectable, humorless Germans of Davenport did not like "chassers," and demanded sight-reading skills as proof of enough skill to warrant the right to play regularly. They repeatedly flunked the most gifted trumpeter in the area until he faked his way on the piano, whipping through several light classical pieces he had memorized by ear.

A case history of how the riverboats spread jazz into the North, Beiderbecke haunted the Davenport docks when Fate Marable paddled in with his star cornet player. "He was a cute little boy," Louis Armstrong remembered. "He'd come down to hear the bands, and then go home and practice what he heard. He and I became friends the first time we met." Beiderbecke too worked on the boats, such as "the mammoth, non-sinkable steamer MAJESTIC," owned by the ubiquitous Streckfus interests, as it worked between St. Louis and Winona, Minnesota. The hours were so long that Beiderbecke soon had a vicious sore on his lip, and he chafed as well under the metronomic discipline. Inevitably, something was lost in translation; Beiderbecke never really assimilated the blues tradition, a good European clarity keeping his tone distinct from that of Armstrong or his black imitators. If anyone set him a mentoring example, Nick La Rocca did. Like so many of his age and location, Beiderbecke slavishly imitated the sounds on ODJB records and heard the NORK whenever he could. With maturity he left them in the dust, developing a "white" style of his own with none of the dirty tones and theatrical effects so common in black jazz and its early imitators.

Beiderbecke essentially led a life appropriate to his talent into 1927, gigging and recording his way to the status of best white cornet/trumpet player in the country. But both he and the musical economy were steadily disintegrating by that time. He was an increasingly self-destructive alcoholic, a legend of consumption levels, absentmindedness, and domestic squalor. Big band leader Paul Whiteman recognized his talent and took him on, but although Beiderbecke had far more respect for Whiteman's abilities than seems musically warranted, his voice was simply lost in the outpouring of that oxymoronic product of entertainment capitalism, "symphonic jazz." He first played for Whiteman on 27 October, 1927; by 6 August, 1931, he was dead. He was twenty-eight years old.[20]

Benny Goodman, by contrast, was from a poor, Jewish home, and never let alcohol or any other substance stand in the way of a methodical rise upward in American music and social status. His parents were immigrants from what became Poland and Lithuania; his father worked as a piecework tailor, with an occasional period in the stockyards—sweated labor, in other words. As babies arrived almost annually, merely finding food was a problem, let alone musical instruments or encouraging teachers. Yet for whites as well as blacks, music could be a way out, a vehicle of upward mobility where talent and perseverance could make up for the lack of education and cultural support. David Goodman took three of his boys to the Kehelah Jacob Synagogue, where they could get instruction and cheap instruments. Benny got a clarinet because he was the smallest, or so he always said. When that band disintegrated, he joined a band at Hull-House. He was especially glad to wear the uniform that went with it.

Unlike Beiderbecke and most blacks, Goodman adapted well to conventional teaching. He was soon taking lessons from Franz Schoepp, one of the best pedagogues in Chicago. As a result his fingering, breathing, tonguing, and embouchure were all correct by European standards. Goodman thus could read, grow, and adapt to the changing demands of both jazz and popular music, and in maturity play Mozart as fluently as Jelly Roll Morton. He also learned valuable lessons about color in music, for Schoepp made no racial distinctions. His pupils included Buster Bailey and Jimmy Noone, as well as members of the Chicago Symphony.

As a teenager, Goodman heard all the jazz in the air in the mid-1920s in Chicago, both black and white. Reliable records remain skimpy, but since he was underage and deplorably financed, Goodman presumably learned the most from recordings, especially those of the NORK, the chief inspiration available to white boys in the area. Although never a student at Austin High, he was soon jamming regularly with its members. He joined the musicians' union at the ripe old age of thirteen and was soon playing regularly at colleges in the area, playing the sax when occasion demanded it. On 28 August, 1923, he met Beiderbecke, and apparently only after that did he begin assimilating black music directly, in person, at the black-and-tan clubs. His name pops up in memoirs listening to Louis Armstrong, Earl Hines, King Oliver, Jelly Roll Morton, and Jimmy Noone. Noone made the greatest impression: "I loved Jimmy Noone's clarinet playing," he recalled. "He was an excellent clarinet player, period." Thus, when he left for a job in Los Angeles in August 1925, Goodman had no real limits to his possible growth: Black or white music, jazz or classical, he was essentially a professional who could play anything for an appropriate fee. What was immediately available was work playing dance music. More than anyone, Goodman would tie all these elements together, bringing blacks and black creations into the mainstream of American culture. And he did it not because of any instinctive liberalism or enlightened educational prompting, but because great art spoke to great artists and largely ignored the petty barriers of prejudice and taste that shackled the larger democracy.[21]

ETHEL WATERS AND MEZZ MEZZROW

In the greatest autobiography any woman has left in the history of jazz, Ethel Waters begins with an illuminating series of narrative free associations:

> I was never a child.
> I never was coddled, or liked, or understood by my family.
> I never felt I belonged.
> I was always an outsider.
> I was born out of wedlock, but that had nothing to do with all this. To people like mine a thing like that didn't mean much.
> Nobody brought me up.
> I just ran wild as a little girl. I was bad, always a leader of the street gang in stealing and general hell-raising. By the time I was seven I knew all about sex and life in the raw. I could outcurse any stevedore and took a sadistic pleasure in shocking people.
> My mixed blood explains this, partly, I think.

She was the product of rape. Her father, "a pianist, a playboy," raped her mother at the age of twelve; another woman murdered him when Ethel was three, and she never saw him alive. She had no identity, usually taking the name of a man her grandmother was in love with. She lived as a castoff, moving from house to house with no place home. For only a brief period did she live in anything like a family unit, and it lay in the Philadelphia prostitution district; she naturally learned to hate the police and to think of vice as the norm, and stealing the proper response to hunger. She swore off sex, drugs, and alcohol at an early age and took refuge in Roman Catholicism and a belief in her psychic powers. She was proud of being the first woman to sing "St. Louis Blues" professionally in public, and made much of her early reputation working with Fletcher Henderson's Jazz Masters.[22]

Or consider the brusquer opening of its male counterpart: "Music school? Are you kidding? I learned to play the sax in Pontiac Reformatory," Mezz Mezzrow says. His family may have been "as respectable as Sunday morning, loaded with doctors, lawyers, dentists and pharmacists," but he felt so out of place as a teenager that he literally could not communicate with them. "I was maneuvering for a new language that would make me shout out loud and romp on to glory. What I needed was the vocabulary," he continued. "I was feeling my way to music like a baby fights its way to talk." No matter how sinful his later life might seem to be, "I was cut out to be a jazzman the way the righteous are chosen for the church." As with any puritan, his course was preordained.

His family might be Jewish and their skin white, but in America color and ethnicity had little to do with race and religion. He learned the blues from blacks at Pontiac and its several successor institutions. Watching the impact of segregationist violence on those makers of beautiful music, he switched sides. "I not only loved those colored boys, but I was one of them." He came out of the school "chocolate brown." He began to develop a "thick Southern accent" and to use "the phrases and intonations of the Negro." He insisted that "being a Jew didn't mean a thing to me"; his "real brothers" were "the colored musicians who made music that sent me." He opted for black music, black friends, a black wife, and a life in Harlem. He appears in both his own book and in those of his friends, as the chief drug pusher of choice for a great many recognizable names.

These connections are not anecdotal examples of lurid gossip. They are points that musicians made repeatedly not just to sell books but because they were true and central to the lives involved. Modernists in America all but universally felt themselves to be alienated outsiders, even when skin color or economic circumstances might indicate otherwise. Declaring that they "could not speak the language" of majority white bourgeois capitalism, young musicians found in jazz an available new language to express personal worth, ethnicity, sexuality, and the right of an artist to pursue art regardless of public approval.

In insisting that sexual violence, drugs, thievery, and prisons were a part of the story they could not omit, Waters and Mezzrow pointed to a key link between Storyville, Chicago, New York, and Kansas City, which were, in that order, the creative centers of jazz until World War II. Vice districts, whether legalized, as in New Orleans and Philadelphia, or tolerated, as in Chicago, New York, and Kansas City, brought together wealth and poverty in a spirit of well-financed carnivalization. Free-spenders needed music, sex, and alcohol together to make the hours pass, and whether legal or not, that meant possibilities of disease, violence, gambling, tax collection and evasion, and so on that encouraged hoodlums and corrupted police. *Something* was always illegal, or contrary to the values of church and propriety.

Mezzrow noted some of the connections in passing. As a young man, he often jammed at the Roamer Inn, "a famous whorehouse that belonged to Al Capone's syndicate," noting among paragraphs of concrete detail: "It struck me funny how the top and bottom crusts of society were always getting together during the prohibition era." At Luigi's Cafe, "run by the head of the notorious Purple Gang, Detroit's bluebloods used to congregate—the Grosse Pointe mob on the slumming kick, rubbing elbows with Louie the Wop's mob." Detroit, Chicago, whatever: The Purple Gang was "so tough they made Capone's playmates look like a kindergarten class, and Detroit's snooty set used to feel it was really living to talk to them hoodlums without getting their ounce-brains blown out."[23]

This situation was not just the result of Prohibition, the end of official tolerance for prostitution, or the large-scale American predilection for gambling. In some basic way, jazz was taking sides in an ethnic war. On the one hand were old-style Irish saloon-keepers, whose musicless male preserves had dominated reform demonology since the potato-famine migrations of the 1840s; and German restauranteurs, whose taste in music has come down to the present in one word: *Schmaltz*. On the other hand were the late arrivals of the 1880s, the Jews and the Italians, whose arms waved, whose feet danced, and whose women were accustomed to coming along on nights out. These later groups proved remarkably tolerant: of fun, of women, of new musical forms, of blacks. And hoodlums. The fact was, these Jews and Italians—usually Sicilians—liked jazz. They were also nepotistic, paternalistic, sentimental, and violent when thwarted. Usually they were into gambling and alcohol and, Hollywood to the contrary, not into violence. They liked blacks and tipped up to a hundred dollars for the playing of a favorite song. Jazz musicians understandably found this supportive. They all shared a common problem: Irish cops. Intimidation and bribery existed on a scale so broad even Hollywood wasn't up to it.[24]

Nothing captured the public imagination like Al Capone; his picture still glowers from uncounted textbooks. No president emerges from the mass of jazz autobiographies with a more burnished image. In the view of Earl Hines, as creative an artist and as respectable in his personal character as anyone could ask, the underworld presence was ubiquitous and Capone a man you wanted to see come through the door at night. Capone "used to run a restaurant twenty-four hours a day where poor people could get free meals, and he took over real estate where these same poor people could move in and live." If, when he came at night, Hines met him at the door, "he might put his hand up to straighten my handkerchief, and there would be a hundred dollar bill. Failing that, he might give me a handshake and put a twenty-dollar bill in my hand." On some nights, his lackeys would arrive and proclaim the night theirs. They usually picked a slow night, and a thousand dollars could be very persuasive. "We'd play one show, and after that everybody used to come off the stand, and then you didn't know what you were, a musician, a show person or a gangster." Indeed.[25]

FLETCHER HENDERSON AND THE SHIFT TO NEW YORK CITY

Major shifts in musical hegemony happen player by player and are often imperceptible at close range. Just as New Orleans players drifted north from about 1915 on, if with many waystations around the nation, so Chicago players began to head for New York in the fall of 1924. They too had many intermediary destinations, but by 1928 the battle was over. The dates are concrete if the choice of them arbitrary. On about 1 October, 1924, Louis Armstrong joined Fletcher Henderson's orchestra in New York City. He retained ties to his wife, Lil Hardin, returning to her band in Chicago early in November 1925, but by May 1929 he was essentially based in New York. As with his shift from New Orleans to Chicago, Armstrong was a little behind the historical forces at work, for on 4 December, 1927, Duke Ellington had opened at the Cotton Club. For half a dozen years, with Ellington as impresario, New York reigned as the creative capital of jazz, until many of the same forces as were at work in New Orleans and Chicago wrought their destruction, and talent shifted to Kansas City, where the first mature generation of jazz modernism died, even as a new one was settling into place.

As with many historical shifts, secondary figures often supply the representative details better than the stars. Wingy Manone was born in New Orleans in 1904; his father was a banana distributor. The family were ethnic Italians who lived near Storyville, and the boy heard black music everywhere. This did not stop the casual violence of youthful territoriality: "Louis Armstrong and Zutty Singleton are famous musicians now," he recalled in 1948, "but I recollect that I used to throw rocks at them." This petty violence in no way impeded musical influence. Manone regularly heard Fate Marable's band in Southern Park whenever his steamer was in the docks, and his "idols were King Oliver, Buddy Petit, and Kid Rena—just as Louis Armstrong is today."

A streetcar accident amputated one arm above the elbow; this gave him a nickname for life, as a horn player with only one wing, but barely slowed him down. By the mid-1920s he was perpetually on the road, taking whatever jobs he could find but leaving the impression that he would have starved without a succession of Jewish and Italian weddings. One route dominated: "Man, I made that trip back and forth between New York and Chicago so many times I was personally acquainted with every cinder on the roadbed." But as the decade started to wane, he placed the center of his jazz life at Plunkett's Bar, "on Fifty-third Street, right off Broadway about four doors." For whites, this was accurate enough; blacks would have chosen a spot roughly seventy blocks north, in Harlem. But the shift was becoming palpable: "In 1926, when all this was happening, if you weren't in New York, you were nowhere."[26]

The man who more than anyone else arranged and orchestrated this shift to New York provides a good check on clichés about jazz primitivism, underworld finances, and the use of drugs or alcohol. Fletcher Henderson was a product of small-town Georgia as it sent its most talented children toward college, respectability, and the leadership of the black community. His father was a school principal, the entire family was musical in a methodical, disciplined way. While attending Atlanta University from 1916 to 1920, Henderson majored in chemistry, served as the university organist at the mandatory chapel services, and indulged in other extracurricular activities in exactly the same way a middle-class white boy might in the North. He took his new B.S. to New York, apparently intending to enroll for an M.S. in chemistry at Columbia.

It didn't happen. Music interested him more and career opportunities for blacks were better in the entertainment industry than in science. That summer, Mamie Smith recorded *Crazy Blues*, and within seven months over 1,000,000 had been sold; black business skills were maturing, from booking agencies like the Clef Club to recording companies like Black Swan. Henderson was soon plugging songs for Pace and Handy Music Company, publishers of *Crazy Blues*. He was accompanying singers on the piano, making his first record—*Dallas Blues* for Victor—on 11 October, 1920. By January 1921, Henderson was music director for Black Swan. The board of the new company indicated its centrality to the black community by including W. E. B. DuBois and John Nail, brother-in-law to James Weldon Johnson. Its advertising slogan, redolent with the various ironies of the black experience in America: The Only Genuine Colored Record. Others Are Only Passing for Colored.

As so often happens in the history of the arts, the available commercial structures shaped musical form and channeled creativity in definable directions. To date, Harlem had developed one jazz dialect of its own, the famous stride piano style forever associated with James P. Johnson. The best-selling singer in the Black Swan organization turned out to be Ethel Waters, and she in turn was devoted to stride. In his talented but malleable way, Henderson adjusted art to business. "I kept having arguments with Fletcher Henderson about the way he was playing my accompaniments," Waters recalled. He was too classical, too traditional. He "wouldn't give me what I call 'the damn-it-to-hell bass,' that chump-chump stuff that real jazz needs." She bought some piano rolls and told him what to listen for. "Fletch began to practice. He got so perfect, listening to James P. Johnson play on the player piano, that he could press down the keys as the roll played, never missing a note." The public soon identified him with that sort of jazz, "which isn't his kind at all."[27]

Henderson's New York career fell neatly into two periods: 1921 to 1923, when he was essentially an accompanist, and 1923 to 1927, when he ran his own band with arranger Don Redman. Originally not a jazzband, the group gradually moved in that direction between August 1923 and August 1924, as it dropped conventional players and picked up new ones, most notably the young Coleman Hawkins. The transition was thus largely complete when Louis Armstrong arrived in October 1924, to make his mark in next to no time. "I went mad with the rest of the town. I tried to walk like him, talk like him, eat like him, sleep like him," Rex Stewart remembered. "I even bought a pair of big policeman shoes like he used to wear and stood outside his apartment waiting for him to come out so I could look at him." The impression of course remained during the succeeding years when Armstrong was chiefly still based in Chicago.[28]

Armstrong came to musical maturity during his year with Henderson and then in his recordings with the Hot Fives and the Hot Sevens, culminating in *West End Blues*, recorded on 28 June, 1928. His tone, his vibratos, and his sense of swing cleared off the competition. The Hot Fives were a recording pickup group, but one whose members were long familiar with each other's work. In addition to Armstrong and Hardin, it included Kid Ory, Johnny Dodds, and Johnny St. Cyr; they began recording on 12 November, 1925. Then and over the next few months the group worked many of the old New Orleans and vaudeville influences out of their system and did their best to bring Hardin's not-quite-idiomatic playing into line. The pick of the lot in terms of Armstrong solo work came in 1926 with *Big Butter and Egg Man*. By 1927, he was recording with the incomparably better Earl Hines on piano, sometimes just the two of them as on the legendary *Weather Bird* (1928), sometimes with the Hot Fives or Hot Sevens, and on occasion with other groups too numerous to name. "By the end of 1927," Gunther Schuller has demonstrated, "Armstrong's style had coalesced into a near-perfect blend of relaxation and tension." He was probably the most creative musician then working in America, and Hines was not far behind.[29]

Creative Chicago, meanwhile, was undergoing death by urban reform. Musicians found themselves increasingly between a rock and a hard place. On their left, the nature of mob violence seemed to be changing. An occasional musician who wanted to change jobs found himself in real danger of physical violence if some hoodlum liked his music where it was. Shoot-outs between rival gangs became more common, and cabarets were bombed, sometimes with musicians playing inside as if their lives depended on it. As the decade went on, the hundred-dollar tips became fewer and the atmosphere gloomier.[30]

Even worse were the police, and the pressures of political reformers eager to rid the community of violence, gambling, prostitution, alcohol, and blacks, in no particular order. Under Mayor Big Bill Thompson, creativity and crime flourished together; vice was an equal-opportunity employer and blacks had their places in the artificial light. But in 1923, a prohibitionist Democrat, William Dever, took over. He soon closed several cabarets and revoked thousands of licenses for liquor or other violations. He put special pressures on the black-and-tans, and racial prejudice was always a factor. Over the winter of 1926/27, anticipating Thompson's return, the Irish police force was especially fierce, raiding, padlocking, and harassing almost at whim. In December 1926, a federal judge ruled that the Volstead Act outlawed not just the sale of alcoholic beverages, but also the operation of any places where customers brought their own. In October 1927, the Supreme Court turned down an appeal and early in 1928 a massive federal crackdown virtually eliminated jazz by closing all the prominent downtown places that had survived. Chicago returned to the speakeasy, the player piano, and the Victrola, and the musicians headed back to New York. Only the Grand Terrace Cafe, with Earl Hines leading a ten-piece orchestra, survived. It had gangland backing, a radio outlet, and precious little competition.[31]

SEVEN

THE BLEACHING OF THE BLUES

CARL VAN VECHTEN'S PARTIES

Ethel Waters rarely felt comfortable with either the rich or the white. She was ever ready to judge them harshly on the slightest of grounds. When, after a show late in the 1920s, a call boy told her that some white man named Carl Van Vechten wanted to see her, she could hardly have cared less. "The name meant nothing to me, though I'd heard of his book, *Nigger Heaven*, and had condemned it because of its obnoxious title—without reading it." Only later did she get around to reading it, and when she did so she "thought it a sympathetic study of the way Negroes were forced to live in Harlem." Slowly they became friends, including Van Vechten's wife, actress Fania Marinoff, "my dearest friends," in spite of the "rich white folks' food" they insisted on serving at their carefully integrated parties. Waters remained convinced for life that cold borscht was "enough to chill your gizzard for a week," but she warmed at the opportunity to meet a playwright like Eugene O'Neill, publishers like Blanche and Alfred A. Knopf, or a critic like George Jean Nathan, not to mention foreigners like Noël Coward and Somerset Maugham. As for her own community, "Carl Van Vechten was credited with knowing at the time more about Harlem than any other white man except the captain of the Harlem police station."[1]

Like so many modernists, Van Vechten came from a place he wished to leave as soon as possible, and from a family in which he could find no place that was psychologically satisfying. Home was

Cedar Rapids, Iowa, located on a branch of the Mississippi River; he called it Maple Valley in his fiction, a place without theater, opera, art galleries, or people sympathetic to his interests. "I want to meet people. I want to learn," one of his disconsolate stand-ins cries out to another, Gareth Johns. "Somewhere, there must be more people like me, heaps of 'em." In Van Vechten's case, it did seem hard to imagine. He had the look of a "domesticated were-wolf," with "the blank stare of an animal, as steady as a cat's, as cold as a snake's," according to his friend and biographer Bruce Kellner. No one easily got by his obtruding mouth. His "outwardly sullen expression was disfigured by two very big and very ugly protruding front teeth, like squares of broken crockery." Mabel Dodge thought they "made him look like a wild boar." Openly bi-sexual, as was she, he "really was queer-looking," his neck "never seeming able to hold up his head, or his knees his body. When he laughed, little shrieks flew out between the slits of his big teeth." Nevertheless he had "nice brown eyes, full of twinkling, good-na-tured malice," and "finely textured, red skin." They became af-fectionate friends almost at once.

Wallace Stevens, on the other hand, had no patience with such affectations, and apparently he was not alone. In a 1915 letter to his wife, he reported that during dinner at the Brevoort, he "caught a glimpse of Carl Van Vechten sitting near-by." Stevens's companion was his old Harvard friend Walter Arensberg, who told him that "Van Vechten bores him to death and he seems to feel even worse about Mrs. V.V." Sensing the disapproval, the couple "hurried out, passing near-by, studying the floor." Arensberg ap-peared much relieved not to have to carry on a contrived conver-sation; Stevens thought Van Vechten was simply the sort of person who had "absolutely no sense that enough is enough." The two assessments were not really all that incompatible. Dodge had trou-ble realizing that enough was enough as well.[2]

In his search for others like himself, Van Vechten fled first to the University of Chicago, where he mostly sampled music and theater from ragtime and black vaudeville to the Chicago Symphony and the touring Metropolitan Opera. He made his first tentative efforts at journalism for the local Hearst outlet, but reserved serious efforts for New York, where he moved in 1906 and joined the *Times*. Even that city was not enough and he was in and out of Paris over the next eight years, until World War I shortened his fourth trip. At heart he was a decadent after the manner of Walter Pater and George Moore, rather than a convinced modernist, but he was open to new experiences and friendly to most modernist experiments, especially when his friends made them, or accompanied him to their exhibition. Through Mabel Dodge he met Gertrude Stein, and they shared so many characteristics that he became her unpaid agent even after death, and their correspondence fills two fat volumes. He was a great admirer of the Ballets Russes, faithfully attending and reporting their performances and being ever ready to praise the music of Igor Stravinsky. Posterity has concluded that he was primarily a dance critic, with music and drama close behind, second best to James Huneker before 1917 and to Paul Rosenfeld thereafter. This sounds generous but isn't; the three had little competition.

In terms of the written word, Van Vechten was actually at his best in a tetralogy of sorts that he published between 1922 and 1925. His intentions in these works were perfectly clear in his own mind. "I *never* invent stories," he assured Mabel Dodge Luhan late in 1924. "I always select a classic theme and write modern variations around it." *Peter Whiffle* (1922) was *Hamlet* or *Elektra; The Blind Bow-Boy* (1923) was his version of *Pilgrim's Progress; The Tattooed Countess* (1924) was *Phaedra*. He was just then completing *Firecrackers* (1925), his *Parsifal* or, "more probably Savonarola." Like most modernists, he felt no ties to his own immediate context, and preferred to choose someplace as far from Cedar Rapids as imagination permitted. But he really belonged in either a Roman or Irish twilight. "My intention in writing is to create moods, to awaken unconscious echoes of the past, to render to shadows their real importance." To himself, his books were about "a man who is alone in the world and is very sad."[3]

Intentions often have little to do with actual achievements. To think of *Peter Whiffle* in a context of *Hamlet* or *Elektra* is sheer whimsy, and of course by the 1920s that face, which in reality was hardly on straight, could seem a straight face indeed. The book announced itself as "a free fantasia in the manner of a Liszt Rhapsody," which implied an even looser sense of form than Liszt assumed, which would be difficult enough in music, let alone in words. But to such a mind, to mix disciplines in this way was to mock the very idea of disciplines. You have to break butterflies on rocks or make soufflés out of smorgasbord to get a visual sense of the oral effusions here. The book scattered names like pieces of parsley around a burned but rare steak, to heighten color contrast rather than to nourish. "What is it about?" Van Vechten asks Peter Whiffle, two decades before John Cage made this sort of *blague* into the origins of postmodernism; " . . . about three hundred pages," Peter answers.

Yes, well. No one really noticed it at the time, for the touch was so light, but something original was actually going on. He put himself in his book repeatedly; he put in Fania Marinoff; he met the Steins, and committed his real publisher, Alfred A. Knopf, to publishing his nonexistent autobiography in 1936, "in two volumes." He also put his friends in the book under pseudonyms, heaven knows why since they loved the attention. Mabel Dodge became Edith Dale, in a sketch so true to that artificial life that dozens of scholarly Simons have pulled it out of their pies and displayed the plummy paragraphs as being true to life. Even Van Vechten's famous ring appeared twice, "an amethyst intaglio, with Leda and the Swan for its subject." This sort of blurring of the "real" and the "imaginary" was not unprecedented in the arts, as Richard Strauss and Marcel Duchamp had demonstrated, but it went well beyond the conventional "I" or "he" of the autobiography or the *Bildungsroman*. Not until Richard Hughes and E. L. Doctorow did something rather like this go on after World War II, but even so the general tone remained unique to Van Vechten. Life, after all, had "nothing whatever to do with art. No more has form." All of which gave Van Vechten a license that even James Bond might envy.[4]

Lest this seem like a lucky hit, Van Vechten became even more blatant about his larger intentions in *The Blind Bow-Boy*. What was clearly going on here was the creation of a bisexual, or androgynous, speech and sense of form, as a variety of modernist discourse. Almost exactly in the middle of a tightly bound book, the Duke of Middlebottom drifted in, flaunting eccentric clothes over an unkempt body. "His name was eponymous for a certain group that frequented the Café Royal in London and with his crest on his stationery was the motto: A thing of beauty is a boy forever." Of course, it would never do, at least in 1923, actually to consummate such a relationship, any more than it would do to confine observations solely to the male sex. When Campaspe Lorillard found herself fascinated with Zimbule O'Grady, she sure-handedly remained voyeuristic. "It was only, she frequently said, those who expected to find amusement in themselves who wandered about disconsolate and bored." You had to derive amusement "from watching others, when one permitted them to be entirely themselves." A paragraph later, she was sure of her response. "'I adore her!' Campaspe ejaculated one day."

Any revolt turned conventions on their heads, and Van Vechten had good fun playing the modernist bull in the Victorian china shop. Harold Prewett's father wanted a daughter but got a son— more or less. He absented himself from Harold's Bildung, but left instructions that his education be as irresponsible and whimsical as possible. All intention seemed fruitless, however, as Harold seemed to have no ego and lacked the energy to want much on his own. In the bisexual novel, clothes had more character than their wearers, tone became more important than content, and the quip replaced the quid. All the arts became implicated. Titus "Bunny" Hugg was the modernist composer, evoking New York City with quarter tones and sixteenth tones, and composing a "Bowery Ballet in two bars." The Duke of Middlebottom somehow managed to have pictures on his walls by a lesbian, a homosexual, and a bisexual: "a bowl of zinnias by Florine Stettheimer, orchids by Charles Demuth, and magnified, scarlet cannas by Georgia O'Keeffe"—all of which decorated the place appropriately, for nothing could be more artificial than painted flowers.

As for time, no one in such a world need take it seriously. "The Duke made it a point to live by the Julian Calendar, thirteen days behind the Gregorian." This enabled him "to evade all unsatisfactory engagements, especially if they were complicated in any way by daylight-saving time, an American refinement of which he was utterly ignorant."

Critics tend to shy away from humor, failing to realize that nothing could be more serious. Campaspe, nicknamed "Firebird," had nothing but contempt for both the uncivilized and the humorless, and her attitudes had relevance for art. "The only way to get the sense of the absurd, contradictory, and perverse existence into a book was to withdraw entirely from the reality," she thought. "The artist who feels the most poignantly the bitterness of life wears a persistent and sardonic smile."[5]

The Tattooed Countess took the androgynous style two steps farther. It played with itself, so to speak, through the punning undertones of the infinitive "to make up." An artist can make up a story, even about Cedar Rapids, Iowa; he can also use makeup to alter the look of things. As the Countess said to her unliberated Midwestern sister: "After my lips are made up I can say things I couldn't have said before." Through the use of such a mask, Van Vechten could then explore space here the way he explored time in *The Blind Bow-Boy*. *The Tattooed Countess* was a study of outward mobility, perhaps the author's most important motive as a teenager. Gareth Johns, age seventeen, needed to get out of Maple Valley, and if a December-May romance with a fifty-something countess will do the trick, he was ready to pack. The language became littered with foreign phrases, generally misused and mispronounced.[6]

All novels in the tetralogy have their merits, each participating at least marginally in the innovations of the others. But *Firecrack-*

ers is the best, somehow managing to be both the last work of American decadence and the first of postmodernism. The title page called it "a realistic novel," which of course it couldn't possibly be. It opened with a young Paul Moody reading a novel, *Two on the Seine*, about "a young American boy kept by a rich woman in her middle years," both an obvious reference to *The Tattooed Countess* and to Paul himself, who was so kept. This mixture of the fictional and the factual no longer seemed formally interesting, and the room filled with a sense of déjà vu. "There is nothing new to think, or to feel, or to do. Even unhappiness has become a routine tremor." Walter Pater, meet Vladimir Nabokov.

As characters from other books and "real" life wandered in and out, the man to watch was Gunnar O'Grady, an acrobat who made his first appearance as a furnace repairman who enjoyed the work of Persian poet Al-Ghazzali. As the androgynous style pattered on about clothes, furnishings, colors, and moods, nothing surprised; even the food was color-coordinated and artificial, the oranges being, for example, soaked in grenadine. Like most of Van Vechten's work, the book seemed weightless even if amusing, until suddenly, like a theatrical device, a curtain fell away. Here it came on page seventy-one, when Edith Dale sent Campaspe Lorillard a letter about a friend, who had just published a little tract, "The Importance of the Facade." Just as Eugene O'Neill was rediscovering the potential modernity of the use of Greek masks, so Van Vechten was theatrically toying with "the basic principle of facial integrity," or how "any meditative person like you or me learns from our own insides how to make our faces." The allusion to Whistler and the use of makeup were fairly obvious; the pamphlet instructed us in "the gentle art of making faces."

By the end of the book O'Grady had a chance to explain himself. As a modernist man, he had an infinite number of masks to choose from. His father was Irish Catholic, his mother Austrian Jewish. Convinced that parents raised children badly, they gave their five to separate adoptive parents of exceptional merit and permitted no interaction with blood relatives until age twenty-one.

Raised by bourgeois Danes, Gunnar became a proficient athlete; in love, he read philosophy to overcome his lust. In a slapstick finale taken straight from silent film comedy—if not Plautus—he ended up in the arms of a brainless actress, as detectives closed in, sure he was someone else.

Insofar as was narratively possible, Van Vechten thus produced the tastiest of modernist soufflés. Nothing in the plot made much sense, any normal sense of time and place disappeared, causes and effects lived in semidetached incomprehension, real and imaginary characters interacted. Occasional references to Proust, not to mention the Duchess of Guermantes, implied not only that the book was in some sense true to Van Vechten's recovery of his own lost time, but also that his method only seemed frivolous. Many people bought and presumably read the book, but few seemed to get the subtle points involved.[7]

Having achieved a certain literary success, and a definite popular one, Van Vechten began to throw it all away. One major virtue of the tetralogy was its blithe way of mixing the real and the unreal, the artist and his environment. Fantastic as the books sometimes seemed, they were hardly more artificial than his life, awash as it was in artists, publishers, and gin. But even a thoughtful hedonism requires ever stronger stimulants to create the same euphorias; even Iowa provincials can exhaust the possibilities of New York City. By about 1924, Van Vechten really was losing his sense of boundaries, his sense of where he stopped and others started, his sense of how he might feel looking at the world and how it might not be precisely the same as how the world might feel looking at him.

He even convinced himself that color was a pigment of the imagination. He definitely had a point. Southern attitudes, and the laws and customs relating to segregation, often seemed to count someone white who was legally or by cultural background black. Many whites of Mediterranean ancestry looked dark enough to stimulate suspicion among the racially paranoid. In his circle of friends, for example, the leading racial spokesman was Walter

White, highly educated and articulate: "He speaks French and talks about Debussy and Marcel Proust in an offhand way," as he wrote Edna Kenton. "An entirely new kind of Negro to me." But although White was white he chose to be black—except when avoiding the inconveniences of segregated travel. "Being a great deal whiter than Waldo Frank he does not travel in Jim Crow cars," and liked to regale his friends with his success in deceiving bigots. Jean Toomer, whose *Cane* (1923) was circulating widely in New York literary circles, could do the same at will.[8]

The famous Van Vechten parties apparently began in earnest in 1924; they included so many blacks that Walter White later took to referring to the Van Vechten/Marinoff apartment at 150 West 55th Street as the midtown branch of the National Association for the Advancement of Colored People. Through White, Van Vechten was soon socializing with James Weldon Johnson, Langston Hughes, and others of the literary side of the Harlem Renaissance, those whom Zora Neale Hurston, in her insouciant way, termed "the Niggerati." Paul and Essie Robeson also became good friends, and even the temperamental Bessie Smith showed up on occasion. The blacks, in turn, could make useful contacts with a publisher such as Alfred A. Knopf or a musician as famous as George Gershwin. Mexican painter Miguel Covarrubias immortalized the general impression Van Vechten made in "A Prediction," that portrayed its subject with darkening skin, thickening lips, and kinking hair. The whole business seemed rather calculated, however, for he was planning a novel and gathering material. "I have passed practically my whole winter in company with Negroes and have succeeded in getting into most of the important *sets*," he bragged to Gertrude Stein in June 1925.[9]

Ever one to mix business with pleasure, to the point of preserving it in alcohol and hard covers, Van Vechten was soon notorious for his forays into Harlem and its cabarets. By profession a critic of music and theater, he did write occasional pieces for local papers on what he heard, and occasional longer discussions of such major singers as Bessie Smith or Clara Smith. Both in print and in private, he preferred dark blacks, and hard-core blues, to anything bleached enough to sell to white America. But either this was not true or he did not know, musically speaking, what he was talking about. This becomes clear in his use of the term "jazz" in several contexts in so loose a way as to dilute it of any meaning more technical than a spirited use of syncopation and glissando. He referred in print to Paul Whiteman as the giver of "a series of concerts devoted to American jazz," and to George Gershwin as composer of the *Rhapsody in Blue*, "a work in concerto form" in which "jazz is utilized in a musicianly manner." In private, he assured Stein that it was the "best piece of music ever done by an American," and seriously considered collaborating with Gershwin on a jazz opera, perhaps based on DuBose Heyward's *Porgy*. It did not come off at the time, but it said something all too accurate about the place of genuinely black culture in America in the mid-1920s that three white men would even consider such a thing.[10]

What did appear was *Nigger Heaven*, the work now forever bonded to Van Vechten's name. In view of the problems the book presented, it needs stressing that the entire Van Vechten family heritage was friendly to American blacks, and that Carl himself had long had a perfectly genuine interest in black vaudeville routines, popular culture, and blues music. To a bisexual writer from darkest Iowa, blacks and Jews could be like-minded "others" when they all shared common interests in writing, music, or merely swapping stories. The most natural event in the modernist cocktail hour would be to bring Langston Hughes, Alfred Knopf, and Van Vechten together for a chat about, say, Paul Robeson's role in *All God's Chillun' Got Wings*, while Gershwin played the piano version of *Rhapsody in Blue* in the background. But so pure did Van Vechten's own motives appear to himself that he was capable of condescending even without consciously intending to do so, of assuming brotherhood across the color line when all his black friends were merely being congenial to a white who was trying so visibly hard, in a bleak period when the Ku Klux Klan was flourishing not too many miles away.

Van Vechten was in fact wallowing in romantic primitivism both in private and in public. Like many Americans with no unusual racial biases, he made casual use of a word like "niggers," even though aware that Negroes might take offense; he does so, for example, in a 1915 letter to Stein, who also prided herself on enlightened racial attitudes. But as he began to get his wind up for the parties and networking that led to *Nigger Heaven*, he started stretching the language to the point where only his closest black friends could remain sympathetic. "I now find that people who don't like niggers bore me," he wrote a bit preeningly to a male friend in Virginia in 1923. As the book approached publication, he noted how offensive the term seemed when a white used it, but appeared to think himself covered since only black characters were doing most of the talking. He knew he wasn't a racist, indeed was spiritually black, so much of the opposition passed him by. Langston Hughes, Walter White, and Wallace Thurman warned him; his own father did as well. White, Rudolph Fisher, and James Weldon Johnson read the manuscript for accuracy and authenticity. He persisted with both title and dialogue and remained unrepentent even as the hostility in some circles became common knowledge. To take the most important example, Hughes kept his reservations to himself and praised the book in the *Pittsburgh Courier*. Van Vechten was grateful, calling the notice "*superb*. The situation is *easy* to explain: You and I are the only colored people who really love *niggers*." He just didn't get it, and even his best friends could not penetrate his capacity for denial.[11]

Nigger Heaven uses many of the same devices that the tetralogy used, and even a few characters, of necessity now on the periphery. But for really the first time, the devices seem tired, the characters stereotyped. The explanation, aside from authorial fatigue, is obvious: Instead of the light satire and the wry game-playing that was Van Vechten's true forte, he had introduced elements of propaganda; a man who had no understanding of functional politics wanted everyone to appreciate black culture. No one in Van Vechten's world ever voted, or even seemed to read a newspaper;

instead they had college degrees, worked in libraries, and sprin-
kled their talk with French phrases. The reader was expected to
find soulmates beneath the skin color; Walter Whites were just a
taxi ride away.

The trouble with turning stereotypes on their heads is that they
remain stereotypes; they merely assume awkward positions. Here
the blood seemed to rush both to head and hips. Mary Love
brooded depairingly on her own aloofness, for culture had separated her from the mass of Harlem. She worked in a library, but
few patrons wanted to read anything worthwhile. Faced with
Schumann or Schubert, they went glassy-eared, "immediately
thereafter losing themselves in a burst of jazz or the glory of an
evangelical Spiritual, recognizing, no doubt, in some dim, biological way, the beat of African rhythm." They were all "Savages! Savages at heart!" Fresh from *The Emperor Jones,* perhaps, Van
Vechten's own ancestral voices were chanting drunkenly, "Jung,
Jung." Mary even convinced herself that "Negroes never premed-
itate murder, their murders are committed under the reign of passion." And so, off to Barron Wilkins's place, perhaps to hear the
natural rhythms of Fletcher Henderson—both came in for specific
reference.[12]

Such an embarrassment had value more as sociopathy than as
literature, but even his best friends didn't know or didn't care.
W. E. B. DuBois, who did understand both politics and the fatu-
ousness of good intentions, might blast away, but Van Vechten had
co-opted most of those who should have known better with his
ebullient, splay-toothed charm. Even Gertrude Stein, a presump-
tive pioneer in writing about blacks who had no problem in her
own social relations with them, offered unqualified approval. She
was "delighted delighted"; the book was "awfully good and made
up of light and delicate work" and she was "pleased and proud to
be in it." He had "never done anything better it is rather perfectly
done and that is one of the things I like about it most, a thing like
the best niggers the Sumners that is actually perfection," and so on
for a remarkable number of lines. She was still "niggering" in her

fecklessly integrated way with their good mutual friend, Paul Robeson, a year later. She didn't get it either; but by then Robeson had had to put up with much worse from the white community.[13]

Van Vechten kept on writing. *Spider Boy* (1928) dealt with fame and Hollywood in the old way, and deserves a place on library shelves only slightly down from Nathanael West's *The Day of the Locust* (1939). He then lost momentum in *Parties* (1930), his worst performance. Instead, in an amateur way, he turned to photography, over the years leaving a visual record of his many friendships and enthusiasms. They included every significant modernist who had worked to make jazz, and black life generally, accessible to white America: not only Sherwood Anderson and Eugene O'Neill, who have been much studied in this context, but also Langston Hughes, George Gershwin, Aaron Copland, and F. Scott Fitzgerald. An examination of these four will establish the contours of a fascinating mosaic of race relations and their impact on artistic creativity.

LANGSTON HUGHES'S WEARY BLUES

The most theatrically aware members of the black community had different perspectives, understandably enough. Langston Hughes, to focus on the most creative member of that community, had grown up as stagestruck as a black child could be in Lawrence, Kansas, and no successive home in a peripatetic life cured him of his desire to see plays, contemplate the dance, and absorb jazz. His mother had yearned throughout her frustrated life for a career as an actress, and the worst burden that segregation imposed on her son was to restrict if not eliminate his chances to see the productions of touring dramatic companies. Hughes did not arrive in New York City until 4 September, 1921, and so he personally could not see the pioneering efforts to put blacks on the stage in significant roles: three one-act plays by Ridgely Torrence in 1917, the first run of *The Emperor Jones* in 1920, and the opening of *Shuffle Along*, the most durable of all black musicals, which had opened on 23 May, 1921, to praise even in conventional white circles. Hughes made an ineffectual stab at the curriculum of Columbia College, and attended lectures at the Rand School of Social Science, but his heart was on the stage. He was soon avidly absorbing, among many more conventional choices, Andreyev's *He Who Gets Slapped*, Kaiser's *From Morn to Midnight*, and of course, O'Neill's *The Hairy Ape*. He usually sat hidden away in high, dark balconies, but didn't seem to mind all that much; the seats were cheaper and cash in short supply.

Eager to escape the burdens of race, poverty, and an unhappy childhood shuttling between relatives, Hughes soon left New York for a time as a sailor, seeking out, among other places, Africa; he was shocked to learn that Africans regarded him as an American and not as a black, refusing to deal with him at any satisfying intellectual level. He returned to the city in 1924, looked up some old friends, and soon found himself at a benefit party for the National Association for the Advancement of Colored People (NAACP). It took place at a well-known nightspot, "Happy" Rhone's at 143rd and Lenox. The black power elite was all there, including W. E. B. Du Bois, James Weldon Johnson, and Walter White. On the dance floor, appropriately enough, he met Carl Van Vechten, already becoming known for *Peter Whiffle* and *The Tattooed Countess:* Walter White was introducing him around. Van Vechten heard the name as "Kingston" Hughes, as he noted in his diary the next morning, and was clearly unfamiliar with Hughes's work. But Van Vechten was always open to new experiences. He welcomed the chance to discover what primitive emotions Hughes might be able to stimulate.

The two men hit it off almost immediately and the relationship proved durable and mutually helpful. Hughes was soon jotting down examples of the blues that he remembered from childhood, and retelling family folktales. He disclaimed much specific knowledge of the blues, but then made an effort to convey their essence. "They always impressed me as being very sad, sadder even than the spirituals because their sadness is not softened with tears but hardened with laughter, the absurd, incongruous laughter of a sadness without even a god to appeal to." He elaborated on the moods and memories the subject stirred in him. "There seems to be a monotonous melancholy, an animal sadness running through all Negro jazz that is almost terrible at times." Always a quick study, and an impressionist in the arts rather more intuitive than most, Van Vechten soaked it all up and said so. He had even more cause to be grateful when he found he had inadvertantly violated copyright in quoting snatches of blues material in *Nigger Heaven*. Hughes wrote out substitute verses almost overnight.[14]

But given his relative youth—he had been born in 1902—his color and his obscurity in terms of public recognition, Hughes profited the most from the relationship. He started getting closer attention at a banquet that Charles S. Johnson of *Opportunity* magazine organized for 1 May, 1925 to publicize a literary contest. The impressive group included not only such literary lions as Eugene O'Neill and Van Wyck Brooks, but also the more innovative publishers, most obviously Alfred A. Knopf. When Hughes won first prize for "The Weary Blues," no less a cultural icon in the black community than James Weldon Johnson read the work to the enthusiastic diners. Hughes shook most of the hands in the room, and since Van Vechten was the de facto adviser to the Knopf firm on all things black, Hughes found himself in the enviable position of having his first book of poems issue from that firm. He was soon safely under the benignly dictatorial wing of Blanche Knopf. Over the next several years, Van Vechten and she collaborated in firmly discouraging any tendencies that Hughes might have toward radical politics, racial and religious extremism, and excessive admiration for the race relations of the Soviet Union. Primitivism, after all, worked most effectively when ethnically sensitive liberals held the strings of purse and publicity.[15]

Hughes had been writing poetry since he was a teenager in high school; his earliest published efforts are in the *Central High Monthly Magazine*, the organ of the Cleveland high school he had entered for ninth grade, in 1916. The first poem worthy of inclusion in his collected poems, "The Negro Speaks of Rivers," had appeared in the black journal *The Crisis* in June of 1921, even before he had enrolled in Columbia. In a brief period, he met the journal's editor, W. E. B. Du Bois, and its literary editor, Jessie Fauset. A highly educated, fastidious woman, devoted to traditional, male ideas of the nature of culture, Fauset always itched to fix the verse of her great friend. With her, as with Blanche Knopf, Hughes had to be tactful and careful not to push too hard at the parameters that tradition established for work to qualify as "poetry." She found it incomprehensible when her protégé ignored the burden of her advice to visit Harlem nightclubs and use jazz rhythmic and linguistic structures to write "The Weary Blues," which Hughes actually composed in one in 1923. Yet two years later, the poem won its *Opportunity* prize, and a year after that was the title work for Knopf's little collection, *The Weary Blues* (1926).

Shortly after the book appeared, the editors of the *Nation* solicited an article in which Hughes explored the nature of his art, and black art in general. In "The Negro Artist and the Racial Mountain," Hughes opened with the regrettable tendency he saw in most young black poets to yearn for whiteness and acceptance as artists for reasons that had nothing to do with race. Hughes found this lamentable; he had trouble seeing the word "white" as "unconsciously a symbol of all virtues." For black artists to feel this way meant that they had to "run away spiritually" from their own race. No one who did this, in his opinion, "would ever be a great poet." Such attitudes constituted "the mountain standing in the way of any true Negro art in America."

Hughes was especially conscious of the strategies of caste and class that the upper echelons of his race accepted with little question. Their homes aped white homes wherever possible. Dark men married light if they possibly could. Professionals attended fashionable circles "where few really colored faces are to be found." They drew a color line as rigid as any of their neighbors. "Nordic manners, Nordic faces, Nordic hair, Nordic art (if any), and an Episcopal heaven. A very high mountain indeed for the would-be racial artist to climb in order to discover himself and his people." Although not himself from the underclass, Hughes thought it the only legitimate source for artistic inspiration. The unself-consciously black lower class was what gave a voice to Paul Robeson and subject matter to Jean Toomer, whose *Cane* (1923) provided the nearest prose parallel to Hughes's own work.

As for himself, he openly claimed that his poetry was "racial in theme and treatment, derived from the life I know." In many of his works, he tried "to grasp and hold some of the meanings and rhythms of jazz." Jazz to him was "one of the inherent expressions of Negro life in America; the eternal tom-tom beating in the Negro soul." For Hughes, that tom-tom sounded a tocsin of revolt against weariness in a white world, a world of subway trains, and "work, work, work"; it sent forth "joy and laughter, and pain swallowed in a smile." It did not share the same basis as white creativity. "Let the blare of Negro jazz bands and the bellowing voice of Bessie Smith singing Blues penetrate the closed ears of the colored near-intellectual until they listen and perhaps understand."[16]

Strictly speaking, this policy position accurately describes what Hughes was trying to do in his verse. On rare occasions, as with "The Weary Blues," he actually succeeded, making that work the most important black contribution to American modernist verse before 1927. But more often he merely described dances, took on the persona of a dancer or appreciative male observer, or, repeatedly, did little more than take a blues song from his childhood and print it virtually unchanged—although when he found out that most journals paid by the line, he doubled his fee by halving the length of the traditional blues line. What seemed fresh to white critics was often enough a result of black speech patterns, of the layered implications of references to shadows, lightness, and darkness in an ambiguously charged racial context, and of an implicit social relevance largely absent from the work of white modernists until 1927. A black poet focused on himself saw an object of discrimination, placed regularly in a situation where random violence if not lynching could result. No black aware of poverty as well as prejudice could ever be entirely free of social pressures, or the economic and political forces that enforced them.

In fact, read in the context of the best white poets of American modernism, Hughes does not seem all that unusual. He chose the Mississippi as the inspiration of his first anthologizable work, the same river that floated past the St. Louis of young Tom Eliot and gave such resonance to his essay on *Huckleberry Finn*. Rivers streamed like consciousness for all close students of William James, and when Hughes floated down the Euphrates, the Nile, or the Congo he was, mutatis mutandis, doing exactly what modernists from Pound to Conrad were doing: analyzing time as place, choosing an ancestry different from the one linear history had bequeathed them, and then perhaps exploring as well the heart of darkness within the soul. Hughes certainly had as much right to visit Egypt as Hilda Doolittle.

Although critics do not customarily note the fact, the ghost of Sherwood Anderson lay behind his narrative technique. No widely read writer in New York at that time could escape knowing about the method of *Winesburg, Ohio*, even if he might absorb it unknowingly through friends, or references in the *Dial*, the *Freeman*, or the *New Republic*. The essence of Anderson's method in prose was to tell tales about the tellers of tales, to make characters out of mythmakers, and thus to distance actual events and emotions from the reader. Events started to happen indirectly, offstage, and to become known only as a storyteller told a reader a story that someone else had told him, perhaps in turn retelling gossip from yet another source. This method reached its limits in William Faulkner's *Absalom, Absalom!*, and of course Hughes never came near to achieving the layered complexity of Faulkner. But his "Aunt Sue" or his blues singers or his betrayed lovers participate in this process, and by so doing cushion the effect on the reader of material that might seem unacceptable if presented in a straightforward, "realistic" manner. Such works also prepared Hughes for his later comic persona in prose, the messages about race, poverty, and violence

seeming more effective because they were more artistically satisfying, indirection enhancing believability.

Langston Hughes was not, technically speaking, a mulatto;
both his parents were of mixed race and thus legally and socially
black in America. But, psychologically speaking, Hughes felt himself to be a mulatto, meaning someone who had no place in either
the white or black communities. Like the speaker in "Cross," after
detailing the dissimilar fates of his wealthy white father and impoverished black mother: "I wonder where I'm gonna die, / Being
neither white nor black?" (58). To be colored was thus to be or-
phaned, a state of the soul rather than a state of pigmentation or
parentage. Scarcely a white modernist from Pound to O'Neill felt
any differently. Hughes had a family history as "historical" as anything in the pedigrees of Eliot or Gertrude Stein, and yet, like
them, he had to flee, for when he looked for genuine sympathy
and understanding from his own people, he found nothing usable.

This mulatto posture naturally created a profound ambivalence
toward America and things American. A "Negro" could evoke
George Washington as well as Caesar, but his was not the conventional posture before such legendary figures: "Caesar told me to
keep his door-steps clean. / I brushed the boots of Washington"
(24). More promising was the example of Walt Whitman, bard of
American individualism and romantic self-development: "I, too,
sing America. / I am the darker brother." Even though "They send
me to eat in the kitchen / When company comes," I am too "beautiful" to remain out of sight forever (46). The situation was psychologically unbearable: Here was a country whose political ideals
and literary role models were entirely sufficient for any citizen, yet
they never seemed to apply in practice to blacks. Men in Hughes's
generation had been asked once, and would be asked again, to
fight for values that were denied them.

The form of the blues was thus a perfect vehicle through which
Hughes could speak the modernist language appropriate for the
black dilemma. "Homesick blues, Lawd, / 'S a terrible thing to

have. / Homesick blues is / A terrible thing to have. / To keep from cryin' / I opens ma mouth an' laughs" (72). And if home were in the South, the welcome back could be ambiguously warm in a very special way, not only warm-affectionate but warm-violent, whites hotly lynching offensive blacks to the tune of lyrics reminiscent of a Stephen Foster favorite: "Way down South in Dixie / (Break the heart of me) / Love is a naked shadow / On a gnarled and naked tree" (104).[17]

Such ambivalence, such two-ness, had long characterized the black experience in America; W. E. B. Du Bois had spelt it out in a famous passage in *The Souls of Black Folk* (1903) and Hughes was merely restating it in a blues format. In fact, viewed in terms of the larger culture, Hughes was in a distinct minority even within his minority group. Of the three other cultural options open to all creative Americans during the early 1920s, progressivism was exhausted: Those, like Du Bois, who had shared progressive moral values and supported Woodrow Wilson and a war to make the world safe for white democracy, found their southern-born president resegregating Washington and angrily refusing to deal with black critics at all. Or a black could follow the Jamaican poet Claude McKay onto the masthead of the *Liberator*, harness art to the revolution and the realistic aesthetics of his mentor Max Eastman, and become a "premature" collectivist, anticipating the socially committed literature of the 1930s.

But the most common position among Harlem renaissance artists was to accept the values of the educated white community and to be conservative in politics, religion, aesthetics, and skin color. Most of those who left a record of their allegiances did not seem to have public positions on political questions, and had small use for emotional Christianity. They liked verse to rhyme, like Jessie Fauset; they felt comfortable with the sonnet, like Countee Cullen; and preferred tonal classical music, like everyone except Hughes. They hooted at "The Negro-Art Hokum" like George Schuyler did in the *Nation* (16 June, 1926), preferring straightforward conventional narratives published by white, solvent, commercial publishers. Above all, they yearned to be white. At least since James Weldon Johnson's *The Autobiography of an Ex-Colored Man* (1912), the subject of passing held an obsessive interest. The best-educated behaved like erstwhile chameleons, assuming that somehow if they adapted to white standards they would lighten up and blend in. The wish seemed as true for the light-skinned Nella Larsen, in *Quicksand* (1928) and *Passing* (1929), not to mention her physicist husband, one of the few black Ph.D.s in the country; as for the very dark-skinned Wallace Thurman, in *The Blacker the Berry* (1929) and *Infants of the Spring* (1932). Thurman's unhappy life leaves a reader with the distinct impression that he drank himself to death because he could never hope to pass. Modernists who could not fit in often drank to excess, as Hemingway and Faulkner amply demonstrated, but they pioneered new dialects and art forms along the way. The Harlem renaissance writers rarely attempted to do this. Jean Toomer was the one real exception, and *Cane* was scarcely in the stores before he began denying that he had any black blood at all.[18]

Hughes was an artist who managed to have two living parents yet be psychologically an orphan in three ways: His parents largely ignored him and he had no real place to feel at home; his country gave him ideals and role models but permitted social circumstances in which they did not apply to him; and his race, while encouraging his art at times, essentially thought him uncouth and likely to lower the tone of black achievement. He earned his right to sing the blues, but no one should have been surprised to see him heading sharply to the left after *Fine Clothes to the Jew* (1927). To anyone feeling black and blue, the expression of collectivist solidarity had a special appeal.

GEORGE GERSHWIN'S BLUE ICE CREAM

Hughes stood almost alone in his comprehension of jazz as a language, and in his ability to express the essence of its meaning in another medium. Most of the Harlem renaissance, and virtually all whites, filtered jazz through ears that were listening for things extramusical. If critical, they heard formlessness, bad taste, sexuality, and even criminality. If friendly, they heard a refreshing primitivism, a liberating search for new forms, a beguiling openness to the validity of emotional expression, something that could conceivably express for perhaps the first time that elusive quality of Americanness that so many had been seeking for so long. Such responses said far more about the listeners than about the players and what they played. Two musicians and a prose writer provided the clearest examples of an influence so pervasive it threatened to escape comprehension. George Gershwin became the most popular.

Gershwin's parents were poor immigrants with no known interest in music. Instability was built into their lives. Having little money, they moved constantly about New York City, staying close to job opportunities and avoiding unsympathetic landlords. The surname went from Gershovitz to Gershwine, to Gershvin, to Gershwin, as Yiddish gave way to English, and George used several pseudonyms as well. George was officially named Jacob on his birth certificate, while brother Ira entered bureaucratic immortality as Israel. Neither, as an adult, could recall their original names as ever having been used, even within the family.

Such instability could work in several ways. The downside could mean an intense dependency on family emotional ties, a need for warmth and approval in constant tension with a fear of suffocation or exploitation. It could mean a shameless cynicism about human motivations, and a scarcely hidden greed for money and accompanying signs of wealth. It could mean as well an inability to form mature ties to members of the opposite sex. On the other hand, a talented boy growing up in ethnic chaos could be open to new influences, gregarious, charming, and uninhibited. Not knowing either social or musical rules, he could break them all with impunity. Greed for new experiences could coexist with other kinds of greed, and freshness balance crudity. Young George could in fact have entered the underworld, as several of his neighbors did; instead, he entered the musical world. He left high school when he was fifteen, eager to scribe his way to the top of the only world where he knew he had talent.

In early 1917, Gershwin was nearing the end of his third year at Jerome H. Remick & Co., a music publisher on West 28th Street in the heart of Tin Pan Alley. Publishers in those days sold sheet music by having a staff of sight-reading pianists able to play pieces for interested customers. Sight, however, did not always convey clear impulses to fingers, nor were pianos always in tune; the results, coming from numerous open doors and windows, sounded much like playful children pounding on tin pans. Like many gifted jazz musicians, Gershwin could not read, and was young even by the most tolerant of pre–welfare state standards. He listened and faked it. Once the score was sold, any discrepancy noted in the home was presumably due to the inadequate technique of the daughter of the house.

At the same time, Gershwin was also commuting to East Orange, across the Hudson in New Jersey, to cut piano rolls at the Perfection Studios. For about a generation, piano rolls were a vital part of the dissemination of musical taste in America. Usually from two to three minutes long, a piano roll could convey a popular tune with precise if colorless clarity to any home with a suitably equipped piano. Classics, dance tunes, or Broadway hits could, through piano rolls, find their ways to middle-class living rooms across the land, and accompany an endless number of teenage parties. Scott Joplin and other ragtimers made them, too; rolls crossed color lines without question. Gershwin at first cut mostly the tunes of others, but soon he did his own. The earliest ones were not very good, but led to better ones; sometimes he even overdubbed himself, becoming a Gershwin with four hands, a technique not common on recordings for another fifty years. In 1917, Gershwin stopped making his rolls at Perfection and switched to Aeolian, making about 130 before he stopped in 1926. He did *Rhapsody in Blue* twice, and it was still occasionally available on recordings at the end of the twentieth century. This was a mixed blessing. The master's touch did not really shine through, and many seasoned critics justly felt that such repetitive activities had a deleterious effect on the way Gershwin composed and performed his own best works.

Early in the 1890s, copyright reform had ended the American habit of cheerfully pirating the best literature and music of Western Europe without the payment of royalties. American vernacular materials suddenly seemed more worthy of exhumation, and the allure of a local career correspondingly more attractive. This refocusing could only have supplied a background of encouragement to someone already intoxicated by the wild variety of the urban sounds that enveloped him. In such a welter of stimuli, black music stood out; it was new, different, and trendy. Gershwin could not get enough of it. He was soon a regular visitor, not to mention the pianist of choice, for many of the parties of his friend Carl Van Vechten. As the most important critic in the city to like jazz, Van Vechten was in a position to push Gershwin's career in print, and did so. He was equally supportive in private. He also went along on many a trip to Harlem. "We all knew Gershwin," Willie the Lion Smith recalled in his memoirs.

Gershwin did not share the primitivistic gusto for all aspects of negritude so evident in Van Vechten's party schedule. He was mostly an eclectic opportunist, taking what he could get wherever he could find it. But he had one large advantage over Van Vechten, and that was the natural affinity of traditional Jewish music for black music, structurally speaking. In the first serious study of Gershwin's life and work, Isaac Goldberg had the advantages of friendship, cooperation, and Jewishness when he came to the making of suggestive insights about Gershwin's music. Oriental and African musics usually shared a pentatonic structure that sounded exotic to listeners of European background. "Perhaps our native theorists have over-philosophized the blue note . . . of the Negro, for the most popular scale of the Khassid has a blue note that is quite as cerulean or indigo as the black man's blues may be," Goldberg wrote, presumably with at least tacit approval from Gershwin. "The Negro blue note . . . has its peculiarities of origin and of use," he continued. "Yet, when the folk music of Ireland and of Jewish Poland . . . betray a similar departure from our own diatonic norm," even someone as unschooled as Gershwin starts to notice. In *Funny Face* he even begins one song with Yiddish inflections, but it "ends up black." Outsiders in American culture once again had ways of finding each other, taking advantage, perhaps, but then making sly jokes about the situation. Humor and music were both preferable to war. After all, what was a little exploitation between New Yorkers?[19]

At one point when he was in his midteens, Gershwin had lived about twenty-five blocks from Barron Wilkins's nightclub, and at such places Gershwin was well situated to hear the best that the newly forming Harlem ghetto had to offer. He heard James Reese Europe direct many a group; for some concerts, Will Marion Cook was concertmaster. Will Vodery was a close enough friend to be recommending Gershwin for jobs. And as for stride pianists, when Gershwin didn't know someone personally, he simply sought him out. "The master of them all" was Lucky Roberts, Ethel Waters recalled many years later. Gershwin went to Roberts and took his pointers from the man himself. The point here is not to search out influences and apportion praise, but merely to indicate that Gershwin was not just slumming as so many whites were. When he borrowed, only the best was good enough. He was as insensitive to racial prejudice as a clamshell, but he was a born pro and knew the type. He didn't look; he listened.[20]

Gershwin was musically mature before he was twenty-five. George White's *Scandals of 1922* was the representative vehicle, as mixed a bag of talent and opportunism as anyone could wish for illustrating how popular culture was working. On the positive side, he put flatted sevenths into his hit, "I'll Build A Stairway to Paradise," a sure sign that he had mastered the blue note insofar as a white man could. But in the same show, he also contributed *Blue Monday Blues*, a mini "opera" about a gambler ashamed of his love for his mother. A rival convinces his girlfriend that his visit home is really to "another woman," and the conflict quickly escalates to murder. Will Vodery helped him to orchestrate it, and some of the writing was apparently effective. But the producers hired whites to act in blackface, as was all too customary, and as a whole the work was out of place and too depressing for its location in a frivolous review. It bombed quickly and was cut from the show, but had two long-term results: it introduced Gershwin to Paul Whiteman, then leading the pit musicians for the show; and it got Gershwin to thinking about the possibilities of a black opera, to bear fruit thirteen years later in *Porgy and Bess*.[21]

Whiteman entered cultural history so appropriately named that he seems overdone, like some of Anthony Trollope's caricatures of British life. He was definitely white, all three-hundred-odd pounds of him, as raffish, charming, tasteless, and pushy as anyone in show biz, which was his game. A *New Yorker* profile in 1926 described him as "a man flabby, virile, quick, coarse, untidy, and sleek, with a hard core of shrewdness in an envelope of sentimentalism, striped ties, perspiration, and fine musical instincts." That was too kind ("sleek?", "fine?") but close enough, since his anti-Semitism never seemed to affect his working relationship with Gershwin. The bottom line was that Paul Whiteman was *l'homme moyen sensuel*, eager to assimilate jazz into the dance halls of white America. Whiteman needed raw talent to debase; Gershwin needed a shill and an orchestrator.[22]

Gershwin's relations to white musicians have naturally come in for much comment. Evidence is scarce and unreliable, and many wished to claim a decisive impact on the man who seemed to dominate popular music in the years after his death. The sparse record shows that Gershwin learned little from any one teacher. He picked up a bit from Charles Hambitzer; he consulted Edward Kilenyi and Rubin Goldmark, among recognizable pedagogues. But Gershwin wasn't a learner, he was an absorber. He got the most from Jerome Kern, beginning with *The Girl from Utah* (1913). Four years later, he actually served as the rehearsal pianist for *Miss 1917*, a collaboration between Kern and Victor Herbert; and the next year he played for Kern's *Rock-a-Bye Baby*. "Kern was the first composer who made me conscious that most popular music was of inferior quality and that musical-comedy music was made of better material," he told Goldberg. "I followed Kern's work and studied each song that he composed." He imitated him devoutly and was happy to acknowledge that "many things I wrote at this period sounded as though Kern had written them himself." He owed less of a debt to Irving Berlin, and small change to a great many lesser Broadway lights.[23]

Such a mixture of white and black influences could not help but bleach any blues Gershwin might compose. In general he used blues effects sparingly in his songs, the word usually implying a mood rather than specific chords, the pentatonic scale, or lyrical patterns. But Whiteman could see money and publicity in domesticating the various elements of jazz for the respectable white patrons that constituted his preferred audiences. He was determined to invest in an evening of jazz-influenced concert music that would include famous names in the audience and introduce new works that proved his point. The experiment would be "purely educational," a handout for the concert read. "Mr. Whiteman intends to point out . . . the tremendous strides which have been made in popular music from the day of the discordant jazz, which sprang into existence about ten years ago from nowhere in particular, to the really melodious music of today which—for no good reason—is still being called jazz." For sheer artistic effrontery, that was hard to beat, implicitly denigrating not only blacks but the music itself. To top it off, he proclaimed himself the "King of Jazz."[24]

Whiteman was so high on Gershwin's talent that he was advertising his participation before Gershwin even knew of the scheme. As the story goes, George was shooting pool on 3 January, 1924, when his brother Ira noticed an announcement of the 12 February concert in the paper. Gershwin, Victor Herbert, Irving Berlin, and others were reportedly writing works for an audience that would include Jascha Heifetz, Sergei Rachmaninov, Efrem Zimbalist, and others almost as well known. Never short of chutzpah, Whiteman was apparently determined to beat out competing bandleader

Vincent Lopez, who was planning a similar event. Whiteman had simply fantasized a suitable program, not caring to notify his composers in advance—even though Gershwin could not orchestrate and Berlin could not even notate music. But Gershwin was amenable. He had long been somewhat in awe of traditional European classical music; in addition to random thoughts about a Negro opera, he had also toyed with the idea of some sort of rhapsody in imitation of the free form experiments of Franz Liszt. He might even have chatted with Whiteman about it. But he had never agreed actually to do it. Still, a pool hall did seem appropriate for thinking about what became the major breakthrough of his brief life.

In a letter to Isaac Goldberg several years later, Gershwin summarized his recollections of what happened. He had been hearing a lot about "the limitations of jazz, not to speak of the manifest misunderstandings of its function." This chatter said that jazz "had to be in strict time" and "had to cling to dance rhythms." He resolved "to kill that misconception with one sturdy blow." He had no plan, and about three weeks, during which he also had to go to Boston to work on a show. The train got his juices flowing, "with its steady rhythms, its rattle-ty-bang that is often so stimulating to a composer." Sitting there he saw the piece as a whole. "No new themes came to me, but I worked on the thematic material already in my mind, and tried to conceive the composition as a whole," he continued. "I heard it as a sort of musical kaleidoscope of America—of our own vast melting pot, of our unduplicated national pep, of our blues, our metropolitan madness." He made his deadline like the pro he was, handing a two-piano version to Whiteman's orchestrator, Ferde Grofé, to finish off. Ira, under the influence of James Whistler's paintings, gave it its name. The result, *Rhapsody in Blue*, was the hit of an otherwise dull evening.

To conservative devotees of mid-nineteenth century piano music of the kind associated with Liszt, Edvard Grieg, or their American counterpart, Edward MacDowell, the work was decidedly a mixed blessing. Writing in the *Tribune*, Lawrence Gilman readily acknowledged that the "rhythmical structure of these pieces, and the manner in which they are scored for the small orchestra of so many wind and percussion instruments and so few strings cannot but delight the observant musician." He acknowledged the "daring, and imagination, and ingenuity, and the trail of an adventurous spirit." But he insisted that the "melodic and harmonic structure of the music" was inadequate. "How trite and feeble and conventional the tunes are, how sentimental and vapid the harmonic treatment, under its disguise of fussy and futile counterpoint!" He asked his readers to "weep over the lifelessness of its melody and harmony, so derivative, so stale, so inexpressive."

The other extreme understandably predominated among Gershwin's friends. The concert was "a riot," and the piece "the foremost serious effort by any American composer," Carl Van Vechten wrote his frequent guest. "Go a little farther in the next one and invent a new *form*." Van Vechten thought "something might be done in the way of combining jazz and the moving-picture technique. Think of themes as close-ups, flashbacks, etc!" He was so enthusiastic that by late in 1924 he was seriously considering "a serious jazz opera, without spoken dialogue, all for Nègres." They discussed the proposal, but nothing came of it.

On the whole, the popular response in both America and Europe was strongly on Van Vechten's side. In 1928, for example, Gershwin found Europeans unusually responsive to the work of a foreigner. Even in distant Austria, restaurant musicians were able to play the work creditably when informed that the composer was a customer. One chef became so carried away that he tried to make blue ice cream for one visit. He failed, and had to substitute a dessert of more gastronomical hue, but with little American flags flying on top.[25]

It took time to achieve a measured professional response, but in 1959 Leonard Bernstein published "Why Don't You Run Upstairs and Write A Nice Gershwin Tune?" By then, forty-four measures of piano solo had been cut, and Grofé had reorchestrated it twice, the 1942 version for full symphony orchestra becoming the version most commonly played. A rare combination of pianist, conductor, and composer, Bernstein denied that the work was "a composition at all. It's a string of separate paragraphs stuck together—with a thin paste of flour and water. Composing is a very different thing from writing tunes, after all." The tunes themselves "are terrific—inspired, God-given . . . perfectly harmonized, ideally proportioned, songful, clear, rich moving. The rhythms are always right." Gershwin was a gifted composer of songs and possibly the most "inspired melodist" since Tchaikovsky. But the *Rhapsody* "is not a real composition in the sense that whatever happens in it must seem inevitable." If you cut it, you just make it shorter, without affecting the whole. You can even interchange sections without doing real harm; indeed, in practice, people did such things and more all the time. Not jazz so much as the Broadway show and the 78 rpm record seemed to have become the permanent form into which Gershwin poured whatever flowed through his fertile brain.[26]

One of the respectable conductors who was following Gershwin's career at the time was Walter Damrosch of the New York Symphony. In general a devotee of Central European, especially Germanic, music, Damrosch nevertheless held a longer range view of musical evolution than certain of his colleagues. To him, music in any culture began with songs and dances and other folk expressions and only evolved slowly into lieder, operas, symphonies, and sonatas. America lacked any true folk music, being rather a collection of immigrants all bringing disparate traditions with them. Damrosch had at first thought of jazz as a "very low form of art" expressive mostly of "nervous excitement." But his daughter Alice had other ideas, as daughters so often do. She liked jazz, and the tunes of Kern, Berlin, and Gershwin, and played them at parties where her father found them hard to avoid. An incessant theatergoer, she was soon a personal friend of Gershwin, and he became a frequent guest at her house.

Walter Damrosch was thus in attendance at both the dress rehearsal and the première of *Rhapsody in Blue*. He noted the use of syncopation and the now plentiful blue notes, but what he intuited was the essential Russianness of the spirit behind it. He heard the echoes of Anton Rubinstein and even Tchaikovsky, not at all a preposterous lineage. Impressed despite himself, he arranged for the Symphony Orchestra to commission a "New York Concerto" from the young composer. Flattered, Gershwin accepted, and then had to run out to buy Cecil Forsyth's *Orchestration* (1914), a standard text, which he needed; he was not even sure what a concerto technically was. He figured it out, more or less, once again because he had to. He also did most of the orchestration himself, with some polishing from his close friend and collaborator William Daly. But what attracted attention was not this "European" proficiency, but the black inspiration. Not only did the second movement make extensive use of the blues, still a novelty in concert halls, but the first made highly unusual use of the new Charleston dance rhythm—a dotted quarternote and an eighth note in a four-beat bar—which James P. Johnson, the famous Harlem stride pianist had introduced in *Runnin' Wild* (1923). The final movement then reverted to the style of the first, and as Gershwin said in its program notes: "It is an orgy of rhythms, starting violently and keeping to the same pace throughout."

At some point before its premiere on 3 December, 1925, the title changed to *Concerto in F,* so its specifically urban and Harlem inspiration was bleached out of the public perception. Indeed, the color-innocent conductor even preceded the work with Alexander Glazunov's *Symphony No. 5*, a piece that just happened to use the same Charleston-type rhythms in its last movement even though it was the product of a respectable Russian pedagogue. Playing it was a friendly, well-meant gesture that almost compelled the audience to welcome the newly tidied up visitor from Broadway. The *Concerto* itself was a great if ragged piece that has long since earned its place in the canon. Once again, Leonard Bernstein deserves the final word: "The concerto is the work of a young genius who is learning fast. But *Porgy and Bess*—there the real destiny of Gershwin begins to be clear."[27]

AARON COPLAND'S WILD OAT

By all rights, any detached student of New York musical culture in the 1920s would seem justified in assuming that Aaron Copland and George Gershwin would have known each other and have profited from each other's work. Of roughly the same ethnic background, their families emigrating from the Pale of Settlement area of the Russian-Lithuanian-Polish borderlands, members of the same generation in the same city, they both even studied, however briefly, with Rubin Goldmark, a teacher of modest reputation for his connections to Central European classical music. Both experimented with jazz and did so at the same time, on occasion with the same conductor. But as Copland mused many years later, "Gershwin and I had no contact. We *must* have been aware of each other, but until the Hollywood years in the thirties, we moved in very different circles." In fact, the witty jack-of-most-musical trades Nicolas Slonimsky recalls introducing them at one of Serge Koussevitzky's New York concerts, but even the company of a man who could get the water fountains to talk did nothing to facilitate discourse: "We found nothing to say to each other!" Copland continued. He enjoyed popular music but knew his talents lay elsewhere. "I have no idea today whether Gershwin's concerto of 1925 influenced me toward composing a piano concerto the following year. I doubt it." No one hearing the two works back-to-back would doubt it. Jazz had clearly headed in several directions at once. The two men shared nothing except the obvious.[28]

New York encompassed many worlds, but few were farther from Tin Pan Alley, or Harlem for that matter, than middle-class Brooklyn. The Coplands and many close relatives were dry-goods merchants of the most sober, stable, bourgeois sort, secularized Jews with no significant interest in music. Aaron's Brooklyn "had none of the garish color of the ghetto, none of the charm of an old New England thoroughfare, or even the rawness of a pioneer street. It was simply drab." He remained for life "filled with mild wonder" each time he realized "that a musician was born" on his street. "In fact, no one had ever connected music with my family or with my street. The idea was entirely original with me." He had trouble finding teachers, scores, or friends with similar interests. He gravitated toward those modernists who experimented on the piano, especially Alexander Scriabin, Claude Debussy, and Maurice Ravel. Both the war and a feeling of cultural decline made Germany less appealing than might have been the case a few years earlier, so he looked to France for liberation. "I belonged to the postwar generation, and so for me 'abroad' inevitably meant Paris."[29]

He was hardly a child of the jazz age; tin pans were something to sell, not bang. At the age of eight and a half he was making up songs; at eleven he noodled away at an opera; in 1917, at the same age as the century, he played a Paderewski polonaise at his debut in the auditorium of the Wanamaker department store. Precocious and lonely, he found stimulation in an occasional recital by Jascha Heifetz or a concert led by Walter Damrosch. He was aware of the experiments of Charles T. Griffes and John A. Carpenter, both men of conservative temperament willing to sample modernist innovations, but recalled writing a friend that Leo Ornstein playing *Danse Sauvage* was the most controversial event of his late teens. Above all he followed the *Dial*, where Paul Rosenfeld "wrote perceptively about controversial figures such as Schoenberg, Stravinsky, Ornstein, Mahler and Sibelius." He thus arrived in Paris in 1921 innocent not only of jazz, but also of most popular culture of any sort.

One of the many results of World War I was a sense that France needed to thank America for its assistance and ensure that it would be available again if needed. The French government decided that one way to do this was to appoint Francis Casadesus to set up a school for American musicians at the palace of Fontainebleau. He worked closely with Walter Damrosch in hiring faculty and publicizing the plan in such journals as *Musical America*. Copland, Virgil Thomson, and several other Americans were soon competing for the nine available fellowships.

Copland had something of a gift for being where the action was, even if he never sensed it to be especially active. On the boat over, he befriended none other than Marcel Duchamp, although their casual times together yielded nothing of cultural import. At the school, he found life "very sleepy," enlivened chiefly by frequent American films in the Paris cinemas a short trip away. The faculty included the famous piano teacher Isidor Philipp, such legendary organists as Charles Marie Widow and Marcel Dupré, and the young nephew of the founder, Robert Casadesus, destined for a major career as a pianist. A formal portrait from 1921 shows Copland standing three rows behind Camille Saint-Saëns, the ghost of an age truly distant. Duchamp had warned him that the place would be "a waste of your time," and told him bluntly that he "would do better" to take his classes "in Paris." At first glance, Copland agreed. He did not intend to stay long.[30]

Damrosch was apparently crucial in urging the appointment of Nadia Boulanger as a teacher of harmony. The homosexual Copland had not come to Paris to learn from a young woman and was reluctant even to visit her classes; besides, he had already studied harmony in New York. But a friend, harp student Djina Ostrowska, urged her abilities on Copland so enthusiastically that he agreed to sample a class session. She was analyzing Modeste Moussorgsky's *Boris Godunov* in a way that captivated Copland. "Her sense of involvement in the whole subject of harmony made it more lively than I ever thought it could be. She created a kind of excitement about the subject, emphasizing how it was, after all, the fundamental basis of our music, when one really thought about it." He realized that he had finally found his composition teacher, and was gratified to be included in the select group of students that "Mademoiselle" often invited to her home for tea. He was soon meeting socially with many of the brightest lights of the Parisian firmament, including Gabriel Fauré and Igor Stravinsky. Through her as well he met Damrosch and Serge Koussevitzky, those conductors who would be most crucial to his early American success.

In time, Nadia Boulanger became the legendary mother of modern American music, her fame enduring into the years after World War II. She did not accomplish this through ebullience or the excessive reinforcement of weak provincial egos. "Nadia was not an easy taskmistress," her modern biographer has noted. "She fussed constantly about every detail, because she could admit of only one correct way to do anything." A true obsessive, "she could not abide a speck of dust, or a book without a proper dust-jacket, or an article of furniture a millimeter out of place, nor would she tolerate lateness or any other sign of weakness or a relaxation of discipline." The burden of the memoir literature seems to be that she was "of personal rather than musical utility," a builder of confidence more than a genuinely insightful teacher, as Thomson noted in a private letter of 1926. By 1931, he was writing about her in quite caustic fashion. Although he had gotten much out of his early studies, Thomson had found things "all changed" by 1926. "The guidance wasn't worth a damn. On the contrary, quite troublesome," he wrote Copland. She wanted everyone to write in the tradition of her deceased sister Lili, a devotee of Roman Catholic church music; meddled in her students' personal lives; and incomprehendingly ruined compositions in progress. "Her lack of comprehension of everything that is vivid or simple is complete."[31]

Even Copland was surprised at himself for finding such satisfaction with a conservative Catholic spinster who seemed older than her thirty-four years. "She understands the kind of modern music I like to write," he informed his family, and her fees were low besides. It helped that she had great faith in American music, and rather enjoyed mothering young males who were no sexual threat. But two factors in her teaching remain striking. First, although she believed in strictly teaching the rules, she also believed that: "To create music, we must forget them," and was eager to encourage her best students to go off on their own. Second, she was completely in sympathy with the neoclassical style that was de rigueur for both French and American modernism in the years immediately after the war. As Jean Françaix said: "Nadis had two polestars, God and Stravinsky." As long as a young person was in tune with Stravinsky's stress on winds and his use of the piano as a percussive instrument, he could work happily with her, leaving out anything German or stringed. Anyone like Thomson, who preferred Erik Satie and the deceptive simplicities of Les Six, was destined for irritation and withdrawal.

It took time for Copland to find his voice in this environment. He was by nature "the same as now—careful, judicious, balanced," his roommate Harold Clurman recalled many years later. They were at heart cultural rubberneckers, "going around to places like Sylvia Beach's bookstore and catching glimpses of famous writers like Hemingway, Joyce and Pound." Of course they hardly knew anyone, but kept up as best they could. "We kept comparing French culture to what we didn't have at home, wondering why Americans were not as interested in the arts." Boulanger helped here as well. "It was not at all unusual to find the latest score of Stravinsky on her piano, still in manuscript, or those of Albert Roussel, Milhaud, or Honegger," Copland recalled. He even discovered a late romantic Austrian such as Mahler, while studying intensely with her *Das Lied von der Erde* in 1922. But she hardly observed disciplinary boundaries: "Also, the latest literary and artistic works were examined: Kafka, Mann, Gide, Pound."[32]

Only in this cosmopolitan, modernist context did jazz begin to assume a place. Stravinsky had been experimenting with new rhythmic structures since before the war, and when Ernest Ansermet brought several ragtime scores back to Europe with him in 1918, Stravinsky immediately set about writing—awkwardly—his own versions of this music that he may never have heard played idiomatically. Along with other dances from popular culture, rag material appears most effectively in *The Story of a Soldier* (1918, 1923). Darius Milhaud, a devotee of Harlem in the Van Vechten mode, produced the most effective, sustained work of jazz assimilation in *The Creation of the World* (1923), and not even the fastidious Ravel remained unaffected, as the "Blues" movement of his *Violin Sonata* soon testified. True to form, Boulanger picked up jazz as well: "I can still remember the eagerness of Nadia's curiosity concerning my rhythms in these early works, particularly the jazz-derived ones," Copland recalled. "Before long we were exploring polyrhythmic devices together."

Copland thus discovered jazz in Paris as part of an environment of neoclassic experimentation. If Gershwin went back to Anton Rubinstein and even to Liszt, Copland went back to Stravinsky and by heredity to Nicolai Rimsky-Korsakov—to dance, to the folk, and to Russian nationalism as an example for American nationalism. "I was particularly struck by the strong Russian element" in Stravinsky's music. "He borrowed freely from folk materials, and I have no doubt that this strongly influenced me to try to find a way to a distinctively American music." He thought it "easy to see a parallel between Stravinsky's powerful Slavic rhythmic drive and our American sense of rhythmic ingenuity."

By the time he collected his ideas in *Our New Music* (1941), Copland had jazz placed firmly if a trifle awkwardly within a context that would have raised every eyebrow in Storyville. Modern music was in essence "a history of the gradual pull-away from the Germanic musical tradition of the past century," especially in Russia. German romantics were "highly subjective and personal" in expressing emotion. "The 20th-century composer seeks a more universal ideal," tending to be "more objective and impersonal in his music." Since the war, the emotional climate has changed. "Romanticism, especially in its later stages, now seems overexpressive, bombastic, self-pitying, long-winded." Modern times call "for a music that is more matter-of-fact, more concise—and, especially, less patently emotional." Russia and France thus shared a common enemy in Germany, in culture as in war; and moderns had more in common with medieval and eighteenth-century music than they did with nineteenth-century music.

Much of musical history reduced itself to a chronicle of what happened to folk inspiration. Germans, following Carl Maria von Weber and heading toward Wagner, took folk materials to increasingly nationalistic as well as romantic extremes. In many other countries, local folkloric materials seemed to open up comparable national destinies; in practice they fell under the "clichés of German musical procedure." Only the Russians truly managed to escape. Led by Glinka and Moussorgsky, they proved capable of "taking their native songs as the basis for their work," and constructing "a music on formal and emotional lines independent of the German tradition." This meant an abandonment of "sonata form, fugal treatments, development sections, and so forth." It also meant "the setting up of new criteria for the judgment of music that existed outside the realm of the standardized German product."

At this point in Copland's analysis, German music becomes chiefly the work of Wagner, and leadership of the cause moves to France. With Claude Debussy, "we have the first example of a composer who openly shouted, 'Down with Wagner,' and who willingly accepted leadership of the anti-Wagnerian forces." He took his inspiration from symbolist poetry and impressionist painting, producing in his music "an exquisite transcription of an ideal world of sensations." Displaying great harmonic originality, creating unprecedented chordal progressions, substituting the whole tone for the diatonic scale, he gave a final shove to a system of harmony that had slowly been breaking down throughout the nineteenth century. "In essence what Debussy did was simple enough: even more truly than Moussorgsky, he dared to make his ear the sole judge of what was good harmonically." Copland pointed especially to the piano preludes, a few songs, the orchestral nocturnes, and *Pelléas et Mélisande*.[33]

With the center of musical gravity moving to France after the war, Copland could shift his attention to Stravinsky, Ravel, and Les Six, most of them interested in jazz for at least a few years. But jazz, for them, had to be largely a device, a tool, a reference point almost entirely detached from any real familiarity with black life or the actual performance of jazz. By essentially discovering jazz in France, Copland severely limited his conception of what jazz was. "From the composer's viewpoint, jazz had only two expressions: the well-known 'blues' mood, and the wild, abandoned, almost hysterical and grotesque mood so dear to the youth of all ages," he insisted a generation later and repeated yet another generation after that, when far richer materials were available to him. "These two moods encompassed the whole gamut of jazz emotion." A composer like himself who tried to use elements of jazz for serious art music "sooner or later became aware of their severe limitations." Jazz actually "had much wider implications, since these were not necessarily restricted to the two moods but might be applied to any number of different musical styles."[34]

Such a view removed most of the color from jazz as surely as Gershwin's immersion in Broadway theater. In fact, as he moved toward his first work to show at least superficial signs of jazz influence, Copland's eyes were chiefly on films and ballets. He and Clurman had attended *Nosferatu*, "with vampires and graveyards and other gruesome things," as Clurman recalled. Igor Stravinsky and the Ballets Russes were also the focus of musical attention in Paris, and in the Boulangerie no one could escape the heat. Copland decided to spend 1922/23 writing a ballet, and chose the film as his subject for the libretto. He had "no choreographer, commission, or contact with a major ballet company," but nevertheless turned out thirty-five minutes of serviceable music. It began with the title, *Le Necromancien*, that he later changed to *Grohg*, the name of a magician in the work. More pagan ritual than plot, the work has four coffins that are placed before Grohg. Three dances bring each of three corpses alive, including an adolescent, an opium addict, and a prostitute. The magician tries to kiss the girl, he loses his temper when she slaps him, and when the corpses jeer him he tosses the girl at them. Other dances occur around the coffins, and a "Cortège macabre" follows them off stage in the same mood in which they came on. "There was a taste for the bizarre at the time, and if *Grohg* sounds morbid and excessive, the music was meant to be fantastic rather than ghastly."

By 1922, Copland had done little with jazz, only brief piano works using jazzy rhythms. But Boulanger was fascinated by them, and encouraged him by noting that Copland seemed to have a rhythmic sense different from the Europeans'. He earnestly left instructions written on the score for conductors so disabled, but never managed actually to choreograph or stage it. He and Boulanger did perform a four-hand piano version in 1924, and Copland later worked the "Cortège macabre" sections into a concert piece that was played twice in the 1920s, withdrawn, and only recorded after his death. Some other materials went into the *Dance Symphony*. But the real effects were two: For the short run, he was interested in making broader use of jazz; for the long run, he wanted to produce ballets, a form in which he later made his greatest mark as a composer.[35]

In the summer of 1923, Copland and Clurman spent several months in Vienna sampling German modernist music. Copland was especially excited by the works of Paul Hindemith, Ernst Krenek, and Alois Hába, especially the experiments Hába was then making with quarter tones. But Copland also haunted bars; in those bars American jazz was often the music of choice; "and hearing it in a fresh context heightened my interest in its potential." Only then, in such a roundabout way, did he begin "to consider that jazz rhythms might be the way to make an American-sounding music."

Upon his return to Paris, Copland found Serge Koussevitzky conducting a series of concerts of modernist music and often in close social contact with Boulanger and her students. He very much liked the score of "Cortège macabre," and when he accepted an offer to become permanent conductor of the Boston Symphony Orchestra, he put everything together, permanently changing Copland's life in the process. Walter Damrosch had already invited Boulanger to play for him in her capacity as an organist, and Koussevitzky turned to them one day and intoned in his magisterial Russian accent: "*You* vill write an organ concerto, Mademoiselle Boulanger vill *play* it and *I* vill conduct!" Copland had not yet heard a note of anything he had actually orchestrated, nor had he ever written anything for organ. She assured him he was up to it, and he devoutly hoped that she knew what she was talking about.

In June 1924 Copland returned to New York City to base his life there. Now fluent in French and a Francophile in tastes, he nevertheless did not confuse roots with musical style. As a Francophile, he knew that jazz provided him with useful experimental techniques, and of course he had a commission to get started on. As he tried and failed to find pupils; as he made friends in the literary as well as the musical community, he struggled away, producing on a disciplined schedule. Boulanger had great influence over her long-time friend Walter Damrosch, and when she pressed Copland's unheard work on him, he accepted politely without realizing how it would feel to his orchestra or sound to his subscribers, both groups noted for stuffiness. The scherzo especially made effective use of raw jazz material, and later had a long life on records in the version led by Leonard Bernstein. But on 11 January, 1925, New York heard it without preparation in Boulanger's New York debut; it got by, despite nerves all around, but only because of the conservative auspices of the respectable Damrosch and his matronly soloist.

After the performance, Boulanger asked Virgil Thomson how he had liked it; he replied that he had wept. "But the important thing is why you wept." "Because I had not written it myself." He meant it. As he wrote in his memoirs: "The piece was exactly the Boulanger piece and exactly the American piece that several of us would have given anything to write and I was overjoyed someone had written." Koussevitzky repeated it a month later in Boston.

In such subsequent works as *Music for the Theater* (1925) and the *Piano Concerto* (1926), Copland continued his jazz experiments, with less success and almost audible boredom. In reviewing his career in an essay published in January 1932, Thomson described his friend's music as "American in rhythm, Jewish in melody, eclectic in all the rest." Occasionally he could work up some nervous excitement of a rather cerebral kind. "This tendency gave him a year or two of jazz-experiment. That has been his one wild oat. It was not a fertile one." No, it wasn't. It got him started, but he was the wrong color, the wrong religion, and the wrong person all around to profit from a spontaneous Harlem improvisation that had to go to Paris and Vienna before he could assimilate it into a set of assumptions already in place. An oat is not black, and neither is the music.[36]

SCOTT FITZGERALD'S AGE

Well into the long hangover known as the Depression, F. Scott Fitzgerald worked himself out of a severe case of writer's block by publishing essays. Always an autobiographical writer in terms of mood, social relationships, and the portrayal of character, he did his best when summing up the associations evoked by the word "jazz": "The word jazz in its progress toward respectability has meant first sex, then dancing, then music," he wrote in 1931. "It is associated with a state of nervous stimulation, not unlike that of big cities behind the lines of a war." As early as 1917, college newspapers in the Ivy League were beginning to note the pleasures of petting, especially in automobiles; the war then speeded everything up. But "only in 1920 did the veil finally fall"; kisses no longer implied that engagement and marriage were imminent, and "the Jazz Age was in flower." For a couple of years, boyishly shapeless young women with bobbed hair seemed perpetually in motion, shaking the foundations of Christianity as well as the local dance floors. The year 1922 "was the peak of the younger generation, for though the Jazz Age continued, it became less and less an affair of youth." By 1923, elders had taken over the children's party, "had discovered that young liquor will take the place of young blood, and with a whoop the orgy began." The whole race went "hedonistic." By 1926, what had seemed new and fresh increasingly seemed a "nuisance": "We looked down and found we had flabby arms and a fat pot and couldn't say boop-boop-a-doop to a Sicilian." By 1928, "Paris had grown suffocating" abroad, while at home, "such phenomena as sex and murder became more mature, if much more conventional."[37]

The very titles of Fitzgerald's early books provided a pop history of this first jazz age. A bright young man with no visible academic interests could nevertheless live just *This Side of Paradise* (1920), which seemed to be a well-appointed eating club in Princeton, N.J. Vigorous Saturday evenings found *Flappers and Philosophers* (1920) doing the fox-trot and the shimmy when not embracing in their autos. Too much alcohol and too little work produced *The Beautiful and Damned* (1922), a gilded subcaste of post-adolescent party-goers, capable of originality in sin but not in art. Their frantic gyrations inspired many trendy *Tales of the Jazz Age* (1922) but only a few proved worth remembering for very long. One young man of several identities, shallow sentimentalities, and one golden, self-deceptive memory, known to his sycophants as *The Great Gatsby* (1925), seemed to embody whatever it was that the age was trying to accomplish. When a demented cuckold did him in, for one of the few crimes he did not commit, *All the Sad Young Men* (1926) had to drift elsewhere for inspiration, party food, and young women. Then the words failed to come for a long time; violence mounted; but the bands played on. Only they didn't sound quite the same.

Anyone with a serious interest in music faces a problem with these volumes: Fitzgerald not only had no knowledge of music beyond the humming of an occasional tune, he scarcely even pretended to fake it. The entire absence of classical music from both his life and his art is no surprise; what surprises is how few references he makes even to jazz, and how spurious and inaccurate he is when he tries. The word "jazz" scarcely occurs in the first two novels, and when it does it is in the context of an attractive young woman being a flapper or "jazz baby," or a young man hearing dance music with an occasional barbaric rhythm. Things are only slightly livelier in the stories. Jazz seems to be fox-trotting in "Bernice Bobs her Hair," and remains implicitly a white collegiate dance form in most references that go beyond vague nods at the "jazz age." When black musicians do appear, as in "The Offshore Pirate," Fitzgerald has them playing in integrated circumstances, on instruments hard to find in standard histories of jazz. He has one musician "teasing ragtime out of a battered violin," (79) and two friends, "he with a bassoon and me with an oboe, and we'd blend minor keys in African harmonies a thousand years old" (84). These references might sound plausible to white readers of college age, but could only move a serious black to singing the blues. Ragtime, while integral to jazz development, was hardly synonymous with it and existed only as a dance cliché by the 1920s; no one seriously played it on the violin. "Minor keys" are common to European art music and are not synonymous with the pentatonic scale, which seems to be what Fitzgerald intended to say; and only an overprivileged college boy would have two funky musicians playing bassoon and oboe on a New York wharf as if they were saxophone and trumpet. When it came to firsthand knowledge of jazz at any level, Fitzgerald's hand was white and clean.

But at some point in 1923, a subtle intuitional shift appears. In "Dice, Brassknuckles & Guitar," an otherwise inconsequential story of that year for *Hearst's International*, James Powell lists himself on his professional card as "J.M.," the way someone else might have "M.D.," or "Ph.D." He is a self-proclaimed Jazz Master whose "school" gives regular instruction in gambling, violence, and music, and even a course in "southern accent," a subject apparently unitary for whites, but with special sessions on "straight nigger—for song purposes" (247). Naturally, anyone completing the course became a "Bachelor of Jazz." Behind the farrago of whimsy, anecdote, and the contrasts between yankee and rebel culture, Fitzgerald was free-associating his way into the mix that rose into *The Great Gatsby*: Because of the origins of jazz in the sexual underworld, and its raucous adolescence in the alcoholic underworld, musical form, criminal status, and violent behavior all reinforced each other, and in so doing, they inadvertently but inevitably included blacks.[38]

As for himself, Fitzgerald was coming from an entirely different direction: He was the second most important American modernist to emerge from a Roman Catholic background, and like Eugene O'Neill, whom he much admired, he was very Irish. Fitzgerald didn't know anything substantive about jazz, but he knew what an outsider was. Catholic in a world of Protestants, Irish in a world of Anglo-Saxons, poor in a world that valued wealth, a Mid-westerner never at ease in the East, Fitzgerald like O'Neill almost drowned his gifts in alcohol. Yet in one brief novel he pulled himself together. He somehow came to represent "the jazz age" to everyone who never listened seriously to jazz, and *The Great Gatsby* came to represent the spirit of that age. Understood in its very special context, the book did represent the first jazz age, but perhaps not in quite the way most people thought. It was a Catholic study of Protestant sin: of lust, greed, pride, and materialism. But because this particular Catholic author had lost his religion, he could offer no redemption. Instead, he displaced salvation, a concept implicitly of the future, into the past, which was as irrecoverable as youth. Music helped recover that past: Its disruptions of dance times were of relevance to anyone who associated dancing with youth. A blues lyric became the American madeleine: recall its taste and back you went, one violation producing another. The only black elements to remain were the color of Irish hair and the mood of gloom that inevitably set in as linear time went Protestantly forward.

Fitzgerald had grown up in a staunchly Roman Catholic family in St. Paul, a city friendlier to the faith than most in America. But somehow he was never comfortable in any church-oriented institution. More sensitive and observant than his peers, he seemed doomed by nature to being the least liked, least assimilated boy wherever he went, whether to the local St. Paul Academy or to Newman, then in far-off Hackensack, N.J. It didn't help that his father, to whom he was devoted, was something of a business failure, and a gentleman inclined to romanticize the Old South of his

Maryland background. Early Fitzgerald themes emerge from these family attitudes: the sense of being a failure in a country that valued success; the sense of being devoted to a lost cause in a country that valued only winners. Religion, when it did become an influence, could build on these: Irish Catholicism as a lost cause to English Protestantism, American Catholicism as a religious minority that would always have to fight for its rightful place in a materialist democracy.

Two important mentors developed these themes as Fitzgerald emerged from adolescence. The first, Father Cyril Sigourney Webster Fay, was then a Newman trustee. A chubby albino with a high-pitched voice and a startling giggle, Fay was a recent convert from the Episcopal Church who brought a good deal of social prestige with him. His family tree ablossoming in Philadelphia aristocracy, equally comfortable chatting in Latin or putting on religious charades with young children, he was a High Church hostess' dream dinner guest, and his social skills carried him as far as the house of Henry Adams, whom he enlightened on the details of medieval church architecture. He was fully up to the psychic strain of fencing with an old skeptic like Adams one day, and conferring on matters of significant church diplomacy with James Cardinal Gibbons the next. The young writer was entranced: "He made of that Church a dazzling, golden thing, dispelling its oppressive mugginess and giving the succession of days upon gray days, passing under its plaintive ritual, the romantic glamour of an adolescent dream."[39]

Once Fitzgerald matriculated at Princeton, his religion became something of a stigma; the college was Presbyterian by tradition, although undemanding either doctrinally or academically. Throwing himself into social and dramatic activities, Fitzgerald became increasingly secular in outlook without Father Fay to hover over his soul. As he drifted, Fitzgerald found his mailbox regularly contained advice from Irish novelist Shane Leslie, a friend of Fay who frequented Newman during these years. Also a convert, Leslie too could claim friends and relatives in high places in Great Britain and Ireland, including his cousin Winston Churchill. Fay and Leslie together seemed determined to merge religion and literature in the life of their novitiate, repeatedly holding up as role model the career of Robert Hugh Benson, the son of the Archbishop of Canterbury, who had converted to the Roman rite, joined the priesthood, and expressed himself in serious Catholic fiction. Fitzgerald proved more interested in the achievements of Compton Mackenzie, especially *Youth's Encounter* and *Sinister Street*, and his mind was more on the literature than the theology.

Immersed in Princeton, Fitzgerald was having too much fun to think about the priesthood or even pass his courses. Leaving without a degree in 1917, he was soon without formal faith as well: "Last year as a Catholic," he wrote in a scrapbook summary of 1917/18, as he turned twenty-two. A year after that, an epoch had clearly passed. "I am ashamed to say that my Catholicism is scarcely more than a memory—no, that's wrong, it's more than that," he confided to his non-Catholic friend and literary mentor, Edmund Wilson; "at any rate I go not to the church nor mumble stray nothings over crystalline beads." This is the point where his religious orientation transcends antiquarian gossip and becomes important for literature, and within five years for the larger culture. The same letter has him "deep in the throes" of what became *This Side of Paradise*, and the very text of that work betrayed the permanent importance that Catholicism as a vision would have for him.[40]

On the surface, *This Side of Paradise* is just one more callow novel of educational experience, about a young man coming of age in fairly comfortable circumstances. It is an exuberant, energetic work, infinitely shallow in most of its characterizations and ideas. Much of the attention it gets worries about how accurately the author portrayed the "real" people and places of his life, an approach of mind-numbing trivialization. Everything that needed saying along these lines Edmund Wilson put in a personal letter that has long been publicly available. He enjoyed the work in many ways, recognizing immediately that Fitzgerald had based his writing at least as much on the literary constructs of Compton Mackenzie and other British writers as he had on his own school experience. He noted the influence of the pseudoscientific journalist H. G. Wells, then the refuge of choice for young intellectuals losing their conventional religious beliefs. As a fellow Princeton writer, Wilson could also vouch for Fitzgerald's eye and ear. "The descriptions in places are very nicely done and so is some of the college dialogue, which really catches the Princeton tone," Wilson noted. But he knew his author only too well: "Your hero as an intellectual is a fake of the first water and I read his views on art, politics, religion and society with more riotous mirth than I should care to have you know."

Clearly, Fitzgerald was too close to his material, absorbing it rather than understanding it. "I really think you should cultivate detachment," and avoid making Amory Blaine "the hero of a series of dramatic encounters with all the naive and romantic gusto of a small boy imagining himself as a brave hunter of Indians." Some passages worked, some didn't; the fact that something may have actually happened was essentially irrelevant. "It would all be better if you would tighten up your artistic conscience and pay a little more attention to form." The dangers were all too obvious. "I believe you might become a very popular trashy novelist without much difficulty." He could also elevate his literary tastes a bit. "Cultivate a universal irony and do read something other than contemporary British novelists: this history of a young man stuff has been run into the ground." Fitzgerald took the criticism in better spirit than many others might have, but in a sense could do little with it: He seemed unable ever to write effectively about anyone but himself and those whom he knew firsthand.[41]

As a New Jersey Protestant of skeptical disposition, Wilson had little interest in the Irish Catholic side of the book. Fitzgerald was the only Roman Catholic he had known in college, and Wilson would never be acute as an analyst of religious writings apart from an inherited Judeo-Protestantism. He did not find it worth noting that on one page (72), for example, Amory Blaine's nickname is

"Original Sin," although he did register shock "when poor old John Bishop's hair stands up on end at beholding the Devil." It is not clear whether the shock is at the treatment of the mutual friend, John Peale Bishop, the activity of his hair, or the presence of the Devil. In context, it seems to be about Bishop; but to understand Fitzgerald and the book, the proper response should have been to ask what the Devil was doing in the book—twice, in fact (106–8, 113)—at all.

The Devil was in *This Side of Paradise* because he was integral to its Augustinian psychology; Fitzgerald may have been losing his religion, but its traces remain in a kind of pentimento to the fictional surfaces he kept imposing on his essentially religious themes. While much Augustinian writing is not directly relevant here, the insistence on Original Sin, on Adam's loss of free choice and the ensuing predestination to sin, remains central. Corrupt individuals must strive after grace, yet never truly deserve it; life becomes a constant striving after what cannot be attained, except through baptism, contrition, and the infinite mercy of an incomprehensible but merciful God. Puritans and Irish Catholics shared the bulk of these ideas, which helps explain why Fitzgerald could come out of a once-despised minority and yet speak in a way that seemed convincing to the larger mass of Americans.[42]

Church writers can get queasy on the subject, but implicit in it is the necessity to sin, for without sin you cannot be forgiven; you must fall before you can rise, and in a sense this makes God the author of sin, a heresy of some persistance in Christian history. And in the strictly male world of most Christian theology, women provided the chief occasions for sin. Greed, sloth, blasphemy, and so on had their honored places, but lust captured the imagination of both the clergy and the concupiscent in about equal measure. A beautiful woman was the greatest threat to male spirituality. Sexual misconduct outside of holy matrimony was the greatest earthly sin an Augustinian could imagine, and even within marriage, sex remained shameful, a deed done in the dark solely to produce more souls for God. The Irish was the most conservative of all

Catholic churches on sexual issues, just as Congregationalists remained among the most conservative of Protestant churches.

Fitzgerald was hopelessly in love with love, glitter, romance,
parties, and all the other nouns that might be used as substitutes
for particular young women. He felt temptation more often than
most people felt the weather, and when such belles as Ginevra
King or Zelda Sayre fox-trotted into his life, he was as predestined
to fall as the sinners in many a homily. He knew he shouldn't, and
with King and numerous others he clearly didn't; but with Sayre
he probably did—she was a liberated Episcopalian and a long way
from Augustinian broodings. Sayre, indeed, fitted the requirements of sin only too well: the beautiful temptress, ever provocative, possibly willing, even desirable socially. But to a friend of
Father Fay, the only thing worse than a temptress who said "no"
was one who said "yes."

This is why, from the very start of the book, sex usually brings
on revulsion rather than excitement, especially when a woman
truly offers a physical part of herself. Young Amory vies for the attentions of Myra St. Claire, made more attractive because she
seems attracted to Froggy Parker. Amory kisses her cheek swiftly
when the moment seems ripe, the audacious adolescent tempted
beyond toleration. Then: "Sudden revulsion seized Amory, disgust, loathing for the whole incident. He desired frantically to be
away, never to see Myra again, never to kiss anyone." She asks for
another kiss, but he refuses. She becomes incensed, and it all ends
badly (21). Clearly, once the woman (or girl) seems willing, even
aggressive, she has entered the Augustinian paradigm; a young
man who accepts is kissing damnation, and in need of a bath and a
trip to the confessional.

This all puts the scenes in which the Devil appears in perspective. In the midst of their alcoholic partying, Amory's superego be-
trays him. A face pursues him, ruining parties and conversations
with pretty girls, all presumably still virginal in a technical medical
sense. Then Amory notices the man's feet, which "were all
wrong." "He wore no shoes, but, instead, a sort of half moccasin,

pointed, . . . with the little ends curling up. . . . They were unutterly terrible" (107–8). He fled, increasingly conscious of bad smells, and "far beyond horror" (110). The next day, the sight of "painted faces" (111), always a euphemism for prostitutes, makes him sick, and he finds everything "filthy." "I've seen the devil" (113) he soon realizes—and the only things he can do are avoid women and read to a male friend from *The New Machiavelli*. In a book dedicated "to Sigourney Fay," this was the right response, but the wrong text.

Still unsure of himself as a writer, Fitzgerald then opted to become a realist or naturalist along the lines of Frank Norris and Theodore Dreiser, a type of work that one of Fitzgerald's favorite critics, H. L. Mencken, was then loudly advocating. Mencken was also supportive of the work of Joseph Conrad, and this proved more fruitful, for Conrad's narrative experiments and his obsession with psychological and geographical evil fitted well with Fitzgerald's predilections. But in the short run naturalistic detail won out, disastrously enough. *The Beautiful and Damned* was, properly understood, a study of the absence of God in a materialistic society, but few read it properly. It sold, as studies of sinners often do, but proved an artistic dead end. "I shall never write another document-novel," he wrote Thomas Boyd early in 1923. "I have decided to be a pure artist and experiment in form and emotion." He had long admired the early work in this area by Sherwood Anderson, but: "I'm sure I can do it much better than Anderson."[43]

Fitzgerald signed off on the mechanics of publishing *Tales of the Jazz Age* in June 1922. In a few casual sentences at the end of a letter attentive mostly to organizational and marketing problems he spoke of his next novel. "Its locale will be the middle west and New York of 1885 I think. It will concern less superlative beauties than I run to usually & will be centered on a smaller period of time," he wrote his editor, Maxwell Perkins. "It will have a catholic element." He had many false starts along the way, and of course the year changed to the five years from 1917 to 1922. Time itself became central, and certain values belonging to 1885 did remain. But in essence, the description held. Especially the Catholic part, which most readers didn't even notice.[44]

Fitzgerald best worked out the ideas that were filling his mind in two stories, both relevant to Catholicism. "Winter Dreams," first published in December 1922 and later reprinted in *All the Sad Young Men*, explores the real eternal triangle of so much of Fitzgerald's best work, the relations between love, money, and memory. Dexter Green caddied for pocket money, but quit after being bossed around by a willful young girl on the edge of puberty. Given to winter dreams of a romantic life, he had trouble dealing with the petty demands of the present. What he wanted was a few of "the glittering things" of life, and he wanted them unsullied by "the mysterious denials and prohibitions in which life indulges" (221). Soon he was making enough money in the laundry business to golf and have caddies of his own. After eight years or so he once again encountered the willful girl on the course, now beautiful but as imperious as ever. She flirted with him, led him on, and made it clear that a suitor's effect on her could be closely dependent on his financial status. When he claimed he was "probably making more money than any man" his age in the area, her kisses took on a compulsive believability (226). She played him like the painted lady she was at heart; he in turn knew full well that "losing himself in her was opiate rather than tonic" (227). Firmly self-deceptive, histrionically miserable, she spoke one of Fitzgerald's classic lines: "I'm more beautiful than anybody else, why can't I be happy?" (232); and then proposed. They had a presumably passionate night together.

Her interest in him survived that night by about a month and she terminated their "engagement." He loved her without illusions and in spite of everything. He lost track of her, as she married and destroyed another man. A chance encounter a decade later revived the memories and brought him to tears, but he knew it was over. He had even left his grief behind "in the country of illusion, of youth, of the richness of life, where his winter dreams had flourished. "Long ago," he said, "long ago, there was something in me, but now that thing is gone" (235–6).

Here is an elaboration and sophistication of the implicit psychology in *This Side of Paradise*. Beautiful women still tempt and destroy, but man has to love them anyway. Money and beauty inevitably taint each other. The moment passes, not "all-too-swiftly" as in conventional writing, but "not-swiftly-enough"; the moment is an act of sin, necessary but disgusting. Now, instead of priest and confessional, only time can grant grace. Grace can live only in the past; the future is a steady declining slope, useful only for an art capable of conveying a single fleeting moment of lost beauty.

"Absolution," first published in June 1924, is even more directly relevant. Fitzgerald originally intended it to be "the prologue of the novel but it interfered with the neatness of the plan," as he wrote Max Perkins at the time. Even more to the eventual point of *The Great Gatsby*, it violated "the sense of mystery" that was to surround the origins of his central character. "Absolution" directly concerned priests, grace, the sanctity of the confessional, and beautiful women as temptresses. Above all, it concerned lies, the telling of stories that weren't true, which was what sinful young boys and imaginative novelists both do.[45]

After lying in the confessional, even insisting to the priest: "I never tell lies" (263), Rudolph Miller indulged his imagination by projecting himself into Blatchford Sarnemington, a double whose "suave nobility" enabled him to live "in great sweeping triumphs" (263). But two figures circumscribed both his lives, a priest and a father, two "father" figures, who both deceived themselves and imposed a spurious order on imaginative escapes from reality. Looming over both, in a crazy way, was the fleeting image of a third, James J. Hill. Hill, one of the great capitalists of the frontier, had been a hero to the young Scott Fitzgerald, a Protestant capitalist married to a devout Catholic and famous for his charities in the Catholic community. In "Absolution," "Hill was the apotheosis of that quality in which Miller himself was deficient—the sense of things, the feel of things, the hint of rain in the wind on the cheek." For two decades, "he had lived alone with Hill's name and God"(264). By the workings of memory and imagination, in other words, Catholicism and capitalism were coming together, not as sources of exploitation, or anything so prosaic as the Protestant ethic, but as sources for charity, for the dispensation of grace, both spiritual and material, in an atmosphere of mystery—in language suspiciously similar to that Fitzgerald had used in describing sexual attraction.

It remained only to plant such associations in an Augustinian contrast between the City of Man and the City of God, and Fitzgerald did this by the end of the story. The priest ridiculed Rudolph's half-spoken fears and, obsessed by his own repressed problems, told Rudolph, "go and see an amusement park." It resembled "a fair, only much more glittering. Go to one at night and stand a little way off from it in a dark place—under dark trees." Observe the ferris wheel and the boatslides. "A band playing somewhere, and a smell of peanuts—and everything will twinkle." The priest then frowned in free association. "But don't get up close, because if you do you'll only feel the heat and the sweat and the life" (271).

As the priest sank into what seemed to be a nervous breakdown, Rudolph felt somehow liberated. He was ready to change his name to Jimmie Gatz and to leave the church of his two fathers—three if you count Hill—and strike out for the city of man. He will watch Blatchford Sarnemington grow into Jay Gatsby, his life full of sweeping triumphs yet hollow at its core; he will displace his religious emotions onto sexual idealizations, knowing full well that the woman of his choice is unworthy; and he will live as if in a carnival, his house as glittering as its women, and as empty as any city of man. Watching it all, obsessed but detached, will be Fitzgerald himself, married to Zelda, dancing slowly downhill into Long Island Sound.

The Great Gatsby is a study of an America that has lost its God and become totally secular. As someone who began as a minority group member, rigidly educated in values highly critical of those in the American mainstream, and who slid away, Fitzgerald was thus not just an outsider, he was an outsider even from the one group to which he could claim allegiance. He took with him all the Catholic conviction of sin and human degradation, but retained none of the Church's promise of grace and resurrection. This world became palpable at the famous opening of Chapter 2, where on the road to West Egg a driver had to pass through the valley of ashes, a huge dump that was taking on the appearance of a fantastic city of dust, with ash-gray men swarming about. The valley of the shadow of death, ashes to ashes, dust to dust—Christian imagery even has its Ash Wednesday, peculiarly emotional to a Catholic—it all prefigured the lives and relationships to come, which will all turn to ashes. Over it all brooded the blind eyes of Dr. T. J. Eckleburg, the remnants of a forgotten ad. God was dead but still selling, so to speak. Through it all ran a foul river, a cloaca minima, that immediately reminded the narrator of Tom Buchanan's flashy, tasteless mistress.

To anyone looking for the fragments of this post-Christian world, the book provided all too many opportunities for symbol hunting. In one famous passage, Gatsby had the conception of himself as "a son of God" who "must be about His Father's Business, the service of a vast, vulgar, and meretricious beauty" (77). He was given to stretching his arms out in a priestly way when he looked toward Daisy's house, while she conveniently provided him with a green votive light at the end of her dock—this from an author who had, quite consciously and openly, written to a mutual friend: "You're still a catholic but Zelda's the only God I have left now." Even nature cooperated suspiciously, providing the tearful reunion of Gatsby and Daisy with enough rain for a thousand romances—it lasted for most of Chapter 5, surely one of the most pathetic fallacies to survive in a major work of art—and included her famous sobbing into Gatsby's rising pile of shirts. Conspicuous consumption had strange effects on the Protestant daughters of capitalist America. And, of course, Gatsby will lay down his life as a vicarious sacrifice for Daisy in her sin, so she could rise again to tempt others.[46]

Such a religious grounding should have made the book a triumph of conservatism, deserving a place on the shelf near *The Age of Innocence* or *Death Comes for the Archbishop*. In many ways Fitzgerald was conservative, insofar as a man innocent of politics could be so-called. But here as elsewhere, a conservative vision of original sin and social pathology went with experimental views of how to portray it in an artistically effective manner. Fitzgerald had already learned a good deal from Sherwood Anderson; Mencken had ushered him into the heart of Conrad's darkness, and Edmund Wilson had him "wild" to read *Ulysses* just as he was starting to conceptualize *The Great Gatsby*. On at least three fronts, Fitzgerald was preparing to write in a modernist manner. Instead of Winesburg, we get East and West Egg; instead of Marlowe we get Nick Carraway; instead of *Ulysses* we get a Long Island *Parsifal*.[47]

In terms of structure, the most striking uses of modernistic technique are in Fitzgerald's treatment of factuality, indirect apprehension of events, and time. Put another way, the reader does not get a linear tale of active people doing real things; the reader hears bits and pieces of information, out of order, that may or may not constitute a believable narrative. This is most obviously true of the eponymous hero. "They say he's a nephew or cousin of Kaiser Wilhelm's. That's where all his money comes from" (28), we hear as the first substantive reference. "Somebody told me they thought he killed a man once," a chattering girl soon remarks, while a companion has heard "he was a German spy during the war" (36). A visitor to his library reports in astonishment that the books are "real" and "have pages and everything" (38). Gatsby then appears in the unmediated flesh, and Nick sees "an elegant young roughneck, a year or two over thirty, whose elaborate formality of speech just missed being absurd" (40). This clearly is not someone equipped to quest for the holy grail of virginal femininity, especially for a narrator who works at Probity Trust and eats at the Yale Club. Others report that Gatsby is a bootlegger, a friend of gamblers, a shipper of illegal oil to Canada, a yachtsman, an Oxford man, and "a penniless young man without a past" (116).

All this chaos of indirection actually has a unifying thread. Having seemingly created himself, Gatsby also wanted to repeat the past, not realizing that both his goals were chimerical. He fooled no one by his act, nor could he recover the idealized moment of his frustrated ecstacy with Daisy Fay. No modernist could make that error: You could never slip into the same stream twice, only attempt to recapture it after the Proustian manner. But when Nick told Gatsby, "You can't repeat the past," Gatsby was incredulous. "Why of course you can!" he insisted, looking a bit frantic. "I'm going to fix everything just the way it was before" (86). A true conservative, he had wandered into the wrong novel as well as the wrong relationship.

Naturally enough, therefore, when Gatsby and Daisy dance, they do a "graceful, conservative fox-trot" (82), and a reader returns inevitably to the role of music, not only at all those parties, but as occasions of memory, the 1920s equivalent of a snapshot, a scrapbook, or a madeleine. The book contained a great deal of quasi-musical noise, a few fragments of popular songs (75), "a neat sad little waltz" (85) and Gatsby's dismissive: "Old sport, the dance is unimportant" (85). At one point there was a reference to saxophones wailing "Beale Street Blues" all one night (118). As for blacks, they came in for two brief, unimportant references. And with one exception, that's about it.

That exception spoke decibels about Fitzgerald's attitude to jazz, his distance both from the black and the jazz communities, and thus the absurdity of his being regarded as a spokesman for any jazz age. Fitzgerald had a habit of using the names of his characters to hint ambiguously at their natures or destinies. Gatsby is thus the man of the gat, slang of the time for gun; Nick Carraway allows himself to get carried away by the glitter, by Gatsby and by Jordan Baker. Daisy Fay is perhaps the most suggestive: the fey Daisy, of course; but also the fairy, so popular at the time in several well-known ballets; and also the occasion of an auto-da-fé, an act of faith, usually the burning of a heretic. And then there is Vladimir Tostoff.

In this context, Tostoff equals tossed off, which is what Fitzgerald thought jazz musicians did. It was all so spontaneous, these folks just tossed off improvisations whenever pretty girls needed a dance tune. The music only had value in its extramusical task of providing a memory aid for passionate kisses, and so on. The piece here is called "Vladimir Tostoff's Jazz History of the World." Since Fitzgerald had no known firsthand knowledge of jazz, it can be taken for granted that a white band on Long Island was not really playing jazz at all; the accompanying reference to its performance at Carnegie Hall makes this definite, since jazz of any legitimate kind was unwelcome there until 1938. But Fitzgerald assimilated bits of musical knowledge from all over, most obviously from conversations with Edmund Wilson, or the reading of Paul Rosenfeld's columns. He could have been referring to a Leo Ornstein work, like "Danse Sauvage," although the idea of genteel couples dancing to Ornstein should give anyone pause. Or Fitzgerald could have been referring to "*The Creation of the World*, which Darius Milhaud based directly on music heard during his Harlem visits—it premiered in Paris on 25 October, 1923. Or, most likely, he was stretching his dates even more and thinking of Gershwin's *Rhapsody in Blue*, which made its New York splash literally as he was writing the book. Whatever Fitzgerald was thinking of, it wasn't jazz; he just tossed off the reference in playful passing.

Finally, along with the casual jazz goes the casual violence, legitimately inseparable. Much of the gossip about Gatsby concerned bootlegging, gambling, and guns. Aside from the rumors directly about Gatsby himself, Fitzgerald carefully built up the circumstances of the corruption that gambling and prohibition have brought to America. The key figure here was Meyer Wolfsheim, the gambler friend presumably based on the actual Arnold Rothstein. Wolfsheim talked casually of business and murder in the same paragraph and wore human molars for cuff-buttons; he was famous for having fixed the World Series in 1919, among other achievements. He also claimed to have raised Gatsby, "right out of the gutter" (133). In the long run, it turned out that Gatsby did owe his money to drugstore bootlegging. His murder, though a mistake, thus came as no real surprise. It even seemed appropriate, the sort of thing that would happen in the City of Man.[48]

Much has been written elsewhere on *The Great Gatsby*, and no more of it needs elaboration here. The book remains an American modernist classic for its embodiment of the new attitude toward time, narrative unreliability, and implicit attack on Protestant notions of progress, but perhaps above all for its post-Catholic sensibility, its being the major achievement of an outsider from a group already outside the American mainstream. Its subsequent acceptance as an embodiment of the American dream, as well as its supposed validity as an example of "jazz age" prose, will long remain among the more amusing errors of cultural analysis in America.[49]

PART THREE

THE ANXIETIES OF

INFLUENCE

EIGHT

FIGHTING FREE OF
THE FIRST MODERNISTS

Late in life, in an autobiography that left out more than it included, Georgia O'Keeffe recalled the visit she made to 291, long before she and Alfred Stieglitz became one of the most famous couples in art history. Stieglitz had hung a show of her work just days before America entered World War I, and hers was the last to appear in the legendary little gallery. Weary and discouraged, he had just dismantled the exhibit when she arrived unexpectedly. With hardly a murmur, he rehung the entire show solely for her benefit. He also photographed her for the first time, "my face twice—my hands several times." During her brief visit, they also made a quick trip to Coney Island with a few friends. "The only thing I remember about Stieglitz from that trip is his black Loden cape. It was a cold, windy day and it was put around me. In later years a cape was always part of his costume."[1]

O'Keeffe rightly claimed that she was a nonverbal artist, but in this single paragraph she brought together several vital themes relevant to herself, to her work, and to an important given in the history of American modernism. She had a pathbreaker whom she greatly admired, both in terms of his work and his person. He definitely reciprocated her feelings, for just as disciples need teachers, teachers need disciples, a situation that sexual attraction only heightened. Artists, of course, always separated their lives and works and always failed, and never more obviously than here, where one art form—painting—excited a response in another—

photography. Indeed, in the small, not to say incestuous, 291 circle, painting and photography interacted constantly, standards and assumptions from each medium affecting the other in ways that sometimes defy clear explanation. But the core of metonymic truth lay in that loden coat. Stieglitz had literally put his mantle on his favorite disciple. The resulting picture could excite his camera as well as her memory; after all, they both looked good in it. But coats could smother as well as warm. Pioneers might break convenient trails, yet their very progress implicitly denies the need for followers to deviate into the underbrush or onto the beckoning plains along the way.

At some point in the decade after America entered World War I, a second modernist generation had to deal with the problems that that coat embodied. The generation of Alfred Stieglitz, Ezra Pound, and Gertrude Stein had to deal with all the religious, moral, and social pressures of late Victorian America, and to withstand as well the ruthlessly Protestant pressures of the progressive impulse, which implicitly demanded that artists produce novels that would expose the evils of the meatpacking industry, poems that exhorted Salvation Army General William Booth to heaven, and paintings that restored self-esteem to the poor as they struggled to survive among the ash cans of lower Broadway. The generation of Georgia O'Keeffe could profit from their efforts, but in turn faced a different problem: how to fight free of these heroic, admired, and all too imitable figures. A newly emerging tradition could stifle talent quite as effectively as any moral policeman snouting out the latest nudes.

Critics at least as far back as T. S. Eliot have analyzed aspects of the problem, usually with explicit reference to poetry from Shakespeare through Coleridge. Eliot insisted that no artist could be entirely original. Some sense of tradition, of indispensable predecessors, was essential to provide context and meaning for any legitimate act of poetry; a poet concentrated experience, he did not originate it. In the early 1970s, both Walter Jackson Bate and Harold Bloom reinvigorated and expanded the discussion. Bate dwelt on the anxieties poets felt about how to be original in the face of such great achievements as those of Shakespeare. Artists felt dwarfed, and escaped if they could by seeking out newer subjects where precedents were fewer and sincerity could often pass for originality. Bloom made the most sustained analytical effort. Battling Nietzsche and Freud even as he wrote, Bloom insisted that strong poets made history "by misreading one another, so as to clear imaginative space for themselves." Since the Renaissance, the main tradition of Western poetry "is a history of anxiety and self-saving caricature, of distortion, of perverse, wilful revisionism without which modern poetry as such could not exist."[2]

None of these critics suggested that their ideas applied equally to all the arts; Bate explicitly thought musicians had an easier time of it, and critics perhaps the easiest of all. Further analysis does not really bear this assumption out. All artists rightly experience anxieties along these lines, but each does so in a spectacularly different way—the divisions are not by art but by talent and circumstance. And America's second generation had much to be anxious about, for giants really were in the woods, capable of trampling the unwary, eating them alive, or rolling over in their sleep and smothering any small creatures who were merely seeking animal warmth.

Four of the lesser-known examples of generational influence indicate the range of possibilities: the close, warmly personal, but stylistically incompatible relationship between the Swiss Jew Ernest Bloch and the purest of purebred yankees, Roger Sessions; the largely posthumous, somewhat dotty precedents that Erik Satie left for a church organist that a secret passion for the illogical named Virgil Thomson; the alcoholic, sterilizing warmth of the relationship between the shy, impecunious James Joyce and the well-funded Robert McAlmon, where hero worship and generally good personal relations produced anecdotage but seemed to extinguish any creative achievements; and finally, the straightforward, honest-disciple relationship that seemed to pertain between Marcel Duchamp and Man Ray, where the chemistry often seemed as difficult to analyze as the works of art themselves.

ERNEST BLOCH/ROGER SESSIONS

In his self-dramatizing way, Ernest Bloch realized early in life that he seemed destined never to belong anywhere. Born in 1880 to a Geneva family that made its living retailing cuckoo clocks, music boxes, and related souvenirs, he had to fight staunch paternal opposition to obtain musical training. He managed nevertheless to make use of what he could find to win quick preferment, in one instance using largely Hebrew melodies that his father habitually hummed into an "Oriental Symphony" at the age of fifteen. Always on the move, he studied with Eugène Ysaye in Brussels and Ivan Knorr in Frankfurt, before moving on to Munich, Paris, and then back to Geneva. He churned out a remarkable number of works, lectured extensively on aesthetics, but felt chained for several years to the family business. The death of his father in 1913 seemed to trigger a racial outburst, and several explicitly Jewish works of striking originality poured forth. The most successful was *Schelomo* (1916), a Hebraic rhapsody for cello and orchestra inspired by the Book of Ecclesiastes, the cello being presumptively the voice of King Solomon.

War conditions forced an economic crisis and Bloch grabbed at a straw. Dancer Maud Allan needed someone to organize and conduct an orchestra for a projected American tour, Bloch got the nod, and thus arrived in New York on 30 July, 1916. Thanks to a letter from his friend Romain Rolland to Waldo Frank, Bloch quickly impressed Paul Rosenfeld, and the *New York Times* critic Olin Downes was not far behind. The tour collapsed in short order but Bloch managed to parlay his real abilities and gregarious character into a position as head of the theory department at the new school that David Mannes was just opening up. On 3 May, 1917, he collaborated with Artur Bodanzky in putting on four major Jewish works with the Society of the Friends of Music. The Philadelphia Orchestra repeated most of the program the next January.[3]

So swift was Bloch's rise to prominence in the rather arid New York scene, that when a precocious graduate of both Harvard and

Yale named Roger Sessions felt the need for competent professional advice, he wrote him "because he was the only composer living in the United States at that time whose judgment" he felt he could rely on. He made a quick study of Bloch's works in between teaching duties at Smith College, then went down to New York "in a state of terrific enthusiasm." Bloch was no pushover and treated the young man "quite roughly." As Sessions went through a piano reduction of his Symphony No. 1, Bloch stood behind him calling out the names of the obvious influences. "I wasn't really fazed by it. It finally got so that I joined in with him just to show him what the situation really was." Bloch told Sessions to put aside composition for two years until he knew what he was doing, and then illustrated what he meant by an impromptu analysis of an early Beethoven piano sonata: "these ten or twenty minutes or however long it took to go through this were about the most important thing in my whole musical education." It was respect at first hearing, the guru had his disciple, and when Bloch accepted an offer to become the first director of the Cleveland Institute of Music, Sessions joined him there in 1921.

In the course of his two years rethinking what he was about, Sessions discovered the work of Igor Stravinsky—another "influence" to be sure, but the most fruitful available at the time. Given the extraordinary availability of piano reductions of even the most complex modernist works in those years, Sessions had possessed four-hand versions of both *Petrushka* and the *Rite of Spring*—he recalled playing the latter for Harvard's Edward Burlingame Hill in 1914, but long remained unsure as to whether or not he actually understood it. He was relieved to learn later, when the full score became available, that he really did, and admitted that the piece "had an enormous influence on me. Bloch didn't like that at all," and Bloch himself took many years before he reached a true understanding of Stravinsky. Sessions thus produced his first important work under conflicting auspices: the personal relationship to his teacher Bloch, and the professional allegiance to an Igor Stravinsky whom he did not meet personally until Nadia Boulanger introduced them in Cleveland in 1925.[4]

The Black Maskers (1923) was a commission from a group at Smith that needed incidental music for a performance of the play of that name by the Russian expressionist Leonid Andreyev. "It is a very strange play, and I don't wholly get it yet." But his mother was in charge of an off-campus dormitory, Sessions had taught there and married one of the students, and was thus willing to accept appropriate commissions. The play consisted of five scenes in the life of "an Italian Renaissance nobleman who's the son of a Crusader, supposedly. And he comes upon a document which convinces him that he is really the offspring of an affair that his mother had with a groom, probably." This ambiguous sense of identity unhinges him, amidst a profusion of symbols. The play includes masked balls, a confrontation with one's double resulting in murder, and a funeral. Such material was foreign both to the psychologies of Bloch and of Sessions, although its Russian origin clearly shared kinship with the strongest tradition in Stravinsky's early career. In the event, it had little in common with anything that followed it.[5]

With this impressive achievement behind him, Sessions had to face an increasingly unpleasant situation in Cleveland. Although he dedicated *The Black Maskers* to Bloch, he was becoming increasingly distressed by his mentor's behavior in a stolid, philistine environment. From Bloch's point of view, America was a country of stones, iron, and tar, culturally inorganic, lacking flexibility, human affection, and subtlety. His family had had numerous troubles in New York but had adjusted to Cleveland fairly well—indeed, he remarked in several private letters that they had become more Americanized than he. He had long settled into a persona that was and would remain "toujours, sans doute, un solitaire." He had tried to institute much-needed pedagogical reforms, but the powers that be were hostile to both himself and his theoretical perspectives. His destiny was to be always "un Juif Errant" stranded among "110 millions de *tubes digestifs* qui composent les U.S.A." At least as early as his unhappy year in Paris he had thought of himself as a Wandering Jew beleaguered by anti-Semites, and doubtless prejudice was never entirely absent, but it had become a routine approaching vaudeville predictability and a self-fulfilling prophecy.[6]

Publicly Sessions defended his teacher down the line. Possessing the highest of musical ideals, Bloch had encountered insensitive, practical bourgeois who wanted chiefly to capitalize on his name for advertising purposes. He wanted a theory department; they wanted a "practical" curriculum. He wanted pupils to have "direct musical experience"; they wanted grades and textbooks. Neither side proved willing to compromise. "Cleveland's rejection of Bloch was a rejection precisely of the best that he had to give. His very geniality, his force of conviction, his ironic laughter—his richness of temperament and culture, in other words—stood in his way." Cleveland was unready for "just those disinterested and humane conceptions which form the indispensable background for artistic creation of any kind." Privately, Sessions recalled for an interviewer years later, Bloch seemed to oscillate between identities as a "petit bourgeois Jew from Geneva" and "a background of French culture which gave him an ironic streak, a very sardonic streak in his nature. These things would fight with each other." He refused to pay socially necessary calls or eat placatory dinners. He treated his own wife with something approaching contempt and engaged in extramarital affairs. He made a histrionic suicide attempt through an overdose of Veronal. He was his own worst enemy and his 1925 resignation inevitable.[7]

Sessions was clearly growing away from Bloch by the summer of 1924. We "must not for a moment let ourselves become involved with the emotions of the Bloch family," he wrote his wife Barbara. "I have become convinced this summer more than ever that the Bloch point of view and all it represents is *not* for *me*, and I feel nothing but repugnance for all their 'alarms and excursions.'" Once of the belief that work with Bloch would be more productive than postgraduate work in France, Sessions was rapidly shifting to a more cosmopolitan perspective. He went to Paris during that summer of 1924, met Aaron Copland and Nadia Boulanger, and discovered that his allegiance to the works of Stravinsky fitted in with trends in a Paris that had refused to pay Bloch more than passing attention. Going on to London, Geneva, and Florence, he felt himself going through "a complete readjustment of values for me," as he wrote his wife from Florence late in August. He was working toward what he later called "fluency. It was a question of not only harmonies specifically, but the whole movement. What I really did was to go into more of an emphasis on line and less on color."[8]

Even a brief acquaintance with Europe was leading Sessions insensibly in the directions Ezra Pound and T. S. Eliot had already pioneered in poetry. "All my questionings about the value of culture" were leading him back "to the conclusion that whatever reality Michelangelo and Giotto and Leonardo and Dante and Botticelli" might have for the masses, "they have an intense reality for me." Whatever discontinuities he might feel with his oppressively American family and the mossbacked universities he had attended, the past of Europe contained a greatness "not only valuable but necessary to us, to the development of a really strong and great personality." He thought the past "as much a part of reality as the present or the future"; it "finally came to seem to me a part of life." At the same time he craved the experience of his own time, of modernity: "of the most elementary sensations; a closer touch with nature, with all the fundamental facts and conditions of our existence—the elementary sensations of the organism and the most intense and vivid experience of them." He wanted to get beyond *The Black Maskers*, and the names that inspired him the most were Dante and Bach.

The next year, 1925, Bloch resigned his position in Cleveland and headed for San Francisco; Sessions resigned in support and headed for Europe, where he stayed for most of the next seven years. He tried to write a piano quintet, but he seemed only to be able to think Stravinsky's thoughts in orchestral terms. The result, with its odd combination of syncopated jazziness and austere neoclassicism, perfectly reflected two of the available modernist languages. The *Symphony No. 1*, which Serge Koussevitzky performed with the Boston Symphony Orchestra on 22 April, 1927, no more represented the mature Sessions than *The Black Maskers*, but no one could mistake it as the result of the inspiration of Ernest Bloch.[9]

ERIK SATIE/VIRGIL THOMSON

Virgil Thomson was a man of many opinions, most of them firm, many of them idiosyncratic. Just as musically aware people conventionally looked at nineteenth century art music in terms of the three German Bs of Bach, Beethoven, and Brahms, he insisted that "the three S's of modern music—in descending order of significance," were "Satie, Schoenberg, and Stravinsky." He thought so in the early 1920s, repeated himself in the early 1940s, and took back nothing in describing his life in the middle 1960s. The ranking was true enough for him, although it reversed the order most analysts would accept then or later; it also unjustly excluded Busoni, who had the misfortune not to be French nor to have a name beginning with S. But Satie *was* crucial, and not just for Thomson. Satie rather combined the roles of both Jules Laforgue and T. S. Eliot in poetry: He was the chronologically distant bearer of popular urban culture and its aesthetic consequences; and he was the geographically distant teacher who successfully manufactured a new language for those who might never have met him, let alone studied under him.

To his credit, Virgil Thomson never let a prejudice slip by without at least a vestige of plausible support. "The Satie musical esthetic is the only twentieth-century musical esthetic in the Western world," he continued. "Schoenberg and his school are Romantics; and their twelve-tone syntax, however intriguing one may find it intellectually, is the purest Romantic chromaticism." He dismissed Hindemith as "a neoclassicist, like Brahms, with ears glued firmly to the past." He assumed that the "same is true of the later Stravinsky and of his satellites." By 1941, the date of this essay, this all had the smell of a pot sniffing at three black adjacent kettles, not to mention the problem of hearing much of anything by Paul Hindemith that resembled anything by Johannes Brahms. But with reference solely to Satie, the statement provoked thought and compelled agreement. "Satie is the only one whose works can be enjoyed and appreciated without any knowledge of the history of music." They are "as straightforward, as devastating as the remarks of a child." Although to the uninitiated they might sound trifling, to "those who love them they are fresh and beautiful and firmly right." They have also "long dominated the musical thought of France." Conventional musicologists assume Debussy was the first important French modernist, but even "Debussy is growing less and less comprehensible these days to those who never knew Satie." For Thomson, the aesthetic values involved "quietude, precision, acuteness of auditory observation, gentleness, sincerity, and directness of statement."[10]

Speaking historically, something contrary to Satie's usual practice, Satie really had two phases clearly relevant to French modernism. As Roger Shattuck suggested in the first truly shrewd scholarly assessment, "he was twice a composer. During the closing years of the century he attained notoriety as an extravagant, Montmartre Bohemian" who "watched his best friend, Claude Debussy, begin a successful career," and then "helped his first protégé, Maurice Ravel, pick his way safely around Wagner and César Franck." He himself seemed merely the composer of "a motley collection of works whose innovations were generally passed off as eccentricities." Around 1898 he seemed to sink into oblivion, not to return until 1910, when his two protégés dubbed him a precursor and found him relevant once more. He promptly confounded "everyone by composing works in a totally new style and fiercely refused to rest on his first and acknowledged career." He was, in short, both the Laforgue and the Eliot of French modernist music.[11]

Seen in context, Satie I was the bard of the new cabaret culture that arose in Paris toward the end of the nineteenth century. The salons that had been so important since midcentury had entered a slow decline in vigor and importance, and artistic cabarets were displacing them, led by Chat Noir, founded in 1881. Intensely casual, intentionally ad hoc, planned to be spontaneous, such cabarets specialized in a prototypically modernist tone. They were ironical and eccentric. They adored deadpan absurdity and the overstatement of the obvious. In time, the Cabaret des Quat'Z-Arts (1893) would sponsor tame bears, horses, singing poets, and outdoor parades. Songs might be earthy, obscene, or bearing the hair of very shaggy dogs, intentionally repetitious and boring. By the 1920s, after Darius Milhaud's *Le Boeuf sur la toit* gave its name to the most famous of all, the anarchy was traditional. Such places rightly appealed to Americans, for aspects of American vaudeville, ragtime, cakewalk, lassoing horses, military marching bands, and worship of the machine had long permeated the scene. Listeners too easily forgot that the American West was even farther from Paris than Paris was from New York City, and thus even more exotic.[12]

Erik Satie was fond of repeating that he had been born very young in very old times, as usual a truism open to multiple ambiguities. An indolent student who rarely impressed his teachers, he became a bohemian fixture in the late 1880s, playing, composing, and studying as he felt the mood and money. Works like his *Sarabandes*, *Gymnopédies*, and *Gnossiennes* began appearing in 1887, often with neither bar lines nor keys indicated. They continued into the 1890s, even as the composer dabbled in various religions and mystical interests usually related to Rosicrucianism. He became friendly with Claude Debussy in about 1889 and Maurice Ravel in 1893, influencing both. Massively skeptical of everything German, especially anything having to do with Richard Strauss or Richard Wagner, he repeatedly urged composers to "be brief," to scale down their orchestras, their aspirations, and the length of their pieces. He loved the light, the parodic, the allusive, the ironic, suggesting that his friends compose "sans choucroute si possible." One did not, after all, consume sauerkraut in a Parisian cabaret.

This worthy but obscure phase petered out at the turn of the century and Satie seemed destined to survive solely as a whimsical eccentric in footnotes to the lives of his friends. As he wrote in a letter of 1901: "I'm getting more and more fed up, for I can see clearly that I was not born into my proper period—a period I can't accommodate myself to, even by putting in something of myself." At the same time that he enrolled rather belatedly in the Schola Cantorum to sophisticate his musical skills, he turned to the other arts. Perhaps more than any other modernist composer, he learned from literature, ballet, drama, painting, and sculpture ideas that he could put to use. He was especially grateful to the painters in his life, once remarking that "it was painters who taught me the most about music."

By 1911, he seemed to revive. Ravel performed and Debussy orchestrated several of his early works, and he began turning out striking piano solos again. He met Serge Diaghilev and Jean Cocteau, and by spring of 1916 plans were afoot for the ballet that became *Parade*. Late in August, Picasso signed on to help design the sets. A reduction for two pianos was in hand early in January 1917, and on 18 May the Ballets Russes premiered it at the Théâtre du Châtelet. An epic scandal ensued that involved a libel suit, fine, and detention for eight days, but Satie's immortality was assured. He became the role model and father figure for Les Six, the avant-garde of the 1920s. With Jean Cocteau as spokesman and mascot, and Darius Milhaud as the most Satie-esque of the six, the group enacted many of the values Satie had been expressing for decades.

Satie was soon friendly with French-speaking Americans who knew of his music or who encountered him at the famous bookshops of Sylvia Beach and Adrienne Monnier. When Virgil Thomson participated in a performance of *Socrate*, Gertrude Stein became interested in his work, and Henri-Pierre Roché arranged an introduction that went well; soon Satie was a valued fixture at many Stein soirées. He met James Joyce and Ezra Pound; he seriously considered collaborating on a ballet of *Alice in Wonderland* with Louise Norton, not yet Mme. Edgard Varèse; he impressed Man Ray, who thought him "the only musician who had eyes." Regardless of the order of the rank of the three S's, in terms of personal contacts with Americans Satie did come in first during the first jazz age.[13]

Thomson first heard of Satie at Harvard. He was friendly with a young instructor of literature named S. Foster Damon, later to win renown as a pioneering Blake scholar. Damon was then in the circle of imagist poets around Amy Lowell and au courant with the most recent European developments in both literature and music; *Tender Buttons* was another of Damon's enthusiasms. He had a collection of Satie's piano works "four inches high" and they made an indelible impression. Shortly thereafter, safely under the pedagogical wing of Nadia Boulanger, Thomson used another Harvard connection to meet his new idol and the innovative musicians of his own generation. He looked up historian Bernard Faÿ, who was just beginning his career as the most influential French scholar of American history, and in his family's flat "met at tea Darius Milhaud, Francis Poulenc, Georges Auric, and Arthur Honegger, all near my age and all well-disposed to accept me as a colleague. There came also my revered Erik Satie," and later Jean Cocteau as well.

In the process Thomson discovered dada. "As explained to me by Emmanuel Faÿ, the Dada principles were simply that all is convention, that all conventions have equal value (or none), and that an artist is therefore free to work in (or vent, if he can) any convention whatsoever that may please him." To a free-spirited young refugee from Kansas City, such a stance "was congenial to my natural rebelliousness." Although dada was by some accounts already dead, "for me it offered an ethical ideal, as well as an expression of my inmost temper: so relentlessly . . . frivolous, at the same time so resistant to being governed."

Thomson oriented himself to modernism by observing the impact Satie had on Les Six, Picasso, and the Ballets Russes. "And I knew his music as the test, almost of any composer's really inside twentieth centuryness." In it, he intuited "an attitude of reserve which by avoiding all success-rhetoric has permitted the creation of a musical reality as real as an apple or a child." He found especially congenial Satie's "way of speaking, as if nobody were there." Events conspired to keep it that way in terms of a mentor/student relationship. "I had not in Paris sought companionship with Satie, wishing to get inside his music first, then make my homage later through performance." Unfortunately, Satie died in 1925, just before Thomson returned from a stay in America to live continuously in Paris, and this severed the personal part of the relationship. But writing after more than forty years of living with it, Satie's music "has never ceased to be rewarding. People take to Satie or they don't, as to Gertrude Stein."[14]

The dating here is important. During the summer of 1925, Thomson wrote the following near–stream of consciousness to his friend, Briggs Buchanan: "The Stein things also mature slowly, because they are a knotty problem. . . . Satie died. I've lost my faith in Stravinsky. And jazz (high-brow or low-brow) is a dead art already. The world is blank and lovely like a clear blackboard." He was evidently associating three modernists and the art form of jazz into one palpable turning point in cultural history. His personal inspiration, Satie, was gone. The most significant musical figure for many, Stravinsky, no longer seemed to have anything useful to say. Jazz, which had been exciting Debussy, Ravel, Milhaud, and others for a full generation, had exhausted its technical originality and the avant-garde was restlessly looking elsewhere. What was left for him was Gertrude Stein. Just as Satie had taken inspiration from other disciplines, especially painting, so Thomson would take his chiefly from literature.[15]

In September 1925, therefore, Thomson returned to Paris and a flat that he would rent for the next fifty years, retaining it even when world affairs forced him to remain in New York. "I prefer to starve where the food is good," he later remarked, presumably with musical as well as gastronomical applications. Through George Antheil, an American composer then living above Shakespeare and Company, he managed an invitation to the salon of Gertrude Stein and Alice B. Toklas. Antheil faded quickly, there as elsewhere, but "Gertrude and I got on like Harvard men," and Thomson was soon profitably involved with the new generation of painters and writers who cycled in and out of her orbit. He began work almost immediately setting her poetry to music, including "Susie Asado," "Preciosilla," and "Capital, Capitals." But unlike so many other American artists, he was now a collaborator, not a disciple. A generation had passed with Satie's death.

"My hope in putting Gertrude Stein to music had been to break, crack open, and solve for all time anything still waiting to be solved, which was almost everything, about English musical declamation," he recalled in his memoirs. "My theory was that if a text is set correctly for the sound of it, the meaning will take care of itself." He found Stein's texts perfect for the purpose, since their meanings were often opaque. "You could make a setting for sound and syntax only, then add, if needed an accompaniment equally functional." He was so pleased with the results that he asked her for an opera libretto, and the path was open toward *Four Saints in Three Acts* (1928).

By midsummer 1927, he knew that he and his friends were in a new phase of cultural history. "As I began to observe a little time ago, a new generation exists," he wrote Buchanan on 17 July. "Cocteau says it became possible about the middle of January. No one knows why, but it suddenly did." All around, in different ways, the same people seemed to be off in new directions. For him, Stein had replaced Satie. For others, Arnold Schoenberg had codified his twelve-tone system and was about to lead German music into a cul-de-sac. Painters were ignoring cubism and the Galerie Surréaliste was coming into its own. A new sense of romantic melody increasingly questioned the dictatorship of Stravinsky's neoclassicism. Les Arts Décoratifs dominated the Paris World's Fair with work that assimilated the modern age and left established painters with nothing compelling to do. *Finnegans Wake* replaced *Ulysses* as the work-in-progress of choice. T. S. Eliot abandoned the wasteland of modernity for classicism, royalism, and Anglo-Catholicism. The list could go on indefinitely, with all its stylistic inconsistencies and seeming irrationalities, the elements always unique to each modernist. But something had happened, and in the case of Virgil Thomson it is most easily defined as the death of a teacher and the discovery of a collaborator.[16]

JAMES JOYCE/ROBERT MCALMON

When Robert McAlmon arrived in Paris in the spring of 1921, he arrived with a new wife and a letter of introduction to James Joyce. His wife, Winifred Ellerman, was friendly with Harriet Shaw Weaver, a woman of some prominence in London journalism, and Weaver welcomed the opportunity to introduce her new American friend to a writer from whom she expected great things. McAlmon presented himself at the Joyce apartment on Boulevard Raspail at the first opportunity, admired the beauty of Nora Joyce at first sight, and met the author of *Dubliners*, a collection of stories that McAlmon already much admired. "Within a few minutes it was obvious that he and I would get on," McAlmon recalled in his memoirs. Both lonely provincials in a city whose language remained foreign, both inclined to accompany discourse with alcohol, they were soon making arrangements for dinner.[17]

In the midst of writing *Ulysses*, Joyce appreciated having a companion who both admired his work and filled the hours between creative spurts. He regularly initiated their meetings, writing his friend Frank Budgen that he found the American "very simple and decent." A poet and short story writer of modest talent but shrewd intelligence, McAlmon could serve as companionable colleague without offering any competitive threat, and his ability to pick up the checks afterwards was an especially useful skill for the ever-impoverished Joyce to appreciate. Something of an overqualified gofer, McAlmon was soon filling in as Joyce's typist, to the point of reworking Molly Bloom's thoughts when the mood hit him. Amused and tolerant when he wanted to be, Joyce noticed the changes but left many in *Ulysses:* "I agreed with you," he re-marked.[18]

For his part, McAlmon decided early on that he understood Joyce "better than most people because of the Irish in me," as he wrote to William Carlos Williams after a few meetings. "I find him less split open than you; less sensitive to many things. More of a detached in-telligence in a way; but more given to cliches of thought, and atti-tudes." McAlmon revelled at being the audience of one when Joyce chose to read long passages of *Ulysses* aloud; and when McAlmon spoke for himself, Joyce would be "constantly leaping upon phrases and bits of slang which came naturally from my American lips." The man had a lifelong infatuation for words, seizing on lengthy latinate ones like "metempsychosis"—"gray, clear, abstract, fine-sounding words that are 'ineluctable' a bit themselves." As alcohol watered their meetings, conversation would free-associate over all of the An-glo-Saxon and Romance literatures, usually climaxing with Joyce "reciting Dante in sonorous Italian. When that misty and intent look came upon his face and into his eyes I knew that friend Joyce was-n't going home till early morning."[19]

McAlmon had come a long way in a very short time. Born in Kansas in 1896, raised largely in South Dakota, he had encoun-tered all the problems anyone would expect in the boyhood of a physically small son of a rigid Presbyterian minister who hated sports and theology with equal fervor. He sampled college and the air corps, but nothing significant happened to him until he started contributing to *Poetry* in 1919. He briefly checked out the pallid Chicago literary scene of the postwar years and headed for Green-wich Village on the theory that it simply had to be more stimulat-ing than the country he had been living in. Knowing no one, owning nothing, he worked as a male model for students at Cooper Union. Marsden Hartley befriended him, and in short order McAl-mon was welcome at Lola Ridge's salon, as an aspiring poet on the periphery of Marianne Moore's circle of contributors to the *Dial*, and an increasingly close friend of William Carlos Williams and the poets contributing to *Contact*.[20]

In his autobiography, Williams gave McAlmon credit as "the instigator in the *Contact* idea," although the idea was never all that clear and the "journal" barely managed to make five appearances between December 1920 and June 1923. The publication was to be in contact with the basic elements of American reality, which in practice seemed to include Pound, Stevens, and Moore as well as the editors, but beyond that no clear philosophical light shines through. What still does shine through is the closeness of the relationship that developed. In the few months when they could work closely together, Williams felt he had finally found a close literary friend in whom he could confide and with whom he could collaborate. But by early 1921, McAlmon was clearly lost to marriage and Paris and Williams confessed to Kenneth Burke that he was "knocked out by Bob's going away"; he was even blunter to Amy Lowell: "I must confess that I am heartbroken." Burke remained cold-eyed, and in a long letter rehearsed McAlmon's several incapacities. In the event, he himself soon replaced McAlmon as Williams's chief literary buddy.[21]

What had happened to break up the relationship was the sudden marriage of Williams's protégé to Winifred Ellerman, who was already calling herself Winifred Bryher, or even just Bryher, both of which in time became her legal names. Bryher had arrived in New York with poet Hilda Doolittle, once the close friend of both Williams and Ezra Pound at the University of Pennsylvania and a gifted sensibility as well as an eccentrically beautiful woman. Doolittle, Bryher, and McAlmon were all bisexual in occasionally self-destructive ways, and the belligerently heterosexual Williams was often at a loss to perceive the various complications that ensued. In shortest compass: McAlmon was impoverished, eager for Europe, and attracted to Bryher; she, the daughter of one of the richest and most emotionally controlling fathers in the entire British Empire, desperately needed a plausible husband to escape a life under the parental thumb. Doolittle acted as matchmaker and on 13 February, 1921, the singularly opportunistic nuptials took place. Williams, Moore, Hartley, and Doolittle were all at the celebratory dinner that evening, and the next day, Valentine's Day, the mismatched couple sailed for England on the *Celtic*, one of many possessions of McAlmon's new father-in-law, Sir John Ellerman. McAlmon's well-financed and thoroughly miserable white marriage had begun, leaving *Contact* in its wake.

The age prided itself on its growing openness toward all aspects of sexuality and marriage, and McAlmon especially strove for blunt honesty in both prose and conversation. But as always, professions of openness only concealed motives more cleverly. McAlmon apparently felt some attraction to Bryher both physically and intellectually, and had no idea of her family wealth. He soon realized that his wife preferred Doolittle to himself then, and other men as well as women later. "The marriage is legal only, unromantic, and strictly an agreement," he wrote Williams later that year. Bryher simply could not travel nor function autonomously as a single woman. "She thought I understood her mind, as I do somewhat, and faced me with the proposition." He then added, rather ominously: "Some other things I shan't mention I knew without realizing. . . . You can use your imagination and perhaps know what I mean." He increasingly thought he'd been a "damn fool" but was learning to cope with what he couldn't change. Many years later his sister Victoria was even blunter, insisting to Williams and his wife "about how lied to he had been from the start, what a blow this was in London, and the distaste he had for Bryher's crowd there." She met Bryher in 1923: "I thought her arrogant, very conceited and pontifical; determined to have her way." The Ellerman family were not the ogres of Bryher's fantasy life, "much humaner and really suffering from their peculiar daughter." Indeed, McAlmon got on well with everyone in the family better than he did with his wife.[22]

The account in Bryher's memoirs sounded cold-blooded, but appropriate to a set of circumstances where almost anything seemed justified. She simply had to marry her way to freedom, and here was a presentable male who "wanted to go to Paris to meet Joyce but lacked the passage money." She would give him a sub-

stantial allowance, and except for occasional obligatory family visits "we would live strictly separate lives." In the Ellerman world
arranged marriages were not unusual and she still saw nothing "ir-
regular" in her proposal. In Paris, they quickly followed those separate paths. Hers was almost entirely lesbian, centered on two
institutions: Shakespeare & Co., the bookstore crossroads of Sylvia
Beach, Adrienne Monnier, and the authors for whom they were essential; and the home of Gertrude Stein, where the major attraction was Alice B. Toklas, "whom I loved. She was so kind to me."
If she were not with Beach and Monnier, 27, rue de Fleurus "was
the only place in Paris where I felt at home."[23]

McAlmon's Paris life thus had underlying stresses unknown to
most of his friends and all of his acquaintances. All they could see
was a small, literate, available companion who had ready cash, and
as the abstemious Beach noted in her memoirs, "The drinks were
always on him, and alas! often in him." True enough, but at best a
partial truth, as she must have known. Beach's great mission in life
became the publication of *Ulysses,* and this was not the only book
of the place and period that required alcohol to make it go. McAlmon talked and listened to the often shy Irishman, steadily subsi-
dizing an unsteady and impoverished family. Ezra Pound, Harriet
Weaver, and others helped as well, but McAlmon was at the vortex, the gofer who more than paid his own way.

Joyce, Hemingway, and others whose opinion mattered often
found merit in McAlmon's stories, but their quality dissolved in alcohol and as the years floated past McAlmon refused to rewrite or
reform. He became a man of two important skills: He was first the
great facilitator, bringing talented people together who might otherwise have been too poor, inhibited, or ill-informed to find each
other . . . "Bob had a gift for meeting people and bringing the most
incongruous groups together," Bryher recalled. "He introduced
me to my lifelong friend, Sylvia Beach, to Joyce, Hemingway,
Gertrude Stein, Berenice Abbott, Man Ray and many others." He
bought and read the works of the newest poets, such as Cummings
and Stevens. "He received, in his turn, the freedom of the Paris of

the twenties." He wrote and he published, but "his real contribution was in introducing people to each other . . . and thus helping many to find themselves through talking out their problems."[24]

Publishing was McAlmon's other skill, and the one where he genuinely earned his place in cultural history. Through his efforts to publish his own works as well as to help Joyce through *Ulysses* he gradually concluded that the *Contact* idea could motivate a publishing concern as well as a poetry journal. In 1922, "Contact Editions" produced only his own *A Hasty Bunch*, but in 1923 he was expanding into Mina Loy, with *Lunar Baedecker*; Hemingway, with *Three Stories and Ten Poems*; Marsden Hartley, with *Twenty-five Poems*; and Williams, with *Spring and All*. The year 1925 brought his most famous work, Stein's *The Making of Americans* unabridged; subsequent years included books by Robert M. Coates, Djuna Barnes, and Nathanael West, for a total of twenty-two. Any publisher knows the importance of lunches, and McAlmon was a champion luncher.[25]

His life peaked during the three-year period 1923 to 1926, when his drinking, facilitating, and publishing made him an obligatory presence in the lives of several important writers. The period began with his relationship with Ernest Hemingway, another hard-drinking exile from the effeminacies of the Victorian Midwest. They first met in Rapallo in 1923; McAlmon found him hard to characterize. "At times he was deliberately hard-boiled, case-hardened, and old; at other times he was the hurt, sensitive boy, deliberately young and naive, wanting to be brave." He often seemed defensive and suspicious. "He approached a cafe with a small-boy, tough-guy swagger, and before strangers of whom he was uncertain a potential snarl of scorn played on his large-lipped, rather loose mouth."

McAlmon was struck by the "falsely naive manner" of some of Hemingway's stories, musing in his memoirs about how original and effective it was. But each found the other socially tolerable, and several photographs that turn up in biographies document their friendship, both in Paris and on a trip to Spain where bull-fighting and whiskey filled their time. Although skeptical of bull-fighting as a rite, McAlmon willingly paid most of the bills; even so, close proximity strained the friendship. Hemingway was becoming the insulting bully of the later 1920s, and perhaps his economic and literary dependence was accelerating the decline of his personality. He got his book published, but he had made an enemy for life. Relations thudded to a close with a left hook in 1934, Hemingway's preferred way of venting his frustrations.[26]

The period climaxed with a visit Williams and his wife Flossie made to Europe for six months early in 1924. For the first time, Williams heard the story of McAlmon's marriage and began to understand why the man was so bitterly drunk so often while leading what seemed to be a rewarding and well-financed life in Paris. McAlmon showed the couple around Paris, producing impressions that later went directly into *A Voyage to Pagany* (1927), where McAlmon appears as Jack Murry. McAlmon was at great pains to introduce the Williams to the Joyces. Both couples were ill at ease, with McAlmon drinking too much, and Joyce nearsightedly missing the glasses when pouring wine. At the first lunch, only Joyce's interest in Flossie Williams's Norse linguistic ancestry kept the conversation from stagnating into silence. A later party was more successful. Despite awkward moments it brought together the Antheils, Sylvia Beach and Adrienne Monnier, Marcel Duchamp and Man Ray, and several others moderately well known. McAlmon paid the bills, of course, and the event gets a paragraph or two in numerous volumes. McAlmon then accompanied the Williamses to the Riviera and the Alps, and their friendship grew stronger, Williams even praising McAlmon's writing rather beyond its merits.[27]

After the Williams's return to America, McAlmon went into a slow decline. Several works in progress appeared, and he continued to publish Contact Editions, but after issuing four volumes in 1926, by Hilda Doolittle, Djuna Barnes, Robert Coates, and himself, he clearly ran out of gas and material. Nothing else appeared until 1929, and only four more works appeared between 1927 and 1931, one a translation and none of long-range significance. In the fall of 1926 he returned to America for a long visit, and in 1927 divorced Bryher. Her father made him so generous a settlement that he received the nickname "McAlimony," but even after his return to Paris he could never regain his former place. Everyone had moved on.

Yet he remains historically important. "McAlmon is the overlooked man," Morley Callaghan has noted in the best of the memoirs of North Americans in Paris, even if his personality proved too difficult for many people to deal with for very long. But if Williams remained loyal, Joyce did not. McAlmon read him portions of *Being Geniuses Together* in 1934, and while Joyce laughed and sounded amused to the author, he was furious at his own portrait. He felt "actionable," he told Harriet Weaver, and took to referring to the book as "the office boy's revenge." It was, but McAlmon deserved better.[28]

MARCEL DUCHAMP/MAN RAY

In 1916, Man Ray completed his greatest painting, *The Rope Dancer Accompanies Herself with Her Shadows*. Inspired by a vaudeville show, he was trying to capture motion in terms of color changes. The son of an immigrant tailor, he was long used to seeing fragments of colored cloth on the floor, and when his original conception did not work out as he wished, he found renewed creativity from observing comparable accidental designs as an adult. He made no attempt "to establish a color harmony; it was red against blue, purple against yellow, green versus orange, with an effect of maximum contrast." He laid on the color "with precision, yet lavishly," entirely depleting "the stock of colors." No one understood the completed work. "I began to expect it and even derived a certain assurance that I was on the right track. What to others was mystification, to me was simply mystery." The next year he gave up painting and only returned to it later in special circumstances. He turned instead to ideas and the ways in which photographic procedures could reduce objects in the three-dimensional world to two dimensions. In the process, he found a friend and guru for life in Marcel Duchamp, and a place for himself as the only American in the world of dada, and one of the few to participate even in such successor movements as surrealism.[29]

In mid-1917, Duchamp had already spent two years in America. A marginal figure in French art, he seemed central to American notions of modernism. His work had been the successful scandal of the 1913 Armory Show, and since his arrival in America on 15 June, 1915, he had been at the center of the salon of Walter and Louise Arensberg, his works on the wall, his charisma fascinating numerous attractive women, and his mind seemingly most often on chess. Duchamp had assimilated several fashionable styles, including fauvism and cubism, during his apprentice years in France, but lingered with none. Instead, he turned against painting itself, becoming more interested in contemporary theories of time and space than in aesthetics; his was always a playful hyperspace philosophy rather than a sophisticated physics, a pataphysics that owed more to *Alice in Wonderland* and Theosophy than it did to Albert Einstein and his more respectable predecessors. "I wanted to get away from the physical aspect of painting. I was much more interested in recreating ideas in painting," he recalled years later for an interviewer. "I wanted to put painting once again at the service of the mind." He took to referring to himself not as a painter but as a breather, a *réspirateur*, and as such his silences often seemed to say more than most painters' and critics' statements.

In 1911, Duchamp began finding objects, like coffee mills and chocolate grinders, to reproduce on canvas or merely to "choose" and title. He cast his choosing eye on a bicycle wheel, a bottle dryer, a comb, and so on, and by 1916 was referring to them—in English, to his sister Suzanne in a private letter that was otherwise in French—as "a sculpture already made." He liked the irony involved and the implicit put-downs of "Art." Matters reached a climax of sorts when he submitted the most publicized urinal in art history to the April 1917 show of the Society of Independent

Artists. More conventional artists predictably had fits, while Alfred Stieglitz immortalized *Fountain* in a photograph—a photograph that, of course, reduced a very three-dimensional object of daily use to a two-dimensional object someone could hang on a gallery wall and think of as art, or perhaps the coming of the end of Art.[30]

As a frequenter of the Arensberg salon, Man Ray met Duchamp shortly after his arrival. Although at first they shared no common language, they soon established a sense of common purpose; they abandoned conventional painting techniques, for example, within months of each other. While Duchamp found objects and then turned obsessively to his *Large Glass* in progress, Ray turned from paintbrushes to palette knives to airbrushes, even etching on glass plates and then filtering light through the results onto sensitive photographic paper. He tried drawing on exposed film, or on old negatives—anything that might produce a new effect. Cameras soon became more essential than brushes. First he used them to document paintings, but soon he was also using them instead of painting. He took an interest in music as well, hanging out at the Brevoort Hotel bar with Edgard Varèse as well as other painters, and titling one aerograph of 1919 *Jazz*.[31]

Duchamp left New York City on 13 August, 1918, and did not return until January 1920. Just before and during this separation of a year and a half, Ray established one policy for his work that did not seem to have bothered his guru. Man Ray loved to manipulate. He might find strips of wood, an eggbeater, or a pair of light reflectors, but he did not usually leave them as "found." He arranged, he sculpted, and above all he juxtaposed, placing objects together in striking and increasingly incongruous ways. He then usually photographed the results, seeming to care little about the original objects. It became customary, in other words, to find, to rearrange, to photograph and to label his created works. All four of these processes became integral to modernism. Some works even encouraged audience response, to push a button, for example, or to straighten something intentionally crooked, thus adding aspects to aesthetic experience that would not reappear until the 1970s.

With Duchamp's return, Man Ray became as well his "documentarian"—to use the useful term of Francis Naumann—meaning that Duchamp created and Ray recorded, although some scholars have understandably seen the works that emerged as collaborations. More institutionally significant, the two men teamed up with Katherine Dreier to found the Société Anonyme, under the auspices of which modernism achieved most of its audience exposure during the years when Alfred Stieglitz essentially paid no attention to European developments. Between its opening show on 29 April, 1920, and its famous run at the Brooklyn Museum, which opened 19 November, 1926, Dreier was right where she wanted to be, in apparent control of the field, and as close as she could get to Marcel Duchamp.

The relationship only looked like a triangle from a distance. Dreier had met Duchamp at an Arensberg salon gathering in 1916, and fallen hopelessly if platonically in love. Duchamp, as was his wont, kept his distance without offending, and may even have found Man Ray useful as a male buffer. The three of them cooperated with such other artists as Henri-Pierre Roché and Joseph Stella in the Society of Independent Artists, and when Duchamp departed for Latin America in 1918, Dreier gave the distinct impression of being in hot pursuit; in time he showed her around Paris and perhaps instructed her about where to go in Germany afterwards. She barely preceded him back to New York City late in 1919, for what became the two-year high-point of Société Anonyme activity. They showed, they held symposia, they published. Unfortunately, she and Man Ray held each other in casual contempt, and only a mutual fixation on Duchamp held things together. Ray immortalized her, after his own fashion, as *Catherine Barometer* (1920), always presumably foreseeing "Dreier" weather regardless of either facts or functionality.[32]

Like Kurt Schwitters in Germany, Ray gave every appearance of being overwhelmed by the detritus of the city. A statement of psychology as well as sanitation, the feeling of being buried in the excreta of modernity produced varieties of *Merzkunst*, an invented

German word that encapsulated the junk collages that resulted. In Ray's case, he became fascinated by the dust gathering slowly on Duchamp's *Large Glass*, publishing the result as *Dust Raising* (1920), a rather ominous homage to a work later celebrated as incomplete, uncompletable, and thus forever gathering dust; and by the petit garbage of the city itself, its assembled ashes, matchsticks, and fragments of burned paper receiving the title of *New York 1920* (1920). In their wildly differing ways, Stieglitz, Dos Passos, and William Carlos Williams were saying much the same thing. Ray operated on his own intuitions and in 1921 headed for Paris, where he arrived on 22 July.

No other American arrived with quite so cordial a reception. Duchamp met the train and took him directly to a modest hotel in Passy; so primitive was his French that the sign, Hotel Meublé, seemed to him a sign of class instead of what amounted to "furnished rooms for rent." He took quarters that the founder of dada, Tristan Tzara, had just vacated, and by late that afternoon he was dining with André Breton, Louis Aragon, Paul and Gala Eluard, Philippe Soupault, and Jacques Rigaut—all figures more identified with literature than painting. The New York dada of Duchamp and Picabia had seemed far more staid in its social behavior, and Ray remained amazed even forty years later at how his new friends "rushed from one attraction to another like children," and courted "the abandon of all dignity" with their public playfulness. Thanks to Duchamp's letters from New York, Ray's reputation had preceded him and the pattern was set that first day: He would live and work among the French and not the Americans, and take his chief cues from writers more than painters—artists of ideas, in other words, not traditional retinal forms.

Although Ray picked up French fairly rapidly, facility in the dialects of modernism stood him in better stead during that first year. Nothing demonstrated this more clearly than the speed of his acclimatization, leading to the opening of his first show on 3 December, 1921, and the appropriately accidental meeting that took place there. "A strange voluble little man in his fifties" came over to him and showed intense interest in one of his paintings. "With a little white beard, an old-fashioned pince-nez, black bowler hat, black overcoat and umbrella, he looked like an undertaker or an employee of some conservative bank." The soul of gentlemanly kindness, the man spoke enough English to appreciate Ray's being cold and fatigued by the rigors of the show, and took him to a nearby café for hot grog. With only the grog and a few phrases between them, he soon found himself friends with Erik Satie. When they left, Ray felt so inspired by the occasion that he casually picked up a flatiron at a housewares store and used Satie's French to acquire a box of tacks and some glue. "Back at the gallery I glued a row of tacks to the smooth surface of the iron, titled it The Gift [*Cadeau*, 1921], and added it to the exhibition. This was my first Dada object in France."[33]

With such a start, Ray led at least two relatively separate lives in Paris. He would socialize with the dada writers, with painters who knew Duchamp or Picabia, or with musicians he met through Picabia's friend Jean Cocteau and Cocteau's close involvement with Les Six. On weekends, he often went out to Puteaux, where Duchamp's brother Jacques Villon lived; they might amuse themselves with such found objects as a bicycle wheel, or do experiments with a movie camera. Such pleasantries brought in no income, however, and Ray became the photographer of choice for both the French- and English-speaking artistic communities, with opportunities increasingly opening up for business documentation as well. He soon was doing Gertrude Stein and James Joyce as well as Satie, Picabia, Matisse, and even a *Deathbed Portrait of Marcel Proust* (1922). Some contacts were more amusing than others: Henri-Pierre Roché saw Ray for an extended session of shots on 7 May, 1922, and in the process Ray showed him numerous lesbian and heterosexual shots he had developed. Roché claimed to recognize one of the girls, something the bulk of his diary proves was entirely possible. The next day the two joined Ray's companion, the famous Kiki (Alice Prin) and Tzara for dinner, an event that occurred more than once.[34]

In a sense, the dada impulse began and ended in France, however much its spirit may have wandered east into Switzerland and Germany or west to America or Argentina. But even more than Duchamp, Man Ray tied its loose historical ends together. Its ur-dada was Isidore Ducasse, who under the pseudonym of Comte de Lautréamont, stressed the importance of chance and surprise, most often in the surprise an observer might feel at the chance juxtaposition of dissimilar objects. The most quoted example of this, the example that Bréton and Max Ernst were always using, was: "Beautiful . . . as the chance meeting of a sewing machine and an umbrella on a dissecting table," from *Maldoror.* Subsequent writers such as Mallarmé and Apollinaire elaborated these themes, and the result was the literary basis for such experiments as collages, assemblages, readymades, sculptures, and found objects. Ray put the whole tradition together in the rather messy package called *The Riddle,* or *The Enigma of Isidore Ducasse* (1920)—basically an army blanket and twine around a sewing machine, but soon photographed and dismantled. Ray insisted in later interviews that Lautréamont revealed "a world of complete freedom" to him, stimulating him "to do things I was not supposed to do."[35]

But the dada influence, forced into quick bloom and early decay by wartime conditions, was already dying even as Ray arrived to administer a final stimulant. He had a typically American interest in dreams, whether Freudian or not; he loved the accidents involved in games such as chess, especially with Arensberg or Duchamp; he loved to sport as well with light and shadow, in ways sometimes suggestive of Paul Strand's early work; and he too occasionally experimented with moving pictures. But his one major contribution during these years was the one to which he gave his name. The Rayograph was a cameraless photograph, and he stumbled onto it by mistake. A sheet of unexposed photopaper got into his developing tray with those already exposed, and he happened to place "a small glass funnel, the graduate and the thermometer in the tray on the wetted paper." He turned on the light and "an image began to form, not quite a simple silhouette of the objects as in a straight photograph, but distorted and refracted by the glass," which was "more or less in contact with the paper and standing out against a black background, the part directly exposed to the light." He made subsequent experiments with his "hotel-room key, a handkerchief, some pencils, a brush, a candle, a piece of twine," and the next day was pleased with the result. He hung a couple on the wall that so impressed Tzara that they were soon collaborating on making more examples of these "pure Dada creations." He was simply trying to do with light what painters did with pigment, but the effect was so striking that the Rayograph became a bit of a fad; Cocteau even commissioned one to be the frontispiece for his next book of poems.[36]

Dada had its last spasm with the performance of *Relâche*, which opened despite its title on 4 December, 1924. Although dying himself, Satie managed to complete the work while living in the Hôtel Istria; Ray, Duchamp, and Picabia all had rooms there, and Ray had his studio next door. All performed, Ray and Duchamp naturally playing a game of chess together on the roof of the Théâtre des Champs-Elysées. The work caused yet one more memorable Parisian musical scandal, although most critics abused the composer and ignored the chess players. Dada and Satie were seemingly spent forces, yet their spirit lived on in at least one American. He was still playing chess with his mentor, and still had several more roles to play.[37]

NINE

ALFRED STIEGLITZ/GEORGIA O'KEEFFE

Alfred Stieglitz had been aching to put his protective mantle on an attractive woman for a long time. He came from a family where all the males apparently married for prudential reasons and then carried on extensive extramarital liaisons. Alfred had spent an extended youth in a Germany tolerant of aberrant young bourgeois, but then his family pressured him into marriage with an eligible but dreary woman from its rather circumscribed circle of friends. He was soon seeking out the aesthetically pleasing wherever he could find it, and as his marriage degenerated into separate and hostile spheres, he found increasing numbers of attractive acquaintances who shared his interests, his lunches, and his gallery shows. Romantic, opinionated, and garrulous, he was not every woman's ideal, especially since he came encumbered with wife and daughter. But he was clearly on the watch for both suitable artists and suitable companions, and like many men of strong opinions, he knew what she would be like before he ever caught sight of her body or her work.

The body had visited 291 on occasion since 1908 and had been an avid reader of *Camera Work* and *291*, but Stieglitz only became aware of her talent on New Year's Day, 1916. Georgia O'Keeffe had sent a "batch of drawings" to her friend Anita Pollitzer, a person less talented than O'Keeffe but nevertheless a vibrant woman much interested in gallery and concert life and a reliable reporter of the goings-on at 291. Much impressed, Pollitzer had tucked the pictures under her arm and hurried first to the Empire Theatre to see Maude Adams in *Peter Pan*, and then in the twilight of an already early winter evening, continued on to 291. She explained her mission to Stieglitz and he invited her into the back room so she could unroll her treasures. He looked, absorbed, and looked again in the dim, quiet room, taking his time. "Finally, a woman on paper," he said portentously, in a phrase destined to become one of the most quoted in all of American art history. He called over painter Abraham Walkowitz, who often kept him company in the gallery, and began to ramble in the stream-of-consciousness style he had evolved. "Why they're genuinely fine things—you say a woman did these—She's an unusual woman—She's broad minded, She's bigger than most woman, but she's got the sensitive emotion—I'd know she was a woman—Look at that line." Walkowitz's eyes "got big & swan like" and he agreed: "Very fine"—but then Walkowitz generally agreed with anything Stieglitz said. Stieglitz asked Pollitzer if she would be writing the artist soon, and when Pollitzer said yes, he asked her to pass on the message: "They're the purest, finest, sincerest things that have entered 291 in a long while," and he would be happy to show them for her. Madly excited if dead tired, she refused to go to bed until she had written it all down. At 11:00 P.M. she assured her distant friend: "You're living Pat in spite of your work at Columbia! South Carolina!"[1]

This was love all but without first sight. O'Keeffe got her first show at 291 from 23 May to 5 July, 1916, apparently without warning. She heard indirectly that her work was on display, and as soon as she could, hurried down from Columbia Teachers College to get it off. She introduced herself and demanded her rights, which presumably included some say about exhibitions. Stieglitz was unperturbed: "You have no more right to withhold these pictures," he recalled later, "than to withdraw a child from the world." She argued with him, but as countless other combatants later discovered, he just plowed over opposition. She was soon mollified, then more than mollified, and by July he was preserving her work photographically with her enthusiastic cooperation. Indeed, she preferred the photos to the originals.[2]

By the summer of 1918, things were coming to a head. He became increasingly obsessed with his new disciple, photographing her without paying the slightest attention to the assumptions of Victorian morality or wifely pride. Furious at what she assumed was implicitly if not explicitly adultery, his wife accelerated his departure in a melodramatic scene that only drove the artists closer together. "O'Keeffe is truly magnificent. And a child at that," he exulted to Arthur Dove, glossing over her chronological age of thirty. "We are at least 90% alike—she a purer form of myself.— The 10% difference is really perhaps a too liberal estimate—but the difference is really negligible." A few weeks later, they had finally consummated their relationship and were "One in a real sense." He was still on a high. "O'Keeffe is a constant source of wonder to me—like Nature itself—& . . . every moment I am full of gratefulness that I am a great fortunate." When she began to produce her first oils, he assured Paul Strand that her achievement would "stagger" him. "Loveliness—Savage Force—Frankness— the Woman—all is there—Beautifully expressed," he effused late in 1918.[3]

Lovers of course enjoy a considerable license for hyperbole, among other things, but these remarks were freighted with dubious assumptions all round. Only in the most literal sense was O'Keeffe a woman on paper; she was an artist who happened to be a woman, and such compulsive gendering was implicitly demeaning. She was not a child, nor a Savage Force, nor like Nature itself, to reproduce Stieglitz's Germanic lexicological excesses. And as for his artistic recreation of the statistics of the relationship, he probably had the percentages reversed. They were 90 percent unlike, as their marriage ultimately proved.

Alfred Stieglitz's gendering oddities would only be an amusing undertone in a long and troubled artistic relationship were it not for their effect on even the best critical opinion of the first jazz age, and their long-range impact on both the shape and the reception of the work of a major artist. Stieglitz talked incessantly and impressed his circle and their friends with his authoritative assumptions, and so naturally when a painter like Marsden Hartley or a critic like Paul Rosenfeld wrote reviews of exhibitions, later including their opinions in respected books, lesser voices tended to echo their views. Since the wider circle included such figures as Freud's translator, Abraham A. Brill, and the chief American modernist novelist then exploring the nature of sexual behavior, Sherwood Anderson, Stieglitz's personal obsessions dovetailed perfectly with advanced critical opinion. O'Keeffe herself was reading books like Anderson's *Many Marriages* with enthusiasm, and should not have been surprised when critics read her work with Anderson, D. H. Lawrence, and Havelock Ellis all too close to the surface of their minds when they looked at O'Keeffe's works.

Rosenfeld repeatedly showed how this atmosphere could fix an artist in critical cement so securely that nothing O'Keeffe herself could say seemed to have the slightest effect. Gregarious, heterosexual, well read, and as familiar with art history as anyone writing at the time, Rosenfeld above all others should have been the perfect interpreter; he had even become a Lake George houseguest during the early 1920s, privileged to view the developing relationship literally from the next room. Yet while he looked at O'Keeffe, he listened to Stieglitz. In contrast to such masculine painters as John Marin and Arthur Dove, he was informing readers of the *Dial* by December 1921, O'Keeffe was "polarizing herself, accepting fully the nature long denied spiritualizing her sex. Her art is gloriously female," and her "great painful and ecstatic climaxes make us at last to know something the man has always wanted to know." Her perceptions were "anchored in the constitution of the woman," and the "organs that differentiate the sex speak. Women . . . always feel, when they feel strongly, through the womb." Her paintings thus speak "a sort of new language."

Within a year, Rosenfeld was almost a coal miner of the unconscious, shining his lamp into murky depths indeed. Her new works "make one to feel life in the dim regions where human and animal and plant are one, indistinguishable, and where the state of existence is blind pressure and dumb unfolding." They repeatedly evoked "mysterious cycles of birth and reproduction and death, expressed through the terms of a woman's body." Her subject matter signified little, for every stroke of her brush was "arrestingly female in quality," based on "the mysterious brooding principle of woman's being." He then compared her to that self-appointed connoisseur of womb power, D. H. Lawrence.

Reproduced in similar language in *Port of New York* (1924), these judgments have shaped male and even female attitudes right up to the present day. Only an occasional note of common sense provided a welcome dissonance. Let us "once and for all dismiss this talk of 'a woman's painting' and 'a man's painting,'" Marya Mannes snorted in 1928. "Any good creative thing is neither aggressively virile nor aggressively feminine, it is a fusion of the best of both." Great art transcends mere sexuality. "Therefore, if we are to exalt the work of Georgia O'Keeffe, let us not exalt it because it seems to be a rare psychic perception of the world peculiar to a woman, but because it is good painting." But Stieglitz never listened, to O'Keeffe, Mannes, nor anyone else, and his disciples had ears only for the master's voice.[4]

When Mitchell Kennerley sent her Rosenfeld's 1921 and 1922 essays, O'Keeffe was not amused. "Rosenfeld's articles have embarrassed me," as did those of Hartley and the rest. "The things they write sound so strange and far removed from what I feel of myself," since they "make me seem like some strange unearthly sort of creature floating in the air—breathing in clouds for nourishment." The truth, she assured Kennerley, "is that I like beaf steak—and like it rare at that." She only calmed down a bit when Hutchins Hapgood laughed at the seriousness of her reaction. He assured her that "they were only writing their own autobiography—that it really wasn't about me at all." But she still steamed up regularly, and properly so. "Im full of furies today," she spluttered at Sherwood Anderson a year later. "I wonder if man has ever been written down the way he has written woman down." She doubted it, firmly convinced that "some woman still has the job to perform."[5]

The publication of two volumes of letters and half a dozen biographical and critical works have amply demonstrated that she was right; indeed, if anyone had sex on the brain in the decade, the men did, imputing their desires and anxieties onto the women. The case for O'Keeffe and rare beefsteak has several vital aspects.

She was, first of all, well trained; the best men in the best male-dominated institutions taught her well, if sometimes condescendingly. She had studied with John Vanderpoel at the Art Institute of Chicago during the 1905/6 academic year, and with William M. Chase and others almost as distinguished at the Art Students League in New York City during 1907/8—at which time she visited 291 and took in the Rodin and Matisse exhibitions of January and April 1908. During the summer of 1912 she learned the principles of Arthur W. Dow, the reigning dogma in the field, from his disciple Alon Bement at the University of Virginia. She later attended Columbia Teachers College to work with Dow himself, meanwhile attending the Braque, Picasso, and Marin shows at 291, over 1914/15. Concurrently, she formularized her views by teaching them to students in Texas, Virginia, and South Carolina. Even when far from New York, she stayed abreast of current developments through correspondence with friends who shared her interests, and through such periodicals as the *Masses*, *Camera Work*, and *291*.

The correspondence with Anita Pollitzer remains a mine of information on such things. Usually based in New York but from an elite Jewish family based in Charleston, Pollitzer shared O'Keeffe's interests to a remarkable extent, even though she was younger and more intensely feminist and political than her friend. The major books on aesthetic subjects that they mention repeatedly, and that O'Keeffe clearly rereads and consults, were Arthur Jerome Eddy's *Cubists and Post-Impressionism* (1914) and Wassily Kandinsky's *Concerning the Spiritual in Art* (1914). Ideas from both books permeated *Camera Work* and were as crucial in the development of such male painters as Marsden Hartley as they were for O'Keeffe.[6]

Forced to translate such books into her own words, O'Keeffe became verbally constipated. Even to Stieglitz, she insisted that "Words and I are not good friends at all," and for the next half-century few found reason to doubt her. She would pour over books as well as pictures and indicate approval or disapproval, but that was about it—in words. But she would then burst forth with a picture, or turn to her violin, to achieve release. Russian modernists such as Kandinsky and Alexander Scriabin experimented a great deal with synaesthesia, and with O'Keeffe the tendency seemed congenial. She painted words, or played them, in preference to saying them. That did not mean she was innocent of theory or sophistication.

She also read widely, often choosing authors who have easily withstood the test of time. Among novelists, H. G. Wells and Thomas Hardy occur, and O'Keeffe even read occasionally in such examples of inspirational feminism as Floyd Dell's *Women as World Builders* (1913). One of O'Keeffe's male admirers, Arthur W. Macmahon, was a Columbia University political scientist who had roomed with progressive essayist Randolph Bourne, and so of course the couple followed Bourne's progress from pragmatic educational reform to passionate opposition to American participation in World War I, in journals that included the *Seven Arts*, where both Bourne and Paul Rosenfeld were major contributors. And despite her aversion to words, especially theoretical words, when duty called and O'Keeffe had to give a public lecture on aesthetics, she dutifully added the works of Willard Huntington Wright, Clive Bell, and Marius de Zayas to her arsenal. Few men did better; certainly Stieglitz never did. And she accomplished this educational level entirely before she had had more than fleeting contacts with Stieglitz.[7]

In addition to her sophisticated training and wide reading, O'Keeffe was far more truly cosmopolitan than Stieglitz or most critics were willing to credit. Rosenfeld was a genuine cosmopolitan, and both Stieglitz and Hartley had once been intimately familiar with the culture of Paris and especially Berlin. But often enough such a worldly patina hid a rigidly circumscribed provincialism—Stieglitz cared only for a narrow range of German culture until about 1917, then suddenly switching to an equally narrow sliver of American culture. Hartley traveled from one homosexual coterie to another; he was so rigid he even disliked the cooking of Paris! O'Keeffe, by contrast, had lived in Wisconsin, Virginia, Chicago, New York, Texas, and South Carolina, in conditions ranging from the most urban to the most rural. Because the country air, sky, flowers, and buildings spoke to her eye most appealingly, men thought her a bit of a bumpkin. Of course, she let them chatter; no one could slow Stieglitz in full voice anyway. For more than one modernist artist, less was more. Silent sophistication would never be the rage in cosmopolis.

The fact was that, like most American modernists, O'Keeffe felt out of place everywhere, from her own home to 291. During a depressing Saturday night in small-town South Carolina, she could note sadly to Pollitzer: "I haven't found anyone yet who likes to live like we do"; and continue in a subsequent letter: "It always seems to me that so few people *live*—they just seem to exist, and I don't see any reason why we shouldn't *live always*." Yet things seemed no different in New York City. In the heart of the city shortly thereafter she suddenly stopped to exhale: "I am lost you know." All this could, of course, lead to art, as she drew a splattery impression on a letter the next month from back in South Carolina: "That's the hole I kicked in the wall because everyone here is so stupid—I never saw such a bunch of nuts." In her personal life, O'Keeffe was clearly getting to the point where she was as prepared to magnify Stieglitz as he was to mythify her.[8]

Although she explicitly told Pollitzer that she was "unable" to answer the question, What is Art anyway?, O'Keeffe was not entirely dumb in the presence of aesthetic questions. "I feel that a real living form is the natural result of the individuals effort to create the living thing out of the adventure of his spirit into the unknown—where it has experienced something—felt something—it has not understood," she wrote to Sherwood Anderson in 1923. Anderson had become a good friend and confidant and she felt a kinship for him and his characters. From such an experience "comes the desire to make the unknown—known." By "unknown," she meant "the thing that means so much to the person that he wants to put it down," to "clarify something he feels but does not clearly understand." Sometimes an artist—she regularly used the generic "he"—"partially knows why—sometimes he doesn't—sometimes it is all working in the dark—but a working that must be done." She then used the phrase that she would use repeatedly over the years when she received questions of form or methodology: "Making the unknown—known—in terms of ones medium is all absorbing." Anyone stopping to think about form directly was lost. "The artists form must be inevitable." She then exhorted Anderson to get over a failure of nerve and follow her example. "What others have called form has nothing to do with our form." She wanted to create her own without stopping to think what anyone would say about it. He should do the same. In fact, Anderson had already done that in *Winesburg, Ohio,* and would never again be able to recapture his gift for the insightful prose fragments that were still impressing young writers.[9]

This sort of expressionism runs contrary to many theories of art, modernist or otherwise. But artists did know what they were doing on occasion, and in her case the words helped explain both practice and result. By 1923 O'Keeffe had experienced European modernist art, the light, sky, and landscape of the arid Southwest, and the obsessive camera of her lover, Stieglitz. In ways that recall the rapid evolution of such Munich painters as Wassily Kandinsky and Franz Marc, she had focused her art on specific subjects, changed perspective on them away from any conventional representational realism, and abstracted their essence as she expressed her personal responses. As the object disappeared, she made the unknown known—almost a lay rendering of a portrayal of the unconscious. "Unformed," as it were, when she became intimate with Stieglitz, she took shape in fragments, as he portrayed her hands, breasts, and torso in hundreds of frames. By taking her apart and then putting her back together, both as an artist and as a woman, Stieglitz had made many unknowns known. And just as she preferred Stieglitz's pictures of her drawings to the actual drawings, so for awhile she preferred his pictures of herself to her real self. It could not and would not last, but it made all the difference in launching her career. Indeed, Stieglitz was clever enough, both aesthetically and financially, to picture O'Keeffe in fragments before fragments of her recent pictures, which were of course for sale. Much of modernist achievement thus became a presentation of realistic fragments, pieces of author highlighting pieces of art that portrayed magnified pieces of objects.

But credit for such achievements remains elusive. O'Keeffe was not Trilby in the hands of Svengali. She produced abstract work of originality before having significant contact with Stieglitz; her work, after all, attracted him in the first place. She was briefly in love with both Paul Strand and the pictures of Paul Strand, which in the period around 1917 were deeply original new angle shots, often enough, of machines or objects ranging from automobile tires to cameras themselves. Major artists were heading in the same general direction and reinforcing each other, as well as interpenetrating each other's work. If Stieglitz influenced O'Keeffe much at this stage, it was old Stieglitz influencing young Strand influencing young O'Keeffe, and not a direct influence at all.

In fact, pictorially speaking, O'Keeffe did more for Stieglitz than he did for her. More than one critic has pointed out the uncanny ways in which Stieglitz's photos seem to imitate O'Keeffe's paintings in these years—the "realistic" medium in effect imitating the "artistic" one—life imitating art to the point of co-opting technology. However this may be, O'Keeffe unquestionably met

Stieglitz at a low point in his life, reenergized him, and sent him forth to do his "Equivalents" as well as his portraits of her, adding roughly fifteen years to his productive longevity. "Mr. Alfred never would have been the photographer he later was if he hadn't got with Georgia," Margaret Prosser, a family housekeeper for forty years, recalled to Pollitzer years later. "I saw his early photographs, I saw his late photographs, the negatives would hang up in my kitchen to dry." She claimed to have seen them all, heard his talk about them, and remembered his explanations. "He did wonderful street scenes, portraits, railroad tracks and all that before Georgia came. But after Georgia came, he made the clouds, the moon, he even made lightning. He never photographed things like that before." O'Keeffe returned the mantle, in short, in better condition than she received it.[10]

Not only did O'Keeffe probably have more effect on Stieglitz's art than he did on hers, whenever he offered her quotable advice he was usually wrong. Not only did he put her in a gendered conceptual prison, preventing anyone from seeing her work clearly until the 1980s, he also was so imperceptive as to think of charcoal as her most appropriate medium and advised her to avoid color and stick with black and white! When she wanted to develop her series of flower studies, he was opposed, trivializing the whole notion as if she were still decorating teacups or traditional floral still lifes, such as women had done in art schools for decade after sterile decade. When he took up photographing the sky, she felt the competitive atmosphere so threatening that she gave up her own sky-oriented works and did not attempt them again until safe in the smogless, Stieglitz-free air of New Mexico in 1929. When she subsequently turned to the city and painted her now much-reproduced views from the Shelton Hotel, he told her only men could paint the city and temporarily resisted her efforts to show her first achievements. He regularly interfered in her professional contacts outside of his own gallery, to the point where she had a complete nervous breakdown under the stress. More than once, in other words, the mantle became a straitjacket.[11]

Indeed, not only did the flowers become crucial, they became representative examples of how external pressures could change the nature of art. In fact, she found flowers an appealing way to get out from all the gendered absurdities that Stieglitz, Rosenfeld, and the rest were foisting upon her. Realism of her own highly specialized variety was the best response she could muster to males with their brains fixated on body parts. "I suppose the reason I got down to an effort to be objective is that I didn't like the interpretations of my other things," she confided to Sherwood Anderson early in 1924. So "here I am with an array of alligator pears—about ten of them—calla lillies—four or six—leaves—summer green ones," not to mention "horrid yellow sunflowers" and "some white birches with yellow leaves. . . . Altogether about forty things." She had an exhibition coming and would appreciate anything he might contribute to the catalog, but did not wish to put words into his mouth. Unfortunately, Anderson was small improvement. He might also be a stammerer when it came to explanations of art or life, but he was too male, and too close an earshot from the 291 set of pseudo-Freudian assumptions to be of much use.

Yet in public she was careful to avoid yet further misunderstanding, for realism to the untutored usually verged on simpleminded replication. "Nothing is less real than realism—details are confusing," a reporter quoted her in the *New York Sun* for 5 December, 1922. "It is only by selection, by elimination, by emphasis, that we get at the real meaning of things." Any good photographer would have known exactly what she meant.[12]

Such remarks linking photography and painting, and the way males gendered certain types of art as intrinsically male or female, have gradually become staples of the best O'Keeffe criticism. But such formal emphases tend to gloss over perhaps the single most important link between the entire 291 circle and other crucial groups such as Margaret Anderson's *Little Review* group. An astonishing percentage of these modernists were devout mystics, either openly advocating the ideas of such figures as Mme. Helen Blavatsky, Annie Besant, and Georges Gurdjieff, or developing views compatible with the essence of a Theosophical worldview. When Stieglitz shot the clouds in his famous "Equivalents" series, he clearly associated celestial abstractions with God, almost as if he were a gypsy interpreting the tea leaves. But O'Keeffe presents a more difficult, more serious, and in the long run a more important example.

Stylistically, the early O'Keeffe was partial to art nouveau and symbolism even before she became fascinated by the camera. Chicago was especially persistent in its devotion to art nouveau during her student days there, and many of her early charcoals, far from being either American or female in essence, were clearly following the precedents of Odilon Redon or Hermann Obrist. She always gave primary credit to Arthur Dow for influencing her work, and his stress on Japanese techniques and formal values certainly captured her imagination for a crucial decade and more. In terms of more conspicuously modernist influences, certainly Whistler, Rodin, Picasso, Picabia, and Matisse belong on the list. But the key person here should surely be Wassily Kandinsky: the mystic, the devotee of the spiritual in art, the man to whom Marsden Hartley had paid homage during the heady days of 1913 to 1915, the man whose words as well as whose paintings received special attention from Stieglitz, including a purchase from the Armory Show.

Kandinsky had been important to Arthur Eddy, Stieglitz, Walkowitz, and Hartley, and his theoretical ghost lies behind not only the 291 art of the first jazz age, but much of the rest of the art O'Keeffe produced in New Mexico throughout her long and mystically aware life. "I was very interested in Kandinsky's book *Spiritual Harmony in Art,* and liked his paintings," she wrote with uncharacteristic precision to Gail Levin many years later. To Kandinsky, she owed her allegiance to color, when Stieglitz scorned it; and from him she found support for her lack of interest in cubism. Kandinsky was also a prime reinforcement for the essentially Whistlerian idea that painting could take inspiration and form from music. His views had special force as well because he was probably the clearest voice explaining the connection between the objective and the abstract that was central to O'Keeffe's assumptions. Strand adapted these ideas to photography and O'Keeffe learned them straight from him.[13]

Arthur Dove was the most overt mystic in the 291 circle during this period, but as it came to a close, a series of events made mysticism both more central and more overt in O'Keeffe's work. Things began to come to a head in 1925. In March, Stieglitz put on his famous *Seven Americans* show at the Anderson Galleries, featuring her work in large flowers along with works of Stieglitz, Dove, Marin, Hartley, Strand, and Charles Demuth. Summer at Lake George proved acutely stressful, with both Stieglitz and O'Keeffe in poor health, and the extended Stieglitz family driving O'Keeffe to prostration with its incessant invasions of her privacy. Stieglitz then turned his energies to organizing the Intimate Gallery, which opened in December. This personal venue absorbed far more of Stieglitz's time and energy than any efforts had during O'Keeffe's time with her mentor and, since December 1924, her husband. It also brought to his attention Dorothy Norman, who would become Stieglitz's muse and O'Keeffe's hated rival for the rest of Stieglitz's life.

In the midst of all this turmoil, the couple made the crucial decision to move to the new Shelton Hotel in New York City—a place where they could live independent of the Stieglitz family and devolve all cooking and housekeeping duties onto the hotel staff. This placed O'Keeffe in an advantageous place in a city in which she did not want to live—and even the hopelessly urban Stieglitz grumbled incessantly about its pressures. For material she turned increasingly to urban subjects, usually a view from her window or some scene from a nearby vantage point. Sometimes with sly humor but usually with serious artistic intent, she applied the lessons she had absorbed to the geometries of tall buildings, contrasts in shading, the effects of sunspotting—seeming to echo the work of Strand and Sheeler but in her own way. But as a woman, and the wife of the boss at that, she knew that members even of the 291 circle did not always take her work as seriously as they would a man's, to the point of denying that any woman could have anything significant to say on the city at all. Only when she persisted, and then made sales, did the eyebrows lower a bit.

What the Shelton unexpectedly did provide for her was a new guru, a charismatic spiritual guide who could talk to her about mystical values while Stieglitz instructed Dorothy Norman. Claude Bragdon was an architect and designer who devoted an inordinate amount of his time to writing Theosophical tracts, and to translating such central works as P. D. Ouspensky's *Tertium Organum*. She was ready. From Max Weber to Marcel Duchamp, artists associated with 291 or *Camera Work* had been talking of the fourth dimension; Stieglitz's favorite niece, Elizabeth Davidson, and her husband, Donald, among the most amenable of those in residence at Lake George, had a long-term interest in Hinduism. O'Keeffe herself seems to have been born that way, which was why the sky, light, and flowers so appealed to her: She was always seeing through them. By March of 1926 she was making passing references to Bragdon in private letters; by summer she was calling herself "one of the intuitives" to Waldo Frank, and clearly mulling a great many things over as her health and domestic situation deteriorated.

She always had trouble being precise in words, but early in 1927 she brought it all together: "I have come to the end of something," she wrote Frank. It took several operations and numerous domestic scenes, but by the end of the decade she was off to New Mexico whether Stieglitz approved or not, and what she found there was a great deal more than desertscapes and cow skulls.[14]

TEN

GERTRUDE STEIN/SHERWOOD ANDERSON/ERNEST HEMINGWAY

Perhaps the best-known instances of the anxiety of influence in the first jazz age were those that Ernest Hemingway felt toward Sherwood Anderson and Gertrude Stein. Both Anderson and Hemingway are on record as paying homage to Stein and the lessons she presumably taught, but readers of these three remain puzzled by a number of unresolved problems. The most obvious ones concern the distinction between human relationships and verbal ones. The three simply do not ever really sound alike as writers, however much they may have liked or listened to each other. In addition, the historical framework is difficult to establish. None of the three is especially reliable about either facts or chronology.

The chief source on Anderson's response to Stein has long been *A Story Teller's Story*, in which Anderson goes on lyrically about how *Tender Buttons* (1914) affected him. "How it had excited me! Here was something purely experimental and dealing in words separated from sense," an approach "I was sure the poets must often be compelled to make." He ruminated over the book for awhile, and "decided to try it." Many laughed about Stein in those days, but "I did not laugh." Her work "excited me as one might grow excited in going into a new and wonderful country where everything is strange." She laid words "before me as the painter had laid the color pans on the table in my presence." His "mind did a kind of jerking flop and after Miss Stein's book had come into my hands I spent days going about with a tablet of paper in my pocket and making new and strange combinations of words." The familiar became new, and "I became a little conscious where before I had been unconscious." This all has a wonderful, insightful sound to it, but if he hadn't told us about her so explicitly, no one would have guessed.[1]

The Hemingway debts have no such single source. He clearly had personal obligations to both Anderson and Stein for encouragement when he needed it, and help in getting his earliest stories into book form, but Hemingway was visibly anxious about the influence of both Anderson and Stein. He had used both of them to further his career, and then turned on both in public and in private. The key events were the publication of both *The Torrents of Spring* and *The Sun Also Rises* in 1926.

Torrents hit Anderson in a number of painful spots, and many friends regarded it as an example of Hemingway's character flaws more than as a literary achievement. Hemingway was progressively losing his right to ready access to the company of his mentors and peers. Originally the soul of adolescent charm, he permitted psychological limitations to take over whatever had once been attractive in his character. He turned on Anderson chiefly because Hemingway could not bear to be indebted to a man whose work was in obvious decline. He turned on Stein not only because he was both attracted and repulsed by her maternal sexuality, as scholars have long recognized, but also because he was a hopeless anti-Semite, whose personal correspondence concerning her in the years after their breakup remain among the permanent embarrassments of American letters.

Hemingway will always retain a certain historical importance. In *Sun* and a handful of short stories, he reoriented American prose toward the simple, the concrete, and the reticent; and he changed the way countless readers acted and spoke. It remains something of a critical mystery precisely what he received from which influence, but perhaps matters are not so complex as they seem in the redundancies of academic criticism. The problem comprises several obvious parts: What literary technique did Hemingway bring to Paris? What did he learn from Anderson and then from Stein? What was Hemingway really trying to accomplish in 1926, especially in *The Torrents of Spring*? And what actually does that slight work accomplish?

Critical opinion has been virtually unanimous since 1954 that Hemingway brought the skills of a trained journalist with him to Paris, and that he learned those skills on the *Kansas City Star.* Only eighteen when he went to Kansas City, Hemingway had really wanted to participate in the war in some exciting way, but his father would not permit it and newspaper work was a compromise that worked briefly to channel youthful energies. He began in the middle of October 1917, and lasted roughly seven months, until his 30 April, 1918, departure for New York City and Europe. In that brief apprenticeship he internalized the essence of the Hemingway style, and the substance of the *Star* lessons prepared him for what Anderson and Stein had to teach.

Like most high school students in the twilight of Victorian prose, Hemingway had displayed a wordy, even flowery style in his jejeune work. It could not possibly survive the single galley page–sized set of 110 rules that instructed reporters at the *Star* and that in pamphlet form soon had wide influence among newspapers around the country. Although recent criticism of English prose has tended to credit the impact of the war experience with chastening the language, American newspapers were already well on the way. The *Star* wanted its writers to use short opening paragraphs and continue using short sentences throughout their stories. It preferred basic Anglo-Saxon words to lengthy Latinate ones. Sentences should be positive, not negative. Reporters should avoid slang words unless the slang were fresh and appropriate. Above all, they should avoid extravagant adjectives, especially "splendid," "gorgeous," "grand," and "magnificent." Over the next half-century, Hemingway gave oral advice to many interviewers about his style, and it usually boiled down to a synthesis of the *Star* rules: be clear, straightforward, concrete, and brief.[2]

Hemingway first met Anderson in Chicago in January 1921, and for about five months they were friendly as mentor and student as well as fellow journalists whose larger ambitions were creative. Anderson was the great hinterland father figure for many young, urban writers in the first jazz age, chiefly for his abandonment of a career in business for the higher calling of writer, and secondarily for his successes in portraying repressed sexual anxiety. Always kind and often helpful, Anderson was too middle-aged and provincial to give Hemingway more than verbal encouragement and a helping hand with publishers, but those things he did and would do. Nothing in his prose style appealed much to Hemingway, and no serious Hemingway prose bears any resemblance to anything Anderson had written. Anderson himself realized this, and in his posthumously published memoirs insisted that, regardless of what critics might have said, he himself had never claimed to have influenced the younger man.[3]

At this point, Anderson went off on the big travel adventure of his life, to Paris with Paul Rosenfeld acting as guide and paying most of the expenses. Two relatively selfless men in the circle around Stieglitz and O'Keeffe, they clearly enjoyed themselves experiencing a Europe unmediated by Stieglitz's monologues. In fact, Anderson and his second wife enjoyed themselves so much that when Hemingway planned to "go Woplands" with his new bride Hadley in 1921, Anderson strongly urged that they go to Paris instead. Italy was all very well for recreation and cultural ambience, but Paris was far more appropriate for a writer—not only cheap but abounding with publishing opportunities and influential contacts. Anderson even volunteered letters of introduction to Gertrude Stein, Ezra Pound, Sylvia Beach, and Lewis Galantière. Stein could introduce him to prose, Pound to poetry, Beach to current literature and James Joyce, and Galantière to suitable apartments. As a reporter, Hemingway could establish a base in Paris and then range as far afield as assignments required. With such an opportunity so suddenly available, Hemingway grabbed at it. Thanks to Anderson, Hemingway and his wife were settled in the

Latin Quarter by the second week of January 1922, and planning holiday excursions to Switzerland.

Hemingway was grateful and thanked Anderson for his aid in letters sent immediately upon arrival and a couple of months after settling in. "Lots of things happen here," he reported happily in the second of these. "Gertrude Stein and me are just like brothers and we see a lot of her." Anderson had recently completed a preface for Stein's *Geography and Plays* (1922), and Stein deeply appreciated the approval, in print as in private, of such an established writer. More exciting yet, "Joyce has a most goddamn wonderful book." Sylvia Beach had just published *Ulysses*, and Hemingway was in awe of the achievement. Sections had been appearing for years in the *Little Review* and scarcely a writer in Paris was unaware that an "event" had occurred. What Hemingway did not convey was that he could not get through the book; in his personal copy, which Sylvia Beach herself presented to him and which survives in the Hemingway collection at the John F. Kennedy Library, only the first half of the volume, and the closing soliloquy of Molly Bloom, have been cut. Meanwhile, Hemingway waxed sardonic about Joyce, delighted to be in the middle of it all: "The report is that he and all his family are starving but you can find the whole celtic crew of them every night in Michaud's," a place the Hemingways could only afford "about once a week."

This letter remains important not only for these glimpses of Stein and Joyce, but for the next two paragraphs, which focus on Pound and include the much-quoted description of Hemingway and Pound boxing despite great disparities of weight and experience. Such exertions were peripheral. The meat of the letter was the information that Pound had forwarded six Hemingway poems to Scofield Thayer at the *Dial*, and one story to the *Little Review*. The combination of physical bravery and literary assistance was a sure path to Hemingway's good graces. "He's really a good guy, Pound, wit a fine bitter tongue onto him. He's written a good review of Ulysses for April Dial." The conclusion almost leaps from the page: Hemingway is learning his critical opinions chiefly secondhand, most obviously from Pound, but secondarily from Stein. His subsequent correspondence, and his behavior concerning Stein's *The Making of Americans,* bear this out, providing useful lessons on how cultural history functioned and how critical opinion really circulated.[4]

For a time, Hemingway managed the considerable feat of remaining on good terms with both Stein and Pound, who disliked each other. By early 1923, Hemingway was in regular correspondence with Pound, dropping references to Major Clifford Hugh Douglas, Pound's favorite monetary theorist, making casual anti-Semitic slurs ("Dave O'Neil the Celto-Kike," Ella Winter the "objectionable 22 year old Bloomsbury Jewine"), and even visiting Pound in Rapallo—where, as it turned out, he saw more of Robert McAlmon than of Pound. Concurrently, he was buttering up the very Semitic Gertrude Stein: "I've been working hard and have two things done," he wrote from Rapallo. "I've thought a lot about the things you said about working and am starting that way at the beginning. If you think of anything else I wish you'd write it to me." And with the opportunistic hypocrisy that was becoming second nature, he even asked Stein to serve as godmother to his new son, usually referred to as Bumby. Stein agreed, as did the equally Jewish Alice B. Toklas, and the ceremony took place at St. Luke's Episcopal Church on 10 March, 1924.[5]

The man whose ear for dialogue would soon be legendary also displayed a tendency to sound like his correspondents whenever he wrote to them. In trying to describe New York City to Stein in the fall of 1923, he came out with rather pallid Steinese:

> All the time I was there I never saw anybody even grin. There was a man drawing on the street in front of the stock exchange with yellow and red chalk and shouting "He sent his only begotten son to do this. He sent his only begotten son to die on the tree. He sent his only begotten son to hang there and die." A big crowd standing around listening. Business men you know. Clerks, messenger boys. "Pretty tough on de boy," said a messenger boy ab-

solutely seriously to another kid. Very Fine. There are really some fine buildings. New ones. Not any with names that we've ever heard of. Funny shapes. Three hundred years from now people will come over from Europe and tour it in rubber neck wagons. Dead and deserted like Egypt. It'll be Cooks most popular tour.

Wouldn't live it for anything.

Two days later, he was writing Pound about the legendary tedium of life in Toronto, in a tone of scatalogical hyperbole that shows an acquaintance with Pound's increasingly idiosyncratic epistolary effusions:

I am at work on a work called OH CANADA which will take the wind out of [B.C.] Windeler. There is no doubt about it being the fistulated asshole of the father of seven among Nations. In every Postoffice, ie. Bureau de Poste there is a big sign, "WRITE OFTEN AND YOU WILL KEEP THE FAMILY TOGETHER.". . .

On Sunday when I wanted to take a box of Chocolate pepruments to Hadley in the hospital I had to buy them from the bootleggers. The Drug Stores cannot sell candy on Sunday.[6]

Things might have gone no farther, and become no more offensive, than this sort of private chaffing, had not Edmund Wilson published his highly intuitive early assessment of Hemingway's first brief volumes. With his unerring instinct for self-promotion, Hemingway had noticed in the Sunday edition of the *New York Tribune*, for 21 October, 1923, in the column "A Bookman's Daybook," that critic Burton Rascoe had called on Wilson and learned of Hemingway's work, which Wilson had received from Lewis Galantière. Seizing the opportunity, Hemingway wrote Wilson from Toronto that in addition to *in our time*, he was sending a copy of *Three Stories and Ten Poems* and hoped for a joint review. Did Wilson know four or five other critics who might like review copies? Wilson replied encouragingly and intuited more influence from Anderson than Hemingway was willing to acknowledge. "No I don't think *My Old Man* derives from Anderson," Hemingway replied late in 1923. "It is about a boy and his father and race-horses." Anderson had written about boys and horses, but "very differently." The stories were not at all alike. "I know I wasn't inspired by him." Besides, Anderson's recent work "seems to me to have gone to hell." Even so, Hemingway remained "very fond of him. He has written good stories."

Hemingway looked Wilson up when he came through New York City and made sure Wilson had both the original *in our time* and the expanded, and now capitalized edition, *In Out Time*, as well as *Three Stories and Ten Poems*, which between them constituted Hemingway's claim to fame in 1924. In the resulting review, "Mr. Hemingway's Dry-Points," Wilson ignored Hemingway's protestations and established what for many years remained the assumption of influence on Hemingway's early work. Wilson rightly dismissed Hemingway's poetry but found his prose "of the first distinction." He remained sure that Hemingway and Anderson were the only two modernist writers who had "felt the genius of Gertrude Stein's *Three Lives*." He argued that "Miss Stein, Mr. Anderson and Mr. Hemingway may now be said to form a school by themselves," the chief characteristic of which was "a naivete of language, often passing into the colloquialism of the character dealt with, which serves actually to convey profound emotions and complex states of mind." He thought this "a distinctively American development in prose." He went on to conclude that *In Our Time* had "more artistic dignity than anything else about the period of the war that has as yet been written by an American." Grateful for positive notice, Hemingway refused to pick a fight and thanked Wilson for the review.[7]

Hemingway's relationship to Stein from about 1922 to 1926 remains something of a biographical muddle because of later recriminations in their widely disseminated autobiographical works, and Hemingway's slighting allusions in presumably fictional writings. On a personal level, things went rather well. Stein doted on her godson, Hadley Hemingway dutifully discussed domestic matters with Toklas, and Ernest went about the laborious task of interesting publishers in *The Making of Americans,* a mountainous pile of manuscript that even his best friends preferred not to touch. He praised it as "wonderful" to such of her friends as Anderson, never raising the problems it presented. Since no commercial publishers were interested, Hemingway prepared portions of it for the *Transatlantic Review,* where it began to appear in April 1924. The parallels to the appearance of *Ulysses* in the *Little Review* were too obvious to miss, even without delving into Stein's intense feelings of jealousy toward James Joyce.

At this point, inaccuracies of language as well as the ambiguities of "repetition" distort literary history. Stein, Hemingway, and many subsequent writers persist in referring to the work as an entity, as if it preexisted its unabridged book publication form and readers somehow took it straight and took it whole, like snakes ingesting animals. But neither Hemingway nor anyone else took it this way. Hemingway took it one hunk at a time, and so readers did as well. When one of the essences of a work is repetition, to encounter it for a few hours every few months was a very different reading experience than to face almost one thousand printed pages all at once. It is the difference between chewing a cooked drumstick, one sensible nibble at a time, or ingesting the entire raw chicken, with feathers, bones, and beak, in one prolonged swallow. To make matters even more deceptive, Hemingway did all the editing chores, and so Stein never had to face up to the results of her careless writing and stubborn refusal to rewrite.

Thus for the "typical" reader the appealing, relatively accessible excerpts did duty for the whole; casual usage then as now never distinguished these short excerpts from the interminable whole. Given the precedents of *Ulysses* and Stein's small cheering section of younger disciples, high expectations were in order when Robert McAlmon published it as a Contact Edition in November 1925. But even that early, Hemingway was himself drawing back from the book, and especially its style, which now seemed beyond parody. Letters to those not of her entourage sounded a note different from those to Anderson. "Stuff like Gertrude Stein isn't worth the bother to show up," Hemingway snorted to Ezra Pound. "It's easier simply to quote from it."

Everyone was happy to discuss the book but few read it and almost no one bought it. As food, it was a dead chicken, with digestive tract still in place. Hemingway was not a competent editor, nor would Stein have paid the slightest attention had he suggested rewriting. What she lacked was a Maxwell Perkins. Faced with the misspellings and grammatical howlers of a Scott Fitzgerald, or the formless logorrhea of a Thomas Wolfe, Perkins would set tactfully to work and cut away or reshape manuscripts until they became coherent and marketable. Stein was capable of short bursts of competent prose, but she had little capacity for focus and none at all for the architecture of an extended fiction. Always autobiographical, she kept remembering things that had happened to her or members of her family and confusing the clarity of memory with the need to evoke some believable reality on the page. She had ambiguous feelings about being Jewish and about the role of Jews in American history. She had no capacity also for dealing either with her own lesbianism or the heterosexual preferences of her brother Leo and most of the rest of her family. Even a later, commercial abridgment could not repair the damage.

The sense of letdown in the literary community comes through most clearly in the correspondence of Scott Fitzgerald. Eagerly absorbing the excerpts as they appeared, he was delighted to offer encouragement to Stein and help her place what he assumed would be an accomplished work. "I am so anxious to get *The Makeings of Americans* + learn something from it and imitate things out of it which I shall doubtless do," he wrote her in June 1925. "That future debt I tried to repay by making the Scribners read it in the *Transatlantic* + convinced one, but the old man's mind was too old." Six months later the tome was on the table and he realized that the excerpts had misrepresented the whole. "Its good you didn't take my advice about looking up Gertrude Stien's new book (The Making of Americans)," he wrote Perkins. "Its bigger than Ullyses and only the first parts, the parts published in the Transatlantic are intelligible at all. Its published privately here."8

The matter of influence poses a different problem. Both Stein and Hemingway have long been known for somehow being masters of "repetition," and nonspecialists at least assume she taught it to him, but here again no functional reader would ever confuse the two styles. The influence, in fact, was actually through personal contact and pithy advice rather than through imitation. Hemingway had admired and respected her for several years, and in reading through his work she had always stressed the sort of focus and compression that journalistic cablese required: Pare down the adjectives and cut description but be willing to repeat nouns and verbs when they help establish the bottom nature, the characteristic habits of thought, of a given person in a specific situation.

This type of compressed repetition gave Hemingway's early stories their peculiar flavor—making them sound unlike Stein's work or anyone else's. A reader can see the results simply by taking the early short stories in the order in which they were originally published, beginning on page eighty-one of *The Short Stories of Ernest Hemingway*. "Up in Michigan" opens with an almost laboratory example of the use of the word "like." It appears eight times in the third paragraph, and "liking" once, and the sexual encounter that constitutes the climax follows almost without saying. "On the Quai at Smyrna," which follows, uses "screamed" in the first two sentences and "screaming" in the third, setting the proper pitch for the deadpan horrors to follow, chiefly concerning dead babies and not containing any further repetition of "scream." "Indian Camp" uses varieties of "row" and "rowboat" six times in the three brief opening paragraphs; "The End of Something" opens with five uses of "lumber" in the first paragraph.

All this would be worthy of note but little more if it did not lead somewhere significant. In fact, the killing of adjectives was intimately related to the killing of soldiers, Indians, and babies, all the language-stretching violence that Hemingway had experienced during World War I, and on his journalistic forays into the war between

Greeks and Turks in the early 1920s. The narrative conventions that Hemingway and his generation had inherited were incapable of conveying the realities of war, starvation, cruelty, and death. He knew instinctively that narrative had to change and with no contact at all with Erik Satie ("be brief") or Mies van der Rohe ("less is more") he was coming to parallel solutions in prose to what was also happening in modernist music and architecture. Insofar as Stein contributed to this process, it seems to have been through ad hoc criticisms of individual stories and not through her prose at all.

The most extended example of this brevity combined with repetition comes in "Soldier's Home." Krebs has been through the worst of the war and finds he can't talk about it. He returns to his home town in Oklahoma to find that no one wants to listen. The lies nauseated him; the peace asphyxiates him. Communication is dead even within his family and he seems virtually catatonic. He focuses instead on young women, whose growth becomes a measure of time and whose beauty becomes the opposite of the ugliness of war:

> Most of them had their hair cut short. When he went away only little girls wore their hair like that or girls that were fast. They all wore sweaters and shirt waists with round Dutch collars. It was a pattern. He liked to look at them from the front porch as they walked on the other side of the street. He liked to watch them walking under the shade of the trees. He liked the round Dutch collars above their sweaters. He liked their silk stockings and flat shoes. He liked their bobbed hair and the way they walked.

On the other hand, he did not like them in town and thought that on the whole women were too complicated. He wanted a companion but could not work out the necessary logistics. He felt unable to say anything not flatly true.

> He did not want any consequences. He did not want any consequences ever again. He wanted to live along without conse-

quences. Besides he did not really need a girl. The army had taught him that.

And so on, free-associating over the same core attitudes: the trouble a man gets into from the consequences of lying in politics or love. Language being in part the point here, he recalls preferring European girls because communication was difficult and primitive due to the differences in language. Krebs retreats into a detached art, a "pattern," in order to avoid any frightening commitment. A phrase like "no entangling alliances" could apply as much to marriage as to war.

> He liked the girls that were walking along the other side of the street. He liked the look of them much better than the French girls or the German girls. But the world they were in was not the world he was in. He would like to have one of them. But it was not worth it. They were such a nice pattern. He liked the pattern. It was exciting. But he would not go through all the talking. He did not want one badly enough. He liked to look at them all, though. It was not worth it.

Another paragraph goes by, full of history but lacking maps. He wants more maps, being able to find his way neither abroad nor at home. The reverie concludes: "He had been a good soldier. That made a difference."[9]

This was great art, but beyond anything Stein herself could accomplish. Her own prose remained diffuse, garrulous, and domestic, repetitious words burying their subjects instead of clarifying by allusion or omission. Hemingway did as she said, not as she did, building on his journalistic training rather than changing it. Soon *The Sun Also Rises* (1926) synthesized the new prose options, adding attitudes of cryptic cynicism and narcissistic opportunism to the postwar weariness. Rituals of church and bullfight replaced those of war and exploitation. Even the women spoke through clenched lips, as if they too had been through hell and struck almost dumb.

As Hemingway slowly absorbed Stein's lessons, she in turn experienced him as part of a broadening and deepening of what still remained a coterie. Although Stein had been writing steadily since the earliest years of the century, literary publication and recognition had been frustratingly slow, based largely on *Three Lives*, *Tender Buttons*, and the gossip of a few friends. Stein had been a hostess for painters and a purchaser of paintings before the war, and a writer largely through courtesy. After the war, she broadened her circle considerably. While keeping a Juan Gris, she added a Man Ray and thus attained firsthand familiarity with experimental photography. She entertained Jean Cocteau, a poet close to Les Six and the music scene. Above all, she began to cultivate writers and editors who would not only stimulate her, they might also aid her quest for *la gloire* by printing her work in quarterlies and placing it between hard covers. Anderson thus came to her bearing the unsolicited praise of an influential novelist whose work was selling in increasing quantities. Hemingway appeared as a handsome war hero who not only played the role of disciple, he dealt with New York book editors and European journal editors. Wandering in and out of the Stein apartment at roughly the same time, say 1922 to 1926, were *Broom* editor Harold Loeb and the everavailable Ford Madox Ford, whose editorial skills had been legendary since the *English Review* had had its gloriously expensive year and a half (1908–10) under his hegemony.

Stein, in short, was basking in praise but also using her new friends to further her publishing plans. As long as Hemingway remained potentially useful in this regard, she was unlikely to push any disagreements to the point of rupture. Friction was inevitable between two such egos, however, and once Hemingway had forced portions of *The Making of Americans* into the *Transatlantic Review*, and the two of them had persuaded Robert McAlmon to bring out the unabridged version, things began to deteriorate. During 1922 and 1923 all was cordial, and she was so enamored of her handsome equerry that she gave him what he later described as "the run of the studio," welcome to have a drink and look at her paintings should he drop in while she was out. The baptism for

John Hadley Nicanor Hemingway was on 16 March, 1924, coinciding roughly with the final refusals of Knopf and Liveright to publish *The Making of Americans* in New York, and its placement with Contact Editions, where McAlmon apparently entertained ludicrously high hopes for sales.

By 1925, the book was out and selling badly, paternity was proving onerous to Hemingway, his marriage was showing strain, and jealousy was coming between him and Stein. Even if few bought the book, many knew of it, and she enjoyed a bit of glory. Anderson published *Dark Laughter*, which got more praise and far more sales than it deserved, Scott Fitzgerald published *The Great Gatsby*, which offered competition indeed. Stein got along well with both Anderson and Fitzgerald, and neither did much to exploit the connection. Neither needed to, and neither confused the public and the personal the way Hemingway did. Other favorites, like painter Pavel Tchelitchew and musician Virgil Thomson, seemed increasingly in evidence. Hemingway had reason to feel a bit abandoned, his own glory still not in evidence. He became petulant and discontented. He showed up once, drunk, and was insultingly familiar; Stein threw him out in a rage.

She relented after a few weeks, and at this point they had their discussions of the character of Robert Cohn and the role Jewishness would play in *The Sun Also Rises*. But then Hemingway apparently overheard a bitter fight between Stein and Toklas; the details remain obscure, but certainly their lesbian relationship and Stein's "weakness" for Hemingway must have played a part. Hemingway withdrew and expressed his revulsion to his wife; things were never thereafter the same. The women realized that they had been overheard, and when Hadley later dropped by with Bumby, the maid turned her away. The pain seems to have been universal, but whether the occasion was its only cause remains problematic. Both Stein and Hemingway were psychologically ready to move on.[10]

A casual anti-Semitism was endemic in the Chicago suburbs where Hemingway had grown up, but he went out of his way to make slurring remarks in private discourse, even when Jews were not directly involved. At times in his letters the effect is a bit surreal. On facing pages of the *Selected Letters*, for example, on 16 November, 1922, he is writing Harriet Monroe about how his new friend Stein has just mailed him "an enormous candied casaba melon . . . pretty nearly as big as a pumpkin," surely a sign of personal amity; on the very next page he is writing Hadley Hemingway twelve days later that Frank Mason of Hearst's International News Service "has kiked me so on money that I can't afford taxi's," and in general pays "little baby kike salaries." Neither Mason nor anyone else in context appears to be Jewish, nor would Hadley be the sort of correspondent who might stimulate her husband to spontaneous bigotry in a moment of stress; if anything, the reverse was true.

For a brief period, Hemingway's ethnic animosities focused on his friend Harold Loeb. A wealthy member of the banking families of Loeb and Guggenheim, Loeb was a minor novelist who published with Liveright and who was instrumental in getting that firm to republish *In Our Time*. He was a generous soul, always eager to treat impecunious friends to drinks and meals, or to provide a competent tennis partner. He was also coeditor of *Broom* and thus in a position to help friends get into print there as well. Loeb's companion was the lovely Kitty Cannell, a frequent confidante of Hemingway; a good friend was Mary Duff Twysden, the "alcoholic nymphomaniac" who was the inspiration for Brett Ashley in *The Sun Also Rises*. Surrounded by friends and potential lovers, which Twysden quickly became, Hemingway should have been grateful at least for the literary material they supplied. But no, he discussed Loeb over with Stein, made remarks about getting "that kike" in Cannell's presence, and created a classic example of overt literary anti-Semitism in the character of Robert Cohn. Handsome, rich, Jewish, good at tennis and at love, Loeb was just too much for Hemingway to deal with. Stein was appalled, as were other mutual friends, but Loeb proved so essentially good-natured that he left most of the unpleasantness out of his own account of those days, *The Way It Was* (1959).[11]

Hemingway, in short, had something close to a compulsion both about Jews and about close friends who did favors. No good deed went unpunished for long, and as *The Sun Also Rises* progressed toward publication, he turned on Loeb, abandoned Liveright, and headed toward a divorce from the woman who loved him selflessly and had just born his child. Stein was the next most obvious target, and she began to appear in an unfriendly light in still unpublished letters late in 1925. Always eager for printed praise, Hemingway wanted his friends to review his works, favorably of course. Stein rarely wrote book reviews; pithy oral instructions were her line. Occasionally she relented, as in the case of *Three Stories and Ten Poems*, but she spoiled the effect a bit for the touchy author by using "turgid" in describing the style of his prose. He seemed to take it well enough at the time, writing Stein and Toklas on 9 November, 1923, that he "will try not to be turgid" in the next "good stories" he was planning. But he never forgot, and when she did not review *In Our Time*, he exploded to Ezra Pound: "What a lot of safe playing kikes."[12]

The mutual exploitation ended at some point late in 1925 or early 1926, as books appeared and opportunities for review became fewer. But as Stein accumulated the evidence that Hemingway disliked both her religious origins and her sexual orientation, he became for her yet one more deplorable example of the "patriarchy" that was coming to be a dominating theme in her writing. The rapid composition of *The Autobiography of Alice B. Toklas* late in 1932 gave her the opportunity for sly revenge. The section on Hemingway began innocuously enough, with the young admirer of the sage older woman sitting, listening, and taking advice to concentrate his prose and give up newspaper work for creative work. Emotionally immature, he came across looking petulant when his wife become pregnant and his carefree lifestyle seemed threatened. He was too young to be a father, he repeatedly proclaimed, while the spinsters consoled him, presumably chuckling behind their deadpan faces and unemotive sentences. The voice of Toklas then went over the odd circumstances of the multicultural baptism, the active phase of their being godparents, and then the inevitable "cooling of friendship." Stein admitted that she had "a weakness for Hemingway," and this made the cooling gradual; but Toklas most decidedly did not, and the sound of her fingernails going into his coffin rasp yet again across literary history.

"Gertrude Stein and Sherwood Anderson are very funny on the subject of Hemingway," continued Toklas's voice. "Hemingway had been formed by the two of them and they were both a little proud and a little ashamed of the work of their minds." Their young protégé had seemed promising but had not developed properly; instead he had betrayed Anderson gratuitously in print and behaved hypocritically in private. Stein and Anderson agreed "that Hemingway was yellow" in his literary and personal relationships. His chief redeeming quality besides charm was that "he is such a good pupil." It was really very "flattering to have a pupil who does it without understanding it, in other words he takes training and anybody who takes training is a favorite pupil." Hemingway's modernism was a fraud: "He looks like a modern and he smells of the museums." She insisted that he had learned his craft chiefly through working on the galleys of *The Making of Americans*.[13]

Eternally thin of skin, Hemingway would make gratuitous remarks in his fiction for years after, denigrating the woman with whom he had seemed so close, but his most illuminating screeds once again went into his private correspondence. The dating of his letters remains problematic, but presumably in response to either the serial or the book publication of *The Autobiography of Alice B. Toklas*, he launched into an unusually detailed analysis. She was "a smart woman and, *if she had worked*," if she had accepted the discipline of prose as he had, "could have written damn good stuff," he wrote Ezra Pound. Instead, "she got a way by which she could write *everyday*, without corrections, and by writing make herself feel swell." Troubled by writer's block, devoted to cablese, cryptic allusion, and the psychological need to omit the most important materials, Hemingway was appalled. The woman seemed to write just because it made her feel good. But then, to keep on feeling good, "she had to get it approved and accepted and accoladed etc." She no longer wrote literature, and her career had "become a racket."

He remained convinced that his early perceptions of her work had been valid. "I think at the start she had something and was writing good stuff—i.e. Melanctha, the First part of Making of Americans, but it was simply panned." She got bitter and determined to ignore the criticism. She "thought all right if the reader is so damned dumb to hell with the reader and wrote for herself," eventually falling into "automatic writing—However some of the short pieces in Geography and plays and some others are darned good legitimate stuff—(to me)." Faced with *The Autobiography of Alice B. Toklas*, he lapsed into the scatology that is so common in the entire Hemingway/Pound correspondence. It was "bullshit," full of errors, and discussions of events where neither Stein nor Toklas were present. "I learned more about how to write and how not to write from you than from any son of a bitch alive and have always said so." He readily admitted to some Stein influence, though. "I learned from her too—in conversation. She was never dumb in conversation. Damned smart—in conversation." Just thinking about it all heated him up. "But it seems she and old mother hubbard Anderson made me in their spare time. Well by Jesus that will be something for them to be remembered by if its true."

As he so frequently did by the early 1930s, he then launched into the sexist mode, as if to complement the anti-Semitic. "I stuck by that old bitch until she threw me out of the house when she lost her judgement with the menopause but it seems that I'm just a fickle, brittle brain-picking bastard. She gave me some damned good advice many times and much shit to boot." The only thing he seemed to recall fondly was the way her work affected Ford Madox Ford. He had never cared for Ford himself, but recalled his sufferings gleefully.[14]

Biographers of both Hemingway and Stein have noted that major changes occurred in the lives of their subjects during the period from 1925 to 1927. Hemingway divorced Hadley and married the very different Pauline Pfeiffer; the change in wives meant a change in geographical location and circle of friends, and the Paris of the Hemingway legends changed significantly. Stein cut off her long hair in January 1926 to adopt the monklike style of her middle age; the tone of her salon shifted accordingly. She became more aware of anti-Semitism and more comfortable around women, especially, who claimed Jewish blood. She became more self-consciously lesbian, increasingly open in her allegiance to those who felt as she and Alice did. Of the men who remained, an increasing number were homosexual, like Virgil Thomson and Hart Crane, or bisexual like Paul Bowles. A second jazz age had begun, and the notes and rhythms would be different.[15]

As some of the remarks from both Hemingway and Stein indicate, Anderson was somehow implicated in the squabbles, and not just as the mutual friend who had brought them together. A man who actually liked Stein's art as much as he did herself, Anderson had gone out of his way to help Hemingway get published as well as introduced around Paris. Both artistically and personally insecure, Anderson never took his feelings of inadequacy out on anyone outside his four long-suffering wives and occasional girlfriends. It was not his fault that Edmund Wilson and others repeatedly discussed his influence on Hemingway. Yet as he soon discovered, Hemingway was perfectly capable of thanking him for his help with one hand and writing a malicious and unprovoked parody with the other.

Hemingway was in a widely parricidal mood by late November 1925, and he claimed to have turned out *The Torrents of Spring* in one frantic week, apparently the 20th through the 26th. Aside from glancing blows at Stein, Scott Fitzgerald, and Wyndham Lewis, his chief target was Anderson's *Dark Laughter* (1925), with occasional notice of *Many Marriages* (1923), the short stories in *The Triumph of the Egg* (1921), and the autobiography *A Story Teller's Story* (1924). Numerous other references pass in an eye-flick, and although Hemingway never mentioned either surrealism or

William Carlos Williams directly, *Torrents* may well owe something to *Spring and All*, which Contact Editions published in 1923; and *The Great American Novel*, which Three Mountains Press issued that same year.[16]

Hemingway had a devastatingly accurate ear for certain types of dialogue, and an eye for redundant narrative techniques, and he nailed Anderson effortlessly in the parody. Characters wonder simplemindedly if spring will follow winter, they are capable of going on a long walk with a wife and somehow losing her, they seem stupefied with wonder that high school kids actually learn things in school. Off in the distance, Indian war whoops make primitive, atavistic noises; close up, black bartenders break suddenly into "high-pitched uncontrollable laughter. The dark laughter of the Negro." Scripps O'Neil even managed to pick up a dead, frozen bird and bring it suddenly to life just through the animal heat of his American chest: It pecks; he cries. The reader giggles. It was all so tacky and unfair, missing Anderson's many virtues as it went. But it was true enough, right down to the fog of rhetorical questions Anderson had taken to using when his creativity burned low.[17]

Hemingway made a token effort to sell the novel to Horace Liveright, since he owed the firm a first refusal on his next book, but he knew that since it also published Anderson and made good money so doing, it was unlikely to take it. He compared the work to that of Henry Fielding, although *Many Marriages* was no *Pamela* and *Torrents* hardly a *Joseph Andrews*. He indirectly but firmly indicated his displeasure with the way Liveright had advertised *In Our Time*, blaming bad sales on business incompetence after the fashion of generations of disgruntled authors. But Hemingway had no case whatsoever. Liveright had treated him well; short stories usually did not sell, and Hemingway was hardly a commercial name before *The Sun Also Rises*. The real problem was anti-Semitism on the one hand, and its obverse, Anglo-Saxon prestige, on the other. Hemingway wanted to distance himself from a Jew with a reputation for high living and flashy salesmanship, and ally himself with the suave and very competent Maxwell Perkins, and the old-line

firm of Scribner's. Shabby as it was in terms of conventional assumptions about friendship and social debts, *Torrents* was an effort
to step up in class as well as to deny influence to a predecessor.[18]

Hemingway couldn't leave the subject alone, as if a guilty conscience were eating at him. He wrote Anderson that Anderson was
well aware of Hemingway's criticisms of *Many Marriages* and *A
Story Teller's Story,* and that *Torrents* was simply one way of legitimately criticizing *Dark Laughter,* an act of literary honesty. "You see
I feel that if among ourselves we have to pull our punches, if when
a man like yourself who can write very great things writes something that seems to me . . . rotten, I ought to tell you so." Without
such honesty, "we'll never produce anything" much. "It looks, of
course, as though I were lining up on the side of the smart jews,"
he continued with an intriguing twist of logic; "and that because
you had always been swell to me and helped like the devil on the
In our time I felt an irresistible need to push you in the face with
true writer's gratitude." Well, yes it did. But Hemingway saw the
episode as one of craft over character: "It goes sort of like this: 1.
Because you are my friend I would not want to hurt you. 2. Because you are my friend has nothing to do with writing. 3. Because
you are my friend I hurt you more. 4. Outside of personal feelings
nothing that's any good can be hurt by satire." With such tortuous
logic he distanced himself from his own behavior.

Remarkably forgiving, Anderson looked up Hemingway on his
next trip to Paris, and "we had two fine afternoons together,"
Hemingway informed Perkins early in 1927. Perhaps, although
Anderson hinted to other friends over the years that in time Hemingway would be parodying himself more effectively than ever he
had parodied Anderson. It was all too true. As a student, he not
only had moved beyond both Stein and Anderson, he would soon
go beyond himself, and end up in self-parodies as distressing as
anything in *Dark Laughter.*[19]

ELEVEN

IGOR STRAVINSKY/GEORGE ANTHEIL

As the first jazz age was drawing to a close, Aaron Copland surveyed his friends in the field, who included Roger Sessions and Henry Cowell, and concluded that George Antheil "possesses the greatest gift of any young American now writing." He thought that no one could "venture to dictate just how he may make the best use of his talents," but that one could "simply remark that so far the very violence of his own sincere desire to write original music has hindered rather than helped the attainment of his own ends." Always kind in public, Copland was somewhat more skeptical in private. As participant pianist as well as auditor of the notorious performances of the *Ballet Mécanique*, he was well qualified to express skepticism, and he did so after its public première in Paris on 19 June, 1926. After describing the audience, the noise, and the scandal, he returned to the composer he had been praising in public. "I am in all honesty bound to repeat my unshakeable conviction—the boy is a genius," he wrote Israel Citkowitz. "Need I add that he has yet to write a work which shows it. If he keeps on exactly as he has started the sum total of all his genius will be exactly nothing. Voilà."[1]

Virgil Thomson, a far more waspish commentator on both composers and compositions, was equally a friend and admirer. Antheil's appreciation for Thomson's own music had meant a great deal to Thomson, especially since it was "the first time in history another musician liked my music." Antheil in person was "the chief event of my winter," and "the first composer of our generation," Thomson informed Briggs Buchanan privately. Antheil "has

admired me, he has quarreled with me about theories, he has criticized my pieces, he has consulted me about his, he has defended
me to my enemies, to his enemies, to my friends, to his friends,"
Thomson continued. "He has talked, walked and drunk me by the
hour. He has lodged me and fed me and given me money. At this
very instant he is trying to persuade a rich lady to give me money
instead of to him, although he is perfectly poor himself." Yet despite such gestures, Thomson concluded later that "for all his facility and ambition there was in him no power of growth." The
self-proclaimed "bad boy of music," "merely grew up to be a good
boy." He peaked at age twenty-five, and *Ballet Mécanique* remained
"his most original piece."

Forty years after its première, Thomson struck another note:
"Antheil was the literary man's ideal of a composer," he wrote an
unnamed correspondent. While there was more to it than that, Antheil unquestionably came closer than other American modernist
composers to literature, most obviously the literary empire of Ezra
Pound. In Pound's hands, Antheil sounded like an imagist poet
loose in the percussion section of an orchestra: "He demanded
short hard bits of rhythm hammered down, worn down so that they
were indestructable and unbendable." Pound went so far as to produce a short book, *Antheil and the Treatise on Harmony* (1924) and to
send advertising flack to numerous small journals. In turn, Antheil
collaborated on Pound's opera, *Le Testament*, and allowed the poet
to turn pages during piano performances. He even put a small
drum part in a violin sonata so that Pound could participate when
Olga Rudge served as Antheil's violinist. Yet close as it was, that
relationship also did not last; after 1926 it petered out, each man
having exhausted the other as of no further use in what were actually two very different careers.[2]

George Antheil clearly had talent and problems. He knew it
both at the time and a generation later, when he went over his career in one of the more useful expatriate memoirs, *Bad Boy of Music* (1945). A bumptious late adolescent, he proved to have facility
but not originality when presumably grown up. But perhaps the

real problem appeared only occasionally in the autobiography. As a composer, Antheil died at least in part from an obsession with Igor Stravinsky, and Antheil's letters of the first jazz age to Pound remain among the most indicative examples of the anxiety of influence and what it might mean when everyone wanted to appear "modern" and "modernist."

Like a disproportionate number of American modernists, Antheil had grown up in a German immigrant home and was fully bilingual as a matter of course. His father was proprietor of "Antheil's, A Friendly Family Shoe Store" in Trenton, but he was also friendly to both literature and music. Although Antheil never properly graduated from high school or even attempted college, he composed music, poetry, and prose from an early age. His writing mostly got him into trouble, both in school and in Europe, but his musical studies certainly began more respectably than most. He started piano when he was about six, and by sixteen was commuting regularly to Philadelphia to work with Constantin von Sternberg, a pupil of Franz Liszt and a pedagogical conservative. Antheil professed to "adore" him and revere him as his "musical godfather" even while ignoring the essence of his advice. In 1919, Antheil moved on to Ernest Bloch, then just establishing himself as the greatest teacher of composition in the country, a short train ride away in New York City.

Unwilling at first, Bloch unbent in the face of the sheer energy Antheil projected. Antheil was soon into an ambitious symphony, but ran out of money before he could complete it. Bloch, by now sympathetic, returned most of his fees, but Antheil abruptly quit in fiscal shame and accepted an invitation to spend a weekend in Bernardsville with Margaret Anderson and a small group of friends. He ended up staying six months, and made friendships that stood him in good stead in Europe shortly thereafter.[3]

He was nineteen, short, with an oddly shaped nose that long lingered in Anderson's mind. Bringing with him a suitcase of "modern musics," he arrived one Sunday and was soon at the piano, beating out "a compelling mechanical music"—everything he had ever written, apparently. He then launched into transcriptions of Debussy and Stravinsky, and even Chopin. Mechanical Chopin? "He used the piano exclusively as an instrument of percussion, making it sound like a xylophone or a cymballo."

The singer Georgette Leblanc, widow of Maurice Maeterlinck, and pianist Allen Tanner were there as well, and they all "lived the life of several musical colonies," practice by day, recital by night. They tried almost everything, always returning at some point to *Pelléas*, "with Georgette singing the two roles." A workaholic of rigid habits, Antheil "kept his room in fanatical order. His work table never held more than a pad of paper, laid straight with the lines of the table, an inkwell, pen, and pencil placed with the precision of mechanical music," she continued. During these weeks, no one passed his open door "without discovering the pencil in any but a vertical relation to the paper." He set modern poetry to music, worked on a piano concerto, and composed "the first of his famous Mechanisms." He lived chiefly on peppermint, green apples, and letters to Ernest Bloch.[4]

Desperate for funding, Antheil eventually left Bernardsville for Philadelphia, where von Sternberg suggested he apply to Mary Louise Curtis Bok, a wealthy patron of the arts whose funds derived from the Curtis Publishing Company, best known for the *Saturday Evening Post*. In 1924, she would endow the Curtis Institute with $12.5 million and formalize her remarkable range of artistic interests, but for the moment she was willing to play lady bountiful to talented young artists. Von Sternberg declared Antheil a genius of good family and spotless character in his letter of recommendation, and assured Bok that Bloch concurred. Impressed, she handed Antheil ten dollars on the spot and enrolled him in what was still the Philadelphia Settlement Music School; she promised one hundred and fifty dollars a month for a year, with renewals possible if the results warranted them. Although she had the tastes and bearing of the upper class, she would tolerate Antheil's barrage of begging letters for almost twenty years, even as she frowned on his behavior and his most famous achievements.[5]

With this precarious financial security in hand, Antheil sailed for Europe on 30 May, 1922, determined to both compose and play modernist music. He lined up Martin H. Hanson, once the representative of Leo Ornstein, to manage his performances, and on 22 June gave his first European concert at Wigmore Hall in London, featuring his own works but including Debussy and Stravinsky as well. He then passed through Donaueschingen, with its annual chamber music festival, to settle in Berlin for a year, intending to work with Artur Schnabel. He also took occasional forays to give concerts in Budapest, Vienna, and points between. These concerts achieved notoriety but few financial rewards. Often he had to fund all or part of the expenses himself. He besieged Mrs. Bok; she reduced his regular stipend 50 percent but proved open to special grants strictly earmarked for specific events, whether renting a hall or printing scores.

Once he had heard examples of the sort of music young German modernists were producing, he became clearer in his own goals and sense of context. "We of the future find our sense of organization from Picasso rather than Beethoven or Strawinsky for that matter," he informed Mrs. Bok in August. "We should find our sense of form and time-spaces molded by months and months of studying the sculptores of Brancusi or Lipchitz," rather than in the sense of architecture that gave Debussy's music a perfection seldom attained by any master. "His generation looked to Joyce and Stein for psychological inspiration, and felt no need to restrict themselves to local musical talent"; he reserved specific scorn for Jean Cocteau, often spokesman for Les Six.[6]

In the fall of 1922, Antheil introduced himself to Igor Stravinsky, telling the Russian exile how much young American composers already admired him. Flattery in the music world was a great facilitator of discourse, and for several months the two apparently shared ideas on a daily basis. Given the disparities between their later reputations, recapturing the context of such a creative relationship remains difficult, a bit like recovering the feelings of true passion long after the marriage has ended in bitter divorce.

But at least one retrospective paragraph seems true enough. "Stravinsky's music, hard, cold, unsentimental, enormously brilliant and virtuous, was now the favorite of my postadolescence," Antheil recalled in his often bitter *Bad Boy of Music*. "In a different way it achieved the hard, cold postwar flawlessness which I myself wanted to attain—but in an entirely different style, medium."

The contemporary response was, if possible, even more overwhelmed than the disillusioned later one might suggest. He called the meeting "the greatest event in my life," in his December letter to his patron. "I met Strawinsky, and because I met him, he changed his Berlin visit of two days to fifteen, and refusing to see all other people spent his time only with me, and it ended by our swearing the deepest and most eternal of friendship." When they parted both wept and embraced, and Stravinsky kissed him on both cheeks, Russian style, "and asked that the time before our next meeting be as short as possible!!!!!"[7]

The German journalist, critic, and biographer H. H. Stuckenschmidt provided the best guide to musical innovations and their context in the Berlin of the first jazz age. Now known chiefly for *Arnold Schoenberg* (1977), Stuckenschmidt was the most acute German critic to examine Antheil's work seriously. Sharing, unfortunately, the common musical fallacy that progress came in definable linear steps, Stuckenschmidt insisted during the summer of 1923 that Antheil was the only composer to have gone beyond Stravinsky as an innovator of composition. Harmony and melody were becoming less significant, while machines were promising new rhythmic possibilities. Steel buildings and electrical circuit boards were now metaphors for musicians: "The face of art work, up to now distorted, ecstatic, shameless, becomes hard, objective and transcendent." Stravinsky had broken trail; Milhaud, Poulenc, Hindemith, and the rest were following along, but only Antheil was dealing with the fundamental problems of recent music.

For Stuckenschmidt, Antheil's Berlin concert had made the rest of the season irrelevant. "His style is today a most lively polyrhythmical homophony. He sets amorphous, motionlessly rhythmical blocks against one another and welds the totality into a wonderfully clear, crystalline form." Although melodically he might stem from fairly banal Russian and American folksongs, Antheil "makes (and fulfills) the demand to each an elementally rhythmical music and fights against the supersensitive decadence of the atonalists, whom he far surpasses in the boldness of his harmony and sound." He was without sentimentality. This from the friend and future biographer of Arnold Schoenberg![8]

For someone still almost a boyish adolescent, this was heady stuff. Not everyone has his role model kiss him fervently good-bye after two weeks of intense conversations, and then finds himself singled out for praise in an august German journal for being in the forefront of the avant-garde. Antheil's change of residence from Berlin to Paris thus seems almost inexplicable, but his letters clarify matters. "The reason I rushed to Paris was because of Strawinsky. He wished to see me immediately about his appearance in America," and since "I was the only one of his American friends whom he could talk like a brother to, he asked me for private counsel," he told Bok excitedly late in July 1923. They had discussed the possibility of going to America together, Stravinsky to conduct his own works and Antheil to be the piano soloist, "for he says that I am the best pianist for his piano works." The plans did not work out because "so much had taken place since then . . . that it was practically hopeless. I renewed, however, my friendship with Strawinsky, and decided to stay here for good while it is less expensive than Berlin." He had, indeed, arrived on 13 June, 1923, expressly to attend the premiere of *Les Noces*, the piece that seemed to haunt the rest of his life.[9]

The view from Stravinsky's vantage point was predictably more pragmatic, and ultimately exasperated. The major point of connection was less mutual admiration and more Martin Hanson, Antheil's manager. Stravinsky never made any bones about what was on his mind: "My principal objective is to publish the works that I compose. I will go anywhere, with you and with them, but they must find a way to arrange for publication," he wrote Swiss conductor Ernest Ansermet about Antheil and Hanson. Stravinsky seemed personally unfamiliar with Antheil's work: "I think that Antheil has considerable power, for, if not, Hanson would not give the impression of wanting to do what the boy desires." Unknown to Stravinsky, Antheil was chasing women, including one he eventually married, all over Central Europe, and was being totally irresponsible about answering the mail or arranging concert dates in any reliable way. "I do not know the reasons for Antheil's delay"; "I hope you will light a fire under Antheil"; "No news from Antheil. What does that mean?"; "I receive letter after letter from Antheil, who always asks me to inform him by telegram where I am or where I will be, so that he can come to see me. But he fails to give me his address"; and finally, in total exasperation: "I have just received a letter from G. Antheil, as idiotic as the others." The self-proclaimed "bad boy of music" was acting out his role only too boyishly.[10]

A date that became fraught with significance on many fronts was 13 June, 1923. It marked a reunion of these two new friends for what might have been a long and fruitful avant-garde relationship. It also marked a watershed in modernist music, for on the program that night were both *Les Noces* and *Pulcinella*, wildly different in style and tendency. *Les Noces* was in many ways an homage to the machine, especially the pianola, and the role of the piano as a percussive and rhythmical instrument that could presumably be mechanized and synchronized into a machine aesthetic compatible with so many parallel trends in painting, photography, and architecture. *Pulcinella* was a firmly neoclassic ballet, an homage to the work presumably of Pergolesi, and hardly the sort of thing to frighten aging subscribers to concert series. Like Stravinsky, Antheil had tendencies in both directions; indeed, he had had them for what in his brief life was a long time, perhaps six years.

Untangling questions of originality and influence is as thankless a job in music as it is in science. Everything from fame to wealth seems to depend on who did what first. The facts indicate that

Stravinsky and Antheil, not to mention Leo Ornstein and Edgard Varèse, were often working along similar lines at the same times; documenting absolute priority is not possible. Stravinsky was the most gifted, but he was also an absorptive sponge of the ideas of others and a pasticheur who trod a very fine line along the edges of plagiarism, as he cheerfully admitted—no visible anxieties about influence in that extraordinary ego! The other three were less stable, less effective, and more subject to burnout. But such composers are often strikingly original, even when unable to sustain and develop their own ideas. All tended to be narcissistic, sure the true center of creativity was inside their own heads.

Even in his own writings, Antheil needed an occasional reality check—an anachronistic term for a serious talk with an older, detached father figure who could explain life and art as ordinary mortals usually understand them. Antheil felt for life that his own experiments with percussive pianos, and with a machine aesthetic, deserved priority and influenced his dear friend Stravinsky, and it may be true. But on the record, Ornstein seems to have been first, and Stravinsky well along the way, without input from Trenton. If any country started such a creative dead-end it was Old Russia, as any piano reduction of the prewar *Petrushka* would indicate, including the composer's; not to mention the ragtime experiments Stravinsky built on these foundations with Ansermet's help. Much like Satie, Stravinsky was summing up and even ending a brief creative flurry in the 1923/24 period, and while Antheil may well have provided congenial companionship and the odd suggestion, he was more an historical footnote than a topic sentence. This part of his creative psyche completed its work in the *Ballet Mécanique* and then moaned to anyone who would listen that in fact he had influenced Stravinsky and not the other way round. When word of his remarks got back to Stravinsky, the Russian cut him dead for life. The story wasn't pretty, but Antheil was asking for it; adolescent charm only goes so far in the real world.

One of the odder ironies of this situation was that, for all the noise surrounding the use of percussive pianos, pianolas, and the assorted musical toys that went into the *Ballet Mécanique*, Antheil was actually heading the other way. "I cannot explain the next four years of my life in Paris unless we thoroughly analyze the word 'neoclassic,'" he remarked in his memoirs; and in this, at least, he was correct. However rambunctious or boyish he might seem to audiences and critics, he remained the rigidly ordered workaholic of Margaret Anderson's memory. The beauty of machine-made sounds was that they were orderly, repetitive, and responsive to definable laws of physics, math, or gravity. "I am, I consider, basically a classicist," and "the fun in 'classical' music consists, as in chess, *of a strict keeping of the rules*, operating to best advantage within *them*." The words recall Marcel Duchamp, and it comes as no surprise that Man Ray took a well-known photograph of Antheil at about this time. But, unable to let go of his grievances, Antheil insisted that Stravinsky did not qualify: "Stravinsky's 'neoclassicism' was no new classicism at all, but a primitive-romanticism—if for no other reason than that Stravinsky so violently opposed all limiting rules except those which he made and destroyed daily for himself." Stravinsky was "no classicist, no classicist at all."[11]

Participants in movements rarely have a clear view of themselves in context and tend to have proprietary feelings about terms—words in many cases providing something like the meaning of life. In Antheil's case, his creative career was largely over by 1945, although he was still composing gamely; outside Hollywood, few paid him the slightest attention. All he could say in painful hindsight was that *Pulcinella* was "dangerous-to-me," and mutter that "the virus of neoclassicism had now made its first inroad upon me." This is largely nonsense. Musical styles are not diseases, and even if they are, healthy bodies expel them eventually and move on to other creative efforts. Stravinsky gleefully pillaged the past regardless of its classicism, the past having already included heavy doses of Rimsky-Korsakov, the hurdy-gurdy, ragtime, and the tango—*The Soldier's Tale* being virtually contemporaneous with *Pulcinella*—and *The Fairy's Kiss* (1928) was coming up, an homage to Tchaikovsky, of all people. Modernists violated time and space, collected garbage, and photographed dust accumulating. Above all they provoked people, something Antheil was at the time rather good at. But he was starting to stiffen up, to become conservative and cautious, as so many modernists did—minor ones who seemed unable to sail serenely through their own backwash.

At this point, perhaps appropriately, Antheil and his fiancée moved into a small apartment at 12, rue de l'Odéon, in the Latin Quarter, above Shakespeare and Company, the famous bookshop run by Sylvia Beach. While she entertained the likes of James Joyce, Ezra Pound, and Ernest Hemingway downstairs, he wrote violin sonatas and the *Ballet* upstairs. Both works involved Pound on their margins, and Antheil so admired Joyce that he devoted a good deal of energy to a futile attempt at turning the "Cyclops" section of *Ulysses* into an opera. In other words, Antheil had almost accidentally joined a literary milieu, and become something of a bridge between the worlds of music and literature. In so doing, he left a paper trail of his creative rise and fall.

The letters to Pound are a motley collection of items both typed and handwritten, some both, some fragmentary, and most difficult to date reliably. Overadapting to his correspondent, Antheil sometimes imitated Pound's epistolary quirks, accents, hyperbola, and so on, occasionally even writing messages over each other, producing a pseudosynthetic cubist style not quite appropriate for the snorts about "psdo Klassmus," "Cubismus," and how "picabia's is still too Dada-Gaga." What appears to be page one of a fragmentary first letter also begins the record of Antheil's persistent habit of free-associating diseases with musical trends. He just *has* to inform Pound that the results of three recent clap tests have been uniformly negative, so that life below the belt can return to normal. He then passes quickly to how Stravinsky was "learning pseudo-classicism and going to write his next work like the II Violin Sonata," thus of course strongly implying that even in 1923 the Russian was following the path laid out by the American. His sense of priority knew few bounds: "Relache of Satie was even an attempt to follow the technic of II Violin Sonata—in every way." He was sure "a new swing to the extreme left seems indicated. All the little smug dada's who are now eating well and following the modes A LITTLE LATE will now be left high and dry for a LIT-TLE WHILE." Even Picasso had abandoned "Ps. Cl." for a "neue Cubismus." Antheil himself was serene at the vortex: "There seems to be a constant eye on me, who am hanging back and finishing my opera." Two pages of the letter are missing, but by page four he has already returned to the permanent flea in his ear: "*No one . . . can dare to accuse me of Strawinskyism after this. . . . I have not used the cramped slavic modes which today means Straw-insky.*" Pound had apparently suggested that his "next work will have to establish your position against Strawinsky," and Antheil was sure his "Mecanique" will leave his critics "ground out *flat.*" "*At any rate,* I know that I'm in the very front of the big swing soon coming, and the rest are now following me *if they admit it or not. I fought them all with their own weapons first.*"

Subsequent letters speak somewhat disconnectedly of Antheil's efforts to raise funds, especially from Natalie Clifford Barney; of the two operas, his *Cyclops* and Pound's *Le Testament,* which were both in progress and would be expensive to mount; of Olga Rudge, for whom Antheil wrote much of his chamber music; of H. H. Stucken-schmidt, "an elegant and intelligent German," and his loyal efforts to line up concert dates; of the *Xiliphony,* the working title of what became the *Ballet Mécanique:* "I GUARANTEE the biggest scandal of the day"; and sometimes of more mundane matters: "I seem clap-less. . . . I seem to be steering towards a nobler old age than was promised." He assured Pound that he was "spending all my spare money buying condoms and sticking them about in reserved places. My suits each contain one (I have two suits) while in my drawer lies a hyperdromic with a boxfull of anti-toxin."[12]

Yet even as Antheil itched and gave praise to the achievements of French medicine, Stravinsky was never far from his mind. Never all that interested in either the violin or the sonata form, Stravinsky should have been largely irrelevant to such concerns, but Antheil was no longer sensible on the subject. "The violin sonata [presumably no. 3, 1924] is wild. . . . The fiddle of the Tziganes, but it seems mostly like Holy Poland. A few of the new themes have a certain new shape that I think is totally new to *written* music." He thought it "barbaric, but not the barbarism of the first sonata which is often as not African (thus differing from Strawinsky, who is never African) nor has it the slightest barbarism of the Sacre du Printemps. . . . Not the least." The only influence he would admit here was that of Moussorgsky, and of Mongols barely Christianized. He neglected to add that another descendant of Mussorgsky was the ubiquitous Stravinsky.

Pound's side of this correspondence has not survived, but apparently he lacked a certain tact—a possibility no one would doubt for a second. The next letter in the Yale sequencing takes offense. "Please get me straight. This is the last time I am ever gona mention Strawinsky's name in my life in this connection. I AM NOT GONA REVISE THE 1ST SONATA. I NEVER SAID I WAS GONA CUT THE STRAWINSKY OUT OF IT." He was merely trying to clarify its texture. "STRAWINSKY COULD NOT HAVE WRITTEN THE FIRST SONATA IF HE TRIED." And furthermore: "HAS A SINGLE WORK OF STRAWINSKY ANY GUTS . . . ANYMORE??????? If you answer that question we will stop the discussion." But he just couldn't let go. "I AINT STRAWINSKY." No, he sure wasn't.[13]

Antheil scarcely seemed aware of it, but he was not quite so important in Pound's view of the world as he was in his own. Pound had long held ideas about the role of music in poetry, which he worked out as early as his Hamilton College days, when he studied the late medieval *canso,* and the works of a wide variety of Provençal and Italian poets, most obviously Dante. He had become a friend and self-styled manager of Katherine Ruth Heyman, a pianist of concert hall ability. He had informally studied the work of Arnold Dolmetsch, as that peripatetic Swiss restored or created harpsichords and clavichords and then sponsored appropriate performances, publishing *The Interpretation of the Music of the XVIIth and XVIIIth Centuries* (1915) along the way. Pound had even lived for several discontinuous months with the Franco–German pianist Walter Morse Rummel during visits to Paris between 1908 and 1916; Rummel was at that time an intimate of the circle around Claude Debussy. Pound could not carry a tune to save his life, but in his fragmentary way he had plenty of opportunity to pick up musical knowledge as it related to his primary interest in poetry.[14]

World War I had ended London's centrality in poetic creativity, and as Pound became increasingly discontented with the literary scene, he took up music with avocational enthusiasm. He began an opera, *Le Testament*, shortly before leaving for Paris toward the end of 1920. He floundered for awhile, but realized when he met Antheil in 1923 that he had found an ideal gofer, a surrogate son who was soon heading his letters "my ole Fadder" or close variations. If to Antheil Pound was a sympathetic ear who could help him raise money and get publicity, to Pound Antheil was an orchestrator and copyist who could make a poet's opera more than a quaint dream. This was the atmosphere in which Antheil tactfully included the part for drum in the Violin Sonata No. 2, so that Pound could "accompany" Olga Rudge on stage as well as off. Several memoirists have recalled Pound's enthusiastic thumping; more often he just turned pages, a "second fiddle" for a few special occasions in a life not noted for self-effacement.

As *Antheil and the Treatise on Harmony* (1924) hints strongly, Antheil took the place of Henri Gaudier-Brzeska in Pound's imagination. Gaudier was the gifted sculptor that Pound had placed at the creative vortex of London just before the war in which he had lost his life. Pound immortalized him in *Gaudier-Brzeska* (1916). By the 1920s Pound's interest in sculpture had waned just as his interest in music waxed, and Antheil's advent allowed him to integrate music into his sense of the avant-garde beyond anything that Heyman, Rummel, or Dolmetsch could have provided. But Pound was always literary in his chief focus, and modernist in his sense of both time and disciplinary boundaries—meaning essentially that he saw music, like sculpture and painting, as sources for poetic insight, fragments for a poet to re-arrange as free associations warranted.

Either as himself or as "William Atheling," Pound had long been arguing that "music and poetry had been in alliance in the twelfth century, that the divorce of the two arts had been to the advantage of neither, and that melodic invention declined simulta-neously and progressively with their divergence." As the "rhythms of poetry grew stupider," it became all the more necessary to use the sculpture of Gaudier and Brancusi, the painting of Picasso and Wyndham Lewis, to reinvigorate the language. Thus Antheil, who was "making his hearers increasingly aware of time-space, the di-visions of time-space." Pound had clearly been reading his mail, and was probably familiar as well with the published snippets of Antheil's ideas.[15]

At this point, however, the customary use of words that ce-mented the Antheil-Pound relationship caused trouble. They were used to extreme, blunt, casual conversation, and tossed-off letters in the same way. Pound habitually free-associated in prose, taking poetic license when it came to precision. He produced his critical pieces on Antheil in the same spirit, making no apparent effort to temper the phraseology, tighten the logic, or tone down the clever quips. To make matters worse, Pound put significant portions of his work in quotation marks, quoting from Antheil es-says, private letters, and plain chatter. Antheil was perfectly capa-ble of saying outrageous things, as many in Paris were discovering, but in cold print Pound presented him as a sort of idiot savant of musical innovation, shrewd about machines and possibly matters relating to time and space, capable as a pianist, but undisciplined, catty, and ill informed even about modernist music.

The Antheil of Pound's book accepted Satie "as a master," but denigrated Stravinsky as "nothing but a jolly Rossini." Debussy had the "soul of an ardent virgin, clear and sentimental implanted in great artistic nature"; but impressionism had better be left as "a term for painting alone." Les Six were "charming and fickle peo-ple. Everything they imitate with the utmost freshness and understanding." Bartók, while in some respects original, "has done much bird-stuffing with folksongs of Hungary." Schoenberg was a composer "whose musical machinery is based fundamentally upon Mendelssohn." At which point Pound adds in his own voice: "All of which appears to me to be very good sense." Speaking as a professional composer, R. Murray Schafer has insisted that despite the inadequacies of the remarks, the part of Pound's book devoted to the treatise on harmony was a "real achievement," with "a beautifully succinct and individualistic conception of the purpose and function of harmony." It ranked with Schoenberg's *Harmonielehre* (1911) and the work of Heinrich Schenker. That is a question best left to experts in the discipline. To nonmusicians, such judgments seemed at best irresponsible, acts of autointoxication rather than serious criticism. Antheil realized immediately that the book was a miscalculation, written more to advance Pound's ideas than Antheil's career. In a lovely example of memory repression, he even got the title wrong when he referred to the book in his memoirs, and insisted that "Ezra was never to have even the slightest idea of what I was really after in music."[16]

Restless, never able to find a real niche in Paris the way he had in London, Pound gradually moved to Rapallo in Italy, to remain on the periphery of modernism—at least to those who reject the notion that wherever Pound was, was the center of modernism. He made strategic trips back to Paris and was present at the creation of several modernist events, and no one ever entirely forgot him, but as the first jazz age drew to a close, Pound was becoming the author of the ongoing Cantos more than the editor in chief of English-language modernism. Actually in Paris, Antheil could take little advantage of his opportunities. As he continued to work on *Cyclops* and *Ballet Mécanique*, and to put down Stravinsky at every opportunity, what really comes through in his letters is the need for money. He wheedled more out of Mrs. Bok; he skillfully played on Robert McAlmon's guilty conscience about his marital endowment, and for good measure hit up McAlmon's mother-in-law, Lady Ellerman, along the way; he begged from Sylvia Beach,

Harriet Shaw Weaver, his parents, and even from Pound. He applied unsuccessfully for a Guggenheim. He needed to eat, print scores, produce pianola rolls, rent halls, and pay performers. Meanwhile, the clap returned; "I'm a living sewer."[17]

These were not the random flailings they sometimes seemed, for poverty, printing, and performance were intimately tied to publicity—and all were relevant to his daily shadowboxing with Stravinsky over who pioneered modernist piano techniques and deserved the credit for being most original. "I am hell-bent upon the production of my work, and to immediate publication," he wrote from Tunis. "If my piano sonatas had been printed a month or two after they were written, like Stravinsky's music is always, there wouldn't be any of this 'Noces' nonsense"—his usual refrain about any use of the percussive piano. The *Ballet Mécanique* was potentially even more important. "And the technic of my present works is complete and new, and I don't want to give it out until I can show up the thieves if necessary." He was still at it upon his return to Paris, and indeed such was his need to rewrite musical history that he soon broadened his claims: "I was one of the very first players in a jazz orchestra in America . . . a real Negro orchestra, where I was the only white. I almost invented the madder jazz, for our organization became the first famous one, and was extensively copied." He was, as well, "the first in America to draw attention to jazz as being the only folk music we had." But of course some unnamed "they" "swiped that idea and hopelessly muddled it." And he was off again about Les Six, and the ubiquitous Stravinsky. He would have been about seventeen, and living in Trenton, that creative hotbed of musical inspiration.[18]

Lessons come in the oddest ways, and the one everyone really seemed to have learned from the première of the *Rite of Spring* (1913) was that an audience riot was a highly useful advertising device. Antheil later bragged that he had acquired the habit of going around to some of his Central European concerts, especially during the German hyperinflation, and placing a highly visible pistol on the piano while he played to discourage too enthusiastic an audience response—and thus insuring an adequate level of anecdotage afterwards. Paris in 1923 was not that elemental in its expressions of disapproval, but Antheil could excite spectacle if anyone could. At his 4 October concert at the Théâtre de Champs-Elysées, for example, he had performed his "Sonata Sauvage," "Mechanisms," and the "Airplane Sonata" to an audience that included Pound, Joyce, Léger, Man Ray, and the Prince of Monaco. Georgette Leblanc had wanted to film a riot for inclusion in *L'Inhumaine*, on which she was then working, and Antheil provided the occasion for an incident that was literally planned, staged, and filmed. Satie reportedly applauded; Milhaud reportedly tried to discourage him. It hardly mattered. The music was somewhat secondary to the film, and both were news rather than art.[19]

As the *Ballet Mécanique* went through trial runs with reduced forces, Antheil amused himself with advertising ploys. One involving a sudden disappearance in Africa actually occurred, more or less. He decided that he would be off in the desert seeking out African rhythms for incorporation into his work, only to be taken prisoner by camel-driving seekers after ransom. He wanted newspaper headlines to read something like: "American Composer Menaced by Desert Tribes, No Trace Found of George Antheil." With the help of friends, chiefly Bravig Imbs at the *Tribune*, he began sending back quotable letters and telegrams, and suitable photographs. Imbs and the others planted the stories and talked them up, and wire services as far away as Chicago began to run stories, to the distress of his parents who were worried in Trenton. As the temperature of luridity rose, friends began dropping in on Sylvia Beach to find out the latest reports. He was about to be rescued by the Foreign Legion when a few editors smelled desert rats and slowed things down. In on the plot from the beginning, Beach finally ran out of patience with the ludicrousness of the whole thing, and cabled him: "FOR GOODNESS SAKE GEORGE COME BACK TO PARIS IMMEDIATELY AND DENY THIS IDIOTIC NEWSPAPER STORY LIONS ATE YOU IN AFRICA OR ELSE YOUR NAME WILL BE MUD FOREVER STOP

TIME IS OF ESSENCE STOP SYLVIA BEACH." He soon reappeared, more notorious than ever, more money came in from yet more patrons, and the "secret" remained one until Imbs cheerfully confessed all a decade later.[20]

The concert on 19 June 1923 was perhaps the closest Antheil ever came to equalling any success of Stravinsky's. Vladimir Golschmann, a man with "a matinee-idol face, lustrous black curls, a distinguished limp and considerable musical ability," had trouble even preparing the equipment. The score originally called for sixteen pianolas, and even with the aid of Virgil Thomson, Antheil could not get them coordinated. Printers sabotaged the advertising posters, making George a Francophile Georges, and only an accident prevented a very public misidentification. Moths put noticeable holes in the composer's best trousers, which only quick sewing by pianist Allen Tanner covered up. Finally, a frantic composer arrived to take his place in Beach's private box, "his hair slicked back so straight and shiny that he looked like a scared rabbit." Pound was much in evidence, "jumping up from his seat in the parterre like a Jack-in-the-box." T. S. Eliot, James Joyce, Nadia Boulanger, Serge Koussevitzky, Alfred A. Knopf, Marcel Duchamp, and Aaron Copland were among those scattered throughout the hall.

A painless Handel concerto grosso made little impression, and Antheil's own relatively innocuous *Symphony in Fa* mostly puzzled those who had been overprepared by the spurious advertising. Finally, Antheil himself appeared on the stage, giving directions for the now real pianos, reduced to five, and the small electric fans, which, with the help of an amplifier, would substitute for the airplane propeller that the score called for. Antheil himself sat down at one of the pianos, and the bedlam began. The audience was soon as noisy as the music, but Golschmann "continued to conduct imperturbably as though he were the dead Centre of a whirlpool." During a momentary lull, Pound jumped to his feet to shout, "Vous êtes tous des imbéciles!" among other things. Once the loudspeaker became functional, the crowd was overpowered, and one "fat bald old gentleman" took out his umbrella and raised it as if to ward off the lashing storm. Sympathetic fellow sufferers quickly followed suit, until the theater seemed full of "black mushrooms." All in all, it was a great success, as an event if not as a creative achievement. A month later, with suitable modifications in scoring, Golschmann led both a private performance at the home of Mrs. Valentine Gross (16 July, 1926) and a public one the next day at the Comédie des Champs-Elysées. With customary modesty, Antheil informed Mrs. Bok that he had become "easily the leading young composer of Paris."[21]

Taking these and other performances into account, Pound wrote a summary judgment of Antheil's entire career. He recalled the conversations they had shared, concerning the "tuning up" of whole cities and the use of silences of up to twenty minutes long. These ideas may have been "jejune" but Pound said he had no regrets about "any comparison of Antheil and Stravinsky that I then made in the former's favour." The *Ballet Mécanique* permitted a listener to imagine "the possibility of organising the sounds of a factory let us say of boiler-plate or any other clangorous noisiness, the actual sounds of the labour, the various tones of the grindings." Antheil had given his audience "the chance, a mode, a music that no mere loudness can obliterate," one that could serve "as the primitive chantey for rowing, for hauling on cables." By inevitable comparison, "'Noces' falls to pieces, after the Ballet it sounds like a few scraps of Wagner, a Russian chorale (quite good) a few scraps of Chopin, a few high notes 'pianolistic.'" He approved the liberation of the pianola, and the use of "longer durations than any other musician has ever attempted to use."[22]

In actuality, Pound was conveying only a small part of what Antheil was trying to do. In a document signed "Paris 1925 (Mai)" and included in the Pound papers so presumably sent to him for his use in writing up criticism, Antheil had laid out "MY BALLET MECANIQUE: WHAT IT MEANS": "My Ballet Mecanique is the new FOURTH DIMENSION of music . . . the first piece of music that has been composed OUT OF and FOR machines, ON

EARTH." It "has found the best forms and materials lying inert in a medium that AS A MEDIUM is mathematically certain of becoming the greatest moving factor of the music of future generations." He was sure he had pioneered "a form that is NOT TONAL." It took its inspiration from "the new fourth-dimensional phenomena wherein TIME FUNCTIONING IN MUSIC DIFFERS FROM ORDINARY TIME and the series of deductive and also purely physical phenomena that follow it." The ballet was thus "the first TIME-FORM on earth." It "is of no kind of tonality at all. It has nothing to do with tonality. It is made of time and sound . . . the two materials, FUNDAMENTAL materials, that music is made of. All else is literary association."

He was dismissive of all the experimentation going on in Vienna. "I am certain that the people who have decided that they can evolve new forms out of the tonal, will find that Beethoven, who did likewise, has finished their work for them long ago. The innocents believe that in the difference between tonality and atonality lies the phenomena out of which the new forms will be created." He, by contrast, was "too sophisticated to try to finish that which has been absolutely finished by greater and kinder talents before me. And with one stroke is all of the modern Central European music eliminated for me." Points west, whether in France or in America, were no better. The new music of Paris or New York "relies mainly upon its charm (as Strawinsky tells me he always and fundamentally searches) and its intelligence in clearing away the mass of music rubbish that accumulated after Wagner," which was essentially "archivistic," was "even less interesting to me."

His sense of form had an entirely different source for inspiration: "TIME. Is not TIME, and TIME ALONE the SOLE canvas of music? Notes, vibrations, and sound are merely our drawing pencils . . . our paint-box. Can you dare to deny that TIME is the sole canvas of music?" He then returned with marvellous illogic, to the industrial analogies he so loved: "The Ballet Mecanique is the first piece IN THE WORLD to be conceived in one piece without interruption, like a solid shaft of steel." He seemed determined to confuse the composer's experience with the listener's, and composition with experience. "I am now writing a work which is four hours long and without interruption or the break of a second's time. After that I shall write one which is ten hours long." He had "started with mechanism and pieces that were only a minute long. Even these produced hysteria and riots. The time was too short, and the nuclei too explosive. A few concerts throughout Europe and I retired to my laboratory." Now he was prepared to make the big leap. "Now I hope to present you not with an explosion, but the FOURTH DIMENSION . . . THE FIRST PHYSICAL REALIZATION OF THE FOURTH DIMENSION. I am not presenting you with an abstraction. I am presenting you with a PHYSICALITY LIKE SEXUAL INTERCOURSE."[23]

Well, perhaps. Creative people make use of the oddest ideas. Antheil is still shadowboxing with Stravinsky, keeping his eye on Schoenberg, and tossing ideas at Les Six. He sounds like a slightly obsessed Duchamp, or perhaps a Man Ray manqué. The work, although it has its merits, has proved about as durable as Alexander Mossolov's *Iron Foundry* (1927) and rather less so than Satie's *Parade*. It does look forward in a few moments to John Cage, but by the time Cage appeared Antheil was writing film music and in full retreat from recognizable modernism.

Built in about equal measure of precosity, energy, and chutzpah, Antheil's reputation began to slip almost as soon as it became visible. As it did so, Antheil took a parting bow at what for most nonmusicians was becoming the dominant popular achievement of the postwar years, jazz. For someone capable of claiming to have "almost invented the madder jazz" as a teenager, and for whom time itself amounted to an obsession, Antheil remained curiously inept in practice. Like Stravinsky, he could recognize the technical importance of the new music, he just couldn't do it himself. He put elements recognizable as jazzy in the violin sonatas, but really only made one serious attempt at a full-length work. Hoping to repeat his success with *Rhapsody in Blue*, bandleader

Paul Whiteman commissioned *A Jazz Symphony* for a 28 December, 1925, concert. Sandwiching his work somehow between the time/space experiments of the *Ballet* and the neoclassicism of the *Symphony in Fa*, Antheil churned out the work on the grounds that such an opportunity was one "every composer who calls himself an American should take." He took to referring to it as a "superjazz" piece, "which even Gershwin's best friends assure me will put Gershwin in the shade." Knowing Mrs. Bok to be conservative on matters of taste and decorum, however, he went on to assure her that, secretly, he hated the "America of today. I hate 'jazz'; my infatuation with it belongs to a period long past in my musical development."[24]

It is difficult to recapture the original quality of this work, as with so many others of Antheil's compositions, since current recordings almost always use revised, shortened, and thinned versions. In one form or another, the *Jazz Symphony* has won the approval of authorities as diverse as Virgil Thomson and Gunther Schuller, and was recorded in the 1990s by Maurice Peress. But at the time, it was not what Whiteman had had in mind. Contrary to the account in Antheil's biography, he completed the work with his usual manic energy between 6 October and 2 November, 1925; although "absolutely a crackerjack in the line of jazz," it came back almost by return ship: "they no sooner got, than they sent right back. I don't know yet what their reason is," he fumed to Pound. "I just think the music (which is absolutely possible for their orchestra) just knocked 'em flat, bug-eyed, and nutty. They aint never seen nothing like that before, and hope they never will again." He snorted at the idea of "serious" jazz, and here he was probably correct—Paul Whiteman had no taste for serious art music, and his attention span was about that of a three-minute Gershwin tune to which paying customers could dance. "I guess that I was rather gullible to think my music would slip over into America so easily. Why it took Strawinsky 13 years!!!"[25]

Such a setback looms more ominously now than it did at the time. Paris remained oblivious to Paul Whiteman and pleasantly outraged at what it took to be Antheil's main thrust, the time-space, percussive experiments of *Ballet Mécanique* and the sonatas for violin and piano. Outwardly confidant that he was a composer with a major future, Antheil prepared to storm New York City. With something bordering on sheer childish perversity, he behaved as if to alienate those in Paris to whom he owed the most. To Pound, he complained repeatedly that Olga Rudge was not up to the demands of the concert hall. She preferred to play a "stunt social program" rather than practice enough to perform his works properly, and even when she proved capable of playing well in private was prone to "nervousness" in the concert hall. Intimately involved with the violinist, who had borne him a daughter on 9 July, 1925, the poet apparently remonstrated in a lost letter. Antheil backed off a bit, but couldn't stop. "Olga's got the kind of violin tone which I hev 'woven' several sonatas around. I hev told so many people politically that Olga is the seventh gate of violin playing that Olga doesn't take the trouble (so it seems TO ME) with *my* violin music that she did ONCT!" As if to will a change in her attitude, he then put into caps: "SHE WILL PLAY BETTER THE NEXT snate I am now planning to write for her." He then swore and shifted direction again. "They's no use telling people they're doing swell when they're just so cockeyed sure they know an old piece that they forget it. You got snap 'em back into the pace." Of course, he realized he wouldn't "find another fiddler like Olga in a hurry." No, he wouldn't, nor a friend like Pound, either.[26]

Having alienated Pound and Rudge, he then turned on his wealthy diplomatic sponsor, Mrs. Gross, displaying more than a little of the anti-Semitism and homophobia that Hemingway had shown in his dealings with Gertrude Stein and Alice B. Toklas. While Antheil had been licking his wounds and recovering his health in Tunis during the summer of 1926, "a New York Jewess, one Bernardine Szold, a really filthy specimen, got into the good graces of Mrs. Gross" and flattered her way to influence. Szold was a friend of Glenway Wescott and his circle of gay friends, and she persuaded Gross to shift her charitable sponsorship from music to painting and writing. Although she had already been quite generous to Antheil, and he still had eight hundred dollars coming to him from a previous commitment, he petitioned her to finance his "autumn orchestral concert." "She refused pleading economy." He received her negative answer on the same day that he read in another source that she "had bought the Empress Katherine of Russia's emeralds." Surely if she could afford jewels she could afford George, but that news plus the news about "that God-be-bitched-and-damed jewess Szold . . . the infernal slut" sent him through the ceiling.

Tactful as ever, he "wrote Mrs. Gross a letter mentioning the Emeralds, and the Szold plans in such a way that Mrs. G. suddenly got off everybody, including myself and especially Szold." His letter "dwelt upon the necessity of a sense of hierarchy in the arts among patrons—lacking which they can lose their usefulness just as a bank that makes bad investments." "Shocked" and "hurt" by the letter, Antheil had learned from a third party, she never answered. He took solace from hearing as well that he had ruined "the Bernardinian plans" to subvert Wescott and his group. Despite his petulance, Gross persisted in treating Antheil generously. "But Mrs. Gross is continuing to heap coals of fire upon my head by continuing the $100 per. Silly woman! In all cases, if she thinks it over again and stops it, I don't especially care." It was such a comfort to curse all the way to the bank. He was still ranting several weeks later.[27]

Moving about, from Paris to Tunis to Chamonix to Budapest, he may simply have felt that his Paris phase had ended and that a few burned bridges were in order, but to offend one's most eminent friend, ablest interpreter, and a major subsidizer all in less than a year took genuine obtuseness. All but oblivious, Antheil still was sure Pound was devoted to his every creative whim and took care to keep the poet posted. As 1926 drew to a close, he had completed sketches for "a new neo-classic piano concerto" and was preparing to abandon that style *"forever."* He was sure he had "done two much better works in it than Strawinsky, who still plods along in it." He was positive that "all of the young musicians, including Les Six, and the still younger school of Frenchmen recognise this." The world, after all, "is just now YAPPING for a bomb, and its coming—and they are *watching* me. Keep you eyes open my direction." The piano concerto, the *Sinfonietta*, and the *Symphony in Fa* "are designed, to swip Strawinsky's present admirers over to me, and at the same time rake me in a little necessary coin." He would then work up a manifesto about the new direction his music would be taking, presumably toward the opera with *Cyclops* as the first step. "I've really a gigantic audience now."[28]

This state of autointoxication lasted until he arrived in New York City for the 10 April, 1927, première of *Ballet Mécanique*, an event with rather a complex history of its own. Aaron Copland had gone to a party at the apartment of theater promoter Donald Friede, and at some point had played an excerpt from Antheil's *Sonata Sauvage*—that had been printed in *This Quarter*. Lewis Galantière, as familiar as Copland with Paris reputations, had suggested that Friede bring the composer over and capitalize on the notoriety of *Ballet Mécanique* by sponsoring it in New York. He had cabled into the dark, otherwise Shakespeare and Company, offering Antheil all the profits from a concert devoted entirely to his music. All Friede had wanted was "the fun and glory." Three days later he received an acceptance from Budapest.

Friede booked Carnegie Hall, arranged transportation, and consulted friends. One interested the Baldwin Piano Company in helping to sponsor the ten pianos the score then called for in exchange for the usual "Baldwin Pianos used exclusively" logo, and got Welte-Mignon to supply a modified player piano, the sole survivor of the sixteen the early version of the score called for. Letters poured in from the composer, from Pound, and from others, usually making unintelligible or unusable suggestions. For the program as it evolved—a string quartet, the second sonata for violin, piano and drum, the *Jazz Symphony*, and the *Ballet Mécanique*—they would need six xylophones, two bass drums, electrical bells, a wind machine, and a fire siren, not to mention ten pianists and more conventional instruments. Eugene Goossens agreed to conduct the *Ballet Mécanique,* and Copland himself to play a piano. Paul Whiteman again refused to have anything to do with the symphony, but then W. C. Handy agreed to lead it. While these events were unfolding, Joseph Mullen designed backdrops: one a black couple doing a suggestive Charleston for the symphony; the other "practically a cyclorama with a futuristic city of skyscrapers as a background; and in the foreground a series of enormous noise-making machines: whistles, riveting machines, airplane propellers, spark plugs, excavating machines."

Things slowly disintegrated. The xylophonists and drummers had one rehearsal in Horace Liveright's apartment, with Antheil trying to operate a player piano, humming the missing parts as best he could. Union musicians, rarely the soul of charm in New York under the best of circumstances, thought the music a hoax and said so, loudly. Tenants in the building complained. A pane of glass crashed to the courtyard during the final delirious ending. A subsequent full rehearsal at the huge Welte-Mignon studios went better under Goossens's competent direction, but then Handy proved totally unable to understand his score, and rehearsals of the symphony degenerated into aimless fiasco. It took roughly twenty-five rehearsals under his replacement Allie Ross, usually at the luxurious Harlem home of Alelia Walker, before it began to sound the way the composer thought he had written it. As publicity escalated and parties multiplied, printers greatly overprinted the number of tickets. Expenses rose, but even a hall packed to suffocation could not have repaid them.

On the night of the performance, only the symphony went well. The two chamber works were lost in the vast hall. Then it turned out that the space available on the stage was not really adequate, and it had to be set up in full view of the intermission crowd, a spectacle that seemed to amuse everyone and prepare them more to laugh than to experience art. As the piece unfolded, the wind machine went on, its propeller aimed at about the eleventh row of the orchestra seats. As it reached excessively full power, women wearing hats had to hang onto them, some with both hands. One old gentleman tied a handkerchief to his cane and waved it wildly as if to signal surrender. Many laughed; some left. It then came time for the fire siren, recently borrowed from a small New Jersey fire station, but never tested in an actual performance. Goossens cued, a man cranked, but no sound came forth. The man cranked more and more frantically, to no avail. The moment passed, the ballet ended, and the man quit, disgusted. Then, as first Goossens and then Antheil took their bows, "it reached its full force." Everyone had forgotten that "a fire siren does not start making any sound until it has been energetically cranked for almost a full minute"; and that "it does not stop shrieking simply because you stop cranking." Its wailing covered the sound of the audience leaving, and at least in New York City they would never return. When Mrs. Bok heard about it, she was horrified.[29]

"Heartsick and broke," Antheil found upon his return that "Paris too had changed. Not only to me. It was less friendly to all Americans." Even simple tolerance for the new and foreign had moved: "Whatever else had been new and amazing in old Paris now migrated to Germany." Stravinsky was working on *Oedipus Rex;* indeed, everyone seemed suddenly drawn to opera. "I had no knowledge of opera construction whatsoever." But ignorance had never slowed him down before and it didn't now. He began *Transatlantic,* a new form, in a new country, in a new age. But Stravinsky's monocle continued to glare over his shoulder.[30]

PART FOUR

THE VARIETIES OF

RELIGIOUS EXPERIENCE

TWELVE

JEAN TOOMER'S QUEST FOR COSMIC CONSCIOUSNESS

The conventional history of the 1920s, jazz age or not, rarely gives much serious consideration to religious experiences. Billy Sunday might thunder on in his ill-mannered way; Prohibition enforcement officers might do what they could to impose the last thirsty gasp of progressive moralism on a contemptuous citizenry; but the prevailing image remains a synthesis of the satirical implications of Sinclair Lewis's *Elmer Gantry* (1927) and the sarcastic contempt of almost any screed by H. L. Mencken. God might not be dead in the boondocks, but he no longer seemed viable in most intellectually respectable venues.

This picture is a false one in many ways. Conventional institutional religion was certainly in disrepute in many circles, but much of the religious energy of Americans has always expressed itself in fringe groups and solitary mystical epiphanies. Among American modernists in the first jazz age, religion remains the forgotten topic, duly noted in study after study but rarely seeming central either to the lives or the art of those involved. Religious visions obsessed several figures to such an extent that they effectively ended creative capacity. They surface as clouds in photography or color relationships in painting, conveying the nature behind the flower or the power inherent in the sea. Exotic races, especially the black and Native American, came to stand as examples of either moral purity or primitive force. Numerous poems and musical compositions are incomprehensible without some knowledge of the beliefs of their creators. In at least one area, architecture, the creative product was negligible even as architects pursued higher levels of consciousness and influenced their friends to rethink the fourth dimension.[1]

The rapid metamorphosis of Jean Toomer provides the best introduction to the problem. At the time he was writing *Cane* (1923), he was all but inseparable from Waldo Frank, in close contact with Paul Rosenfeld, Sherwood Anderson, and Hart Crane, and a friendly visitor to the houses of Alfred Stieglitz and the salon of Lola Ridge, then the gathering spot of choice for Malcolm Cowley, Kenneth Burke, and the younger literary set. On one occasion, Toomer even moved into the spare room of editor Gorham Munson, and thus lived for awhile in the very vortex of modernism during the first jazz age. His book won praise and respectable sales, and he seemed the preeminent experimental writer of both prose and poetry to have a significant amount of black blood. Yet instead of enjoying his achievement and perhaps starting another book, he felt exhausted and depressed and began desperately exploring religious texts.

Even as a high school student, Toomer had displayed an obsessive need for rigid frames. Perhaps because he had never enjoyed stability of identity in home, place, or racial heritage, he insisted on having it in literature. Disliking poetry as too vague and incoherent, he "liked composition and rhetoric, rules and structure and order. The business of drilling and discipline was attractive to him," his biographers have noted. When his physical condition seemed subpar to him, he bought Bernarr MacFadden's *Encyclopedia of Health and Physical Culture* and followed its regimen of weightlifting, dieting, and the pursuit of a physique that resembled that of a Greek statue. In need of a vision of society, he absorbed socialist dogma to fend off capitalist uncertainties. When he listened to Clarence Darrow and read Ernst Haeckel, he found their atheism convincing but infinitely depressing. A world without God's ordering hand made him feel like a man about to be hanged. "For several days I was so stunned and broken that I could hardly do more than lay on my bed in a darkened room and feel I was dying. . . . In truth, I did not want to live."[2]

The external man found solace in the arms of Margaret Naumburg, then in the process of separating from and finally divorcing Waldo Frank; the internal man and woman both found another variety of oneness in the *Tertium Organum* of P. D. Ouspensky, which had appeared first in English in 1920 and was rapidly displacing Wassily Kandinsky's *On the Spiritual in Art* as the vade mecum of artists who felt the world too cold to bear. Hart Crane was perhaps the first in the circle to find it, and was using its vocabulary in his letters by February 1923, although it clearly built on religious attitudes in place by the summer of 1918. He passed it on to Gorham Munson and his wife, dancer Elizabeth Delza, and they passed it to Toomer, who read it in December, 1923, in the midst of his postpartum depression over *Cane*.

Through Kandinsky, Max Weber, and Marcel Duchamp, ideas of a fourth dimension of reality had been in the air — and in *Camera Work* — for more than a decade, but artists of the word were slower than those of the eye to absorb them. To Ouspensky, human beings had three levels of perception in their normal lives: sensation, representation, and concept. But only mystics knew moments at least of a fourth, a noumenal world beyond time and space. Ouspensky urged his followers to cultivate knowledge of a "cosmic consciousness" where opposites would find unity, conventional logic would lack validity, and the living and the dead communicate. Such a vision would by implication transcend racial barriers as well, and Toomer was still in turmoil about whether he was a Negro author, or more accurately the American author of a book that peered behind the veil concealing black America from white eyes. Toomer also needed a religious structure that would transcend the boundaries of marriage and friendship, and his religious libido marched hand in hand with his physical one. No wonder he had no hand left with which to write. "I have given up art," he announced to Munson the next summer, "to undertake the Gurdjieff discipline."[3]

Ouspensky had originally been a follower of Georges I. Gurdjieff, but the two had drifted apart and were not working together at this time. In 1922, Gurdjieff had purchased the Château du Prieuré, an unused structure near the Château du Fontainebleau, not far from Paris. There he established the Institute for the Harmonious Development of Man, where he proved capable of structuring the physical and emotional lives of up to two hundred visitors in need of wholeness and transcendence. He lectured, he played the harmonium, he wrote books, and became the guru of choice for an odd assortment of creative people, especially writers. Katharine Mansfield was only the best known, seeking the Institute out as a sort of non-Catholic Lourdes as her tuberculosis became terminal. No miracle ensued.

As the Institute gained popularity, Gurdjieff sent Alfred Orage to America to gain publicity, converts, and funds. A legitimate literary intellectual with many American contacts through his work on the *New Age* in London before the war, Orage seemed ideal to work through the *Little Review* and the *New Republic* sets and get writers up for the arrival of Gurdjieff himself. He did very well. The ceremonial dances, gymnastics, costumes, and the rest provided a rather exotic show, with names like "The Obligations," "The Stop," and "The Initiation of the Priestess," and for a former pupil of Bernarr MacFadden, the sight of well-trained containers of three dimensions boded well for their ideas of a fourth. Toomer and Margaret Naumburg, approaching the most sexually intense few months of their relationship, went together early in 1924. He never forgot his first impression of Gurdjieff himself. His head shaved, his eyes dark, his nose "finely moulded and almost delicate in comparison to the strong jaw," he also sported a "mustache, most unusual and large, curling down and sweeping up to the tips." Dressed in a tuxedo, he moved like a powerful animal; "there was something panther-like about him." Toomer was in ecstasy, stayed to the end of a long evening, and returned another night with Crane and the Munsons. They too were impressed. Here was a structure that could replace Christianity, bodybuilding, and socialism, and make the despair of atheism a repressed memory.[4]

Converts are notoriously zealous, and Toomer was a classic case. He threw himself into the regime and helped spread the word. Like a medieval crusader obsessed by a distant Holy Land, he could not rest until he could head for Paris and his own version of psychological liberation. He went in July 1924 with virtually no knowledge of the French language or geography; when he arrived he could not even convey his destination to a taxi driver. He could hardly have picked a worse time: Gurdjieff was in the hospital in serious condition after a car wreck. In culture shock in two ways, Toomer insensibly fell into the laborious routines of the Prieuré, his muscles protesting every demand he made on them. He became, by his own account, inarticulate, cheering up only slightly as Gurdjieff unexpectedly recovered from a severe concussion. Toomer then faced another blow: Gurdjieff decided to close the Institute officially, and merely make the place a home in which he could meditate and write. He might receive visitors and contributions, but would not be running a holistic training institute. Toomer returned home in late October and spent the next year and a half as a missionary for the new faith in New York City.[5]

Orage was already in New York, and Toomer was soon working with him as well as taking detailed notes like a dutiful undergraduate. The Orage technique was to form cells of six to ten people and then hold regular meetings. The most famous now centered on Jane Heap, an editor of the *Little Review;* it included architect Hugh Ferriss and hostess Mabel Dodge Luhan. She threw herself into this new enthusiasm with characteristic panache and financing, even offering $15,000 to help the faith get a toehold in Taos, where she usually lived with her fourth husband, Tony Luhan, a Native American who sometimes endured the meetings with her, silently. Orage made Toomer his chief negotiator on that deal, and it was all the handsome convert could do to evade her physical demands when he traveled to Taos to work out details during the

Christmas season of 1925. She paid, but the money later caused a rift between the hardworking but impoverished Toomer and the rather profligate guru.[6]

Yet another group has long had a minor place in literary history because Langston Hughes devoted a few sardonic paragraphs to it in his autobiography. Orage determined to form a beachhead in Harlem by annexing key black writers and thus gaining not only publicity but also proving that Gurdjieff's teaching was one way of transcending American racism. Thus even as Toomer was beginning to deny that he was black at all, he was trying to convert the budding Harlem renaissance to the cosmic consciousness: Wallace Thurman, Nella Larsen, and Dorothy Peterson were among the writers who attended, and Aaron Douglas among the painters. But as Hughes noted, "the trouble with such a life-pattern in Harlem was that practically everybody had to work all day to make a living, and the cult of Gurdjieff demanded not only study and application, but a large amount of inner observation and silent concentration as well." Anyone who got seriously involved might lose his job, and so Harlem's "advance toward cosmic consciousness was slow," and its "hope of achieving awareness distant indeed." Hughes feared, through a raised eyebrow, that "very few there have evolved souls."[7]

In *The Varieties of Religious Experience*, William James made a classic analysis of extreme religious beliefs and their impact on a wide variety of individuals including his father and himself. In *Tertium Organum*, Ouspensky quoted James, as well as such kindred writers as Plotinus and Jakob Boehme, and it was probably only a matter of time and occasion before Toomer's yearnings followed the established pattern. It finally happened one "April evening in 1926," on the platform of the elevated railway at 66th Street. He felt "a mysterious working in my depths," and as if he were "being taken apart, unmeshed and remeshed." He knew himself to be "as if decentered," his body and life "in the power of a Power." His mind seemed to leave his body and to experience "Grace." He became free: "Liberation is the exact term. I was being freed from my ego-prison."[8]

As soon as he could digest the experience he packed and headed for Fontainebleau, arriving 29 May, 1926. He spent the summer with his guru, and when he left in October he had a commission to found a center for the faith in Chicago. He arrived there in November and did in fact establish one of the crucial outposts. His literary friendships lapsed, even with true believers like Waldo Frank, Gorham Munson, and Hart Crane. Over the next decade he would write prolificly, but to no effect. He had been able to evoke the varieties of the black experience but became a garrulous bore on anything touching religion.

THIRTEEN

WALLACE STEVENS AND THE
SATISFACTIONS OF BELIEF

Georges I. Gurdjieff was fond of speaking of man as a plural being. He insisted that each human was not a single "I" but rather a
multiple of "I's" even into the hundreds and thousands. A physical body and a single name implied a unity that was spurious. A
book like *Cane*, with its multiplicity of unrelated characters, its geographical shifts, and its mixture of genres, seems implicitly to assume this, although Gurdjieffian ideas had no known effect on its
composition. With Wallace Stevens, this multiple sense of self
contributed in a basic way to the structure of his best poetry. The
poet never speaks directly for himself, but rather implies his
stance in the distance between multiple speakers. A reader has to
locate himself as well as "the poet" in some act of abstracting
meaning from the discordances of speech, genres, attitudes, and
ideas. One reason for the appeal of a guru like Gurdjieff was that
he formulated and charismatically presented something artists
were already doing. Indeed, although Stevens seems to have done
major work of this kind by 1923, he only began phrasing the prose
implications of his achievements over a decade later.[1]

Unlike Toomer, who only began the pieces that made up *Cane*
in about 1918, Stevens was an accomplished modernist when the
first jazz age began. A Harvard friend of Walter Arensberg, Stevens
had been a regular visitor to the famous salon where Walter and his
pianist wife Lou entertained the likes of Marcel Duchamp, Man
Ray, William Carlos Williams, and Edgard Varèse. Like modernists

in painting and photography, Stevens focused his aesthetic energies on the relation of subject to object, of the imagination to reality, of surface to depth. Neither clear nor consistent before the mid-1930s, Stevens held deeply conflicting emotions towards religious questions. He seemed not to believe in God, nor wish to join any established church, yet urged his fiancée to believe and attend, and entertained a deep respect for religious attitudes toward nature and order in the universe. Alternately disciplined and decadent, devoted to selling insurance by day and writing poetry by night, he held religious ideas in tension as well, producing poetry whose conflicting voices echoed his own as well as his age's inability to settle any important question with finality.

Before 1917, Stevens had completed that great masterpiece of early American modernism, "Sunday Morning," as well as such enduring works as "Peter Quince at the Clavier" and "Disillusionment of Ten O'Clock." He knew ragtime, cubism, pragmatism, and modernist drama. But he was a picker and a chooser, rejecting imagism, for example, for advocating the notion that all objects were equal. Having assimilated the stream of consciousness long ago, he had no trouble hearing music as an evoker of memory or assuming with Carl Jung the truths of atavism and archetype. But he seemed too aesthetic, too detached to many of his friends. Since he sold insurance and was a master of the arcane subject of surety bonding, this was an odd misjudgment; only Dr. William Carlos Williams could possibly have been more "hands on" to the world than Wallace Stevens. But two events conspired to make the situation seem even more serious: in May 1916 he moved permanently to Hartford to join the home office of Hartford Accident and Indemnity Company; and in April 1917 America entered World War I.[2]

Stevens had long been an economic realist. He realized as a college student that to enjoy the kind of artistic, imaginative freedom that he required, he would have to have a vocational anchor. He wanted the money that would supply the rich food, the big cigars, and the pitchers of martinis that all contributed to his ample size, not to mention chronic health problems. But he thought his job far more than that. It required discipline, it imposed order, it matched cause and effect in a world that often did not seem to. Like Arensberg in his love of literary cryptograms or the solving of chess problems, Stevens thought of insurance law as the solving of puzzles—mental exercises in the world of "as if," the phrase Hans Vaihinger was imposing on the world of philosophy. He took to work like an addict might take to the solving of crossword puzzles, as a relaxing warm-up before the real game of the day. Besides, company business kept him traveling, in style, to places he never would otherwise have seen. Like subject and object, business and poetry had a symbiotic relationship not always evident to outsiders, and certainly not to most poets and insurance salesmen.[3]

In terms of geography, the removal to Hartford presented both problems and solutions. By comparison to New York City, Hartford was culturally comatose. It had a good college and many well-educated people, but it could never supply the concerts, the art galleries, the dramas of the big city. The Wadsworth Atheneum, while admirable in its way, was not the Met. Yet Stevens needed a certain distance and detachment in order to function. He still had many friends in New York and visited regularly. He claimed that all his life he wanted to go to Paris, but never did even though he could well have afforded it. Instead, he kept up a large correspondence, often with people he had never met, or only met once or twice in a formal way. Robert McAlmon, for example, conveyed the minutiae of Parisian life, while Alice Corbin Henderson filled him in on Santa Fe. He preferred mental journeys to physical ones, business trips to aesthetic ones. He made his own world—it seemed to feature exotic parrots able to speak French—and it suited him. Literally.

The war was another matter. Appearances to the contrary notwithstanding, "Stevens began his career as a war poet," one of his best critics has recently noted, and he's right.[4] The war spelled an end to many vaguely modernist vogues, most obviously aesthetic decadence. Stevens was sometimes relatively straightforward about this, as in "The Death of a Soldier," where he effectively integrates finality and movement: "Death is absolute and without memorial, / As in a season of autumn, / When the wind stops, / . . . and, over the heavens, / The clouds go, nevertheless, / In their direction" (*CP*, 97). In the very next poem, "Negation," war as a specific subject is gone but the world that remains seems about the same. "The creator too is blind, / Struggling toward his harmonious whole," an "Incapable master of all force." As one who firmly disapproved of President Woodrow Wilson's military and diplomatic proclivities, Stevens seems to conflate the Presbyterian and the cosmos: "Too vague idealist, overwhelmed? By an afflatus that persists." People come, people go. If it all seems to mean anything, it isn't obvious. This is a world beyond Darwin, moving but not evolving, chilling even when the sun is out.

Overt in many poems, most obviously in "Lettres d'un Soldat" (1914–15)[5] (*OP*, 29–36), war becomes the absent presence in many poems that outwardly have nothing to do with war and that do not take place in France or French. The pervasiveness of death, the psychological difficulty of internalizing its meaning, create the need for distance. The writing of a poem was one way to control the emotions regarding the subject, art supplying the satisfactions that religion had once provided, but nonpoets had to seek less subtle means. In parallel circumstances, Jelly Roll Morton has described black attitudes toward the laying out of a corpse in one room, as the living enjoyed a rare feast in the next. Funereal jazz replicated this, with the slow cortege marching to the gravesite and the joyous saints marching out, the feet of those still living presumably signifying the direction of the feet of the departed. Sadness at death, joy at resurrection, the emotions went together, for life must go on and better to go on in the most affirmative way possible.

However different he might look from Morton—the mind boggles at the stretch required by such comparison—Stevens was in tune with the age. War merely supplied a public metaphor for the private indignity; the black community had been at war a lot longer than the U.S. Army. The now-famous poem in this context is of course "The Emperor of Ice-Cream" (1922), with its "roller of big cigars" whipping up "in kitchen cups concupiscent curds," the successive "c" sounds providing a quasi-jazz beat to the voice as to the activity. Food and tobacco were reasons for living, and took the mind off more distressing topics. The use of "wenches" and "boys" establishes a lower class milieu, as do the "flowers in last month's newspapers" rather than being attractively arranged. The moment will pass as truly as the whole of a human life. As the ice cream drips into a less appealing form, mourners in the next room take out a "sheet / On which she embroidered fantails once" to cover the body. But death is never elegant. "If her horny feet protrude, they come / To show how cold she is, and dumb." Flux is the law and this too shall pass. "The only emperor is the emperor of ice-cream" (*CP*, 64).[6]

Like many subsequent critics, Stevens often denigrated the urge to state in clear prose what a poem seemed to mean in its evocative allusions. Poems were and did, they did not mean. This position is perfectly correct, but not applicable to poets; poets intend and assume things like everyone else. The questions in this context were: What was the nature of Stevens's insight into himself and his age? In what forms did he best express his insights?

No final answers to such questions are possible for poets, musicians, painters, or other artists who choose to innovate in unscientific and unphilosophical areas. You cannot sensibly measure ice cream with a ruler. But two works effectively frame the first jazz age as Stevens experienced it, and a look at their implications, if not their meaning, provides a riff to underlay any analysis of more prosaic citizens.

In 1916/17, Stevens seriously experimented with dramatic form, exploring both the use of poetry in drama and, more fruitfully, the use of drama in poetry. In the two generations before his own, Henry James had been only the best known of the artists who ab-

sorbed the works of Ibsen, Strindberg, or Mallarmé in efforts to
add elements of the drama to their extended fictions. These might
include new subject matter, new ideas about God, science, disease, or moral corruption, new types of characters, or, most subtly,
the sense of dramatic relationships obtainable through dialogue or
whatever words might cover its extensions: trialogue, quadrologue,
and so on. Stevens's own generation went even farther, looking
into the "new theater" or the "unstage-like play" of Yeats or Gordon Craig. Such efforts were almost always unsuccessful as plays,
but knowledge of them often illuminates the more important poetry that followed.

At first, the idea of drama seemed fruitful as drama. *Three Travelers Watch a Sunrise* won the Players' Producing Company Prize
for a one-act play in verse and appeared in print in the July 1916,
issue of *Poetry*. The work so intrigued the director of the Wisconsin Players, Laura Sherry, that she commissioned a second; he
sent both *Carlos Among the Candles* and *Bowl, Cat and Broomstick*,
and she put them on in New York at the Neighborhood Playhouse
during October 1917. Both sets and performances were unimpres-
sive and conveyed to Stevens the depressing news that he was
probably out of his depth. He lost interest in playwriting, and not
even a revival of *Three Travelers* by the Provincetown Players in
1920 stimulated him subsequently. He never even attempted to
publish *Bowl, Cat and Broomstick* and it did not appear in print until 1969. It is now most accessible in the revised edition of *Opus
Posthumous*.[7]

This situation was a shame, for it excluded the most suggestive
of the plays from critical consideration until the 1970s. Set in sev-
enteenth-century France, with figures straight out of the comme-
dia dell'arte, it runs changes on many of the obsessions of
symbolist drama: the marionettes and masks, the curtains and the
colors, the symbiosis of tragedy and comedy. It reminds viewers of
Maeterlinck and Gordon Craig in alternate moments, or perhaps
the influence of Santayana at Harvard not only on Stevens but also
on Walter Arensberg and other decadent poets. Drama in such cir-

cumstances readily dissolved into mood, wordplay, and posturing, creating a world that seems to have no relation whatever to the sale of life insurance or the problems of setting up house in a new city, which was in fact what Stevens was doing at the time.

The play opens with Bowl using the French word *rouge* to mean "tawny." When Cat points out that "*rouge* means red," Bowl replies with firmness: "No doubt, when it refers to something red. But when, as here, it refers to something tawny, then it means tawny" (*OP*, 168). A viewer could scarcely ask for a more precise expression of Stevens's point of view in much of his verse. The speaker is in charge and whimsically arbitrary, signs and signifiers have divorced, everything is relative, meaning diffuse, pose affected, and tone haughty-seeming but self-deprecating. Broomstick thus rightly dismisses skeptics who retain any Victorian faith in precision, stability, or consistency: "A man with so firm a faith in the meaning of words should not listen to poetry" (*OP*, 169).

The three then conduct a trialogue about the poet Claire Dupray, whose flowers were supposedly tawny. She is a poetess at age twenty-two but would be a poet at forty-two, words changing with age like cheeses; they interpret her picture in the frontispiece, parodying various critical methods as they proceed. Stevens is slowly achieving the delicate balance he will maintain between comedy and tragedy: usually the comedy inhering in tone and form, the tragedy in the philosophical and religious implications of the content. "How little it would take to turn the poets into the only true comedians!" Broomstick enthuses. "There's no truer comedy than this hodge-podge of men and sunlight, women and moonlight, houses and clouds, and so on." "Nor any truer tragedy," Bowl responds, only to be put down firmly: "No one believes in tragedy" (*OP*, 170). Since translation in Stevens is impossible, one plausible mistranslation might be: The circumstances of modern man, of modern woman in art, are so inherently tragic that only comic tone and repartee can deal with them. The poet, external to the play, not only has to mix comedy and tragedy in this way, he has to communicate his dilemma to readers who no longer believe in tragedy. Such lack of faith is indeed in itself tragic. Funny, isn't it?

In Stevens's best verse, the mood is often about mood, the language about language. Translation is all but impossible, for if you could translate poetry into prose, then poetry would not be necessary. Thus the need for foreignness, for the use of French to evoke what does not come through in English. "These things are atrociously difficult in English," Bowl complains. "In French, they seem almost pellucid." Neither Broomstick nor many of Stevens's somewhat bewildered readers was so sure: "My knowledge of French is not absolutely penetrating" (*OP*, 173, 175).

The ultimate in denotative reduction is the poet's effort to evoke color by listing the names of colors. "You read these rapidly and so produce in the mind a visual impression like that produced by the actual sight of dahlias," Bowl points out helpfully. He then reads: "Green, green, green—no doubt this indicates the stalks—green, green, green, green, green, yellow, green, yellow, green, green, gray, green, yellow, yellow, white, white, white, green." Broomstick interjects hopefully: "We ought to be getting to the flowers soon." Bowl knows he has missed the point. "We're right in them now. The white, white, white, indicates white flowers, white dahlias" (*OP*, 174).

This is very witty in its way, but readers need to resist the impulse to overanalyze, murdering to dissect. The points that need making because they remain relevant for years are that Stevens was philosophically acute and linguistically aware; that he was frequently self-reflexive; that he often spoke in several voices at once, not only in dialogue but in trialogue and more, his own "position" being between or above the voices, not simply using one as a surrogate mouthpiece; and that he often conceptualized spatially, seeing his subject as on a stage, often in motion, rarely stable, and at its best redolent of life in another dimension, "abroad" in France or French, in Cuba or China or the Palaz of Hoon. In the best of his work, balance will often be an issue: tragedy and comedy, subject and object, here and there. The balance itself becomes the object of attention, as if a pierrot were forever juggling some lethal object that might prove fatal if not kept forever in the air. Like so many modernists, Stevens had no final answers for anything; but he enjoyed sampling every object that came his way.

Having given up writing dramas, Stevens continued to be astonishingly productive for another six years. A number of these works have earned places in most anthologies, such as "Le Monocle de Mon Oncle," and "Anecdote of the Jar." But perhaps the most substantial work written during the first jazz age was "The Comedian as the Letter C," a work as crucial for its time as "Sunday Morning" had been in bringing into focus the emotional meaning of a world at war where French was spoken. "How little it would take to turn the poets into the only true comedians!" Broomstick had exclaimed in 1917, going on 1666, when a plague of another sort had been much on the minds of English speakers. "There's no truer comedy than this hodge-podge of men and sunlight, women and moonlight, houses and clouds, and so on" (*OP,* 170).

In 1921, the Poetry Society of South Carolina offered what it called the Blindman Prize of two hundred and fifty dollars for a poem of substantial length. Harriet Monroe publicized it in *Poetry* and Stevens immediately accepted the challenge. He was not always happy about the results. "I have been churning and churning, producing, however, a very rancid butter, which I intend to submit in that competition." After all, "what's the use of offering prizes if people don't make an effort to capture them." He called his draft "from the Journal of Crispin," realized it was "very incomplete and most imperfect," but remained "determined to have a fling at least." The sole judge was Amy Lowell, and she awarded the prize to Grace Hazard Conkling; Stevens won first honorable mention in a field that included Babette Deutsch, Janet Lewis, and Herbert Read. This version then disappeared for half a century while he worked out an extensive revision, which was completed in 1922 and first appeared in *Harmonium* (1923).[8]

The first version starts with what seems to be the hallmark juxtaposition of extremes in Stevens's work: Man, "the Socrates / Of snails, musician of pears, principium / And lex." It seemed clear enough, a satirical jibe at the overeducated, the world of the "nincompated pedagogue." Crispin will escape this world by sea, languidly eyeing "gelatines and jupes, / Berries of villages," plucking visual sweetness as he floats past on his stream of sensation. This is not so much wrong as incomplete, for it passes over one of the standing musical jokes of French dada in music, Erik Satie's whimsical formal pun, usually translated as "Three Pieces in the Shape of a Pear" (1903). Critics had found his works formless, so he gave them the form of a pear, and in his Rosicrucian world, three would form a pair if you juggled a dimension. Stevens knew modern French music well, and Satie was fully assimilated into the Arensberg salon. Satie and Crispin, "the lutanist of fleas," would have understood each other implicitly.

Yet if the ghost of any composer hangs over this poem, it is that of Claude Debussy. The most innovative modernist in French music before the arrival of Igor Stravinsky, Debussy was the harmonic impressionist among composers. Taking inspiration from Whistler's nocturnes, mentoring the cranky creativity of a Satie, the composer of *Pelléas et Mélisande*, whose themes so haunted John Dos Passos, was in this context also the composer of *La Mer* (The Sea). Given Stevens's musical enthusiasms, his genuine passion for things French, and his inveterate punning, it is only a bit of a stretch to think of this work as the "debut of C," the Debussy of the sea's debut, so to speak. For Stevens as for Debussy, the sea and music often seemed interchangeable. "The whole of life that still remains in him / Dwindles to one sound strumming in his ear, / Ubiquitous concussion, slap and sigh, / Polyphony beyond his baton's thrust." Crispin "is a man made vivid by the sea," much like Stevens himself.

In transforming this preliminary version into "The Comedian as the Letter C," Stevens gave both his protagonist and his favorite letter musical significance. When critics immediately confused Stevens and Crispin, the poet was firm. "I ought to confess that by the letter C I meant the sound of the letter C," he wrote to

Ronald Latimer in 1935; "what was in my mind was to play on that sound throughout the poem." He also included "K and S," and thought the various sounds "may be said to have a comic aspect. Consequently, the letter C is a comedian." What he did not want was to have readers hearing program music, as if he were Richard Strauss in verse. Five years later he added the sounds for X, TS, and Z in a letter to Hi Simons, giving several specific examples, concluding: "You have to read the poem and hear all this whistling and mocking and stressing and, in a minor way, orchestrating, going on in the background . . . 'in, on or about the words.'"[9]

Given such encouragement from the author himself, critics have had a lot of fun with this work. Crispin was a C, on the sea, all at sea, in the key of C, perhaps the minor C while the author remained C major. It's all there, mostly diminuendo rather than crescendo, but a "wordy, watery age" did not always grasp the literary and philosophical point that this "introspective voyager" was making. The work of both Joseph Conrad and his great admirer Eugene O'Neill had assumed the dual nature of the sea as both time and motion. While deep-flowing currents, most famously the Gulf Stream, could be carrying everything inexorably north ("America was always north to him"), this lover of Florida and the Caribbean well knew that surface wind could easily make it seem just the reverse. Appearance and reality, motion and stasis, the North in the South, the sea embodied the dialogic world Stevens knew, everything somehow implying its opposite, with "Crispin confronting it, a vocable thing." He knew his voyage "to be / An up and down between two elements, / A fluctuating between sun and moon."

The work was not, of course, "just" a musical contribution to a jazz age. It participated in a century-old romantic tradition of the voyage of self-discovery; it was a picaresque; a Joycean analysis of an artist's growth; an American *Candide;* an American *Petrushka.* The poem is not only about language and "itself," it is as much about sights and smells as it is about sounds, and touches implicitly on numerous philosophical and aesthetic issues. It also needs to be seen in the company of Ezra Pound's *Hugh Selwyn Mauberley,* which had just appeared; Joyce's *Ulysses,* which he had been following in the *Little Review* and finally obtained in book form from Pitts Sanborn in the fall of 1922; and Eliot's *The Waste Land,* which was being written simultaneously. Unlike these three authors, who had become emigrés for life, however, Stevens stayed home and let his imagination wander. It wandered to music, often with lyrics that sounded French, and gave a sound rather different from American modernism.[10]

Stevens easily resisted Pound's influence, and was dismissive about *The Waste Land;* he was on a quest of his own, having conversations with himself, and the larger burden of his quest and his self-interrogations was the need for a substitute for the religion that had sustained earlier generations. The simplest way of expressing his tentative conclusions is to see him as equally the student of William James and George Santayana. As a pragmatist, he felt the will to believe and knew that God was real because belief in him had real effects. Every psychology was different, and so each person's religion would differ from every other. As an aesthete, he valued institutional religion in its proper historical context. Religion stimulated the imagination, enriched the arts, and provided the best substitutes for actual belief. Critics who have cautioned against reading his later views collected in *The Necessary Angel* (1951) into the early poetry definitely have a point, but nevertheless Stevens's work shows a definite consistency. In the early work he talks to himself and ponders the ideas, the poet himself persisting in the spaces between the views. In the later work, both verse and essays, opinion has settled and the voice becomes firmer, more singular. The ideas themselves have always been there, but the poet had at first not yet chosen among them, and really could not until *Ideas of Order* (1935) and after.[11]

What most critics of literary training miss, as they somewhat hermetically compare the prose of essays and letters to the poetry and unsurprisingly find a general consistency, is the way in which Stevens internalizes not only James, Santayana, and the Harvard philosophical world, but the scientific framework of assumptions that his teachers both grew out of and revolted against. The assumptions of Darwinian science and Spencerian political economy were givens in the Boston of the 1870s, and even two decades later, Stevens all but insensibly absorbed and aestheticized them. Even as James—once a Spencerian and later a parodist of the entire Synthetic philosophy—had done, Stevens both swallowed the science whole and then had fun with its gloomy implications. If the world were to be essentially meaningless, a poet could still imply that such dreariness was really for the birds, and toy with implications like a child decorating an exotic plaything.

One especially vivid example of this is "The Bird with the Coppery, Keen Claws" of 1921, the "C" sounds of the title all but demanding comparison to "The Comedian as the Letter C." Rarely receiving attention from those concerned with demonstrating the persistence of romanticism in verse, it actually aestheticizes postromantic science and philosophy. A parakeet is a good bird for Stevens's purposes, all beautiful feathers and meaningless repetition, what you "see" being what you get. Evolution: "Above the forest of the parakeets, / A parakeet of parakeets prevails," but "His lids are white because his eyes are blind." Insight: "He broods there and is still." Divine intervention: "As his pure intellect applies its laws, / He moves not on his coppery, keen claws." In the world in which only the fittest survive, death is the mother of beauty: "He munches a dry shell while he exerts / His will, yet never ceases, perfect cock, / To flare, in the sun-pallor of his rock" (*CP*, 82).[12]

The implications of such a work are simply devastating to conventional Christianity, idealistic philosophy, and most of the assumptions of romantic poetry. Stevens has moved beyond even the scientific materialism to accept everything that Darwin's critics found, however unjustly, in evolutionary theory. He sees no real hope, no real progress, no justice, no wisdom. He knows that pretty sounds are just mimicry, and that lovely feathers mask an organism that ingests and excretes, without taste or decency. And yet

the bird was worth a poem, for he was the negative of a truth behind Stevens's entire career. Unlike a bird, a man can don a business suit, build business structures that help make pain bearable,
and create a beauty in words beyond mere feathers. Of course,
feathers helped. So did cigars, martinis, and concupiscent curds.

This all has an historical importance beyond the determination
of poetic merit. Liberal and radical critics especially have long
wrung their hands over the conservative and even reactionary political implications of the views of leading modernists: Yeats,
Lawrence, Pound, Eliot, and Wyndham Lewis being favorite
whipping boys. Such attacks are largely silly, a bit like fuming over
the taste of Dwight D. Eisenhower for westerns, John F. Kennedy
for the fantasies of Ian Fleming, or Richard Nixon for the heroics
of George C. Scott. Just as politicians with rare exceptions demon-
strate no knowledge whatever of significant art, so artists with rare
exceptions show no comprehension of politics, even when they
write about it directly (like Pound) or even participate (like Yeats).

The palette must be broader and the limits of useful criticism
more restricted. A broader palette means that the entirety of
Stevens's cultural values is the proper focus, not just his presump-
tive views on poetry or politics. A sensibly limited criticism does
not permit the application of some readers' arbitrary standards of
leftist politics, Christian theology, or idealist metaphysics on the
poetry or the poet. Anyone writing sensibly on an artist has to take
historical context and authorial intent seriously, all the while keeping parallel or diverging comparisons at least subconsciously in
mind. Within these parameters, Stevens rather better than Pound
or Eliot illustrates the essentially conservative cultural vision that
lay behind most modernist creativity among those born American.
Stoic in temper, Epicurean in taste, materialist in philosophy, post-
Darwinian in science, skeptical in religion, he comes on even in
the first jazz age as an existentialist with taste. His existence preceded his essence; the first might be bleak, so the second could be
as gaudy as the language and the "I/eye" permitted. "C"-ing was
believing.

Because this complex of values seems remarkably consistent throughout his career, it is inaccurate to conceptualize Stevens as "Janus-faced"—radical in technique yet conservative in politics; or, more simple-mindedly, as simply "reactionary," especially in the 1930s. Careers, like planets, revolve, pursue orbits, warm to suns, and feel gravitational pulls. Business, marriage, war, and depression all had their impacts on the mature poet, and his work often reflected these. He was always radical in insight and technique; he was always conservative in essential political, religious, economic, and sartorial behavior. The blue guitar always had ideas of order to counterpoint the melody line.[13]

Such thoughts were untimely in 1923, when *Harmonium* appeared to an audience unenthusiastic because unprepared. The volume attracted little attention beyond a small group that followed new poetry. Even the most perceptive of critics tended to gloss over truly basic issues to focus on the glittering surfaces. "One resents the temper of certain of these poems," Marianne Moore noted in the best-remembered notice. "Mr. Stevens is never inadvertently crude; one is conscious, however, of a deliberate bearishness—a shadow of acrimonious, unprovoked contumely." She found in even the best work "the effect of the mind disturbed by the intangible; of a mind oppressed by the properties of the world which it is expert in manipulating." True enough, if hardly adequate. But the bulk of her analysis was pointed quotation rather than philosophical implication; she hesitated to go beyond the "riot of gorgeousness in which Mr. Stevens's imagination takes refuge." Most readers did not get even that far.[14]

Like the author of *Cane*, the author of *Harmonium* experienced book publication more as the end of something than as the beginning. He was feeling increasingly isolated, as poet, as businessman, as resident of Hartford. The Arensberg salon broke up, the host and hostess retiring to the West Coast and less exhausting enthusiasms, in the process eliminating Stevens's favorite artistic watering hole. He marked the occasion by donating all his art catalogs to the Wadsworth Atheneum. His marriage had proven emotionally arid, as his wife proved unable to share his interests or his friends. He was in a mood to hunker down, establish himself financially, and put poetry on hold. "I live like a turtle under a bush," he had written to Ferdinand Reyher in April 1922, and while the voice of the turtle would be heard in the land for another two years, it was soon to grow faint indeed.[15]

Harmonium appeared on 7 September, 1923. On 18 October, on the aptly named *Kroonland*, Stevens and his wife took the first real holiday they had allowed themselves since their marriage. As they sailed the Gulf of Mexico (although still technically in October), "In that November off Tehuantepec, / The slopping of the sea grew still one night," and marital concord returned at least once: "C'était mon extase et mon amour." "Then the sea / And heaven rolled as one and from the two / Came fresh transfigurings of freshest blue" (*CP*, 98–102). Blue was always a color of creative achievement for Stevens, and nine months later his only child was born. Along the way, bliss and poetry both vanished. A difficult woman at best, Elsie Stevens did not like being pregnant, nor did she like being a mother. Her customary frigidity returned to the relationship; her customary rigidity would dominate every aspect of daughter Holly's childhood. Stevens poured his frustrations into "Red Loves Kit" (1924) and went dry for six years.[16]

When Stevens returned to his art, it would be subtly different, more recognizably conservative beneath its modernist manner, less harshly Darwinian in implication, less gaudy in externals. But it would remain to the grave primarily a poetry of religious intent and meaning. "In an age of disbelief," he would say, "it is for the poet to supply the satisfactions of belief." (*OP*, 259).[17]

FOURTEEN

ARTHUR G. DOVE AND THE STIEGLITZ CIRCLE'S EQUIVALENTS

For many obvious reasons, American entry into World War I in April 1917 has mesmerized analysts into choosing that month, or at least that year, as the crucial historical watershed: between the Victorian and the modern, between the provincial and the cosmopolitan, between innocence and complicity with the world's corruptions. But history is rarely so tidy, and edges blur under microscopes. In the world of American modernism, change was already well underway, and neither German submarines nor Presbyterian presidents had much to do with the changes that mattered. Almost precisely a year earlier, for example, with Alfred Stieglitz as its chief sponsor, the "Forum Exhibition of Modern American Painters" put on a significant show at the Anderson Galleries. Sensing that a decade of stress on European modernism had done perhaps more than its job of initiating America into the world of fauvism, cubism, and their siblings, the sponsors wished to expose and encourage such American work as deserved publicity and sales. The most worthy of the 193 works by the seventeen artists on display between 13 and 25 March, 1916, were the sixteen by Arthur Dove, all titled *Nature Symbolized*.

Dove had not found the path to recognition easy to negotiate, nor would sales of his work ever lift him back into the middle class into which he had been born in 1880. Dove had grown up chiefly in Geneva, New York. His father manufactured bricks and prospered as a contractor, but had not the slightest interest in painting as a career for a son in possession of a normal set of faculties. The upper-middle class of that period encouraged elementary exposure to art and music, but was visibly more at ease with hunting, fishing, and baseball. Dove moved insensibly along an obvious path to the local Hobart College, and then to Cornell University to study law. It palled rapidly. He sampled physics, a subject that later had an odd resonance in his mature outlook on metaphysical matters, but his heart was increasingly on art. Seemingly the practical son of a practical father, he determined on a career as an illustrator. He took his A.B. in 1903, moved to New York City, and was soon appearing in several mass-circulation magazines. His drawings had wit and charm and so did he. He married a local girl in 1904 and soon fitted easily into city cultural life. He dined at Mouquin's, socialized with John Sloan and others of "the Eight," and seemed at ease in "journalism," which was the operative vocational label that suited many artists during the earliest years of the century.

The next four years remain largely undocumented, but by 1908 Dove was clearly yearning for something more. Late in the spring, he and his wife Florence headed for Paris, where he befriended Alfie Maurer and quickly found a place for himself in the small community of exiles. Maurer was already an habitué at Gertrude Stein's salon, so Dove was soon familiar with the casual chat concerning Matisse and Picasso. He even managed to contribute a work of his own to the "Salon d'automne" of 1908. But Dove rarely felt comfortable in cities for very long. He and Maurer went on sketching trips outside Paris, and he was soon off on his own in the south, chiefly in Cagnes but often on the move toward Spain or Italy. He seemed instinctively a rural modernist of the type who found Cézanne key, rather than an urban neophiliac like so many of his friends. He needed distances, perspectives, and earth tones to feel inspired. Cézanne's ideas about the role of the cone in art, now well known but hardly available at the time to a monolingual visitor, seem so close to Dove's later theorizing as to present an alluring but unlikely possibility of direct influence. But affinity is not influence. Dove simply shared basic attitudes with other modernists and in this case both painters remained painfully inarticulate about what they were up to.[1]

This French idyll lasted roughly fourteen months and the Doves returned in July 1909. But the experience put the painter in something of a vocational bind, not sure of what he could do or where he could do it. He went to Geneva to visit family, brood in the woods, and arrange a small show at Hobart. He returned to New York City and tried halfheartedly to resume his career as a journalist illustrator. He couldn't; France had ripened his wish to free himself to pursue his own agenda. "To understand painting one must live with it. The speed of today" left folks little time "to really live with anything, even ourselves," he recalled in an autobiographical fragment in 1930. He "discovered that at that time it was not possible to live by modern art alone," and that he would have to make "a living by farming and illustrating to support the paintings." The illustrating quickly palled, although he would occasionally revert to it in later life in periods of desperation. Farming was another matter.[2]

Dove resolved his dilemma by moving in two directions almost at once. Over the winter of 1909/10, he and Florence bought a house in Westport, a Connecticut suburb about an hour outside the city. Florence was pregnant and both seemed to wish instinctively for a return to the domestic rhythms of their parents; farming and fishing seemed, at least from a distance, more promising over the long run than illustrating, and so, once William arrived on 4 July, 1910, the family took full possession of the house.

Dove also dropped into 291. Alfie Maurer had long been a friend of Alfred Stieglitz, and had shared a show there with John Marin. Presumably with his encouragement, Dove introduced himself to the man who would be his closest professional friend and sponsor for the next thirty-five years. Opposites attracted as affinities melded: the talkative, arrogant, cosmopolitan Jew taking at once to the reticent, humble, provincial Anglo-Saxon. The "whispering kid," as his nickname was, was sixteen years junior to

Stieglitz, and desperate for guidance and encouragement. He got it. He placed *The Lobster* (1908) in a March 1910 show of "Younger American Painters"; a worthy work, it essentially summarized what he had absorbed in France. A few landscapes dated 1908 and 1909 aside, that opened and closed Dove's career as a representational painter. When he gave up illustration, he gave up direct representation as well.

He moved swiftly into a set of six oil studies, which he never showed; and another of ten pastels, which attracted significant attention when he had his second one-man show at 291, erroneously advertised as "Arthur G. Dove First Exhibition Anywhere," 27 February to 12 March, 1912; it moved to Chicago for the 14 to 30 March period, and attracted a gratifying amount of newspaper attention in both cities. Later entitled "The Ten Commandments," they remain apparently the first publicly shown examples of non-representational art by an American painter. The soul of propriety in both dress and language, Dove found himself the living embodiment of all the horrors of modernism, a lunatic pervert out to degrade American taste and morals. More serious discussions placed him more properly in the company of Picasso, Duchamp, and especially Francis Picabia.[3]

Dove thus became one of the few modernist Americans to appear in Arthur J. Eddy's pioneering study, *Cubists and Post-Impressionism* (1914), where he is "almost the only man in this country who has persistently painted in Cubist fashion for any length of time." Eddy asked Dove how he had come to paint as he did, and Dove had replied that he had never been able to derive many useful principles from earlier painters. As he studied their works rather than their words, he became impressed by the "choice of the simple motif" as the most evident: "This same law held in nature, a few forms and a few colors sufficed for the creation of an object." He thus abandoned impressionism or any kind of representationalism: "I gave up trying to express an idea by stating innumerable little facts, the statement of facts having no more to do with the art of painting than statistics with literature."

He then made what seems to have been his first public reference to the Orient, and the implicitly religious orientation that
would in fact have rather more effect on his art than Eddy's "cubism." He referred to "that perfect sense of order which exists in
the early Chinese painting" and outlined what he meant. "The
first step was to choose from nature a motif in color, and with that
motif to paint from nature, the form still being objective." The
second "was to apply this same principle to form, the actual dependence upon the object . . . disappearing, and the means of expression being purely subjective." Working along these lines, he
observed in a new way, "and not only began to think *subjectively,*
but also to remember certain sensations *purely through their form and
color,* that is by certain shapes, planes, light or character lines determined by the meeting of such planes." He then made clear
what would always be true of his work, its derivation from nature.
Referring to a specific work that Eddy reproduced in his book, he
explained: "It is a choice of three colors, red, yellow, and green,
and three forms selected from trees and the spaces between them
that to me were expressive of the movement of the thing which I
felt." Beyond such skeletal description he thought explanation
useless, like trying to explain sound to a deaf person. "The deaf
person is simply not sensitive to sound and cannot appreciate; and
a person who is not sensitive to form and color as such would be
quite as helpless." Clearly having his recent reviewers in mind, he
assumed that the fault was in them rather than in him or his
works.[4]

For some years, however, Dove seemed to have all but ceased
painting, one of many casualties within modernist ranks. Economi-
ically, Westport was not working out. About 1912, just as his work
was winning its first recognition, he purchased a farm and tried to
make ends meet with chickens, eggs, and vegetables. The food
kept his family alive but never generated enough money to make
the grueling labor worthwhile. His painting ceased and his marriage frayed. His wife opened a summer teahouse that proved
more successful, but that was a mere stopgap. Neither she nor

Dove's family had any sympathy either for abstract painting or economic failure. The marriage broke up in great bitterness in 1919. Protected by the archaic laws and attitudes of that period, Florence took all his possessions right down to his paints and easel and refused him any contacts with his son.

The Westport area came to his rescue in several ways. If some neighbors, like Van Wyck Brooks, were essentially hostile to modernism, others like Sherwood Anderson and Paul Rosenfeld were decidedly friendly, and numerous mentions in letters and diary entries attest to repeated visits both in town and in the city. Dove was a valued member of the Stieglitz circle and could always count on Stieglitz for loans, expressions of support, and, in time, shows at the Intimate Gallery and An American Place. Such friends also kept each other up on the *Little Review* and the *Dial*, with their reports of European literary developments—Dove especially admired the work of James Joyce and Gertrude Stein. Most of all, the area contributed Clive Weed, a newspaper cartoonist of considerable charm, and his wife Helen Torr, usually referred to as "Reds." She too was a painter and a very private person. The marriage had been breaking down for some time, and she joined Dove late in 1921 when he moved into a houseboat then moored off Manhattan—cheaply but conveniently. Dove promptly began painting again, at least when weather conditions did not disturb the boat. The couple eventually married and remained devoted until death parted them.

Dove was no intellectual; indeed, he often seemed to mistrust clarity and fear words, or at least reductionist interpretations of any nonverbal art, especially his. But he was a reasonably educated man, the graduate of a good college, and the friend of numerous others who shared his interests at articulate levels. The New York State area had long been known for enthusiastic religious outbursts, and a subsequent friendliness to the worlds of pure experience. These might include séances, table-rappings, extrasensory perception, and communication with the dead. Even hard-core scientists sometimes shared those interests, demanding only that science be permitted to experiment with such ideas like it might with any other hypothesis. William James was only the most famous of the figures who devoted much time, effort, and wishful thinking to the problems involved, with results that touched the coursework of a good many Harvard graduates. Dove may have studied physics, but he was equally interested in Oriental and South Asian thought, and he was soon into occultism and its most famous offspring in this context, Theosophy.

At the same time artistic and literary romanticism was producing generations of artists throughout the Western world who were convinced that nature was essentially the mind of God, and that all organisms within it partook of divinity. Painters could see God through animals, actions, and large vistas, writers could describe these visions, and citizens everywhere could partake of sublime mysteries while merely taking a country stroll. Thinkers from Emanuel Swedenborg to Ralph Waldo Emerson provided metaphysical superstructures. Theosophy had much to build on.

At first, Dove used his own special vocabulary. In his 1930 autobiographical statement, he recalled the time spent "in search for a means of expression which did not depend upon representation. It should have order, size, intensity, spirit, nearer to the music of the eye." He also searched "for a something in color which I then called 'a condition of light.' It applied to all objects in nature, flowers, trees, people, apples, cows." Soon, he "began to feel the same idea existing in form." The Greeks had known something along these lines, in what were called 'Maenechmian Triads,' and such knowledge seemed to free him "from representation in the ordinary sense."

Then he made a drawing of a hillside when the wind was blowing. He "chose three forms from the planes on the sides of the trees, and three colors, and black and white." From these he "made a rhythmic painting which expressed the spirit of the whole thing." The colors expressed "the substances of those objects and the sky." He had "earth color, the green of the trees, and the cyan blue of the sky." He made these into pastels and used them in making *Ten Commandments*. By the early 1920s he was ready to build on these precedents.[5]

The Stieglitz circle, not to mention family members, provided plenty of stimulation. The old man himself had been printing ideas taken from Wassily Kandinsky in *Camera Work* for years, and Marsden Hartley had made what amounted to a devout pilgrimage to Munich in 1913 to meet the author of *The Spiritual in Art* in person. Georgia O'Keeffe had a strong mystical streak that paralleled Dove's and enabled them to be exceptionally compatible; and of course the early 1920s were a time when Stieglitz himself was busy shooting "Equivalents," usually photographs of clouds with clear intentions of spying out Divinity. Finally, in what in some ways may have been the most significant relationship of all, the Doves had become close friends with Elizabeth Davidson, Stieglitz's niece, and her husband, Donald Davidson. The Davidsons were Vedantists, the couples visited regularly, and books went back and forth: *The Lectures of Bodhananda, Kali the Mother, Raja Yoga*, and so on. On at least one occasion, the Davidsons brought a Swami Nikhilananda with them on a visit. They were also into the occult, astrology, and numerology. And just for fun, they occasionally went off to Hindu restaurants together.[6]

Taken one at a time, these influences each made a certain amount of sense. Taken together, and added to others equally as diverse, the results seem an intellectual chaos: eggs from the farm, cones from Cézanne, force lines from physics; white lights, the fourth dimension, earthtones, and biomorphs—any schematic effort at analysis muddles rather than clarifies one sincere artist's search for modernist forms that suited him. Dove was seeing a larger order within the smallest details and producing work that was original if not always comprehensible. It never sold, and without subsidies first from Stieglitz and later from Duncan Phillips, Dove would have starved. He and Reds came close to it as it was, especially during the 1930s.[7]

None of these confusions really mattered over the short run, however, for among Dove's closest friends in the Stieglitz circle was Paul Rosenfeld, and his lengthy reviews dominated the intelligentsia during the first jazz age. They rarely sold paintings, but they assured Dove a place in the hierarchy—the modernist canon of "Seven Americans," plus the Sherwood Andersons of literature, the Leo Ornsteins of music, and the rest. Dove was the Earth Father, to play off against O'Keeffe: "There is not a pastel or drawing or painting of Dove's that does not communicate some love and direct sensuous feeling of the earth," Rosenfeld wrote in his major survey of the early work. "Dove's compositions are built up of abstract shapes that suggest the body's semi-consciousness of itself: of intestine-like shapes, shapes of fern-foetuses in May, animal udder-forms, forms in nature which doubtlessly had a fascination for the mind unafraid of its own body."

Rosenfeld is here the recording angel of a divine hierarchy, giving voice to the Stieglitz version of the art-world-that-mattered, where Stieglitz ruled as producer and director, Dove and O'Keeffe represented the fecundity of the next generation, with Marin, Demuth, Hartley, and occasional others forming a loving if sometimes closed circle. "For Dove is very directly the man in painting, precisely as Georgia O'Keeffe is the female; neither type has been known in quite the degree of purity before." For her, "the world is within herself." She feels its elements "in terms of her own person." Dove, in contrast, "does not feel the world within himself. He feels himself present out in its proper elements. Objects do not bring him consciousness of his own person." Instead, "they make him to lose it in the discovery of the qualities and identities of the object. The center of life comes to exist for him outside himself, in the thing, tree or lamp, or woman, opposite him." Dove "has moved himself out into the object." This sort of analysis had a beguiling sound to it, coming as much of it probably did, at least in part, from Lake George summer evenings at the Stieglitz retreat; but it remains critically meaningless, as so much of Rosenfeld's writing ultimately was. He was the best in the business, but the tools of the trade remained primitive, and too often at the service of casual intuition.

Rosenfeld got Dove into the canon, but did not explain why the canon was constituted as it was.[8]

The biomorphic Dove of Rosenfeld's analysis predominated during this period, but other Doves competed, often seeming the product of both local and international influences. Every veteran of 291 knew of Duchamp's *Fountain*, which endures to this day chiefly as a Stieglitz photograph, and of Picabia's mechanical abstractions, one famous one being of Stieglitz himself. They knew as well of Strand's photographs of machine parts, the wheel of a car or the structures of his favorite cameras. In *Gear* (1922) and *Lantern* (1922), Dove paid brief homage to this sort of thing, as if to prove he could do it. Within two years, however, he was into a more significant area, and from 1924 into 1926 turned out most of his "arrangements," works that even managed to win a certain amount of popularity. An American version of synthetic cubism, often in three dimensions, they seemed as well to be a variety of Merzkunst in the spirit of Man Ray and Kurt Schwitters, or even Dr. William Carlos Williams in certain moods, rearranging found objects of no intrinsic value into visual poems. Even in a painter as devoted to nature as Dove, the broken things of the postwar world could dance into new shapes. Even Stieglitz could dance: *Alfred Stieglitz* (1924) was a witty "assemblage of lens, photographic plate, clock and watch springs, and steel wool on plywood," now safely entombed in the Museum of Modern Art. *The Critic* (1925), not necessarily an homage to Rosenfeld, was an "assemblage of cardboard, magazine cutouts, cord, and velvet," now safe from revengeful acts in the Whitney.[9]

The period 1925 to 1927 marked a highpoint for Dove, as he experimented successfully, reached something of a synthetic form of his own, integrated his work with the music of the period, and achieved singular exposure in exhibitions. As he digested the mechanical imagery and the collagelike arrangements, he recovered the biomorphic emphasis that never really disappeared from his work and applied it directly to music: *George Gershwin—"Rhapsody in Blue,"* parts I and II (1927), *I'll Build a Stairway to Paradise—*

Gershwin (1927), and *Orange Grove in California by Irving Berlin* (1927). He showed in the "Seven Americans" exhibition at the Anderson Galleries, 2–29 March, 1925, and in the "International Exhibition of Modern Art, Assembled by the Société Anonyme," at the Brooklyn Museum, 19 November, 1926 to 9 January, 1927 (running a week longer than originally announced); and Stieglitz gave him two shows at the Intimate Gallery, 11 January to 7 February, 1926, and 12 December, 1926, to 7 January, 1927. But financial success eluded him. Stieglitz and Phillips gave him enough to survive, but nothing more.[10]

FIFTEEN

CLAUDE BRAGDON'S OTHER LIVES

The interest in Theosophy, Vedanta, the Wisdom of the East—the names and nations change, but the imaginary map seems to stretch from Madras to Kyoto—turns out to be the greatest missing patch in the crazy quilt of modernism, uniting Americans with such Europeans as Kandinsky, Kupka, and Mondrian. Most apparently in painting and literature, an interest in the Occult also provided entrée to the world of architecture and the designs that went with it, designs so commercially appealing that they soon permeated the covers of books and set new standards for the very look of commercial products and assumptions about class and advertising that went with them.

So central to European modernism, architects had had little to do with early American modernism. Americans had proven to be great engineers, the skyscraper alone proving it to the world, but they had been incapable of recognizing genius even when it appeared. Henry Hobson Richardson in the East, Louis Sullivan in the Midwest—neither had won much recognition, received many commissions, nor inspired more than a handful of disciples by the time of the first jazz age. Even Frank Lloyd Wright, who now seems so central in the history books, appeared to be little more than an eccentric adulterer of strictly regional eminence, even though he had been influential as far from home as Berlin for more than a decade; and Tokyo claimed more of his time in the 1920s than any American city. This situation would not really change until the 1930s, when both exhibitions and emigrés brought buildings, politics, and contemporary industrial designs together.

Only two architects' names appear at all in the vast majority of available sources. Hugh Ferriss attended occasional Theosophically oriented events during the first jazz age and was personally friendly to several of the writers and artists more central to the modernist enterprise. He produced little himself during these years, however, his *The Metropolis of Tomorrow* not appearing until 1929. When it did, critics from Lewis Mumford to William H. Jordy dismissed Ferriss as an odd combination of Gothicizing romantic and Corbusieran epigone. "The entire population of this imaginary metropolis seems to have lived a glamorously decadent penthouse existence replete with martinis and costume balls, as though the milieu of *The Great Gatsby* had been transported from East and West Egg to Manhattan," Jordy snorted in the ablest history of the profession. He dismissed Ferriss's "megalomania" and thought his vision "a rhapsodically uncritical projection of trends in skyscraper design current during the late twenties among the more progressive of the Beaux-Arts trained architects."[1]

Claude Bragdon was another story, one as yet only partially told. Never a major creative force in architecture, as he himself was well aware, Bragdon appears in standard architectural histories only as an acquaintance, disciple, and editor of Louis Sullivan. This is less inaccurate than partial: Bragdon lectured on both Sullivan and Wright often enough during the years before World War I, but confessed later that he had been "as unalive to Sullivan's essential *rightness* as were most of my colleagues," but was early convinced that "he alone of us all was honest." What united them more than profession or style was in fact the spiritual substructure beneath the foundation: "With me architecture is not an art but a religion, and that religion but part of a greater religion of Democracy," as Sullivan wrote Bragdon in a private letter. As architecture shifted "from stone and brick masonry to steel frame and reinforced concrete construction," Sullivan became "the first to give dramatic expression to the new engineering." He knew that form should follow function, and that the skyscraper should be tall, "a proud and soaring thing." Whatever the gaps in Sullivan's ideas and their execution, Bragdon took him as a role model, to the point where he went to the trouble of gathering and editing Sullivan's *Kindergarten Chats* (1934), thirty-five years after their composition.[2]

But Bragdon's buildings and editing jobs were merely the outward and visible sign of an inward and spiritual vision. Born to a northern New York State family with "something stony" about it, he recalled his father as being "spiritually akin to the New England Transcendentalists," a man whose outlook on life "was essentially Oriental"; his mother was the daughter of an abolitionist clergyman. As such, Bragdon grew up as a progressive and had much to overcome on his way to being a modernist. On the one hand, he married a fanatic suffragette; on the other, he converted to Theosophy after reading Emerson's *Conduct of Life,* and apparently took his father along with him. The family library acquired the works of Mme. Helena Blavatsky, along with numerous others with titles like *Esoteric Buddhism, The Perfect Way,* and *Light on the Path.* Bragdon was soon off in his own inner Orient, cherishing the *Bhagavad Gita,* the *Upanishads,* and Max Müller's *The Sacred Books of the East.* With a few friends he founded the Genesee Lodge of the Theosophical Society, wrote up *Episodes from an Unwritten History* about his new faith, and competed vigorously with the Gideonites by placing a copy "in every hotel room in Rochester."

Episodes was a small volume of ninety-eight pages, plus a reprinting of an essay by Annie Besant at the end. Rarely cited even by serious historians familiar with Bragdon's later contributions, it was an able synthesis for its time, eminently clear and measured in its judgments. It remains useful not so much for its information about Theosophy as for its clear expression of the core of religious ideas that would underlie Bragdon's impending aesthetic pronouncements. It shows him well versed in the larger context of the American religious flowering that included spiritualism, New Thought, and Christian Science; well aware of the complex and prickly nature of Mme. Blavatsky's character; and an able critic of those who dismissed Theosophy as an imaginative fraud. It also demonstrates a quaint sexism that could write of Blavatsky as "that mysterious being, woman in body, man in intelligence and will," simply taking for granted what he took to be the case, that women were more intuitive about religious questions than men; and an implicit Orientalism, with apparitions such as a "mysterious Asiatic," "an Oriental clad in white garments," and "a Mahatma" with a "mess of dark hair dropping to his shoulders" appearing at predictable intervals.

Using considerable rhetorical skills, Bragdon foreshadowed his core idea early in the book, but withheld its clear expression until the end. After detailing the highly improbable circumstances of the meeting of Blavatsky with her companion Colonel Henry Steel Olcott, he insisted that they were "drawn together there, not by accident, . . . but as the initial move in a great game planned far away and long ago, and played by transcendent beings in whose hands this man and woman were instruments." These were "the Men Behind," the true masters who had attained perfection and won release from compulsory reincarnation. Those coming from the Christian perspective of the Rochester area might pass such phrasing by at first, but the book reached a climax sixty pages later with the bold assertion of Bragdon's three most important ideas:

"I can well imagine the reader unacquainted with the Ancient Wisdom to have followed this veracious narrative with growing incredulity and bewilderment," for it must seem "a cryptogram without a key." The key was one word: *"Reincarnation."* His was "the story of a successive series of *recognitions*." His subjects "did not become acquainted in the ordinary way; they sought one another out to resume relations established and cemented in many antecedent earthly lives." Reincarnation was possible because "time is not, as it is often imagined, a straight line of infinite extension, but a circle, or rather a spiral." In its return, it "brings the to-morrow of the world nearer to some long-vanished yesterday than to the passing hour." It thus seemed to follow that "one of these major cycles has just been completed; that another morning of the world is presently to dawn." The year 1910 was "in a condition analogous to that which prevailed when Christianity arose and swept away the outworn paganism of Rome."[3]

Like some emanation of a Divine spirit, the white light of Theosophy pervaded everything Bragdon wrote. After spending the bulk of his early career as a draughtsman and then as an architect, usually of such public structures as bridges or railway stations, he began to turn his lectures into essays and books. The core of his faith was there from the start. The original Theosophic idea was that everything was an expression of the self, but as an active artist he preferred to rephrase it: "Everything is the expression of the Self in terms of sense. Art, accordingly, is the expression of the Self in terms of sense." Those having an aesthetic experience should think of the various arts as colors that merge into one another. The extremes were music and architecture, the former allied to time, the latter to space. A decade before T. S. Eliot made the case for "Tradition and the Individual Talent," Bragdon was insisting that architecture was always reincarnating past forms, and originality in practice largely a matter of adding elements to achievements already there. This parallelism in ideas on art being grounded in religion, and especially religion with strong affinities for the attitudes of South Asia, said a great deal about the true nature of "modernism" and how historical and seemingly "unmodern" it could be.

Bragdon then went on to argue that the glimpses of divinity he perceived were real. "There is a *Beautiful Necessity* which rules the world, which is a law of nature and equally a law of art, for art is the idealized creation: man carried to a higher power by reason of its passage through a human consciousness." He then stressed two of the major axioms of his faith: The human body was the model for pillars, church designs, ornaments, and so on, for "man is indeed the microcosm—a little world fashioned from the same elements and in accordance with the same Beautiful Necessity as is the greater world in which he dwells." And a latent geometry underlay all design: "it may be said that architecture is geometry made visible, in the same sense that music is number made audible." He concluded, lest anyone remain in doubt as to where he stood: "In every excellent work of architecture, in addition to its obvious and individual beauty, there dwells an esoteric and universal beauty, following as it does, the archetypal pattern laid down by the Great Architect for the building of that temple which is the world wherein we dwell."[4]

At the same time that he was exploring the relevance of Theosophy for art, Bragdon was becoming deeply involved in the craze for the fourth dimension that was sweeping much of Europe. Early in 1907, his friend Gelett Burgess had introduced him to the mathematician Charles Howard Hinton at the Players Club in New York City; as Bragdon later informed his mother, "Hinton demonstrated the Fourth Dimension with different colored cubes of his own invention." Within two years, Bragdon had submitted an article on the subject to a *Scientific American* essay contest, and was toying with an overtly Christian parable, "Man the Square," a pamphlet of essay length that explored the ways in which the line between the second and third dimensions could help students understand how to visualize the line between the third and fourth dimensions. Using arguments from mathematics as well as the religious thought of both Asia and Europe, he insisted that "Our sense of time may be only an imperfect sense of space." Supplying an impressive number of plates demonstrating the aesthetic possibilities involved, he also added materials on magic squares and cubes, a subterranean theme that had been appearing in Western art for centuries. The cast of mind he displayed in doing so bore a striking resemblance to the obsessions of Walter Arensberg and several frequenters of his salon with ciphers and codes in the works of Dante and Shakespeare, and the analogical possibilities suggested by chessboards in more than two dimensions and the possible use of mirror images to convey the conceptual implications involved.[5]

Bragdon demonstrated just how far he could take his extra-architectural ideas into his chosen profession with his most memorable design, the New York Central Station in Rochester, N.Y. Eager to produce a masterpiece, he dallied with such grandiose precedents as the Sancta Sophia, as well as Charles F. McKim's Pennsylvania Terminal in New York City, "that veritable Temple of Fatigue," as he described it after coming to his senses. Finally recalling his allegiance to Sullivan's formula that form should follow function, he instead immersed himself in the world of tracks, locomotives, smokestacks, and driving wheels, repeating the mantra to himself, "This is a railway station," and not a "city hall, a post office, or a court house." He recalled that his own son had mistaken Pennsylvania Station for a library, and took pride in thinking that at least no one could make such a mistake in Rochester.

But the thought processes he went through in reaching his basic design warrant extended quotation, for they display the ways in which a modernist sensibility could contribute to architecture at a time when the profession seemed mired in eclecticism:

> In the proportioning of the facade and of the waiting-room I made use of one of those systems set forth in my book, *The Beautiful Necessity*—what might be called the "musical parallel," by reason of the employment of those numerical ratios subsisting between the consonant intervals within the octave—namely: 1:2, the octave; 2:3, the fifth; 3:4, the fourth; 4:5, the major third; and 4:7, the subminor seventh. The waiting room is twice as wide as it is high—the interval of the octave; or, if one prefers to name it so, the proportions of a root-four rectangle of Dynamic Symmetry. There also occur the ratios of 2:3 and 4:7—the fifth and the diminished seventh. The beauty of the proportions in this room impress everyone as particularly fine.

Lest that sound too technical an example to be "modernist" in this religious context, he then followed it immediately with a deadpan narration of his bringing Mrs. Marie Russak to see his achievement shortly before the official opening. A friend of Annie Besant and "an occultist of note," she had once been an opera singer, and as she looked around, she burst into the notes of the diatonic scale. "At the utterance of a certain note the entire room seemed to become a resonance chamber, reinforcing the tone with a volume of sound so great as to be almost overpowering." She then declared that his station had "found its keynote" and was "alive." Ever willing to integrate the visible with the invisible, Bragdon concluded his account: "This was one of the strangest happenings in all my experience, and I have often wondered if those musical ratios employed in the design had anything to do with it."[6]

Bragdon's ideas seem to have come to him in a fairly brief span of time, roughly 1907 to 1916, which were also the climax of pre-Einstein physics. As reputable scientists, such as Johann Karl Friedrich Zöllner, a professor of physics and astronomy at Leipzig, went to considerable lengths to prove that psychic phenomena could be explained by a hypothesis based on the reality of the fourth dimension, the spread of well-known inventions lent credence to seemingly fantastic notions: the radio, the telephone, electricity, airplanes—the very air was full of extrasensory possibilities. Not even the sophisticated knew where to draw the line, as the entire career of William James repeatedly demonstrated. Sleep, dreams, hypnotism, clairvoyance, curved time—why would Freud be an obvious prophet, but not Sir Oliver Lodge, Arthur Conan Doyle, or Frederic W. H. Myers? Even germ theory had its doubters.[7]

As it so frequently would, Bragdon's personal life seemed to feed his occult predilections. His first wife, the reforming Charlotte, died giving birth to their second son in 1911. After a period of understandable devastation, Bragdon went manfully to work on his New York Central commission and slowly reentered society. He soon met an eligible widow, Eugenie Julier Macaulay, and married her on 13 July, 1912: The date seems worth noting as the most precise way of indicating the permanent shift of Bragdon's psyche from any lingering progressivism to a modernism of heart, soul, and astral planes. While the rest of the nation watched Woodrow

Wilson, Theodore Roosevelt, and William Howard Taft fight it out for the presidency, Bragdon devoted himself to a woman "of the Delphic Sisterhood," who consistently reminded him of those fairy tales in which a man loved "a bird-wife or a sea creature": "For the air or the sea substitute the astral plane, the fourth dimension, or whatever one may name that mysterious demesne which is no less real than this of which our senses make report." Religious in an obsessive but uninstitutional way, she "believed herself to be under the guidance of a daemon, or guardian spirit of supernatural beneficence," to whom she referred as "Oracle, because it gave her warning and counsel, answering questions mentally addressed to it." After seven years of marriage, it also did her in: "her Oracle told her that she must die," and she did late in 1920, of stomach cancer. She continued to send him messages after death.[8]

Given these experiences, Bragdon felt an understandable distaste for life in Rochester. A provincial city with gloomy weather, then known almost entirely for being the location of George Eastman's photographic enterprises, it had little to interest a man of Bragdon's religious and aesthetic preferences. He closed out his architectural life, even as the press that he had established was beginning to achieve notable success in selling various essays on Theosophy, ornament, architecture, and democracy. He moved into New York City, where he had friends, especially Walter Kirkpatrick Bryce, who were actively involved in the literary, musical, and religious worlds that were then in ferment. In his middle fifties, Bragdon slipped easily into a new career as a theater designer, with several available alternatives, such as writer in all his established areas of interest, publisher's adviser, book designer, and companion of choice for those exploring the religious fringes.

Thus, as an "architect," Bragdon was the exception that proved the rule: He was really an exarchitect. He entered into what became a lifelong relationship with the enterprising young publisher, Alfred A. Knopf, for example. Since Bragdon's Manas Press in Rochester was doing so well, Knopf agreed to take over its most promising titles. He reissued old titles and proved remarkably tolerant in accepting new collections of short essays that, to put it kindly, did not contain anything new or remunerative. To judge from the surviving readers' reports and in-house assessments, no one at Alfred A. Knopf, Inc., accepted Bragdon's ideas on religious subjects, they merely acknowledged that he was an "expert" in a field that sold books. In this capacity he advised on manuscripts from Georges I. Gurdjieff and Dane Rudhyar, for example. He also displayed one of his truly genuine talents, that of channeling his ideas on "progressive ornament" into designs for book covers, most notably those of Willa Cather. She was "one of our most fussy and particular authors, but you pleased her enormously with your binding for *Youth and the Bright Medusa* and I hope you can do it a second time," Knopf wrote, with reference to the forthcoming *One of Ours*.[9]

As these activities do not perhaps indicate clearly, however, the big attraction that Bragdon and his press had for the house of Knopf was the rights to what is still in print as P. D. Ouspensky, *Tertium Organum: The Third Canon of Thought. A Key to the Enigmas of the World*, originally translated by Claude Bragdon and Nicholas Bessaraboff (Rochester, 1920). The original copyright was in Bragdon's name, and Knopf was rather careful in dealing with the legalities, personalities, and sensibilities involved.[10]

The bare facts of the relationship between Bragdon, Bessaraboff, and Ouspensky were almost enough to compel faith in thought transferance. Working out of traditions of Russian mysticism of the same sort that so influenced Kandinsky, Ouspensky had published a first edition of *Tertium Organum* in St. Petersburg in 1912, with a somewhat revised second edition appearing four years later. A disciple, "a pale-faced, studious-looking youth" named Nicholas Bessaraboff, had taken a copy of this second edition with him when he fled the war-torn capital just before the Russian Revolution of 1917. He had made his way to Philadelphia, discovered Bragdon's *Four-Dimensional Vistas* in a public library, and somehow made his way to the author in Rochester. The points of view in the two books were so similar that he was convinced that Bragdon would be interested in the text, and in perhaps working out a translation. "I took fire at once," Bragdon recalled later, and the two got to work. Bessaraboff put the Russian text into whatever English he could, and Bragdon then tried to make an idiomatic text. Having worked often enough from memory, showing a disturbing habit of compressing or altering quotations, Ouspensky caused his collaborators endless trouble as they tried to track down the originals of at least the materials that had first appeared in English. By the end of 1919 they were done. At his own expense, Bragdon then printed the book at his Manas Press in Rochester.

Ouspensky of course knew nothing of all this. This most eminent member of the Russian Theosophist community, Pyotr Demianovich Ouspensky (now increasingly spelled Petr Demianovich Uspenskii) had been born in Moscow in 1878 into a family devoted both to the arts and to mathematics. In an autobiographical fragment, he recalled both his mother and maternal grandfather as painters, the latter having made a living painting portraits, executing pastels, and decorating churches. His father, "an officer in the survey," shared many of her tastes and was also fond of music. In addition, he "was a good mathematician," who "had a particular interest in the problems of the fourth dimension to which he gave much of his spare time." The boy early acquired a taste for poetry and the pictures that so often went with it, moved on "to feel a great interest in natural science," and thence to philosophy. "At sixteen I first found Nietzsche," and was soon "anarchistically inclined." He developed an acute distrust for academic science: "I was enormously excited by the idea of the fourth dimension and subsequently terribly disappointed by the usual 'scientific' treatment of it."

He was a perfect candidate for the vogue of occultism, spiritualism, and Theosophy that swept through the Russian intelligentsia: they "are everywhere present, and are, in fact, a major determinant in the artistic and cultural course of the Silver Age" that flourished in the last three decades before World War I. Included under such rubrics should be as well Rosicrucianism, Freemasonry, Martinism, phrenology, and an obsession with tarot cards: Organized religion had lost its appeal, science and materialism had won out on the surface of life but had failed to nourish the soul, and ideas flourished indiscriminantly. Wassily Kandinsky in painting, Alexander Scriabin in music, Andrei Belyi in fiction, Nikolai Berdiaev in philosophy—the names included some of the most eminent across the broad spectrum of late czarist culture. By borrowing ideas from Hindus, Buddhists, and Sufis, by insisting on the scientific nature of their mindsets, and by concealing the rest in esoteric knowledge that only enlightened "Mahatmas," the "Men Who Know," could penetrate, Theosophy seemed to have it all.

In 1907, Ouspensky discovered this literature and spent about seven years in its thrall. He sought further enlightenment by extensive travels throughout the Eastern Mediterranean countries, adding India and Ceylon in the last year before the war. When the war changed everything he returned to Russia, began lecturing chiefly in St. Petersburg, and in 1915 met Georges I. Gurdjieff in Moscow. Gurdjieff's ideas "produced a very great impression on me," for Gurdjieff "had found many things for which I had been looking in India." Ouspensky had encountered "a completely new system of thought surpassing all I knew before." He abandoned Theosophy and was soon arranging lectures and meetings for Gurdjieff in St. Petersburg.

As was so often the case with literary modernism, many texts of theological modernism were written years before their deceptive publication dates. While a convinced Theosophist, he wrote *A New Model of the Universe* over 1911–14, although it did not appear in English until 1931. *The Symbolism of the Tarot* appeared in Russian in 1913, but not on its own in English until 1976—in essence, it got absorbed into revisions of *A New Model*. All the operative ideas of the occult and the esoteric, from the fourth dimension to Yoga, appear in these works and persist from Theosophy, through the decade of association with Gurdjieff, into or alongside the strikingly similar ideas of Bragdon.[11]

Like all too many other Russian cultural figures of the time, Ouspensky largely dropped out of the recoverable record during the war and revolution, and only resurfaced in Constantinople in 1920. A. R. Orage, the respected editor of *The New Age* in London, had been publishing contributions by a P. Uspenski, and through that faint clue and contacts with the Theosophical Society, friends were able to get copies of the translation and a royalty check through to a penniless and thankful exile. Wealthy English followers, led by Vicountess Rothermere, sister-in-law of press baron Lord Northcliffe, offered to help with travel expenses, and soon Ouspensky was in London, writing away and cultivating a growing circle of followers. He professed himself "startled" at the parallels he could perceive between his ideas and those of Bragdon.[12]

A century of scholarship on nineteenth century thought makes the parallels seem much less surprising. In fact, philosophical investigations from St. Petersburg to San Francisco shared a remarkable number of common sources and emphases. They started with the distinctions between the objective and the subjective, the world and the individual, time and space. They quoted a lot of Kant, if not always agreeing with Kant's meaning. Both English and American thought then tended to divide into positivists and spiritualists, with religiously inclined individuals usually feeling most comfortable in a world which still showed a divine origin and offered clues in nature to life of some sort on another plane. Charles H. Hinton, in *A New Era of Thought*, and Richard Maurice Bucke, in *Cosmic Consciousness* were representative thinkers who offered comfort. For Americans, the ubiquitous William James remained crucial, a scientist ever eager to test spiritualist assertions no matter how daft they might appear to succeeding generations. *A Pluralistic Universe* and *The Varieties of Religious Experience* come in for repeated and lengthy quotation in Ouspensky's book, and many American readers had every right to feel at home in its pages.

Although most curious readers did not take it, only a short step separated this core set of religious attitudes from "projective ornament" in spatial design and Theosophy in philosophical practice. Ouspensky too believed that "time is the *fourth dimension of space*," and that a three-dimensional body "is merely the *projection* of a four-dimensional body—its drawing, its image *on our plane*." He too was fascinated by the possibilities of non-Euclidean geometry. He too cited Helena Blavatsky's *The Secret Doctrine* and *Isis Unveiled* and took material from the works of C.W. Leadbeater, one of the most influential of Theosophical popularizers. American Protestantism had long been prone to new religions, often with bases in mysticism, and the apparent triumph of Darwinian science and materialist philosophy merely made the hunger for transcendental truth all the greater.[13]

In his New York City environment, Bragdon was thus an ex-architect with a religious message, and as such only on the fringes of modernist creativity. He socialized chiefly with theater people, working with Walter Hampden on productions of plays such as *Hamlet* and *Cyrano de Bergerac* that were irrelevant to the history of modernism. But he knew and worked with Robert Edmond Jones, Lee Simonson, and Norman Bel Geddes, he thought about the use of masks in the works of Eugene O'Neill, and he wrote up his ideas occasionally for the *Dial* or other journals that participated in formulating modernist ideas. Sibley Watson had been a childhood friend in Rochester, Bragdon was capable of writing simply and clearly, and he had much to say on subjects far from Theosophy. He was rather old for bohemian excesses, and seemed content with his new life.[14]

He did serve, however, in two additional roles before the end of the first jazz age. On 26 November, 1923, A. R. Orage wrote him from London that he would soon arrive to prepare the way for a visit from Gurdjieff in January. Bragdon was underwhelmed at this news. Although an admirer of Ouspensky, he harbored many doubts about Gurdjieff and the Institute for the Harmonious Development of Man; "something deep within me demurred." But the irrepressible Orage kept after him, and so Bragdon reluctantly attended several of the meetings and performances that Orage arranged. A sight of the guru did nothing to change his opinion: "There was something *disturbing* about him." Gurdjieff "impressed me as a man of power, but at the same time I was a little repelled; I did not want to be drawn into that particular act." Besides, Gurdjieff's English was so bad, few could understand him. Bragdon's views would moderate over the 1930s, but he remained more sympathetic to thoughtful books than to gurus or their utopian experiments.[15]

Perhaps too visible in occult circles, Bragdon may well have enjoyed more influence than he realized by virtue of where he lived and with whom he ate. On 25 February, 1924, he was one of the first tenants to move into the new Shelton Hotel; in November 1925, Alfred Stieglitz and Georgia O'Keeffe also moved in. The next February, a mutual friend wrote Bragdon telling him that he should introduce himself to the couple, which he immediately did. With Stieglitz, a man of almost identical age, he hit it off immediately, and they all began to have regular breakfasts together. With O'Keeffe things were a bit cooler, but as the most thorough of recent O'Keeffe scholars for this period has suggested, both were fascinated by the fourth dimension, by "the beyond which is within," and both revered the sort of organic forms for which Louis Sullivan seemed the most obvious mutual source. O'Keeffe was a "maverick mystic," so were Bragdon and Stieglitz, and so indeed was their mutual friend, Arthur Dove.[16]

SIXTEEN

MARGARET ANDERSON'S SEARCH
FOR ECSTASY

During the summer of 1916, the life of Margaret Anderson and the contents of the *Little Review* both entered a period of rapid change that had long-range consequences for both American and European modernism. Having been based in Chicago for the first two years of their public lives, both Anderson and her journal had begun to mutate rapidly with the arrival of Jane Heap in February. By summer, the two women were intensely committed partners, and almost as a honeymoon they took off for California. Leaving behind an anarchist phase devoted to Emma Goldman in politics and Friedrich Nietzsche in philosophy, they also left behind the chance for obtaining much material for their journal from their usual sources. Ever blithe under stress, they published the September issue with numerous blank pages, as a provocative want ad in their quixotic search for new art expressive of the intensity they both sought. Realizing that they had to act decisively or admit failure, they opted to join what had become almost a Chicago renaissance migration and shift their base of operations to New York City.

Sitting in London in 1914, his eye regularly sweeping the American cultural desert for even faint signs of an oasis for writers, Ezra Pound had taken immediate note of the initial issues of the *Little Review*. He was then himself affiliated with *Poetry*, but thought perhaps the new contender would prove encouraging to artists not yet quite up to *Poetry*'s level. By 1916, his irritation at Harriet Monroe's various gaucheries of taste and her meddlesome editorial interventions was growing, and he was contributing the occasional "Letter from London" and looking about for alternative outlets for the work of himself and his friends. He gently mocked the decision of Anderson and Heap to stop in New York, insisting that even in wartime London and Paris were more appropriate cultural centers. But Pound never saw an empty page that he couldn't fill it with a worthy poem, and immediately offered his services on a regular basis. Late in January 1917 he told Anderson that he was in search of an "official organ" in which he and T. S. Eliot could "appear once a month" and "James Joyce can appear when he likes, and where Wyndham Lewis can appear if he comes back from the war." By early February, he had his wind clearly up: "I want to start off the new order of things with a bang."[1]

By the issue of May 1917 Pound had joined the masthead as foreign editor; in July, the magazine featured a subscription premium of a copy of *Portrait of the Artist as a Young Man* at a discount to new subscribers; and the major payoff came with the issue dated March 1918, when *Ulysses* began its serial appearance. Anderson later wrote that when the first chapter hit her desk, she began to read and immediately had a Joycean epiphany: "This is the most beautiful thing we'll ever have, I cried. We'll print it if it's the last effort of our lives." There is no reason to doubt the gist of the recollection, which sounds in character. But as Jane Heap noted, they were both already devoted to Joyce's concept of the artist as the central focus of art in the earlier novel. Modernism, or Ireland, or Greek myth, as such, interested them far less. In an historically significant chronological evolution, Emma Goldman's free individual had metamorphosed into the artist experiencing ecstasy and evoking it in readers. And with both editors, such ecstasy had divine sanction. "Mr. Joyce was talking about the artist of any land, not the youth of England or any other country," Heap wrote. "In this country there is only God to thank that the young artist does not go entirely mad over one and all of its institutions." In anyone else, such a casual invocation of the deity would probably be meaningless, but with both editors, time would prove otherwise.

The history of Stephen Dedalus proved important to them less for its contribution to literature than for its contribution to their acceptance of mystical religion. Joyce never intended any such thing, but then, the history of modernism, like history in general, was full of unintended consequences.[2]

Although Pound stopped being foreign editor of the *Review* in Spring 1919, and did not rejoin the magazine until April 1921, he placed its editors in the hands of the now well-known lawyer John Quinn for the crucial period of the *Ulysses* trial. Quinn was an American of Irish descent much interested in the painting and writing both of his ancestral isle and of Great Britain. Not especially wealthy, he earned enough each month to support both the obsessive acquisition of more paintings than he could display, and the subvention of the careers of Joyce, Wyndham Lewis, and others, usually through the purchase of manuscripts with Pound serving as agent. Pound and Quinn worked out an arrangement where Pound could use one hundred and fifty pounds per year to pay authors for their contributions to the *Little Review*. This meant occasional meetings between its editors and their benefactor, and a good deal of steaming correspondence between Pound and Quinn across the Atlantic.

The points of friction were many. Anderson retained a deep affection for Emma Goldman and remained attracted by much that the word "anarchism" suggested, even though she had moved on; Quinn detested both. Neither Anderson nor Heap were even slightly interested in money, business, or the minimal requirements of conventional accounting practice; Quinn was an obsessive bean counter, especially when his personal funds were at risk. Neither woman understood nor cared about legal tactics; Quinn had to do both. The editors mistrusted all society; Quinn was one of its pillars, and public opinion was important to him. Most of all, largely unmentioned but steaming to the point where it positively fogged his correspondence, was the issue of sexuality. Quinn was a notorious predator. Unable or unwilling to understand Anderson's sexual preferences, he found her "a woman of taste and refinement and good looking," in one letter to Pound; and "a damned attractive young woman, one of the handsomest I have ever seen, very high spirited, very courageous and very fine" in a second. He dismissed the possibly androgynous Heap out of hand. They in turn complained to Pound about his tightness with money, vulgarity of aesthetic expression, and general irascibility. The issues had obviously been coming up for some time. "I have never known anyone worth a damn who wasn't irascible," he shot back.[3]

When it came to censorship, the editors, Pound, and Quinn all knew what they were doing. The literary folks had been attacking American philistia for most of their active lives—it was a key ingredient in their development into modernists in the first place. Not only did war then exacerbate censorious tendencies already lurking within most politicians and preachers, but the *Little Review* knew what was up at first hand, when the October 1917 issue faced suppression for its inclusion of Lewis's "Cantleman's Spring Mate." More irascible in private than he could afford to be in public, Quinn thought the journal went out of its way to be provocative. On the whole, he thought book publications easier to defend in court and preferred evasion to confrontation. Court victories for censorship, he knew, could set dangerous precedents that could make literary publications more difficult rather than less, at least over the short run.

In a sweat as much sexual as legal, Quinn spluttered to Pound in escalating fury as the crisis developed. Anderson suddenly appeared unannounced at his office one day, "dressed in a becoming gray suit; looking a little thinner than before; and smiling and looking almost as embarrassed as a virgin in a law office," to beg for money. There being frontiers of virginity closed to Quinn's imagination, she managed to extract two hundred dollars, but he swore it was "the last contribution I shall make to the Little Review and I perhaps should not have made that." But the fact remained that *Ulysses* was patently offensive to the public taste of 1920, Quinn knew it, and knew as well that its greatness as literature provided little legal ammunition.

Pound was already on record that he thought Joyce "worth be-ing suppressed for," the women proved feckless as ever, and the legal system simply plowed them all under. The daughter of a lawyer had stumbled on a copy of the *Little Review*, been offended, and had asked her father to do something about it. He complained to the district attorney of New York County, he in turn contacted John Sumner, the leading vice crusader of the day, and Sumner swore out a complaint. As Quinn noted acidly to Pound, this was the normal working of a legitimate if unfortunate law, one in fact copied from the British and less restrictive than those on the Con-tinent: "So, don't blow off at your typewriter with the idea that this is a sign of provinciality, or anything peculiar to America." Mod-ernist attitudes misunderstood social change. "Law is changed by public opinion, discreetly organized and not by flagrant violations leading to convictions."[4]

In an argument that often distressed his clients, Quinn admit-ted that *Ulysses* was filthy but insisted that its was the "bracing" filth of a Swift or a Rabelais and should not be subject to suppres-sion. It was, furthermore, largely incomprehensible to the average mind; it could anger people, but not corrupt anyone. This was an ingenious argument in its way, and set precedents for the ultimate acceptance of the book as a book in the 1930s, but in the short run it and the *Little Review* lost. The decision intimidated several American publishers and pushed Joyce to look for an outlet in Eu-rope, which Sylvia Beach soon provided for him; and it helped push Anderson toward a nervous breakdown, a decision to close the review on or about its tenth anniversary in 1924, and a decisive change in partners.[5]

Over the course of a long if sporadically documented life, Mar-garet Anderson had several partners, all closely identified with the arts and fascinated by occult religious experiences. For the four years or so of the *Little Review*'s major phase, 1916 to 1920, when James Joyce as a writer and Stephen Dedalus as a role model dom-inated her imagination, Anderson lived with Jane Heap: Part Nor-wegian, part Anglo-Saxon by ancestry, suicidal by disposition, theatrical in expression, handsome to her lover, Heap remains in Anderson's oblique memoirs largely through "her soft deep eyes, in which you could watch thought take form," thought "that was always clearest when she talked of the undefinable, the vast, or the unknown; thought that made other people's thinking seem unnecessary." They talked endlessly, shared much, and would remain in touch for many years after they ceased being a couple.[6]

On the surface, at least, Georgette Leblanc was very different. A French actress, she had made her way for many years in the world of music as the companion of Maurice Maeterlinck. As in many symbolist circles, mystical religious ideas cohabited with artistic creativity, and she records in her memoirs that Sâr Peladan and numerous Rosicrucians were occasional visitors to her home. Heterosexual at least at first, she married young and may never have terminated that unsuccessful experiment legally. Over the years, the relationship to Maeterlinck evolved into a maternal partnership; nevertheless, she was clearly devastated when Maeterlinck suddenly abandoned her for a much younger woman, whom he married. Leblanc went to America to recover in 1920. Anderson remained convinced for life that destiny had taken a hand: "We cannot have met by chance, Georgette and I, since we knew at once that we were to join hands and advance through life together." Her "marvellous mystic face" was "the land I have been seeking." Twenty years and linguistic incomprehension made not the slightest difference. For Anderson, they had "a true and limitless human communication."

Pianist Allen Tanner brought them together, underlining the personal connections that so often joined the worlds of modernist literature and music. Off men for life, Leblanc too apparently experienced love, or at least fascination, at first sight: Struck by the "grand chic" of Anderson's suit, she stared at this "belle jeune femme si parfaitement élégante," and commented to Tanner: "c'est là . . . la femme sauvage . . . la femme préhistorique." John Quinn couldn't have said it better. Anderson's blue eyes and profound silences said more than a knowledge of French possibly could have. A complicated, melodramatic woman herself, Leblanc read "une totale simplicité" into the character of her new friend. They were soon healing together in exurban Bernardsville, New Jersey, where they met George Antheil and consolidated a growing and binational circle of friends.[7]

Over the next several months, Antheil, then Tanner, and then Anderson decided to go to Europe. She decided to give up the editing of the review to Jane Heap, who rejected the gift and insisted that editorially, if not domestically, things should go on as before. They did, at least on the surface, and Anderson continued to be a literary presence for a couple of years, meeting the faces that went with her correspondence. She met Pound and introduced Antheil to him. She met James Joyce and Nora Barnacle in Pound's studio. She visited Gertrude Stein, Brancusi, and Picabia, meeting Satie by chance. She attended performances of the Swedish Ballet. She had a grand time using her editorial position as a pretext for entering the world of modernist music and literature.

Increasingly, however, Heap ran the review. After visiting Europe in 1923, she returned to New York, and the remaining issues demonstrated the shifting of her responsibility. Dominated by Pound's London orientation into 1921, the *Little Review* quickly became a Paris journal in all but name, reflecting Heap's preferences for dada, surrealism, and an atmosphere of *blague.* As it turned out, Anderson never could get on well with Stein or her repetitious style; Heap, by contrast, got on well with Stein in person and on paper, and the review inevitably drifted accordingly. By 1926, Heap had become interested in theater, and the next year industrialism and the machine. The last issue of any importance, the catalog of a "Machine-Age Exposition," appeared in 1927, and a final whimper of no significance except for a brief obituary, appeared unnoticed in 1929. Looking back from the 1950s, Anderson recalled that Heap had been in complete control from 1924 to 1929, and there is no reason to doubt her. "During those years I stayed in France, and almost nothing that I read in the *Little Review* that came to me there held any vitality for me at all, with the exception of the 'notes' that Jane still wrote."[8]

The search for ecstasy, as she never ceased to say, had been at the core of Anderson's motivations since girlhood. She had found it first in Goldman and Nietzsche, then in Joyce and the portrait of the artist as a universal role model, and third in life with Leblanc at home and distinguished aesthetes along the boulevards. Always, she had found it as well in music, lamentably enough in the bloated late romanticism of Wagner and Rachmaninov; she never did care much either for the likes of Scarlatti and Haydn, nor for the works of her own contemporaries, such as Bartók and Hindemith. But even life with a primary source of her own sex was not enough, although she and Leblanc had two devoted decades together. They both needed a religious center, and they found it in the writings of Ouspensky and the presence of Gurdjieff. And whereas male admirers such as Jean Toomer, Hart Crane, Gorham Munson, and Waldo Frank tended to admire from afar, merely attending lectures and study groups, the women often stayed. As time passed, they became something of a lesbian support group devoted chastely to a male guru. Such were the connecting tissues that sustained the little society through Depression and war and that disintegrated only with Gurdjieff's death in 1948.[9]

The sense of chronology may be weak, but the logic of free association remains clear in Anderson's autobiography. Recalling the most intense period of her life with Heap, in California before the move to New York, Anderson insisted that "we had never thought of art simply as painting, poetry, music, sculpture. We thought art was an expression, through the arts, of a need of something else." In New York, they then read a book of Claude Bragdon's, unnamed, that looked forward to the book Bragdon was helping to translate, Ouspensky's *Tertium Organum*. They admired this book when it appeared, but "what interested us most about Ouspensky was the rumor that he was associated with a greater man called Gurdjieff," about whom he was supposed to be writing a book. At this point, Alfred Richard Orage arrived in his role of John the

Baptist for Gurdjieff, immediately captivating Toomer, Crane, Frank, Munson, and the two women.

The salons of modernism, with that of Walter and Louise Arensberg being the preeminent one in the New York area, had been bringing oddly matched people together for a full generation before the winter of 1923/4, but for sheer unpredictability the Gurdjieff circle deserves at least minor immortality in the intellectual history of cultural behavior. Probably the most representative couple involved was the literary critic and editor Gorham Munson and his wife, dancer and instructor Elizabeth Delza. Jean Toomer introduced them both to Orage on the day in February 1924, when Orage's plans were to come to first fruition with a "demonstration of ancient dances." Music, dance, literature, and religious yearning had helped bond the Munson/Delza relationship fully as much as it had the Anderson/Heap one, and such performances were proving more efficacious in spreading new ideas than formal lectures.

More kinetic than literary in her judgments, Delza first felt Orage's "alertness and his relaxation." She sensed "something always in motion but not hurried, not tense, not forced—an easy swiftness which could change its course deftly and resume the original direction with perfect sureness." She recalled specifically his "quick intelligence, quick feeling and understanding, and an extraordinary speed of perception—a sort of lightning functioning."

Munson filtered the impressions after the fashion of a man of letters. "I felt that this man's *note* was intelligence, and I have never met a man who struck it with as much clarity." The same word kept recurring to him. "The hazel eyes, alive and challenging, were intelligent. The strong nose was intelligent. The mouth, ready to smile at paradox, was intelligent." He brought forth images of the elephantine, for "the elephant is reputed to be the most intelligent of beasts." This was, he quickly added, "a light and swift-moving elephant, not a lumbering one." Although fifty-one, he showed scant signs of aging, and talked "well" that day about those movements of the human body that had been "taken from the art of the Ancient East"—examples of sacred gymnastics, sacred dances, and religious ceremonies "preserved in Central Asia." Gurdjieff, Orage insisted portentously, "was able to prove that in the Orient certain dances have not lost the deep religious and scientific significance they had in the remote past."

Orage tied the various elements of dance, thought, and faith together that evening. He spoke of "a new quality of concentration and attention and a new direction of the mind" that the dance exercises would presumably achieve. Dancing, he went on, meant something different in the East from what it meant in the West. It traditionally held the entry keys to the temples of religion and art. "A person who specialized in a subject communicated his knowledge through works of art, particularly dances, as we spread the knowledge through books." Thus, the dances that intellectuals would view in the New York of early 1924 originated in ancient sacred dances that not only constituted aesthetic experiences, but were books or scripts "containing a definite piece of knowledge." Not everyone could read it, but it was there for all who wished to try. A demonstration followed, which in toto "had a strange impact that can only be described as awakening." Design and detail clearly conveyed knowledge of a sort only available to the aesthetically aware: "One could not read it, only feel it; and the feeling was—tremendous."[10]

Despite her new relationship with Georgette Leblanc in France, Anderson continued to share an apartment with Heap during her visits to New York—*Little Review* headquarters seemed to be wherever Heap was on a given day. They had welcomed Orage, attended lectures and performances, and soon were welcoming Gurdjieff himself: "a dark man with an oriental face, whose life seemed to reside in his eyes. He had a presence impossible to describe because I had never encountered another with which to compare it." They were all expecting, well, "a seer, a prophet, a messiah?"—even many years later, she hedged her words with hand-wringing question marks, perhaps a sign of charismatic shock. She almost literally did not know what to say, although managing three books in the effort to pin down her fascination. "I think I really thought of Gurdjieff, at first, as a sort of Hermes, teaching his son Tat." She prided herself on her devotion to science rather than mystery, but was sure the two had now fused: "What mystics have taught through ecstatic revelation, Gurdjieff would teach as a science—an exact science of man and human behavior—a supreme science of God, world, man—based on sources outside the scope, reach, knowledge or conception of modern scientists and psychologists." Meanwhile the audience could catch glimpses of his face at the performances, exhorting his pupils "to greater, and ever greater, precision."[11]

According to the best historian of the subject, Louise Welch, the program began "with the dancers in an almost military order of seven files and three rows, but costumed with quite unmilitary softness." Regardless of sex, all dancers "wore white tunics over full white trousers gathered at the ankle, much like the Rajput way of dressing, with its yielding responsiveness to bodily motion." Over the tunics, dancers wore belts that were essentially "wide sashes, looped on the left side, in the seven colors of the spectrum, and for the first few movements the dancers stood in that order: red, orange, yellow, green, blue, indigo, violet." Dances were designed "to make the colors change and shift," giving viewers the illusion of "watching white light pressed very slowly through a prism and breaking into its spectral color." Men in Islamic-style costumes then engaged in "Dervish exercises," as well as dances designed to portray an elaborate symbolism, which perhaps only Gurdjieff himself really understood.

After a pause, Orage appeared to explain what would follow, the "stop" exercise that received a good deal of comment both at the time and in subsequent interviews and treatments. Dancers went about conventional motions until the shout to "stop," at which point all had to freeze in place regardless of position. The point was not theatrical effect—nor twisted ankles—but heightened consciousness. "Since the body is made to stop in quite unplanned positions, the dancer cannot help but observe himself in a new situation—between postures, as it were." He had fallen into habitual, rote movements in real life, and through dance could regroove. "This was one way to break the vicious circle of his automatism." The audience was almost always "electrified," some experiencing "fear." "Others were shocked into the vision of a new human possibility."

Ever supportive, Welch admitted that she had heard of reports that "the dancers, still frozen in the stop, fell off the stage into the orchestra pit," but she assured readers in the 1980s that such "did not, of course, actually happen." William Seabrook, an historian of witchcraft, had a less enamored account. Describing Gurdjieff as "a calm, bull-like man, with muscles in those days as hard as steel, in immaculate dinner clothes, his head shaven like a Prussian officer's, with black luxurient handlebar moustaches, and generally smoking expensive Egyptian cigarettes," Seabrook compared him to "a slave-master or wild-animal trainer, with an invisible bullwhip switching inaudibly through the air." Always casual, never shouting, completely in command, he had his troupe race toward the audience on at least one occasion, stopping only as they became "an aerial human avalanche," flying "across the orchestra, down among the empty chairs, on the floor, bodies pell-mell, piled on top of each other, arms and legs sticking out in weird postures—frozen there, fallen, in complete immobility and silence." Gurdjieff, having lighted a cigarette, calmly gave them permission to relax, and miraculously no one was hurt. The audience both applauded and protested. "It had almost been too much." Gurdjieff's chief comment: "If we live calm, monotonous days and peaceful nights, we stultify. We had better torture our own spirit than suffer the inanities of calm."[12]

All during the spring of 1924, Orage continued to lecture and sign up disciples for Gurdjieff. According to Munson, he and his wife joined a group that centered on Anderson and Heap, meeting regularly at 24 East 11th Street. Georgette Leblanc and her faithful servant Monique were also in the city that spring, everyone seemed to be compatible, and although the meetings usually attracted only a small core of true believers, Munson could recall at least one evening that "found Van Wyck Brooks and Padraic Colum sitting inconspicuously in a corner." Over the next couple of years, with occasional absences for visits to Fontainebleau, the meeting place shifted to Muriel Draper's "barnlike quarters" at 24 East 40th Street. Among those who might be in attendance: pianist Carol Robinson, Helen Westley, and Edna Kenton from the world of theater; Mabel Dodge Luhan and her husband Tony, in from Taos; Harlem artist Aaron Douglas; and Herbert Croly and T. S. Matthews, very senior and very junior editors at the *New Republic*. Jean Toomer was the most devoted of all. "If it cannot be said that the visit of Gurdjieff took America by storm," Munson accurately enough noted, "it can be said that it raised a conversational storm in the circles of the intelligentsia."[13]

In June, the *Little Review* entourage was ready to sail, the four of them; "we knew the import of our decision: we had prepared to 'cast aside our nets' and follow." A month later Toomer arrived, only to find that he never really fitted in. On a later visit in 1927, he would bring Waldo Frank along, but Frank was even less compatible. Carol Robinson did better, living at Prieuré for a long time, winning Gurdjieff entirely, and becoming a leading exponent of his music. Back in New York, she and Elizabeth Delza would spend many years in informal collaboration, teaching music and dance alternately to students up to college age. It is, simply, impossible to enumerate all those areas in which Gurdjieff and his disciple Orage had influence.[14]

The Château du Prieuré at Fontainebleau-Avon, to give a version of its official name, had already entered literary history. Seeking much the same spiritual solace, the New Zealand writer Katherine Mansfield had chosen it as a final refuge in her brave fight against tuberculosis; she had succumbed there shortly after it opened, in 1923. Long available for study, her letters have dominated literary discourse about the place, unintentionally leaving the impression of an odd collection of the sick and the maladjusted quixotically seeking on earth what they feared would no longer be available in heaven for the liberated intelligentsia of the 1920s.

Subsequent anecdotal material concerning Gurdjieff's 1924 automobile accident, or the pointless manual labor imposed on tender
literary folk like Orage, have only clouded the scene; subsequent
publication of Gurdjieff's opaque and fanciful teachings has if anything only made things worse. The history of modernism contained a great deal more than the cafés of Paris, and the various
"isms" that flourished there so loudly. However odd life at the
Prieuré may have appeared to those oriented in other directions, it
attracted too many gifted and cosmopolitan people not to deserve
serious attention.[15]

The life of Georges Ivanovich Gurdjieff remains undocu-
mentable in the conventional sense. He was most probably born in
1874, give or take about three years, somewhere in the Russo-Turkish borderland, to a Greek father and an Armenian mother. He wandered all over Eastern Europe and Northern Asia picking up an
endless supply of stories that later served as vehicles for his interminable religious parables. An uncompromising materialist, he was
fascinated by the complexes of ideas now associated with such
terms as occultism, hypnosis, and animal magnetism. He was familiar with the concepts of traditional Western medicine and psychoanalysis, and scornful of both. He experimented with alcohol and
drugs as ways to heighten consciousness. He began to surface in
conventional historical contexts in St. Petersburg in 1913 and
Moscow in 1914. In 1915 he met P. D. Ouspensky in Moscow and
they went back to St. Petersburg together, with Gurdjieff in the role
of religious leader, which Ouspensky had long been seeking.

Although incompatibilities of personality and doctrine would
soon separate them, the two seemed to agree on certain images
and metaphors that yielded teachable doctrines. Mankind was a
collection of sleeping machines, trapped in the mad machine of
World War I, which in turn was but a minute particle of the machine that constituted the universe. The first duty of the individual was to awaken, to become active rather than passive. To assist
individuals to awaken, the "Man Who Knows" would occasionally
appear on earth as a teacher, leaving behind increasing particles of

thought. These constituted occult wisdom, handed down over countless ages. Impossibly complicated in detail and exposition, the ideas meant in practice that a novitiate had to understand the need to achieve psychological balance between the three essential centers in human nature: the intellectual, the emotional, and the physical. In time, Gurdjieff would speak of humans as "three-brained beings," and then expand the three to seven. The work, the exercises, the dances—with their obsessive "threes" and "sevens"—were designed to balance or tune the human machines. And since, in a functioning, self-enclosed machine, the future was the same as the past, memory of oneself became the future of oneself—in effect, a fourth dimension.[16]

The war and the revolution disrupted every life in the area, and such religious seekers instinctively rejected bolshevism. With the help of Orage's editorial commissions, Viscountess Rothermere's subventions, and Claude Bragdon's royalty checks, Ouspensky eventually made it to London. Gurdjieff first tried to put down roots in Germany, failed, and continued on to London. Followers were no problem but public authorities were. Probably due to widespread fears of bolshevism, neither he nor his followers could get permanent visas. The French government was more accommodating, so the group headed for Paris, bought the unoccupied Prieuré out at Fontainebleau, and in October 1922 opened what translated as The Institute for the Harmonious Development of Man (L'Institut du Développement Harmonique de l'Homme).

At the time Gurdjieff bought the property, the Prieuré stood on about 200 acres, a potentially spectacular site. But no one had lived there since 1914, and early arrivals had to achieve their sense of psychological balance by recovering overgrown trails, clearing fallen trees, mowing lawns, digging ditches, moving large stones, and so on. Indoors, the ground floor contained an Empire drawing room, salon, and library, all of which had seen better days. The second floor, "the Ritz" in local slang, had quarters for Gurdjieff and his companion, and guests who were worthy of special attention. The third floor, the "Monks' Corridor," was home for most of the long-term disciples. Children, supervised by one mother for a week at a time in rotation, lived in a separate building. Usually from sixty to seventy people were in residence at any one time, divided about evenly between Eastern Europeans who spoke no English, and English speakers who spoke little else.

The description of such a motley mixture of people, beliefs, and duties hardly explains the appeal of such a place to visitors as individualistic and cultivated as Anderson, Heap, and Leblanc. The presence of Thomas and Olga de Hartmann, close friends of Gurdjieff, and collaborators with him from 1917 on, provides the best example of the reasons why these women might be so attracted, quite apart from the strictly religious or doctrinal aspects of the sect.

Long before meeting Gurdjieff, Thomas de Hartmann had been an established composer in St. Petersburg. A graduate of the Imperial Conservatory of Music, he had studied composition with three of the great composers of nineteenth-century Russia: Nikolai Rimsky-Korsakov, Anton Arensky, and Sergei Taneyev; and piano with Mme. Essipoff-Leschetizky, the former student and second wife of the world-class pianist and teacher, Theodor Leschetizky. De Hartmann composed chiefly for voice and piano, but a ballet, *The Pink Flower,* had included Pavlova, Fokine, and Nijinsky in its 1907 run at the Imperial Opera. The Czar himself granted his petition for exemption from military service so that he could go to Munich to study conducting. There he made friends with Wassily Kandinsky and was on the fringes of *Der Blaue Reiter.* His wife was born Olga Arcadievna de Schumacher, her father being a high official in the Russian government. As if all this were not enough, de Hartmann's uncle was Eduard de Hartmann, whose *The Philosophy of the Unconscious* (1869) was well known in America although available chiefly in German. De Hartmann's main function at the Prieuré was not only to compose for and accompany the dance exercises, but to take Gurdjieff's own improvised "compositions" down from piano to paper and make them publishable.

Early in 1924, he came along when Gurdjieff and the dancers made their first trip to America.[17]

Anderson, Heap, and Leblanc all lived for music, however literary they might seem due to their connections to the *Little Review*. An environment with both Gurdjieff and de Hartmann must have seemed an achieved utopia, even without Orage and others who were in and out. The three women arrived by train and foot from Paris, wandered happily among the newly restored gardens, and then chose "cells" in Monks' Row, which Anderson habitually referred to as "the Monastery," which didn't make much literal sense: "mine over the diningroom, Georgette's toward the forest. Jane chose a room at the back that looked into a farmyard, because she liked to be wakened by crowing cocks." At dinner, Ouspensky "sat at Gurdjieff's left and acted like a small boy, laughing more than he meant to, saying what he meant not to," flushed with alcohol that Gurdjieff pushed on him with frequent Russian-style toasts. It was a winning scene, although Ouspensky and Gurdjieff were close to a break and everyone knew it.

During her first few months, Gurdjieff was usually secluded, writing out his ideas for teaching purposes and perhaps, in the distant future, publication. He would appear at meals and performances, and take the wheel for hair-raisingly inept forays in a car, but was largely unavailable for personal chats, something his primitive English was then hardly up to anyway. Anderson insisted, even a quarter of a century later, that she could not describe her guru. "I would feel as if I had been asked to write a description of Nature in all her moods." Nor could she "talk of the material of his teaching, of its method or its meaning." She could only "tell what it did to me, that is all." His goal in his own words was enough for her: "I cannot develop you; I can create conditions in which you can develop yourself." She wanted to find God, and did find "a place where reverent study filled the days and nights." She loved music, and recalled most vividly the many nights when Gurdjieff sat at the piano composing, with de Hartmann scoring on the spot.

Others choreographed almost as quickly. As always, they talked afterwards.[18]

Bluntly heterosexual himself, usually with wife or companion nearby, Gurdjieff paid no obvious attention to the increasingly disproportionate homosexuality of his most devoted followers. Thomas de Hartmann aside, few males persist in the memoir literature even in minor roles so long as the Man Who Knows lived. Lesbian women seemed implicitly to agree with Janet Flanner, that America was hard, cold, unattractive, and male; Paris, by contrast, was soft, warm, appealing, and female. Whether in Fontainebleau, Paris, or some temporarily available chateau, women found each other, sometimes almost against their individual, unbalanced wills. For some, the salons of Gertrude Stein or Natalie Barney, or the bookshops of Sylvia Beach and Adrienne Monnier sufficed to anchor a secular and often passionate existence. For others, Gurdjieff himself or through his teachings, served: The Man Who Knows did not need their physical attentions, nor were they offered; but somehow he helped even when he wasn't there. Solita Solano was one, so devoted to Janet Flanner during the 1920s that they inspired portraits of Nip and Tuck in Djuna Barnes's *Ladies' Almanack*, the privately published satire of Barney's salon. Solano was unimpressed when she met Gurdjieff in 1927 at Prieuré, bored by the man and his music. Anderson and Heap persisted, and arranged a second meeting at a Paris restaurant. "He seated me next to him and [talked] for two hours in broken English. I rejected his language, the suit he was wearing and his table manners; I decided that I rather disliked him." Yet even years later, "in a crisis of misery," she suddenly felt a change of heart, sought him out at the Grand Hotel, and within days was in a group of intense women who "formed the nucleus of a new group which was to grow larger year by year until the end of his life." Jane Heap having moved to London, the group included Solano, Anderson, Leblanc, Louise Davidson, and Kathryn Hulme: "five highly vibrating beggars waiting for a crumb from the master's table," in Hulme's words.[19]

The ripple effects of such activity were hardly limited to the lesbian literary community, however central it may have been to Gurdjieff's daily activities. Indeed, they seem almost as "unknowable" as Anderson's Gurdjieff and as undefinable as the essential principles of his ideas. But let two examples suffice.

One of the young women studying at Prieuré was a Montenegrin, Olga Milanoff. Primarily interested in music, she studied especially with Carol Robinson, profiting from Robinson's wide network of friends, who ranged from composer Henry Cowell to Katherine Ruth Heyman, the advocate of Scriabin and long-term friend of Ezra Pound. When Olga married Frank Lloyd Wright and became his "Olgivanna," she was soon able to spread Gurdjieff's ideas and music to both Taliesin East and West. With four years of Prieuré living behind her, she shaped the life of her own "Master," obviously a "Man Who Knows," and his disciples, into the peculiar routines that would mark life there for decades. A humorless micromanager, Olgivanna not only choreographed dances based on Gurdjieff's principles, she also introduced the ideas of balance and harmony, of physical and mental labor. She got her famous husband into the habit of delivering esoteric homilies that merged the occultisms of America and Russia into an idiosyncratic approach to creativity. Robinson remained a regular visitor who both gave solo concerts and led chamber-music festivals. So long and close were the relationships formed that in time she taught their daughter Iovanna as well, and when Wright died at ninety, she was still available to play a memorial concert.[20]

No one would assert Gurdjieffian effects on the design of Wright's buildings, however much they might have taken over his domestic habits; although at least one major critic has suggested that Gurdjieff's concepts contributed to the broader context of Wright's Broadacre City plans.[21] With Lincoln Kirstein, the effects seem far more portentous, if equally unmeasurable. Here, Americans had one of the central figures in the world of ballet, a man whose ideas were absolutely crucial to that art form for the next half-century. His collaborator, a Georgian originally christened

Georgi Melitonovitch Balanchivadze, had changed his name to Balanchine at the request of Serge Diaghilev—occultism wasn't the only field where "Russian" origins added a certain charismatic aura. No one with adequate background knowledge has re-created the School of American Ballet and its successors, but on the surface at least, Balanchine was yet another Man Who Knows with very definite ideas of balance that went far beyond what appeared on the stage.

But Kirstein himself could not have been clearer. In 1927, when a sophomore at Harvard, he went with a friend to Prieuré and checked into the "Ritz" section. After a detailed tour of the area, including both the town and the Institute grounds, he went to "The Study House" to observe "two dozen people, an equal corps of men and women, clad in vaguely 'oriental' pajamas, belted around their middles," who were "following patterns of movement with mortal seriousness." The performances resembled nothing he had ever observed. "I began to realize it was governed by counts, that, instead of moving freely, the men and women were mutely counting." Oblivious to the small audience, the dancers worked into increasingly complex routines. Although these seemed "rather static, the sequence of hand signs and shifting steps was accentuated by a steady rhythm." The music, produced by a small harmonium, suddenly accelerated. "In one thunderous surge, the entire body of men and women went berserk, and racing, with a startling jump as from a catapult, the whole mass of bodies came hurtling straight at me." A voice suddenly yelled "STOP!" and everyone froze. Kirstein was observing the increasingly sophisticated stop dancing that had captivated Anderson and the rest in New York.

Mystified at the resulting chaos, Kirstein felt "shaken." The spectacle "gave me a theatrical shudder to which no dance or drama that I had seen could compare." His first sight of Gurdjieff came several hours later: He seemed "an obese, dark-pink male, hairy and with his belly down." Two adult males supported a young boy "who was jogged up and down on the lying man's spine." All were naked, in a room scorching hot, a Russian version of a Turkish bath. Everyone seemed to be having a high old time, and Kirstein was soon as relaxed and jolly as any. At first sight desperate to leave, he was soon contemplating a longer stay. "A surge of well-being, of which I'd had a faint touch before, rushed up from somewhere to overwhelm me." He experienced "one of the last recurrences of those mystical moments which belong to the instinctive, cloudless miracles of childhood, as when I was first shown what notes printed on a page of music meant."

The description of host, meals, drinks, and companions went on for pages, the impressions still vivid sixty-six years later. But: "I feel paralyzing inadequacy trying to write of Mr. Gurdjieff." The man "exerted more influence on my behavior than anyone, including my parents." Encountering him at a time of personal disorientation, when the future seemed totally open, Kirstein internalized the man and "under the influence of a force amounting to a revelation, I surrendered to whatever of his system I could grasp." The effects never totally wore off: "I had no trouble in formulating 'dancing' as praise rather than fun. I credited the entity, which many spelled 'God,' as Order." Much remained unexplained. "Nevertheless, the Gurdjieffian metaphysics kept me warm." His formula, "that most men are sleepwalkers, that most lives pass in mute, self-blinded somnambulism, that there is a factor which compels us to be pleased to exist passively without comprehension—seemed relentlessly reasonable." Modernism, if not "modern dance," had found one of its major voices for the next generation, in a perfect synthesis of self, ideal, and art. "Effort toward self-remembering is the key to all of Mr. Gurdjieff's proposals." Those bodies would be stopping in motion, in America, for many years to come. Kirstein returned to Harvard, Balanchine soon emigrated, and the Russo-Turkish border added yet another source for a maturing American modernism.[22]

CODA

WITH WORDS BY MALCOLM COWLEY

Something about the 1920s, and the generation that found its first voices during its early years, attracted analysis from the start. That most narcissistic of poets, E. E. Cummings, was first out of the gate with *The Enormous Room*, Ernest Hemingway was clearly in an autobiographical mood in *The Sun Also Rises,* and by the 1930s works of genuinely analytical merit were coming out almost annually. Nor were they confined to literature. In time, music provided several of the best, and even the visual arts, so often nonverbal, made a major contribution.[1]

Of all the acts of self-analysis, Malcolm Cowley's *Exile's Return* has had the longest run. Written first during the early 1930s, when Cowley had swung far to the humorless left, the first edition was something of an exorcism, as if modernism had been chiefly an episode of adolescent religious excess. The economic pressures of capitalism and the horrors of war had pushed the talented young to revolt and exile, but the Depression forced a political sobriety on all who wished to retain an audience. The Hitler-Stalin Pact, World War II, and the cold war then imposed rhetorical reality checks, and Cowley took another and more mature look. No more perfect nor complete than Paul Rosenfeld had been at the time, Cowley nevertheless did well, putting a kind of closure to the early experiences of his generation just before more detached scholars, with Frederick J. Hoffman in the lead, would start weighing in with more academic analyses.

Cowley took it as a given that sensitive writers felt alienated by the philistia of a progressive world that had exhausted itself in the futilities of sexual, alcoholic, and military repressions. That conservatives replaced progressives in the elections of 1920 made no difference: "Feeling like aliens in the commercial world, they sailed for Europe as soon as they had money enough to pay for their steamer tickets." Gertrude Stein may have meant her famous quote about how they were all a lost generation for another context, but still, the generation born in the years around 1900 was in fact lost "because it was uprooted" from any attachment to religion or tradition; "because its training had prepared it for another world than existed after the war"; "because it tried to live in exile"; "because it accepted no older guides to conduct"; and finally, "because it had formed a false picture of society and the writer's place in it."

In a classic distinction that shaped all its artistic products, Cowley's cohort assumed that life and art were two different realms. The mass of citizens scorned most artists and contemporary creative efforts, and the artists reciprocated. This went way beyond issues of class, industrialization, or the shift from rural to urban life. "Their real exile was from society itself, from any society to which they could honestly contribute and from which they could draw the strength that lies in shared convictions." A government and a war in which they felt little stake took them to Europe, but did not fundamentally change the relationship. The Ambulance Service was the perfect vehicle, for it took a person to war and took care of him, but it did not force the issue of involvement, let alone death: "It instilled into us what might be called a *spectatorial* attitude."

Behind all this detached movement, Cowley detected eight basic assumptions. 1) "Salvation by the child," let the young flourish naturally and they could remake the world; 2) "self-expression," or the artist's assumption that creative activity was the basic purpose of life; 3) "paganism," the rejection of external religious or moral restrictions and the cultivation of natural drives; 4) "living for the moment"; 5) "liberty"; 6) "female equality"; 7) "psychological adjustment"; 8) "changing place." The last five of these are presumably corollaries of the first three, the net result presumably being that Europeans handled the bulk of these matters more sensibly than Americans, and so artists should join them if at all possible. Cowley then went on, somewhat testily, to point out how well these somewhat imprecise assumptions all too easily fitted into capitalism. Buy now, consume, accumulate, bring women up to speed and then buy tickets to take them elsewhere! The grapes were a bit sour by the 1930s, but speaking in terms of cultural history, he was right, and a great many modernists would find themselves on the right, and not just in America.

"Yet there was one political event of the later 1920s that brought a great many writers together for a common purpose": the lengthy trial and unjust execution of Sacco and Vanzetti was something of a firebell in the night, a sign that artists could ignore society only at their long-term peril. Paris meanwhile changed, especially in its treatment of Americans. "The earlier exiles had been driven abroad by a hatred of American dullness and puritanism, yet primarily they had traveled *in search of* something." Their successors seemed "propelled from behind, pushed eastward by the need for *getting away from* something. They were not so much exiles as refugees," who were trying to escape "some quality of American civilization that they carried within themselves."

But the nature of their welcome had also changed. Parisians had originally welcomed Americans, as creative pilgrims from a country that had been crucial in winning the war and was openly Francophile in sympathy. These early apprentices had learned their trades by about 1926 or 1927, however. New arrivals were different, their numbers swollen as well by seedy emigrés from Russia, Germany, and the rest of Europe. Imperceptibly the atmosphere became crasser, as if "the natives were grasping the opportunity of exploiting all these visitors by raising prices and installing a jazz band in the principal café. Artists complained that it was impossible to work here any longer."

Many went home, the vanguard of an exodus that helped define the second jazz age. They arrived in New York only to find a new generation had somehow taken over at least the setting of trends. They looked and dressed and even talked differently, and for good reason: "They were learning to talk about 'our own' generation, which they contrasted with 'your lost' generation." Cowley and his friends found it hard "to get used to the idea that there were rebels younger than ourselves, who regarded us as relics of an age that was passing." Indeed, they all seemed to talk like Jake Barnes and Brett Ashley. Hemingway had passed from apprentice to role model in less than a decade, and he was not the only one.

As a modernist sympathizer who headed left, Cowley in retrospect found this shift long overdue. "The search itself was ending, and a new conception of art was replacing the idea that it was something purposeless, useless, wholly individual and forever opposed to a stupid world," he wrote somewhat complacently. "The artist and his art had once more become a part of the world, produced by and perhaps affecting it." And he concluded: "They had returned toward their earlier and indispensable task of revealing its values and making it more human."[2]

NOTES

Introduction

1. See virtually any fat textbook or the following: Frederick Lewis Allen, *Only Yesterday* (New York, 1931); George Henry Soule, *Prosperity Decade, From War to Depression: 1917–1929* (New York, 1947); Arthur M. Schlesinger, Jr., *The Crisis of the Old Order, 1919–1933* (Boston, 1957); William E. Leuchtenberg, *The Perils of Prosperity, 1914–1932* (Chicago, 1958); John D. Hicks, *Republican Ascendancy, 1921–1933* (New York, 1960); Roderick Nash, *The Nervous Generation: American Thought, 1917–1930* (Chicago, 1970); Robert M. Crunden, *From Self to Society, 1919–1941* (Englewood Cliffs, 1972); Michael E. Parrish, *Anxious Decades: America in Prosperity and Depression, 1920–1941* (New York, 1992); Lynn Dumenil, *The Modern Temper: American Culture and Society in the 1920s* (New York, 1995).

Overture

1. See Paul Rosenfeld (hereafter PR) to Philip S. Platt, 1910–1915, passim., especially 10 March, 18 April, 22 May, and 7 August, 1913, and 11 February, 1914, Paul Rosenfeld Papers, Beinecke Library, Yale University (hereafter cited as PR-YU); and the wide range of unpublished or partially published memoir material at Yale, both fictional and nonfictional. The published novel, *The Boy in the Sun* (New York, 1928) is closely autobiographical and Jewishness is central to it. The most useful secondary sources are Hugh M. Potter, *False Dawn: Paul Rosenfeld and Art in America, 1916–1946* (Ann Arbor, 1980), ch. 1; and Bruce A. Butterfield, "Paul Rosenfeld: The Critic as Autobiographer," Ph.D. diss., University of Illinois, 1975, DA#75–14,087, ch.1. On Yale, see Dan A. Oren, *Joining the Club: A History of Jews and Yale* (New Haven, 1985); on the general problem, see Susanne Klingenstein, *Jews in the American Academy 1900–1940* (New Haven, 1991).

2. PR, "Grand Transformation Scene, 1907–1915," *Twice A Year* 5–6 (1940–41), 352–360; and "Scriabine," in *Musical Portraits* (New York, 1920), 182 and passim.

3. Potter, *False Dawn*, quotes Ornstein to Reis, 6 August, 1915, and then we both rely on PR, "Grand Transformation Scene," 357–360. See also Alan Trachtenberg, ed., *Memoirs of Waldo Frank* (Amherst, 1973), 64–65.

4. PR, "Ornstein," *Musical Portraits*, 267–280; Leo Ornstein, "The Music of New Russia," *Seven Arts* 1, no. 3 (January, 1917), 260–264. The most extensive discussion of the music is now Thomas Eugene Darter, "The Futurist Piano Music of Leo Ornstein" (DMA diss., Cornell, 1979), 738.

5. Trachtenberg, ed., *Memoirs of WF*, 63–64; PR to Alfred Stieglitz (hereafter AS), 29 December, 1915, and 12 August, 1918, Alfred Stieglitz Papers, Beinecke Library, Yale University (hereafter AS-YU); Peter Minuit (pseudonym for

Rosenfeld), "291 Fifth Avenue," *Seven Arts* 1, no. 1 (November, 1916), 61–65. For additional background see Robert M. Crunden, *American Salons: Encounters with European Modernism, 1885–1917* (New York, 1993), 339–382 and passim.

6. PR to AS, 12 August, 1918, AS-YU.

7. PR to AS, 30 August, 1920, and 14 July, 1919, AS-YU.

8. The best introduction is now Casey Nelson Blake, *Beloved Community: The Cultural Criticism of Randolph Bourne, Van Wyck Brooks, Waldo Frank & Lewis Mumford* (Chapel Hill, 1990). Blake includes Mumford for his work in the 1920s and rather slights Rosenfeld, possibly because Rosenfeld doesn't fit very well—and for good reason.

9. PR to AS, 30 August, 1920, 28 November, 1920, 24 August, 1921, and 29 August, 1922, all AS-YU.

10. PR, "Wagner," *Musical Portraits*, 3–25.

11. PR, "Moussorgsky," *Musical Portraits*, 57–72.

12. PR, "Debussy," *Musical Portraits*, 119–131. On the Moussorgsky-Debussy relation see the hypothetical quality of the discussion in Lélon Vallas, *Claude Debussy* (1928; English translation 1933; reissued New York, 1973), 60–62.

13. PR, "Ravel," *Musical Portraits*, 133–147; PR, *Musical Chronicle (1917–1923)* (New York, 1923), 174–184.

14. PR, *Musical Chronicle*, 144–166.

15. PR, "Rimsky-Korsakoff" and "Strawinsky," *Musical Portraits*, 159–168 and 191–204; and "The Strawinsky Concertino," *Musical Chronicle*, 97–104.

16. PR, "Schoenberg," *Musical Portraits*, 233–243; and "New German Music," *Musical Chronicle*, 293–314.

17. On Ives, see Robert M. Crunden, *Ministers of Reform: The Progressives' Achievement in American Civilization, 1889–1920* (New York, 1982), 116–133, and "On Charles Ives," *Modernism/Modernity*, 4, no. 3 (September, 1997), 154–159; Jan Swafford, *Charles Ives* (New York, 1996) and Frank R. Rossiter, *Charles Ives and his America* (New York, 1975). On Griffes, see Edward Maisel, *Charles T. Griffes* (New York, 1943) and Donna K. Anderson, *Charles T. Griffes* (Washington, 1993). On Loeffler and MacDowell, see Ellen E. Knight, *Charles Martin Loeffler* (Urbana, 1993); Margery Morgan Lowens, "The New York Years of Edward MacDowell" (Ph.D. diss., University of Michigan, 1971). For Rosenfeld's views, see "Loeffler," *Musical Portraits*, 257–266, and "The Fate of 'Mona,'" *Musical Chronicle*, 54–60, inter alia.

18. PR, "The Ornstein Double Sonata," *Musical Chronicle*, 220–227; PR to AS, 31 August, 1922, 1 September, 1923, 11 September, 1923, AS-YU.

19. PR, "Bloch," *Musical Portraits*, 281–295.

20. PR to AS, 7 July, 1922, AS-YU; PR, "The Bloch Concerto Grosso," *By Way of Art* (New York, 1928), 53–58; see also PR, *Discoveries of a Music Critic* (New York, 1936), 164–170; and PR to AS, 6 November, 1923, AS-YU, on the Bloch *Quintet.*

21. PR to AS, 28 June, 1923, and 11 September, 1923, AS-YU; PR, "Roger H. Sessions," *Port of New York* (New York, 1924), 145–152; PR, *An Hour with American Music* (Philadelphia, 1929), 79–91.

22. PR, *By Way of Art*, 58–65. See also the discussion of *Arcanes*, 89–94, *An Hour with American Music*, 160–179 and *Discoveries of a Music Critic*, 256–263.

23. PR to AS, 2 August, 1922, 11 August, 1922, 29 August, 1922, 22 September, 1922, 25 October, 1922, 8 November, 1922, 23 October, 1923, 28 October, 1923, and for the quote, 30 September, 1922, all AS-YU. See also the correspondence between PR and Scofield Thayer in Box 5, folders 180–185, Scofield Thayer Papers, Beinecke Library, Yale University.

24. PR to AS, 8 November, 1923, 1 September, 1923, 28 October, 1923, and 4 November, 1923, all AS-YU.

25. PR to AS, 14 July, 1919, 29 October, 1920, 3 November, 1920, 8 July, 1923; PR to O'Keeffe, ?14 July, 1921, all AS-YU; PR, *Port of New York*, 83–102.

26. PR to AS, 30 August, 1920, 22 September, 1922, and for the quotes, two letters of 22 July, 1923 separated by about twelve hours, all AS-YU.

27. PR, *Port of New York*, 167–174.

28. PR to AS, 26 July, 1922, 2 August, 1922, 11 August, 1922, AS-YU; PR, *Port of New York*, 199–210. For background, see Cynthia L. Ward, "Vanity Fair Magazine and the Modern Style, 1914–1936" (Ph.D. diss., State University of New York, Stony Brook, 1983); and Thomas Patrick Clarke, "Patterns of Radical Intellectual Dissent in the 1920s" (Ph.D. diss., University of North Carolina, 1971).

29. PR to AS, 14 July, 1919, 28 June, 1923, AS-YU; PR, *Port of New York*, 153–166.

30. Waldo Frank (hereafter WF) to AS, 5 October, 1920, 8 December, 1920, 25 February, 1922, 31 July, 1923, all AS-YU. See also William Robert Bittner, *The Novels of Waldo Frank* (Philadelphia, 1958); Daniel Stern Terris, "Waldo Frank and the Rediscovery of America, 1889–1929," (Ph.D. diss., Harvard, 1992), and Jerome W. Kloucek, "Waldo Frank: The Ground of his Mind and Art" (Ph.D. diss., Northwestern, 1958).

31. PR to AS, 24 September, 1920, 29 September 1920, 3 November, 1920, AS-YU. See also PR to Sherwood Anderson, 19 October, 1920, and 19 November, 1920, Sherwood Anderson Papers, Newberry Library (hereafter cited as SA-NL); WF to PR, 1 January, 1921, PR-YU; and WF to AS, 3 January, 1921, AS-YU.

32. PR to AS, 26 July, 1922, 8 November, 1922, 28 June, 1923, the earlier of two letters of 22 July, 1923, 5 August, 1923, 7 September, 1923, all AS-YU; PR, *Men Seen* (New York, 1925), 89–109. On Margaret Naumburg, see PR, *Port of New York*, 117–134.

33. WF, "Emerging Greatness," *Seven Arts* 1, no. 1 (November, 1916), 73–78.

34. See Crunden, *American Salons*, 118–124, and PR to AS, 29 August, 1922, AS-YU.

35. PR to AS, 14 September, 1922, and 22 September, 1922, AS-YU.

36. Sherwood Anderson (hereafter SA) to AS, 1923(?); and to Georgia O'Keeffe, 2 February 1923, both AS-YU; PR, *Port of New York*, 175–198.

37. Frederik L. Rusch, ed., *A Jean Toomer Reader* (New York, 1993), 15–16; Nellie Y. McKay, *Jean Toomer, Artist* (Chapel Hill, 1984), 3–33. The most detailed account of the Frank/Toomer relationship is in Terris, "Waldo Frank," 292–350.

38. Jean Toomer (hereafter JT) to SA, 18 December, 1922, and JT to Gorham Munson, 31 October, 1922, in Rusch, *Toomer Reader*, 17–21.

39. McKay, *Toomer*, 43–58; Darwin Turner, "An Intersection of Paths: Correspondence between Jean Toomer and Sherwood Anderson," *College Language Association Journal* 17, no. 4 (June, 1974), 455–467.

40. JT to Horace Liveright, 5 September, 1923, in Rusch, *Toomer Reader*, 94–95; see also 31–114; McKay, *Toomer*, 179–187; PR, *Men Seen*, 227–233.

41. PR to AS, 13 June, 1926, 23 June, 1926, 18 July, 1926, 15 August, 1926, and 31 August, 1926, all AS-YU. See also Potter, *False Dawn*, and the many memories of the later Rosenfeld in Jerome Mellquist and Lucie Wiese, eds., *Paul Rosenfeld: Voyager in the Arts* (New York, 1948).

ONE

1. For most of his life, Varèse spelled his first name "Edgard," but at the time Rosenfeld met him, it was "Edgar" and remains so in *An Hour with American Music* (Philadelphia, 1929). All quotations in this section are from chapter 8, pp. 160–179, unless otherwise identified. The book was incompetently edited and I have silently corrected an occasional typographical error; other awkwardnesses are from the original. Louise Varèse quotes her husband in *Varèse: A Looking-Glass Diary, Volume I: 1883–1928* (London and New York, 1972), 72. The quote on *Amériques* is from Odile Vivier, *Varèse* (Paris, 1973), 35.

2. L. Varèse, *Varèse*, 121ff., and 203; Jo Davidson, *Between Sittings* (New York, 1951), 126; Beatrice Wood, *I Shock Myself* (San Francisco, 1988), chs. 3–4; and Olivia Mattis, "Edgard Varèse and the Visual Art" (Ph.D. diss., Stanford, 1992), 126–127. For background on Duchamp and the Arensbergs, see my *American Salons: Encounters with European Modernism, 1885–1917* (New York, 1993), 409–443.

3. L. Varèse, *Varèse*, 121–132; Ferruccio Busoni, *Sketch of a New Esthetic of Music* (1911), collected in *Three Classics in the Aesthetic of Music* (New York, 1962), 95.

4. Avis Berman, *Rebels on Eighth Street: Juliana Force and the Whitney Museum of American Art* (New York, 1990), 174–175 and passim; the ICG manifesto, often reprinted, quoted from Mattis, "Varèse," 151–152. See also R. Allen Lott, "'New Music for New Ears': The International Composers' Guild," *Journal of the American Musicological Society*, 36, no. 2 (Summer, 1983), 266–286, for an analysis and list of all programs.

5. In addition to works cited, see for musicians: Nina Marchetti Archabel, "Carl Ruggles: An Ultramodern Composer as Painter" (Ph.D. diss., University of Minnesota, 1979); Marilyn J. Ziffrin, *Carl Ruggles: Composer, Painter, and Storyteller* (Urbana, 1994); and Robert F. Nisbett, "Louis Gruenberg: His Life and Work" (Ph.D. diss., Ohio State University, 1979).

6. L. Varèse, *Varèse*, calls Claire R. Reis's *Composers, Conductors and Critics* (Detroit, 1974), a "carefully misleading (not to use a less euphemistic word) account of the ICG" on page 177. See Lott, "New Music," and David Joel Metzer, "The Ascendancy of Musical Modernism in New York City, 1915–1929" (Ph.D. diss., Yale, 1993), ch. 5. Vivian Perlis also has oral history interviews with Claire Reis and Dane

Rudhyar, which in 1986 were located in her office, Yale School of Music; there is also one of Varèse by John Edmunds. They provided only occasional atmospheric details to this account. On Schoenberg, see Anne Florence Parks, "Freedom, Form, and Process in Varèse: A Study of Varèse's Musical Ideas—Their Sources, Their Development, and Their Use in his Works" (Ph.D. diss., Cornell, 1974), 163–169; H. H. Stuckenschmidt, *Schoenberg* (London, 1977), 283–284; Erwin Stein, ed., Arnold Schoenberg, *Ausgewählt Briefe* (Mainz, 1958), 79, also available in English as Erwin Stein, ed., Arnold Schoenberg, *Letters* (London, 1974), 78–79.

7. See Mattis, "Edgard Varèse," 175–176 for the texts quoted. The original French text, from Ruth Phelps and Henri Morane, "Artistes d'avant-garde en Amérique," *e Figaro Hebdomadaire* (25 July, 1928), 8–9 is: "Le jazz n'est pas l'Amérique. C'est un produit négroide, exploité par les juifs. Tous ces compositeurs d'ici sont des juifs. Le jazz ne représente pas plus l'Amérique que les valses lentes représentaient l'Allemagen. Le jazz est sans idée. C'est un bruit sur quoi on tressaute." See also Ruggles to Henry Cowell, 21 June, 1933, and Edgard Varèse to Carl Ruggles, 19 July, 1926, Carl Ruggles Papers, Yale School of Music Library; and Ziffrin, *Ruggles*, 136.

8. L. Varèse, *Varèse*, 23.

9. Ibid., 17–24, 69, 99; Roche is quoted in Mattis, "Varèse," 1, from her unpublished memoirs in the Pompidou, Paris. L. Varèse does not mention Freud in her memoir but says Varèse was treated by Wilhelm Fliess. She had not at the time met Varèse.

10. L. Varèse, *Varèse*, 33–34, 45, and passim.

11. Ibid., esp. 42. As with many of Varèse's pronouncements, this lecture has appeared in three languages in numerous versions. John D. Anderson, "Varèse and the Lyricism of the New Physics," *Musical Quarterly* 75, no. 1 (Spring, 1991), 31–49, is an essential recent analysis.

12. I have relied heavily on Antony Beaumont, *Busoni the Composer* (Bloomington, 1985), 29 and passim; see also Larry Sitsky, *Busoni and the Piano* (New York, 1986), 84–87, passim. Busoni's "Sketch" in *Three Classics*, 73–102; scattered brief pieces in *The Essence of Music* (New York, 1987), see esp. 23–24; the definitive biography is Edward J. Dent, *Ferruccio Busoni* (Oxford, 1966).

13. L. Varèse, *Varèse*, 49–56.

14. Marius de Zayas to Alfred Stieglitz, 30 June, 1914, Alfred Stieglitz Papers, Yale University. The theme still dominates Henri-Martin Barzun's privately printed lectures, *Orpheus: Modern Culture and the 1913 Renaissance* (New York, 1956). For secondary treatments, see Parks, "Freedom, Form, and Process in Varèse," 97ff.; Mattis, "Varèse," 35ff.; Stephen Kern, *The Culture of Time and Space 1880–1918* (Cambridge, Mass., 1983); and Mark Antliff, *Inventing Bergson* (Princeton, 1993).

15. Albert Gleizes and Jean Metzinger, *Cubism* (1912) as reprinted in Robert L. Herbert, ed., *Modern Artists on Art* (Englewood Cliffs, 1964), 15; Jonathan W. Bernard, *The Music of Edgard Varèse* (New Haven, 1987), 16.

16. Mattis, "Varèse," esp. 10, 19–20, 30, 71, 76–77, 179, 208, 259; Pablo Picasso to Henri-Pierre Roché, 7 April, 1911, Henri-Pierre Roché Papers, Carleton

Lake Collection, Harry Ransom Humanities Research Center, University of Texas, Austin (hereafter cited as HPR-UT).

17. Mattis, "Varèse," 57, quotes the interview from the *New York Review*, March, 1916.

18. See especially the New York dada issue of *Dada/Surrealism* XIV (1985), and the Duchamp issue, 16 (1987), which are more easily obtained as books: Rudolf E. Kuenzli, ed., *New York Dada* (New York, 1986) and Rudolf Kuenzli and Francis M. Naumann, eds., *Marcel Duchamp: Artist of the Century* (New York, 1989); and Parks, "Freedom, Form, and Process in Varèse," 101ff. Beatrice Wood, *I Shock Myself*, 26–36, includes Varèse on several levels. The Roché Diaries, HPR-UT, mention Varèse on several occasions in the context of the Arensbergs, Duchamp and Wood, Francis Picabia, and Joseph Stella. Mattis, "Varèse," 122–149, covers the ground thoroughly and quotes extensively from Wood's Cryptic diaries.

19. Massimo Zanotti-Bianco, "Edgard Varèse and the Geometry of Sound," *The Arts* 7 (January, 1925) 35–36, as reprinted in Parks, "Freedom, Form, and Process in Varèse," 216–218.

20. Bernard, *Music of Edgard Varèse*, 17, first juxtaposed the Jeanneret article and the later Varèse interviews and articles; no contemporary evidence supports him but the logic of the argument remains impressive because of the friendship and later collaboration. For Varèse's words, see "The Liberation of Sound" in Benjamin Boretz and Edward T. Cone, eds., *Perspectives on American Composers* (New York, 1971), 25–33; and in a somewhat different version, in Elliott Schwartz and Barney Childs, eds., *Contemporary Composers on Contemporary Music* (New York, 1967), 196–208; for Jeanneret see Edward F. Fry, *Cubism* (New York, 1966), 170–171; Amédéle Ozenfant was coauthor of the essay.

21. Gunther Schuller, "Conversation with Varèse," in *Perspectives of New Music* 3, no. 2 (Spring-Summer, 1965), 32–37. Parks, "Freedom, Form, and Process in Varèse," reprints the important passages, 213–215.

22. Igor Stravinsky and Robert Craft, *Dialogues* (London, 1982), 109–112; see also *Memories and Commentaries* (London, 1981), 102–103.

Two

1. Paul Strand, "Photography," originally in the *Seven Arts* for August, 1917, 524–526, as reprinted in Nathan Lyons, ed., *Photographers on Photography* (Englewood Cliffs, 1966), 136–144.

2. Alfred Stieglitz (hereafter AS) to R. Child Bayley, 17 April, 1916, Alfred Stieglitz Papers, Beinecke Library, Yale University (hereafter AS-YU).

3. Paul Strand, *Paul Strand: A Retrospective Monograph the Years 1915–1946* (Millerton, N.Y., 1971) contains the best reproductions of this and other works analyzed unless otherwise noted.

4. Lewis W. Hine to AS, 14 December, 1906, AS-YU. For biographical background I have relied on Naomi Rosenblum, "Paul Strand: The Early Years, 1910–1932" (Ph.D. diss., City University of New York, 1978). A much con-

densed version, "The Early Years," appears in Maren Stange, ed., *Paul Strand* (New York, 1991), 31–51, 270–274.

5. For background, see Robert M. Crunden, *American Salons: Encounters with European Modernism, 1885–1917* (New York, 1993), 275–282, 339–353 and passim. On Hine, see especially Judith Mara Gutman, *Lewis W. Hine and the American Social Conscience* (New York, 1967).

6. Hine was never prolific but see "The School in the Park," *Outlook 83* (28 July, 1906), 712–718. Merely to use "real" or "realism" is to raise complex issues that underlie much in succeeding paragraphs. See especially Miles Orvell, *The Real Thing: Imitation and Authenticity in American Culture, 1880–1940* (Chapel Hill, 1989) and David E. Shi, *Facing Facts: Realism in American Thought and Culture, 1850–1920* (New York, 1995).

7. Paul Strand (hereafter PS) to parents, especially 11 April and 6 May, 1915, Paul Strand Archive, Center for Creative Photography, University of Arizona, Tucson (hereafter PS-CCP). See Rosenblum, "Paul Strand," ch. 2, for a secondary treatment.

8. Coburn's works are available from many sources, but most accessibly in Alvin Langdon Coburn, *Alvin Langdon Coburn: An Autobiography* (New York, 1978) and Mike Weaver, *Alvin Langdon Coburn: Symbolist Photographer 1882–1966* (New York, 1986).

9. PS to AS, 28 August, 1916, and AS to R. Child Bayley, 1 November, 1916, both AS-YU; Rosenblum, "Paul Strand," ch. 3.

10. PS to AS, 30 or 31 July, 1917, AS-YU; AS to PS, 18 August, 1917, PS-CCP.

11. O'Keeffe to Anita Pollitzer, 20 June, 1917, in Clive Giboire, ed., *Lovingly, Georgia: The Complete Correspondence of Georgia O'Keeffe and Anita Pollitzer* (New York, 1990), 256. The most detailed discussion of the tangled relations between Stieglitz, O'Keeffe, Strand, and Rebecca Salsbury (Strand) is Benita Eisler, *O'-Keeffe and Stieglitz* (New York, 1991).

12. Most of the letters from O'Keeffe (hereafter GO'K) to Strand, PS-CCP, have long been restricted as to both access and quotation; but see Sarah Greenough, ed., *Georgia O'Keeffe Art and Letters* (Washington, 1987) for GO'K to PS, 3 June, 25 June, 23 July, 24 October, and 15 November, 1917, 161–166.

13. PS to AS, especially 18 May, 1918, but see also 26 May, 29 May, 30 May, 31 May, and 1 June, 1918, AS-YU; AS to PS, 23 May, 27 May, and 28 May 1918 (PS-CCP). The best biography of O'Keeffe is Roxana Robinson, *Georgia O'Keeffe* (New York, 1989).

14. PS to parents, 25 October, 1918, PS-CCP; Strand's old friend from Ethical Culture School, Herbert Seligman, hinted at much of this in his letter to Strand of 2 November, 1918, PS-CCP. Strand had introduced Seligman to Stieglitz, thus initiating one of the more epigonal of 291 relationships and at least one useful book of Stieglitz's conversational meanderings.

15. Paul Strand and Calvin Tomkins, *Paul Strand: Sixty Years of Photographs* (Millerton, N.Y., 1976), profile by Calvin Tomkins, 146.

16. Oddly enough, Sheeler ignores the film in his unpublished autobiography in the Archives of American Art, even though several of his later works clearly

derive from it. The most thorough secondary treatment is Jan-Christopher Horak, "Modernist Perspectives and Romantic Desire: *Manhatta*," *Afterimage* 15, no. 14 (November, 1987), 8–15; also available slightly condensed and with fewer illustrations in Stange, ed., *Paul Strand*, 55–71, 274–275.

17. AS to Herbert Seligman (HS), 27 June, 1923, AS-YU; Sheeler to PS, 22 June, 1923, and AS to PS, 28 June, 1923, both PS-CCP.

18. AS to Sherwood Anderson, 7 December, 1924, 11 March, and 23, March 1925, all AS-YU. Strand showed eighteen photographs, ten of them machines, five of New York City, and three of leaves, all untitled.

19. AS to HS, 30 July, 1924, 16 October, 1927, AS-YU.

THREE

1. John Dos Passos (hereafter JDP) to Walter Rumsey Marvin (hereafter WRM), 12 December, 1916, and 20 April, 1917, in Townsend Ludington, ed., *The Fourteenth Chronicle: Letters and Diaries of John Dos Passos* (Boston, 1973), 60, 70–71; hereafter cited as *14th Chronicle*.

2. William Blazek, "The Norton-Harjes Ambulance Corps and American Literature of World War I" (Ph.D. diss., University of Aberdeen, 1986), ch. 1.

3. JDP to WRM, 23 August, 1917, *14th Chronicle*, 91–93.

4. Blazek, chs. 1 and 4, quote p. 207.

5. JDP to Arthur K. McComb (hereafter AKM), 12 September, and ? September, 1917, in Melvin Landsberg, ed., *John Dos Passos' Correspondence with Arthur K. McComb, or, "Learn to sing the Carmagnole"* (Niwot, Colo., 1991) (hereafter cited as *JDP/AKM Letters*), 67–71.

6. JDP to WRM, 26 October, 1917, *14th Chronicle*, 100–101.

7. JDP to WRM, 9 December, 1917; diary entry for 10 January, 1918; JDP to WRM, June 1918, all *14th Chronicle*, 104, 124, 188–189.

8. JDP, *The Best Times* (New York, 1966), 70; hereafter cited as *Best Times*.

9. JDP, diary for 1 October, 1918; JDP to John Howard Lawson (hereafter JHL), October 1918, both *14th Chronicle*, 212–213, 215; JDP to WRM, October 1918, *14th Chronicle*, 215, 226–227.

10. JDP to AKM, 5 October, 1918, and 21 October, 1918, *JDP/AKM Letters*, 108–109, 113.

11. JDP, *Best Times*, 76.

12. Dos Passos has had two fine biographies, each containing substantial amounts of material not available in the other: Townsend Ludington, *John Dos Passos* (New York, 1980) and Virginia Spencer Carr, *Dos Passos* (Garden City, N.Y., 1984). They will be the chief sources for factual materials unless otherwise indicated.

13. JDP, Diary, 9 April, 1911, John Dos Passos Papers, Alderman Library, University of Virginia, as quoted in Carr, *Dos Passos*, 40–41; JDP, *Best Times*, 15; *The 42nd Parallel* (New York, 1930), Camera Eye no. 7.

14. JDP to WRM, Spring 1916, November 1920, April-May 1921, *14th Chronicle*, 39, 305, 309; *The 42nd Parallel*, Camera Eye no. 25.

15. JDP to WRM, 6 December, 1915, *14th Chronicle*, 30–31; JDP, *Best Times*, 52; *The 42nd Parallel*, Camera Eye no. 25.

16. JDP to WRM, 28 September, 1916, and June 1919, *14th Chronicle*, 47, 252; see also 182.

17. JDP to WRM, 20 June, 1916, and 4 December, 1916, *14th Chronicle*, 41, 57; see also my *American Salons*, Book 1.

18. JDP diaries, 30 October to 15 November, 1914, *14th Chronicle*, 21–23.

19. JDP to WRM, 23 April, 1916, *14th Chronicle*, 36; Amy Lowell, ed., Introduction, *Some Imagist Poets* (Boston, 1915).

20. JDP, review of Louis Couperus, *Small Souls, Harvard Monthly*, 59 (February, 1915), 169; JDP to WRM, 5 January, 1918, *14th Chronicle*, 120; JDP, *Best Times*, 44.

21. JDP to WRM, 28 September, 24 October, 30 October, and 25 December, 1916, *14th Chronicle*, 47–50, 64; see also 238, 247, 363.

22. JDP, *Best Times*, 49–50; the basic history is Robert F. Storey, *Pierrot: A Critical History of a Mask* (Princeton, 1978). It largely neglects music.

23. JDP to WRM, April 1918, *14th Chronicle*, 169; JDP, "What Makes A Novelist," *National Review* 20 (16 January, 1968), 29–32; Lisa Lorraine Nanny, "John Dos Passos and the Visual Arts" (Ph.D. diss., University of North Carolina, 1989), 92. For Armory Show background see my *American Salons*, 357–370.

24. JDP, *Best Times*, 146; Peter de Francia, *Fernand Léger* (New Haven, 1983), 15, 31, 50–62, 71–74, and passim.

25. See Lynn Garafola, *Diaghilev's Ballets Russes* (New York, 1989), 350–351 and passim.; *JDP/AKM Letters*, 45, 47, 52, 54, 63.

26. Diary, 7 October, 1918, *14th Chronicle*, 220.

27. *JDP/AKM Letters*, 130; JDP, "What Makes a Novelist."

28. Carr, *Dos Passos*, 185, quotes the Lawson letter; Nanny, "JDP and the Visual Arts," esp. 205; and Paul Fussell, *The Great War and Modern Memory* (New York, 1975), 221, 306, and passim.

29. JDP to JHL, 12 September and 11 October, 1920, *14th Chronicle*, 300–301. Dos Passos discussed his attitudes about Nock with me in an interview at Yale in the fall of 1961, and in a letter now in the Nock Papers, Sterling Library, Yale University. See also my *The Mind and Art of Albert Jay Nock* (Chicago, 1964).

30. JDP to JHL, 2 November, 1920, *14th Chronicle*, 305; see also 208–211. JDP to JHL, 12 September, 1920, John Howard Lawson Papers, Southern Illinois University Library, Carbondale (hereafter JHL-SIU).

31. JDP, "What Makes a Novelist."

32. JDP, *Manhattan Transfer* (Boston, 1925), 144; hereafter citations will be made in the text to page numbers in this edition.

33. See especially George A. Knox and Herbert M. Stahl, *Dos Passos and "The Revolting Playwrights"* (Lund, 1964).

34. JHL, "Rebellion in the Twenties," unpublished typescript in the JHL-SIU, Box 99, 71, 114, 144, and passim. See also the unusually thorough treat-

ment in Beverle Rochelle Bloch, "John Howard Lawson's 'Processional': Modernism in American theatre in the twenties" (Ph.D. diss., University of Denver, 1988).

35. See especially JDP, *Best Times*, 165–166.

FOUR

1. William Carlos Williams, *The Autobiography of William Carlos Williams* (New York, 1951), xii; William Carlos Williams (hereafter WCW) to Florence Herman Williams (hereafter FHW), 28 September, 1927, John C. Thirlwall, ed., *The Selected Letters of William Carlos Williams* (New York, 1957), 80.

2. WCW, *Autobiography*, 279–280; WCW to Kenneth Burke (hereafter KB), 10 June, 1921, Kenneth Burke papers, Pennsylvania State University Library; I am very grateful to James East for showing me his transcripts of the entire WCW/KB correspondence. Also: "Journal," 15 December 1927, William Carlos Williams papers, State University of New York, Buffalo, as cited in Paul Mariani, *William Carlos Williams: A New World Naked* (New York, 1981), 266–267. This is the definitive biography and the source of factual material unless otherwise noted. The most useful secondary source on Burke is now Jack Selzer, *Kenneth Burke in Greenwich Village: Conversing with the Moderns* (Madison, 1996).

3. David Frail, "Citizen Williams: Thirty News Items from the Rutherford Newspapers," *William Carlos Williams Review* 13, no. 2 (Fall, 1987), 1–8 (hereafter cited as WCWR); KB, *Language as Symbolic Action* (Berkeley, 1966), 286; WCW, *Imaginations* (New York, 1970), 255; and *Autobiography*, 157.

4. WCW, *Imaginations*, 119–120.

5. WCW, *Autobiography*, 286–292.

6. WCW, *Imaginations*, 95–96.

7. WCW, "Marianne Moore," *Selected Essays of William Carlos Williams* (New York, 1954), 121–131; KB, *Language*, 282.

8. WCW, *The Collected Earlier Poems of William Carlos Williams* (New York, 1966), 103 (hereafter cited as *CEP*); see also "The Little Red Notebook of William Carlos Williams," *WCWR* 9, nos. 1–2 (Fall, 1983), 1–34, and William Eric Williams, "The Doctor," 35–43; WCW, *CEP*, 268.

9. The most thorough work in this area is T. Hugh Crawford, *Modernism, Medicine & William Carlos Williams* (Norman, 1993); WCW, *I Wanted to Write A Poem* (New York, 1958), 38–39. For an example too long to quote, see *The Great American Novel* in *Imaginations*, 162–163.

10. WCW, *Autobiography*, 109, 217.

11. Ibid., 135; Alfred Kreymborg, *Troubadour* (New York, 1957, c.1925), 186; Robert M. Crunden, *American Salons: Encounters with European Modernism, 1885–1917* (New York, 1993), 416–423.

12. WCW, *CEP*, 162–166; the best secondary treatment for my purposes is Peter Schmidt, *William Carlos Williams, the Arts and Literary Tradition* (Baton Rouge, 1988), ch. 2.

13. WCW, *Autobiography*, 52, 151–156; William Marling, *William Carlos Williams and the Painters, 1909–1923* (Athens, Ohio, 1982), 25–26; Dickran Tashjian, *William Carlos Williams and the American Scene, 1920–1940* (New York, 1978), 67, 72; Emily Farnham, *Charles Demuth* (Norman, 1971), 5, 14, 40, 72–74, 123, 174.

14. See the manuscript draft of the "Autobiography" in the William Carlos Williams Papers, Beinecke Library, Yale University (hereafter cited as WCW-YU), 40; WCW, *Autobiography*, 380–381.

15. See Crunden, *American Salons*, 288–294; WCW, "A Matisse," *Contact* (January, 1921), n.p.[7], rpt. *Selected Essays*, 30–31; WCW to Marianne Moore, 30 August, 1928, *Selected Letters*, 107.

16. But see "Picasso Breaks Faces" (1950), in WCW, *A Recognizable Image: William Carlos Williams on Art and Artists*, ed. Bram Dijkstra (New York, 1978), 223–224; WCW to Kay Boyle, ?1932, *Selected Letters*, 130; Juan Gris, "On the Possibilities of Painting," *Transatlantic Review*, 1, no. 6 (June, 1924), 482–488 and 2, no. 1 (July, 1924), 75–79, rpt. in Daniel-Henry Kahnweiler, *Juan Gris*, rev. ed. (New York, 1969, c. 1946), 195–201. Henry M. Sayre, *The Visual Text of William Carlos Williams* (Urbana, 1983), makes several useful remarks on these subjects in the introduction and chapter 1.

17. WCW, *Imaginations*, 107–108.

18. See Crunden, *American Salons*, 313–322; for a contrary view, see Christopher J. MacGowan, *William Carlos Williams's Early Poetry: The Visual Arts Background* (Ann Arbor, 1984), 64–65.

19. See Schmidt, *Williams*, 12–19; for a useful bibliography through 1987 see especially 11, n.1. The pioneering study was Dickran Tashjian, *Skyscraper Primitives: Dada and the American Avant-Garde, 1910–1925* (Middletown, Conn., 1975).

20. *Contact* 1, no. 1 (December, 1920), 1, 10; 3 (n.d. [1923]), 14–15, rpt. *Selected Essays*, 32–37. On early imagism, see Crunden, *American Salons*, 208–214 and passim.

21. The definitive treatment from an American point of view is now Francis M. Naumann, *New York Dada 1915–1923* (New York, 1994), see especially 9–10.

22. See the many letters from de Zayas to Stieglitz in the Alfred Stieglitz Papers, Beinecke Library, Yale University (hereafter AS-YU), partially summarized in Crunden, *American Salons*, 354ff.; Naumann, *N.Y. Dada*, 192–194; and Michel Sanouillet, *Dada à Paris* (Paris, 1965), 569, 572.

23. In addition to the references in note 22 above, see Marius de Zayas, "The Sun Has Set," *Camera Work*, 39 (July, 1912), 17–21.

24. See Crunden, *American Salons*, 409–443; the major exceptions would be Schmidt, *Williams*, 91ff., and MacGowan, *Williams's Early Poetry*, 90, 95ff.; WCW, *Autobiography*, 135–138.

25. WCW, *Autobiography*, 165.

26. WCW, *Imaginations*, 109–110, 125. Schwitters has been neglected by most scholars of American modernism, but he had a show at the Société Anonyme in 1920, and by 1926 he was well enough known to be included in the International Exhibition of Modern Art at the Brooklyn Museum. The

most thorough analysis of Williams's dada connection is Schmidt, *Williams*, ch. 3; see also MacGowan, *Williams's Early Poetry*, ch. 6, and Tashjian, *Skyscraper Primitives*, ch. 5 and 9.

27. Ezra Pound to WCW, 18 March, 1922, in D. D. Paige, ed., *The Selected Letters of Ezra Pound 1907–1941* (New York, 1950), 173.

28. WCW, "An Essay on Virginia," *Imaginations*, 321.

29. WCW to Horace Gregory, 22 July, 1939, *Selected Letters*, 187; WCW to Marianne Moore, 10 February and 14 April, 1924, 59–60, 62–63; WCW, *In the American Grain* (New York, 1925), 120, 127.

30. For a book-length study that touches on some of these issues, see Bryce Conrad, *Refiguring America* (Urbana, 1990).

31. WCW, *CEP*, 233–235.

FIVE

1. Marius de Zayas to Alfred Stieglitz (hereafter AS), 23, 27, and 30 August, 1915, 1(twice), 4, 8 (twice), and 14 September, 1915, all Alfred Stieglitz Papers, Beinecke Library, Yale University (hereafter AS-YU), discuss the idea of the Modern Gallery. See also Douglas K. S. Hyland, "Agnes Ernst Meyer, Patron of American Modernism," *American Art Journal* 12, no. 1 (Winter, 1980), 64–81.

2. Charles Sheeler (hereafter CS) to AS, 25 May, 1915, 11 June, 1915, 28 October, 1916; AS to CS, 1 November, 1916, 1 December, 1916, 22 November, 1917; Marsden Hartley to AS, ?Spring, 1918, all AS-YU.

3. CS, "Autobiography," Charles Sheeler Papers, Archives of American Art (hereafter CS-AAA), Roll NSH–1, frames 27–134. Never completed nor published, this document was the chief source Sheeler gave to Constance Rourke when she was at work on *Charles Sheeler: Artist in the American Tradition* (New York, 1938). She quoted it extensively, but often in garbled form. My own quotations will be from the handwritten manuscript, preserving idiosyncratic spellings but silently correcting obvious slips of the pen, as when a syllable gets inadvertently dropped. In this chapter, this "Autobiography" will be my source for all quotations from Sheeler unless otherwise noted. Only scattered letters survive for the 1917–26 period, at which point the letters to Walter Arensberg (hereafter WA), in the Walter Arensberg Papers, Philadelphia Museum of Art (hereafter WA-PMA), provide essential data, especially for the 1930s.

4. CS, "Autobiography," CS to AS, 25 May, 1915, AS-YU. The most useful secondary sources have been Susan Fillin Yeh, "Charles Sheeler and the Machine Age" (Ph.D. diss., City University of New York, 1981); and Theodore E. Stebbins, Jr., and Norman Keyes, Jr., *Charles Sheeler: The Photographs* (Boston, 1987).

5. Francis M. Naumann, ed., "How, When, and Why Modern Art Came to New York," by Marius de Zayas, *The Arts* 54, no. 8 (April, 1980), 104, later expanded to *How, When and Why Modern Art Came to New York* (Cambridge, Mass., 1996). Henry McBride, a critic second only to Paul Rosenfeld in the early 1920s,

said essentially the same thing as de Zayas in much more detail. See Daniel Catton Rich, ed., *The Flow of Art* (New York, 1975), 155–156, reprinting a review of 22 February, 1920. A small correspondence between CS and Mercer survives in the Spruance Library, Bucks County Historical Society, Doylestown, Pennsylvania. Some of the best work in this area is by Karen Davies Lucic, in "Charles Sheeler in Doylestown and the Image of Rural Architecture," *Arts Magazine* 59 (March, 1985), 135–139; and "The Present and the Past in the Works of Charles Sheeler" (Ph.D. diss., Yale, 1989), subsequently published as *Charles Sheeler and the Cult of the Machine* (London, 1991).

6. See especially Carol Troyen and Erica E. Hirshler, *Charles Sheeler: Paintings and Drawings* (Boston, 1987), 5, 44 fns. 17 and 24; Milton W. Brown, *The Story of the Armory Show* (Greenwich, Conn., 1963), 228–230, 290.

7. CS, "Autobiography"; Martin Friedman et al., *Charles Sheeler* (Washington, 1968), 68; CS to Louise Arensberg, 10 November, 1933, WA-PMA.

8. CS, "Recent Photographs by Alfred Stieglitz," *The Arts* 3 (May, 1923); PS to AS, ? June 1923, and AS to PS, 28 June, 1923, both AS-YU; AS to PS, 16 November, 1920, Paul Strand Papers, Center for Creative Photography, Tucson (hereafter PS-CCP); AS to Herbert Seligman, 27 June, 1923, AS-YU. Strand wrote a public letter to *The Arts*, dated 1 June, 1923, copy in PS-CCP, and a similar one to the *New York Sun and Globe*, which appeared in volume 90 (27 June, 1923), 20. On Juliana Force and the Whitney, which did not focus exclusively on modernist artists, see Avis Berman, *Rebels on Eighth Street: Juliana Force and the Whitney Museum of American Art* (New York, 1990), 198.

9. CS to WA, 10 January, 1927, WA-PMA. The classic discussion of the place of "dimensions" in modern art is Linda Dalrymple Henderson, *The Fourth Dimension and Non-Euclidean Geometry in Modern Art* (Princeton, 1983).

10. CS to WA, 25 October, 1927, and 6 February, 1929, WA-PMA.

Six

1. Louis Armstrong, *Swing That Music* (New York, 1993), 16; *Satchmo: My Life in New Orleans* (New York, 1986), 96–97. For the earlier history of jazz as modernist speech, see Robert M. Crunden, *American Salons: Encounters with European Modernism, 1855–1917* (New York, 1993), 125–144; for the role of Chicago in American modernism, 102–124.

2. Alan Lomax, *Mr. Jelly Roll: The Fortunes of Jelly Roll Morton, New Orleans Creole and "Inventor of Jazz"* (Berkeley, 1973), 3–26; 210; Lawrence Gushee, ":A Preliminary Chronology of the Early Career of Ferd 'Jelly Roll' Morton," *American Music* 3, no. 4 (Winter, 1985), 389–412.

3. Lomax, *Mr. Jelly Roll*, 122, 185–187; Stanley Dance, *The World of Earl Hines* (New York, 1977), 34; Gunther Schuller, *Early Jazz* (New York, 1968), 134–174, quotes 145, 170. There is still much of value in Martin Williams, *Jelly Roll Morton* (New York, 1963). The Chicago Red Hot Peppers sessions ran from 15 September, 1926, to 10 June, 1927, at which point Morton began to record out of New York City.

4. Sidney Bechet, *Treat It Gentle* (New York, 1978), 6–7, 30, 44, 50–51.

5. John Chilton, *Sidney Bechet* (New York, 1987), 21, 39–40.

6. Duke Ellington, *Music Is My Mistress* (Garden City, N.Y., 1973), 417, 466; Barney Bigard, *With Louis and the Duke* (New York, 1986), 71; Chilton, *Bechet*, ch. 7.

7. Bechet, *Treat It Gentle*, 45; Chilton, *Bechet*, ch. 9.

8. Walter C. Allen and Brian A. L. Rust, *King Joe Oliver* (London, 1958), 1–7; Armstrong, *Satchmo*, 136–138; *Louis Armstrong—A Self-Portrait* (New York, 1971), 25–27. The best biography is now Laurence Bergreen, *Louis Armstrong* (New York, 1997).

9. Pops Foster, *The Autobiography of A New Orleans Jazzman*, as told to Tom Stoddard (Berkeley, 1971), 106–107; 115; for life on the boats, see Armstrong, *Swing That Music*, 35–69.

10. James Lincoln Collier, *Louis Armstrong* (New York, 1983), 94; Armstrong, *Satchmo*, 234–236.

11. Armstrong, *Satchmo*, 188–189.

12. Dempsey J. Travis, *An Autobiography of Black Jazz* (Chicago, 1983), 43; Willie the Lion Smith, *Music on my Mind* (New York), 127.

13. Bud Freeman, *Crazeology: The Autobiography of a Chicago Jazzman* (Urbana, 1989), 2, 6–7.

14. Milton "Mezz" Mezzrow and Bernard Wolfe, *Really the Blues* (London, 1957), 52–54, 119–120.

15. Collier, *Armstrong*, 98, 109.

16. See especially Ronald C. Foreman, Jr., "Jazz and Race Records, 1920–32: Their Origins and Their Significance for the Record Industry and Society" (Ph.D. diss., University of Illinois, 1968), 49; William Howland Kenney, *Chicago Jazz* (New York, 1993), 11; and Burton W. Peretti, *The Creation of Jazz* (Urbana, 1992), 22.

17. H. O. Brunn, *The Story of the Original Dixieland Jazz Band* (Baton Rouge, 1960), chs. 1–6, quote 29; Schuller, *Early Jazz*, 182.

18. Bechet, *Treat It Gentle*, 114; Martin Williams, *Jazz Masters of New Orleans* (New York, 1979), 121–135; Nat Shapiro and Nat Hentoff, eds., *Hear Me Talkin' to Ya* (New York, 1966), 118–121.

19. The most useful primary sources of information include: Bud Freeman, *"You Don't Look Like a Musician"* (Detroit, 1974) and *Crazeology*; Mezzrow and Wolfe, *Really the Blues;* Eddie Condon, *We Called It Music* (New York, 1947); Benny Goodman and Irving Kolodin, *The Kingdom of Swing* (Harrisburg, Pa., 1939); and the invaluable Shapiro and Hentoff, *Hear Me*.

20. Ralph Berton, *Remembering Bix* (New York, 1974), 14, 19, 348, 99; Richard M. Sudhalter, Philip R. Evans with William Dean-Myatt, *Bix* (New York, 1975), 36–195 passim.

21. Goodman and Kolodin, *Kingdom of Swing*, 15–59; James Lincoln Collier, *Benny Goodman and the Swing Era* (New York, 1989), ch.1–3; Ross Firestone, *Swing, Swing, Swing: The Life and Times of Benny Goodman* (New York, 1993), ch.1, quote 27.

22. Ethel Waters, with Charles Samuels, *His Eye Is on the Sparrow* (New York, 1951), ch.1–2 and passim.

23. Mezzrow and Wolfe, *Really the Blues*, 3, 5, 7, 18, 22, 49, 92, 111–112.

24. For a scholarly overview, see Ronald L. Morris, *Wait Until Dark: Jazz and the Underworld 1880–1940* (Bowling Green, Ohio, 1980).

25. Dance, *The World of Hines*, 61. As Benny Goodman once said, "the bigger the gangster, the better the treatment and pay." See Firestone, *Swing*, 45. See also Freeman, *"You Don't Look,"* 115–116; Condon, *We Called It Music*, 104; Mezzrow and Wolfe, *Really the Blues*, 22, 92.

26. Wingy Manone and Paul Vandervoort II, *Trumpet on the Wing* (Garden City, N.Y., 1948), 19, 27, 50, 54, 77.

27. Jeffrey Stanford Magee, "The Music of Fletcher Henderson and his Orchestra in the 1920s" (Ph.D. diss., University of Michigan, 1992), ch. 1; Waters, *His Eye*, 146–147; Garvin Bushell, *Jazz from the Beginning* (Ann Arbor, 1988), ch. 3.

28. Shapiro and Hentoff, *Hear Me*, 206; see also Rex Stewart, *Boy Meets Horn* (Ann Arbor, 1991); Howard Scott, interview by Chris Albertson, 8 March, 1979, transcript in Jazz Oral History Project (JOHP), Institute of Jazz Studies, Rutgers University, Newark; and John Chilton, *The Song of the Hawk: The Life and Recordings of Coleman Hawkins* (Ann Arbor, 1990).

29. Schuller, *Early Jazz*, ch. 3, quote 109.

30. Peretti, *Creation of Jazz*, 146–147.

31. Kenney, *Chicago Jazz*, 30–31, 148–155; Dance, *World of Hines*, 52.

SEVEN

1. Ethel Waters with Charles Samuels, *His Eye Is on the Sparrow* (New York, 1951), 194–196.

2. Carl Van Vechten (hereafter CVV), *The Tattooed Countess* (New York, 1924), 81; Bruce Kellner, *Carl Van Vechten and the Irreverent Decades* (Norman, Okla., 1968), 16–17; Mabel Dodge Luhan, *Movers and Shakers* (New York, 1936), 14–16; Wallace Stevens to his wife, 3 August, 1915, in Holly Stevens, ed., *Letters of Wallace Stevens* (Berkeley, 1996), 185–186.

3. CVV to Mabel Dodge Luhan, 8 October, 1924, in Bruce Kellner, ed., *Letters of Carl Van Vechten* (New Haven, 1987), 71–72.

4. CVV, *Peter Whiffle* (New York, 1929), 8, 52, 84, 148, 186.

5. CVV, *The Blind Bow-Boy* (New York, 1923), 67, 114–117, 124, 160.

6. CVV, *Tattooed Countess*, 33.

7. CVV, *Firecrackers* (New York, 1925), 1, 3, 71–72.

8. CVV to Edna Kenton, August 1924, in Kellner, *Letters*, 69.

9. Kellner, *Irreverent Decades*, 162, with the Covarrubias work reproduced after 122; CVV to Gertrude Stein (hereafter GS), 30 June, 1925, in Edward Burns, ed., *The Letters of Gertrude Stein and Carl Van Vechten, 1913–1946* (2 vols., New York, 1986), vol. 1: 116.

10. See especially Bruce Kellner, ed., *"Keep A-Inchin' Along": Selected Writings of Carl Van Vechten about Black Art and Letters* (Westport, Conn., 1979), 32, 160–172; CVV, *Red* (New York, 1925), xv; CVV to GS, 15 November, 1924, *Stein/Van Vechten Letters*, vol. 1: 108; see also Kellner, *Irreverent Decades*, 192–194.

11. Kellner, *Irreverent Decades*, 195ff., 208ff.; CVV to GS, 24 October, 1915, in *Stein/Van Vechten Letters*, vol. 1: 48; CVV to Hunter Stagg, 16 September, 1923, and CVV to Langston Hughes, 25 March, 1927, in Kellner, ed., *Letters*, 56, 95; CVV, *Nigger Heaven* (New York, 1926), 26, 30, 239, 259–260.

12. For a summary of the actual people behind the fictional characters, see Kellner, ed., *Keep A-Inchin'*, 73–74; CVV, *Nigger Heaven*, 89–90.

13. For Du Bois and James Weldon Johnson on *Nigger Heaven*, see David Levering Lewis, ed., *The Portable Harlem Renaissance Reader* (New York, 1994), 106–109; On Stein's "Melanctha" and its dubious basis in a knowledge of black culture, see Robert M. Crunden, *American Salons* (New York, 1993), 177–179; GS to CVV, 9 August, 1926, and 11 August, 1927, in *Stein/Van Vechten Letters*, vol. 1: 131–132, 152–153.

14. CVV diary entry 10 November, 1924, Box F, Carl Van Vechten Papers, New York Public Library; Langston Hughes (hereafter LH) to CVV, n.d., and CVV to LH, n.d. (but both ?1925), CVV Papers, Beinecke Library, Yale University, all as cited in Arnold Rampersad, *The Life of Langston Hughes*, I (New York, 1986), 97, 111. This is the best biography and the source of all facts unless otherwise noted. See also Kellner, *Van Vechten*, 212–213; CVV, "The Black Blues," *Vanity Fair*, 24 (August, 1925), 86; and "Langston Hughes: A Biographical Note" *Vanity Fair* (September, 1925), 62. For background on the blues, see Crunden, *American Salons*, 134–136; on Kansas City, see Ross Russell, *Jazz Style in Kansas City and the Southwest* (Berkeley, 1971).

15. See, inter alia, CVV to Blanche Knopf (hereafter BK), 3 April 1933, BK to LH, 12 March, 1934, LH to BK, 15 May, 1934, and CVV to BK, 14 December, 1934, all Alfred A. Knopf Collection, Harry Ransom Humanities Research Center, University of Texas at Austin (hereafter AAK-UT). I am grateful to my student, Randolph Lewis, for drawing my attention to these letters, first in "Prejudice in Publishing: Alfred A. Knopf and American Publishing, 1915–1935" (M.A. diss., University of Texas at Austin, 1990), and then in abridged form in "Langston Hughes and Alfred A. Knopf, Inc., 1925–1935," *The Library Chronicle* of the University of Texas at Austin, 22, no. 4 (1992), 51–63. The same issue includes excerpts from Knopf's unpublished memoirs and Peter Flora, "Carl Van Vechten, Blanche Knopf, and the Harlem Renaissance," 65–83, which includes a useful checklist of CVV's articles on black subjects, 70, no. 8.

16. LH, "The Negro Artist and the Racial Mountain," first appeared in the *Nation*, 23 June, 1926, and is most readily now available in both the basic anthologies of the Harlem renaissance: David Levering Lewis, ed., *The Portable Harlem Renaissance Reader* (New York, 1994), 91–95; and Nathan Irvin Huggins, ed., *Voices from the Harlem Renaissance* (New York, 1976), 305–309.

17. Arnold Rampersad, ed., *The Collected Poems of Langston Hughes* (New York, 1995); pagination in the text refers to this edition. For the context of the refer-

ences to Sherwood Anderson, see Crunden, *American Salons*, 118–124, and passim for Pound, Eliot, and Stein. For a good technical discussion see Steven C. Tracy, *Langston Hughes & the Blues* (Urbana, 1988).

18. Recent scholarship has produced a number of valuable studies on these themes. See, inter alia, Nellie Y. McKay, *Jean Toomer Artist* (Chapel Hill, 1984); Thadious M. Davis, *Nella Larsen* (Baton Rouge, 1994); and Wayne F. Cooper, *Claude McKay* (Baton Rouge, 1987). Several relevant issues also come up in Willard B. Gatewood, *Aristocrats of Color: The Black Elite, 1880–1920* (Bloomington, 1990).

19. Isaac Goldberg, *George Gershwin* (New York, 1958), 40–42 and passim. This volume retains utility as in places almost a primary source. I have also garnered factual material from Charles Schwartz, *Gershwin* (New York, 1979); Edward Jablonski, *Gershwin* (Boston, 1990); and Joan Peyser, *The Memory of All That* (New York, 1993). See also Willie the Lion Smith, *Music on My Mind* (New York, 1978), 225.

20. Ethel Waters, *His Eye Is on the Sparrow*, 145. The best recent study of the Harlem music scene in its wider context is Reid Badger, *A Life in Ragtime: A Biography of James Reese Europe* (New York, 1995).

21. Alec Wilder, *American Popular Song: The Great Innovators, 1900–1950* (New York, 1972), 126–127.

22. Thomas A. DeLong, *Pops: Paul Whiteman, King of Jazz* (Piscataway, N.J., 1983), 85. See also Samuel B. Charters and Leonard Kunstadt, *Jazz: A History of the New York Scene* (New York, 1981), ch. 11.

23. Gerald Bordman, *Jerome Kern* (New York, 1980), 94–99 and passim; Goldberg, *Gershwin*, 80–81.

24. Quoted in Peyser, *Memory*, 75; see also Paul Whiteman and Mary Margaret McBride, *Jazz* (New York, 1926), ch. 4.

25. See Schwartz, *Gershwin*, ch. 5, and p. 156 for the blue ice cream; Jablonski, *Gershwin*, ch. 4; Peyser, *Memory*, 73–86; the quotes are from Goldberg, *Gershwin*, 138–140, 152, 154, and the program 146–147. On Whistler, see Philip Furia, *Ira Gershwin* (New York, 1996), 44. For Van Vechten, see CVV to Hugh Walpole, 18 October, 1924, in Kellner, ed., *Letters of Van Vechten*, 73.

26. Leonard Bernstein, *The Joy of Music* (New York, 1963), 52–62.

27. George Martin, *The Damrosch Dynasty* (Boston, 1983), 288–291; Goldberg, *Gershwin*, 178; Peyser, *Memory*, 102–107; Bernstein, *Joy of Music*, 60.

28. Aaron Copland and Vivian Perlis, *Copland 1900 through 1942* (New York, 1984), 130; this first of two volumes of oral history will be my source for most facts and quotes unless otherwise noted. See also Nicolas Slonimsky, *Perfect Pitch* (New York, 1988), 116.

29. Aaron Copland (hereafter AC), "Composer from Brooklyn: An Autobiographical Sketch," *The New Music 1900–1960* (New York, 1968), 151–154.

30. Copland and Perlis, *Copland*, 32, 43–47; the formal picture is in Léonie Rosenstiel, *Nadia Boulanger* (New York, 1982), 158–159.

31. Copland and Perlis, *Copland*, 48–50; Rosenstiel, *Boulanger*, 192; Virgil Thomson (hereafter VT) to Briggs Buchanan, May 1926, and VT to AC, 26 No-

vember, 1931, both in Tim Page and Vanessa Weeks Page, eds., *Selected Letters of Virgil Thomson* (New York, 1988), 72, 100. Compare to the more neutral description published in Thomson's *Virgil Thomson* (New York, 1967), while Boulanger was still alive.

32. Copland and Perlis, *Copland*, 56–66, 72.

33. Ibid., 67, 71, 73; Copland, *New Music*, 17–31.

34. Copland, *New Music*, 63–64; see also AC's "Jazz Structure and Influence," *Modern Music* 4, no. 2 (January-February 1927), 9–14.

35. Copland and Perlis, *Copland*, 59, 84–86.

36. Ibid., 90–92; VT, *Thomson*, 71; VT, "Aaron Copland," in *A Virgil Thomson Reader* (Boston, 1981), 19–22.

37. F. Scott Fitzgerald (hereafter FSF), "Echoes of the Jazz Age," (1931), in *The Crack-Up*, ed. Edmund Wilson (New York, 1956), 13–22.

38. Matthew J. Bruccoli, ed., *The Short Stories of F. Scott Fitzgerald* (New York, 1989), esp. 79, 84, 247. Subsequent references to short stories will be to this edition, with specific pages in parentheses in text.

39. A highly useful work, not cited as often as it should be, is Joan M. Allen, *Candles and Carnival Lights: The Catholic Sensibility of F. Scott Fitzgerald* (New York, 1978); quote, 37, from FSF's "Homage to the Victorians," *N.Y. Tribune* (14 May, 1922), 4:7. For most readers and purposes, the best biography of reasonable length is André Le Vot, *F. Scott Fitzgerald* (Garden City, N.Y., 1983), well translated from the original French by William Byron.

40. Matthew J. Bruccoli, *Some Sort of Epic Grandeur: The Life of F. Scott Fitzgerald* (New York, 1981), 89; FSF to Edmund Wilson (hereafter EW), 15 August, 1919, in Andrew Turnbull, ed., *The Letters of F. Scott Fitzgerald* (New York, 1966), 349.

41. EW to FSF, 21 November, 1919, in *Letters on Literature and Politics 1912–1972/Edmund Wilson*, ed. Elena Wilson (New York, 1977), 45–47.

42. Citations to *This Side of Paradise* (New York, 1948) will appear in the text from the standard Scribner's edition. On several theological matters, see again Allen, *Candles and Carnival Lights;* the classic statement on Augustinianism in early America is Perry Miller, *The New England Mind: the Seventeenth Century* (New York, 1939), ch. 1.

43. FSF to Thomas Boyd, March 1923, in *Correspondence of F. Scott Fitzgerald*, ed. Matthew Bruccoli and Margaret M. Duggan (New York, 1980), 126; Nancy Milford, *Zelda* (New York, 1971), 55.

44. FSF to Maxwell Perkins (hereafter MP), in *Dear Scott/Dear Max: The Fitzgerald-Perkins Correspondence*, ed. John Kuehl and Jackson R. Bryer (New York, 1971), 61.

45. FSF to MP, 18 June, 1924, *Dear Scott*, 72; FSF to John Jamieson, 15 April, 1934, in Turnbull, ed., *Letters*, 529.

46. FSF to Isabelle Amorous, 26 February, 1920, *Correspondence*, 53. Page references to *The Great Gatsby* will be keyed to the Cambridge edition, ed. Matthew J. Bruccoli (New York, 1991).

47. FSF to EW, ?30 May, 1922, in Matthew J. Bruccoli, ed., *A Life in Letters: F. Scott Fitzgerald* (New York, 1994), 58.

48. In his text, Bruccoli spells the name "Wolfshiem," even though a decade earlier he used "Wolfsheim" in his own biography (for example, 184). It seems that FSF, perpetually unable to spell, used Wolfshiem originally, much the way he spelled Stein as "Stien," etc. as "ect.," yacht as "yatch," and Van Vechten as "Van Vetchten." Following sensible linguistic usage, EW had corrected it to Wolfsheim for all previous modern editions. Wilson as usual was right. The name means, after all, home of the wolf, a connotation lost with Bruccoli's pedantries. I find it also logically inconsistent to leave "errors" in names in despite editorial changing, only to accept editorial corrections elsewhere. FSF *needed* editing. We all do.

49. See, for example, Ronald Berman, *The Great Gatsby and Modern Times* (Urbana, 1994) and Scott Donaldson, ed., *Critical Essays on F. Scott Fitzgerald's* The Great Gatsby (Boston, 1984).

Eight

1. Georgia O'Keeffe, *Georgia O'Keeffe* (New York, 1976), unpaginated but opposite illustration no. 11.

2. T. S. Eliot, "Tradition and the Individual Talent" (1919), *Selected Essays 1917–1932* (New York, 1950), 3–11; W. Jackson Bate, *The Burden of the Past and the English Poet* (Cambridge, Mass., 1970); Harold Bloom, *The Anxiety of Influence: A Theory of Poetry* (New York, 1973), 5, 30.

3. Long out of fashion except in Jewish religious circles, Bloch has received little scholarly attention, and surviving papers are perhaps too thin for an extensive biography. The most useful source is Robert Strassburg, *Ernest Bloch, Voice in the Wilderness* (Los Angeles, 1977); but see also David Z. Kushner, *Ernest Bloch and his Music* (Glasgow, 1973) and Suzanne Bloch with Irene Heskes, *Ernest Bloch: Creative Spirit* (New York, 1976). More technical is William M. Jones, "The Music of Ernest Bloch" (Ph.D. diss., Indiana University, 1963).

4. Edward T. Cone, "Conversation with Roger Sessions," in Benjamin Boretz and Edward T. Cone, eds., *Perspectives on American Composers* (New York, 1971), 90–107; and Roger Sessions (hereafter RS) to George H. Bartlett, 17 December, 1919, in Andrea Olmstead, ed., *The Correspondence of Roger Sessions* (Boston, 1992), 36 (hereafter *Letters*).

5. Andrea Olmstead, *Conversations with Roger Sessions* (Boston, 1987), 14–17. Howard Hanson conducted a suite from *The Black Maskers*, based on a 1928 reworking, that ironically became Sessions's most popular and accessible piece, on Mercury MG50106.

6. Ernest Bloch (hereafter EB) to Romain Rolland, 27 June, 1921, 19 July, 1925, 15 April, 1926, in José-Flore Tappy, ed., *Lettres, 1911–1933/Ernest Bloch Romain Rolland* (Lausanne, 1984), 132, 147–155; see also 10 and passim. This volume contains a wealth of detail not available in English-language sources. For EB's impressions of RS, his "fils spiritual," and *The Black Maskers*, see 141–142.

7. RS, "Ernest Bloch" (1927), in Edward T. Cone, ed., *Roger Sessions on Music* (Princeton, 1979), 329–338; Yale Oral History Collection no. 61, "Roger Sessions," office of Vivian Perlis, Stoeckel Hall, Yale University.

8. RS to Barbara Sessions (hereafter BS), 31 July and 22 August, 1924, Olmstead, ed., *Letters*, 48–49; Olmstead, *Conversations*, 53.

9. RS to BS, 22 August and 6 September, 1924, Olmstead, ed., *Letters*, 48–59; Olmstead, *Conversations*, 20ff. The best secondary source is Andrea Olmstead, *Roger Sessions and his Music* (Ann Arbor, 1985).

10. Virgil Thomson (hereafter VT), "French Music Here" (5 January, 1941), in *A Virgil Thomson Reader* (New York, 1981), 207–210; see also Kathleen Hoover and John Cage, *Virgil Thomson* (New York, 1959), 99–100; and VT, *Virgil Thomson* (New York, 1967), 64 and passim. The definitive treatment of Thomson's life is now Anthony Tommasini, *Virgil Thomson: Composer on the Aisle* (New York, 1997).

11. Roger Shattuck, *The Banquet Years: The Arts in France 1885–1918* (New York, 1961), 114–115.

12. Nancy Perloff, *Art and the Everyday: Popular Entertainment and the Circle of Erik Satie* (Oxford, 1991), has been invaluable in this section.

13. See especially Robert Orledge, *Satie the Composer* (Cambridge, 1990), 254, 52, 205, 240 and passim. See also Rollo H. Myers, *Erik Satie* (New York, 1968), 23.

14. VT, *Virgil Thomson*, 46, 55, 58, 64 and passim.

15. VT to Briggs Buchanan, 4 August, 1925, in Tim Page and Vanessa Weeks Page, eds., *Selected Letters of Virgil Thomson* (New York, 1988), 62–63.

16. VT, interview with Vivian Perlis, 1977, Yale Oral History no. 29, p. 8; VT to Briggs Buchanan, 17 July, 1927, Page and Page *Letters*, 81–83; see also 67–68, including a list of friends; VT, *Virgil Thomson*, 89–91, 112–113.

17. Robert McAlmon, *Being Geniuses Together*, as revised and supplemented by Kay Boyle (New York, 1968), 27–28 (hereafter cited as BGT). See also Jane Lidderdale and Mary Nicholson, *Dear Miss Weaver: Harriet Shaw Weaver 1876–1961* (New York, 1970), 177; and Brenda Maddox, *Nora* (Boston, 1988), 179ff.

18. James Joyce (hereafter JJ) to Frank Budgen, 6 September, 1921, in Stuart Gilbert, ed., *Letters of James Joyce*, (New York, 1957), vol. 1, 172; Richard Ellmann, *James Joyce* (New York, 1959), 528–529.

19. Sanford J. Smoller, *Adrift Among Geniuses: Robert McAlmon Writer and Publisher of the Twenties* (University Park, Pa., 1975), 59–62, especially for McAlmon to William Carlos Williams, ? Spring 1921; BGT, 28–29.

20. Smoller, *Adrift*, 27ff., and passim. See also Robert E. Knoll, *Robert McAlmon* (Lincoln, Neb., 1959), and ed., *McAlmon and the Lost Generation* (Lincoln, Neb., 1962), pts. 1–2.

21. William Carlos Williams, *The Autobiography of William Carlos Williams* (New York, 1951), 175; William Carlos Williams (hereafter WCW) to Kenneth Burke (hereafter KB), 24 February, 1921, Kenneth Burke Papers, Pennsylvania State University Library (hereafter KB-PSU); WCW to Amy Lowell, 6 March, 1921, in John C. Thirlwell, ed., *The Selected Letters of William Carlos Williams* (New York, 1985), 51; KB to WCW, 21 March, 1921, KS-PSU.

22. McAlmon to WCW, ?1921, and Victoria McAlmon to WCW and Florence Williams, ?1959, both quoted in McAlmon, *BGT*, 50–51.

23. Bryher, *The Heart to Artemis* (New York, 1962), 201–211.

24. Ibid., 201–202; Sylvia Beach, *Shakespeare and Company* (New York, 1959), 102.

25. The best analysis is Hugh Ford, *Published in Paris* (London, 1975), 34–94.

26. McAlmon, *BGT,* 175–178.

27. WCW to McAlmon, ?1923, Thirlwell, ed., *Letters,* 56–57; Paul Mariani, *William Carlos Williams* (New York, 1981), 218ff.

28. Morley Callaghan, *That Summer in Paris* (New York, 1963), ch. 10; Ellmann, *Joyce,* 684.

29. Man Ray, *Self Portrait* (Boston, 1963), 66–67.

30. See especially Robert M. Crunden, *American Salons: Encounters with European Modernism, 1885–1917* (New York, 1993), 423–437.

31. For biographical detail, see especially Arturo Schwarz, *Man Ray: The Rigour of Imagination* (New York, 1977) and Neil Baldwin, *Man Ray* (New York, 1988). Calvin Tomkins, *Duchamp* (New York, 1996) is now standard.

32. Francis M. Naumann, *New York Dada 1915–23* (New York, 1994), 76–93, especially 88; Robert L. Herbert, Eleanor S. Apter, and Elise K. Kenney, eds., *The Société Anonyme and the Dreier Bequest at Yale University: A Catalog Raisonné* (New Haven, 1984), introduction.

33. Ray, *Self Portrait,* 107–109, 115.

34. Henri-Pierre Roché, Diaries for 8 May, 1922; see also 25 May and 24 June, 1922, and 1 January, 1923, Carlton Lake Collection, Harry Ransom Humanities Research Center, University of Texas, Austin. Anyone knowing Roché was effectively plugged into the best gossip machine in Paris. Other entries record meals with Stein and Satie, love affairs with Lou Arensberg and Louise Norton [Varèse]; talks with Picasso, Milhaud, and Brancusi, and much more. For the best current scholarship see the articles in Merry Foresta et al., *Perpetual Motif: The Art of Man Ray* (New York and Washington, 1988).

35. Schwarz, *Man Ray,* 133, 161.

36. Ray, *Self Portrait,* 128–131.

37. Foresta, *Perpetual Motif,* 125.

NINE

1. Anita Pollitzer (hereafter AP) to Georgia O'Keeffe (hereafter GO'K), 1 January, 1916, in Clive Giboire, ed., *Lovingly, Georgia: The Complete Correspondence of Georgia O'Keeffe & Anita Pollitzer* (New York, 1990), 115–116 (hereafter cited as *O'Keeffe/Pollitzer*). On Stieglitz up to this point, see Robert M. Crunden, *American Salons: Encounters with European Modernism, 1885–1917* (New York, 1993), 339–382. The standard biography of Stieglitz is now Richard Whelan, *Alfred Stieglitz* (Boston, 1995).

2. Dorothy Norman, *Alfred Stieglitz: An American Seer* (New York, 1973), 130; Anita Pollitzer, *A Woman on Paper: Georgia O'Keeffe* (New York, 1988), 139–142; Pollitzer, *O'Keeffe/Pollitzer,* 174.

3. Alfred Stieglitz (hereafter AS) to Arthur Dove (hereafter AD), late July and 15 August, 1918, in Ann Lee Morgan, ed., *Dear Stieglitz, Dear Dove* (Newark and

Cranbury, N.J., 1988) (hereafter *Stieglitz/Dove*), 61–62; AS to Paul Strand (hereafter PS), 17 November, 1918, Alfred Stieglitz Papers, Beinecke Library, Yale University (hereafter AS-YU).

4. See especially Barbara Buhler Lynes, *O'Keeffe, Stieglitz, and the Critics, 1916–1929* (Chicago, 1991), 171–179, 203–209, 282–283, her Appendix A reprinting 90 examples of critical commentary.

5. GO'K to Mitchell Kennerley, Fall 1922; and GO'K to Sherwood Anderson, ?September 1923, in Sarah Greenough, ed., *Georgia O'Keeffe: Art and Letters* (Washington and Boston, 1987) 170–171, 173–175.

6. Pollitzer, *O'Keeffe/Pollitzer*, 10, 15, 19, 24. For more details, see Crunden, *American Salons*, 309–329, with extensive references to relevant secondary literature.

7. GO'K to AS, 1 February, 1916, Greenough, ed., *Letters*, 150; Pollitzer, *O'-Keeffe/Pollitzer*, 15, 22, 32, 59, 211, 224, 238, and passim.

8. G'OK to AP, ? October 1915, three separate letters; and ? November 1915, Pollitzer, *O'Keeffe/Pollitzer*, 42, 52, 66, 84.

9. Pollitzer, *O'Keeffe/Pollitzer*, ? October 1915, 59; GO'K to Sherwood Anderson, ? September 1923, Greenough, ed., *Letters*, 173–175.

10. Quoted in Pollitzer, *Woman on Paper*, 169–172. For critical opinion see especially Charles C. Eldredge, *Georgia O'Keeffe* (New York, 1991); and Sarah Whitaker Peters, *Becoming O'Keeffe* (New York, 1991).

11. Laurie Lisle, *Portrait of an Artist* (New York, 1980), 82; Roxana Robinson, *Georgia O'Keeffe* (New York, 1989), 223–224; O'Keeffe, *O'Keeffe*, opposite nos. 17 and 18; Sarah Whitaker Peters, "Georgia O'Keeffe and Photography: Her Formative Years, 1915–1930" (Ph.D. diss., City University of New York, 1987), 273–274.

12. GO'K to Sherwood Anderson, 11 February, 1924, Greenough, *Letters*, 176; quoted *New York Sun*, 5 December, 1922, in Peters, "O'Keeffe and Photography," 289.

13. On Kandinsky and America before 1917, see Crunden, *American Salons*, esp. 309–327; and Gail Levin and Marianne Lorenz, *Theme and Improvisation: Kandinsky & the American Avant-Garde, 1912–1950* (Boston, 1992), 25–27, including GO'K to Gail Levin, 22 November, 1974. The most extensive discussion of art nouveau and symbolism in this context is Peters, *Becoming O'Keeffe*, esp. 13–17, 21, 39ff., 78, 94, 99–100, 129–131.

14. See Part 4 for the development of this theme in Bragdon, Dove, and others before 1926. On domestic life see Robinson, *O'Keeffe*, 296ff; Sue Davidson Lowe, *Stieglitz* (New York, 1983), 216ff, and her addendum, "O'Keeffe, Stieglitz, and the Stieglitz Family," in Christopher Merrill and Ellen Bredbury, eds., *From the Faraway Nearby: Georgia O'Keeffe as Icon* (Reading, Mass., 1992), 141–161. The same volume also contains the suggestive Sharyn R. Udall article, "Beholding the Epiphanies: Mysticism and the Art of Georgia O'Keeffe," 89–112. Essential background is in *The Spiritual in Art: Abstract Painting, 1890–1985* (New York, 1986) and Linda Henderson, *The Fourth Dimension and Non-Euclidean Geometry in Modern Art* (Princeton, 1983). The final quotations are from GO'K to Blanche

Matthias, ? March 1926; GO'K to Waldo Frank, ? Summer 1926, and 10 January, 1927, Greenough, *Letters*, 183–185.

Ten

1. Sherwood Anderson (hereafter SA), *A Story Teller's Story* (New York, 1989), 359–362. Ray Lewis White, ed., *Sherwood Anderson/Gertrude Stein* (Chapel Hill, 1972), brings together most of the available primary sources.

2. Charles A. Fenton, *The Apprenticeship of Ernest Hemingway: The Early Years* (New York, 1954) was seminal on the early journalism; the most recent is Shelley Fisher Fishkin, *From Fact to Fiction: Journalism & Imaginative Writing in America* (Baltimore, 1985), ch. 5. For primary material, see Matthew J. Bruccoli, ed., *Ernest Hemingway, Cub Reporter: Kansas City Star Stories* (Pittsburgh, 1970). On the effect of World War I on English prose, Paul Fussell, *The Great War and Modern Memory* (New York, 1975) is a classic, but Hemingway is only mentioned in passing.

3. Kim Townsend, *Sherwood Anderson* (Boston, 1987), 172–174; SA, *Sherwood Anderson's Memoirs* (New York, 1942), 474–475.

4. SA to Gertrude Stein (hereafter GS), 3 December, 1921, in Donald Gallup, ed., *The Flowers of Friendship: Letters Written to Gertrude Stein* (New York, 1979), 142–143; Ernest Hemingway (hereafter EH) to SA, ?23 December 1921 and 22 March, 1922, in Carlos Baker, ed., *Ernest Hemingway: Selected Letters 1917–1961* (hereafter *Letters*) (New York, 1981), 59, 62–63. See also Carlos Baker, *Ernest Hemingway* (New York, 1969), 78ff., and Kenneth S. Lynn, *Hemingway* (New York, 1987), 161.

5. EH to Ezra Pound (hereafter EP), 23 January, 1923, and 2 May, 1924, Baker, ed., *Letters*, 76–77, 114–116; and EH to GS, 18 February, 1923, ibid., 79–80.

6. EH to GS and Alice B. Toklas, 11 October, 1923; EH to EP, 13 October, 1923, ibid., 93–97.

7. EH to Edmund Wilson, 11 November, 1923, 25 November, 1923, and 18 October, 1924, in Edmund Wilson, *The Shores of Light* (New York, 1952), 115–124; see also Baker, ed., *Letters*, 104–106.

8. EH to SA, 23 May, 1925, Baker, ed., *Letters*, 161–162; EH to EP, ? November 1925, Ezra Pound Papers, Beinecke Library, Yale University (hereafter EP-YU); F. Scott Fitzgerald to GS, ? June 1925, and to Maxwell Perkins, ca. 27 December, 1925, in Matthew J. Bruccoli, ed., *A Life in Letters: F. Scott Fitzgerald* (New York, 1994), 115, 131–133, with Fitzgerald's spellings all (sic). For background on the book see Robert M. Crunden, *American Salons: Encounters with European Modernism, 1885–1917* (New York, 1993), 172ff.; on book publications, see Hugh Ford, *Published in Paris* (London, 1975), 56ff. Autobiographical accounts, and secondary treatments largely based on them, are colorful but unreliable.

9. EH to SA, 21 May, 1926, Baker, ed., *Letters*, 205–206; *The Short Stories of Ernest Hemingway* (New York, 1953), 147–148.

10. Linda Wagner-Martin, *"Favored Strangers": Gertrude Stein and her Family* (New Brunswick, N.J., 1995), 168ff., including EH to Donald Gallup, 22 Sep-

tember, 1952, quoted 170, 178. See also Hadley Hemingway's taped memoirs, cited in Gioia Diliberto, *Hadley* (New York, 1992), 191; and EH, *A Moveable Feast* (New York, 1964), 117–119.

11. EH to Harriet Monroe, 16 November, 1922, and EH to Hadley Hemingway, 28 November, 1922, Baker, ed., *Letters*, 72–73. For other examples see 77, 114–115, 120, 135, 171. Diliberto, *Hadley*, 199; the most detailed biographical treatment is Jeffrey Meyers, *Hemingway* (New York, 1985), 154–159.

12. EH to GS and Alice B. Toklas, 9 November, 1923, Baker, ed., *Letters*, 100–102; EH to EP, 8 November, 1925, EP-YU. Stein's one paragraph review is reprinted in Peter Griffin, *Less Than a Treason: Hemingway in Paris* (New York, 1990), 73.

13. GS, *The Autobiography of Alice B. Toklas*, in Carl Van Vechten, ed., *Selected Writings of Gertrude Stein* (New York, 1962), 200–208.

14. EH to EP, tentatively dated 25 February, 1932, by Beinecke, but more likely 1933 or 1934, EP-YU; EH to EP, 22 July, 1933, EP-YU. Hemingway even launched into an "Autobiography of Alice B. Hemingway" but never completed or published it. It remains in the Hemingway Collection, John F. Kennedy Library, Boston.

15. The best treatment is Wagner-Martin, *Favored Strangers*, ch. 12.

16. EH to SA, 23 May, 1925, Baker, ed., *Letters*, 161–162.

17. The most available version of *The Torrents of Spring* is in *The Hemingway Reader* (New York, 1953), 25–86, quote p. 68.

18. EH to Scott Fitzgerald, 31 December, 1925/1 January, 1926, and EH to Horace Liveright, 7 December, 1925 and 19 January, 1926, *Letters*, 172–174, 183–185, 190–191. In addition to the biographies already cited, see Tom Dardis, *Firebrand: The Life of Horace Liveright* (New York, 1995), 251–261; and Matthew J. Bruccoli, *Fitzgerald and Hemingway* (New York, 1994), 28ff.

19. EH to SA, 21 May, 1926, and EH to Maxwell Perkins, 20 June, 1927, Baker, ed., *Letters*, 205–206, 241. See, for example, Ben Hecht, *Letters from Bohemia* (Garden City, N.Y., 1964), 98; and Howard Mumford Jones and Walter B. Rideout, eds., *Letters of Sherwood Anderson* (Boston, 1953), 205.

ELEVEN

1. Aaron Copland, "Americans Young Men of Promise," *Modern Music* 3, no. 3 (March-April, 1926), as reprinted in *Copland on Music* (New York, 1963), 145–146; Aaron Copland and Vivian Perlis, *Copland 1900 through 1942* (New York 1984), 127.

2. Virgil Thomson, *Virgil Thomson* (New York 1967), 81–82; Thomson to (?), 9 June, 1964, in Tim Page and Vanessa Weeks Page, eds., *Selected Letters of Virgil Thomson* (New York, 1988), 319; R. Murray Schafer, ed., *Ezra Pound and Music* (New York, 1977), 243 and passim.

3. George Antheil (hereafter GA) to Mary Louise Bok (hereafter MB), 10 November, 1921, George Antheil Correspondence, Music Division, Library of Congress (hereafter cited as GA-LC); on the contents of this collection see especially

Wayne D. Shirley, "Another American in Paris: George Antheil's Correspondence with Mary Curtis Bok," *The Quarterly Journal of the Library of Congress* 34, no. 1 (January, 1977), 2–22. The most thorough secondary source is Linda Whitesitt, *The Life and Music of George Antheil 1900–1959* (Ann Arbor, 1983), to which I am much indebted. Hugh Ford has a graceful study in *Four Lives in Paris* (San Francisco, 1987), 3–81, that contains new information but is sadly unfootnoted and unindexed. See also the often unreliable autobiography, *Bad Boy of Music* (New York 1945), 16–19.

4. Margaret Anderson, *My Thirty Years' War* (New York, 1969), 234–239. Anderson is no more reliable than Antheil when it comes to minor details, but the impressions remain valid.

5. C. von Sternberg to MB, ? November, 1921, GA-LC.

6. GA to MB, ? August 1922, GA-LC.

7. AC, *Bad Boy of Music*, 29; GA to MB, ? December, 1922, GA-LC.

8. AC, *Bad Boy of Music*, 29; Whitesitt, *Antheil*, 12; H. H. Stuckenschmidt, "Umschau: Ausblick in die Musik," *Das Kunstblatt* 7 (July, 1923), 221–222. His biography originally appeared as *Schönberg, Leben, Umwelt, Werk* (Zürich, 1974).

9. GA to MB, 26 July, 1923, GA-LC.

10. This paragraph is a collage of several separate letters or fragments, dated between January and May, 1923, Igor Stravinsky to Ernest Ansermet, as printed in Robert Craft, ed., *Stravinsky: Selected Correspondence* 1 (New York, 1982), 162–168.

11. AC, *Bad Boy of Music*, 98–108. I have also profited from the most serious overview of these issues, Glenn Watkins, *Pyramids at the Louvre: Music, Culture, and Collage from Stravinsky to the Postmodernists* (Cambridge, Mass., 1994), especially ch. 12. See also Robert M. Crunden, *American Salons: Encounters with European Modernism, 1885–1917* (New York, 1993) 409–443.

12. GA to Ezra Pound (hereafter EP), separate letters each labelled "1923–24?" in a later hand, Ezra Pound Papers, Beinecke Library, Yale University (hereafter EP-YU). GA did not marry Böski Markus until 4 November, 1925. The fullest treatment of the GA-EP relationship is in Humphrey Carpenter, *A Serious Character* (Boston, 1988), 431–436 and passim.

13. GA to EP, both also dated "1923–24?" in another hand, EP-YU. The ellipses within quotations are GA's.

14. Most useful in this context are the collection of primary documents with substantive annotation, in Schafer, *Pound and Music*, and Archibald Henderson III, "Pound and Music: The Paris and Early Years" (Ph.D. diss., UCLA, 1983). Note that Schafer is a Canadian composer of considerable achievement and not a literary theorist.

15. Schafer, *Pound and Music*, 253–256, with a list of his fugitive writings at n. 8.

16. Ibid., 262–264; R. Murray Schafer, "Ezra Pound and Music," *The Canadian Music Journal* 5, no. 4 (Summer, 1961). See also Henderson, "Pound and Music," ch. 3; and AC, *Bad Boy of Music*, 118–119.

17. See the twelve-page letter, GA to EP, Paris, ? 1925; the postcard, Tunis, ? 24 August, 1925; and Tunis, 15 September, 1925, all EP-YU.

18. GA to EP, ? 1925, separate letters from Tunis and Paris, EP-YU.

19. Searcher Ceasinger, "The Greatest Coup of the Age," *Der Querschnitt* 4 (1924), 47–48; AC, *Bad Boy of Music*, 132–134.

20. Bravig Imbs, *Confessions of Another Young Man* (New York, 1936), 78–81; Noel Riley Fitch, *Sylvia Beach and the Lost Generation* (New York, 1983), 192–193.

21. Imbs, *Confessions*, 96–103; Virgil Thomson to Alice Smith, 30 May, 1926, in Tim Page and Vanessa Weeks Page, eds., *Selected Letters of Virgil Thomson* (New York, 1988), 74; Virgil Thomson, *Virgil Thomson*, 75; AC to Israel Citkowitz, n.d., in Copland and Perlis, *Copland*, 127; GA to MB, ? July 1925, GA-LC. See also Sylvia Beach, *Shakespeare and Company* (New York, 1959), 122–125; and Ella Winter and Granville Hicks, eds., *Letters of Lincoln Steffens* (2 vols., New York, 1938), 749, for Lincoln Steffens to Ella Winter, 20 June, 1926.

22. EP, "Antheil 1924–1926," typescript, EP-YU, for article appearing in the *New Criterion* 4, no. 4 (October, 1926), 695–699; see also "George Antheil," *Criterion*, 2, no. 7 (April, 1924), 321–333.

23. GA, "MY BALLET MECANIQUE: WHAT IT MEANS," typescript, EP-YU.

24. GA to EP, ?late 1925, EP-YU; GA to MB, 19 October and 15 November, 1925, GA-LC.

25. GA to EP, ?early 1926, EP-YU; see Whitesitt, *Antheil*, 112.

26. GA to EP, ?Spring, 1926, 13 August, 1926, and 26 December, 1926, all EP-YU.

27. GA to EP, ?Autumn 1926, and 11 December, 1926, EP-YU.

28. GA to EP, ?Autumn 1926, EP-YU.

29. Donald Friede, *The Mechanical Angel* (New York, 1948), 44–61; MB to GA, 27 April, 1927, GA-LC; AC, *Bad Boy of Music*, 192–197. Not yet well known, Colin McPhee also played one of the pianos.

30. AC, *Bad Boy of Music*, 199–200, 204.

TWELVE

1. Limitations of space and inadequate archival sources prevent the detailed discussion the topic deserves. For a useful overview, see Roger Lipsey, *An Art of Our Own: The Spiritual in Twentieth-Century Art* (Boston, 1988).

2. Toomer left extensive unpublished autobiographical writings; many are now available in Darwin T. Turner, ed., *The Wayward and the Seeking: A Collection of Writings by Jean Toomer* (Washington, 1980). The standard biography, Cynthia Earl Kerman and Richard Eldridge, *The Lives of Jean Toomer* (Baton Rouge, 1987), naturally makes heavy use of them, so quotations often occur in both. Here, see the former, 64–66, 101–102, and the latter, 48, 66–68.

3. Hart Crane to Allen Tate, 15 February, 1923; and to Gorham Munson, 2 March, 1923 and ? June, 1918, in Brom Weber, ed., *The Letters of Hart Crane 1916–1932* (Berkeley, 1965), 91–92, 123–124, 129; Jean Toomer (hereafter JT) to Gorham Munson (hereafter GM) 17 July, 1924, as quoted in Kerman and Eldridge, *Toomer*, 112–116. P. D. Ouspensky, *Tertium Organum* (New York, 1981) is

a current standard translation. See also Linda Henderson, *The Fourth Dimension and Non-Euclidean Geometry in Modern Art* (Princeton, 1983).

4. Kerman and Eldridge, *Toomer*, ch. 6, quote 127; Rudolph P. Byrd, *Jean Toomer's Years with Gurdjieff* (Athens, Ga., 1990), ch. 2, esp. 69–71.

5. There are few strictly contemporary letters for Toomer's European months, but see JT to Waldo Frank, 1 October, 1924, Waldo Frank Papers, Van Pelt Library, University of Pennsylvania; and JT to Alfred Stieglitz, 7 October, 1924, Alfred Stieglitz Papers, Beinecke Library, Yale University.

6. In addition to works cited, see Louise Welch, *Orage with Gurdjieff in America* (Boston, 1982).

7. Langston Hughes, *The Big Sea* (New York, 1940), 241–243.

8. See the edited version of an autobiographical recollection written over 1937–46 in Frederik L. Rusch, ed., *A Jean Toomer Reader* (New York, 1993), 31–76, chiefly 33–41.

Thirteen

1. See for instance, Georges I. Gurdjieff, *Views from the Real World* (New York, 1973), 44; and P. D. Ouspensky, *The Psychology of Man's Possible Evolution* (New York, 1974), 13.

2. For Stevens in this context, see Robert M. Crunden, *American Salons: Encounter with European Modernism, 1885–1917* (New York, 1993), 437–443 and passim.

3. Consistently the best analysis of Stevens's relationship to the world is James Longenbach, *Wallace Stevens: The Plain Sense of Things* (New York, 1991).

4. "The Death of A Soldier" and "Negation" are in Wallace Stevens, *The Collected Poems of Wallace Stevens* (New York, 1954), 97–98. Hereafter quotations will be cited in the text as *CP* and page number. The critic cited is Longenbach, *Plain Sense*, 46. For Stevens as correspondent, in addition to Holly Stevens, ed., *Letters of Wallace Stevens* (New York, 1966), see Alan Filreis, "Voicing the Desert of Silence: Stevens's Letters to Alice Corbin Henderson," *Wallace Stevens Journal*, 12, no. 1 (Spring, 1988), 3–20.

5. "Lettres d'un Soldat" is in *Opus Posthumous* (New York, 1989), 29–36, hereafter cited as *OP* with page numbers in text. On jazz attitudes toward death, see especially Alan Lomax, *Mister Jelly Roll* (Berkeley, 1973), 15–18.

6. The imagery persists, as in *An Ice-Cream War* (New York, 1983) by William Boyd.

7. On the issue of drama as a formal influence in Henry James and American modernism generally, see Crunden, *American Salons*, 57–79; on the context of the three plays, see especially A. Walton Litz, *Introspective Voyager: The Poetic Development of Wallace Stevens* (New York, 1972), ch. 3.

8. WS to Harriet Monroe, 21 December, 1921, and to Hervey Allen, 5 May, 1922, in H. Stevens, ed., *Letters*, 224–227. The full text of "From the Journal of Crispin" first appeared in Frank Doggett and Robert Buttel, eds., *Wallace Stevens: A Celebration* (Princeton, 1980), 30–45, and is now most accessible in the revised *Opus Posthumous*, 46–59. Citations will be to the latter in the text.

9. WS to Ronald Lane Latimer, 15 November 1935, and to Hi Simons, 12 January, 1940, both in H. Stevens, ed., *Letters*, 293–295, 351–352.

10. In addition to Litz, *Introspective Voyager*, see also Joseph N. Riddel, *The Clairvoyant Eye* (Baton Rouge, 1965); Guy Davenport, "Spinoza's Tulips: A Commentary on 'The Comedian as the Letter C,'" *Perspective* 7 (Autumn, 1954); Sidney Feshbach, "Wallace Stevens and Erik Satie: A Source for 'The Comedian as the Letter C,'" *Texas Studies in Literature and Language*, 11, no. 1 (Spring, 1969), 811–818; and David M. Linebarger, "'Orchestrating' Stravinsky: Petrushka's Ghost and Stevens' 'The Comedian as the Letter C,'" *Wallace Stevens Journal* 19, no. 1 (Spring, 1995), 71–87. On *The Waste Land*, see especially WS to Alice Corbin Henderson, 17 November, 1922, in Filreis, "Letters to Henderson," 19.

11. Such issues appear in Stevens criticism as early as J. Hillis Miller, *Poets of Reality* (Cambridge, Mass., 1965), ch. 6; for a recent reworking, see David R. Jarraway, *Wallace Stevens and the Question of Belief* (Baton Rouge, 1993), esp. 1–19. See also Margaret Peterson, "*Harmonium* and William James," *Southern Review*, 7, no. 3 (July, 1971), 658–682.

12. Thus, Harold Bloom, *Wallace Stevens: The Poems of Our Climate* (Ithaca, 1977), must have his own special climate in mind. He can barely stand to mention the poem at all, not to speak of the entire absence of Darwin and Spencer.

13. See for example Charles Doyle, ed., *Wallace Stevens: The Critical Heritage* (Boston, 1985), among others.

14. Marianne Moore, "Well Moused, Lion," *Dial* 76 (January, 1924), 84–91, now most readily available in Patricia C. Willis, ed., *The Complete Prose of Marianne Moore* (New York, 1986), 91–98.

15. WS to Ferdinand Reyher, 6 April, 1922, Wallace Stevens Collection, Huntington Library, no. 1568, as quoted in Joan Richardson, *Wallace Stevens: The Early Years 1879–1923* (New York, 1986), 525.

16. See especially the opening pages of Joan Richardson, *Wallace Stevens: The Later Years 1923–1955* (New York, 1988) and H. Stevens, ed., *Letters*, 241.

17. See also WS to Hi Simons, 9 January, 1940, 28 August, 1940, and to Henry Church, 15 October, 1940, in H. Stevens, ed., *Letters*, 346–350, 369–370, 376–378. On the larger subject, the pioneering work was Adalaide Kirby Morris, *Wallace Stevens: Imagination and Faith* (Princeton, 1974). For a more recent study that connects Stevens to others in this chapter, see Leonore Woodman, *Stanza My Stone: Wallace Stevens and the Hermetic Tradition* (West Lafayette, Ind., 1983).

FOURTEEN

1. See especially the diaries of Arthur C. Dove and Helen Torr Dove, which over the years have entries in both hands, for 20 June 1924, Arthur G. Dove Papers, Archives of American Art (hereafter AGD-AAA), on Cézanne. Somewhat mystifyingly, the microfilm sent me had #T3531 on the box and #N70–52 on the label of the film itself; the Helen Torr diaries are frames #67–596 but the frame numbers were not visible on my machine. See also Elizabeth McCausland, *A. H. Maurer* (New York, 1951). The best general biographical source is the lengthy in-

troduction by Ann Lee Morgan to her Catalog Raisonné, *Arthur Dove* (Newark, Del., 1984). I remain indebted to this work for details throughout this section. For occasional references, see Bruce St. John, ed., *John Sloan's New York Scene* (New York, 1965).

2. Dove provided an autobiographical statement for Samuel Kootz, *Modern American Painters* (New York, 1930), now most readily available in Ann Lee Morgan, ed., *Dear Stieglitz, Dear Dove* (Newark, Del., 1988), 188–191.

3. Maurice Aisen, "The Latest Evolution in Art and Picabia," *Camera Work* (June, 1913), 14–21.

4. Arthur Jerome Eddy, *Cubists and Post-Impressionism* (Chicago, 1914) 48–49.

5. Statement for Kootz in *Stieglitz/Dove*, 188–190.

6. See the Dove diaries for June 1924, December 1925, and August 1933, AGD-AAA; the best secondary treatment is Sherrye Cohn, *Arthur Dove: Nature as Symbol* (Ann Arbor, 1985), ch. 3. The Davidsons' daughter, Sue Davidson Lowe, discusses the larger picture in her memoir/biography, *Stieglitz* (New York, 1983).

7. Cohn, *Dove*, wrestles bravely with all these influences, but they can't possibly cohere.

8. Paul Rosenfeld, "Arthur G. Dove," in *Port of New York* (Urbana, 1961), 167–174.

9. The best selection is in Morgan, *Dove*, where *Stieglitz* is #24.1 and *Critic* is #25.2.

10. Ibid., #27.2, #27.3, #27.10.

FIFTEEN

1. William H. Jordy, *American Buildings and their Architects: The Impact of European Modernism in the Mid-Twentieth Century* (New York, 1972), 65–67.

2. William H. Pierson, Jr., *American Buildings and their Architects: Progressive and Academic Ideals at the Turn of the Twentieth Century* (New York, 1972), 97, 259; Claude Bragdon, *More Lives than One* (hereafter cited as *More Lives*) (New York, 1938), 143–150. See also Bragdon's *Architecture and Democracy* (New York, 1926), 113–131 and passim; and *Merely Players* (New York, 1929), 83–93. The most detailed study of Bragdon's work is Dorothy M. Cantor, "Claude Bragdon and his Relation to the Development of Modern Architectural Theory" (M.A. diss., Rochester, N.Y., 1963).

3. Bragdon, *More Lives*, 51–59; Claude Bragdon, *Episodes from an Unwritten History* (Rochester, N.Y., 1910, 2nd ed.), 13, 16, 20, 21, 30, 33, 80–83. For larger contexts, see Peter Washington, *Madame Blavatsky's Baboon: A History of the Mystics, Mediums, and Misfits Who Brought Spiritualism to America* (New York, 1995), and James Webb, *The Harmonious Circle: The Lives and Work of G. I. Gurdjieff, P. D. Ouspensky, and their Followers* (Boston, 1987).

4. Claude Bragdon, *The Beautiful Necessity* (Rochester, N.Y., 1910), 9, 22, 52, 63, 84.

5. Several letters in the Bragdon Family Papers, University of Rochester Library, deal with Claude's relation to Burgess and Hinton. See Linda Henderson,

The Fourth Dimension and Non-Euclidean Geometry in Modern Art (Princeton, 1983), 182–183, 186ff. See also Bragdon's *A Primer of Higher Space (The Fourth Dimension)* (Rochester, N.Y., 1913), quote p. 16; for "Man the Square," 59ff. On the Arensberg obsessions, see Robert M. Crunden, *American Salons*, 409–443.

6. Bragdon, *More Lives*, 163–165, with illustrations following 168. See also Claude Bragdon, *The Frozen Fountain* (New York, 1932), 41.

7. Johann Karl Friedrich Zöllner's major work available in English was *Transcendental Physics* (London, 1880). Bragdon took him very seriously, as in *Four-Dimensional Vistas* (New York, 1923), 53.

8. Bragdon, *More Lives*, 67ff, 79, 88, 291ff.; *Oracle* (Rochester, 1921).

9. See Bragdon, *Projective Ornament* (Rochester, 1915), and Alfred A. Knopf (hereafter AAK) to Claude Bragdon (hereafter CB), 6 February, 1922, Alfred A. Knopf Papers, Harry Ransom Humanities Research Center, University of Texas, Austin (hereafter cited as AAK-UT) and CB to AAK, 15 February, 1922, and 16 November, 1922. See also AAK to CB, 4 November, 1922 on spring book designs and 16 May, 1923, on *Buddenbrooks*. AAK, Inc. to CB, 23 May, 1923, is very specific in its insistence on projective ornament rather than alternatives with which CB was experimenting. On Gurdjieff, see AAK to CB, 20 and 23 March, 1931; on Rudhyar, AAK to CB, 13 and 20 November, 1933, and CB to AAK, 17 November, 1938. The firm humored Bragdon through *More Lives* (1938) but turned down *The Arch Lectures* (1942) and offered highly skeptical criticisms of a subsequent yoga manuscript. See Scott Mabon's caustic remarks dated 31 August, 1942, AAK to CB, 10 September, 1942, and CB to AAK, 12 September, 1942 and 13 March, 1943; all AAK-UT.

10. AAK to CB, 23 January and 18 October, 1922, and 4 January, 1923; CB to AAK, 15 February and 18 October, 1922, AAK-UT. Numerous other letters rather inflate the sales of *Tertium Organum*, somewhat to Knopf's irritation.

11. For an important sampling of primary material and factual information, see Merrily E. Taylor's Yale University Library catalog, *Remembering Pyotr Demianovich Ouspensky* (New Haven, 1978). The best study of the Russian background is now Maria Carlson, *"No Religion Higher than Truth": A History of the Theosophical Movement in Russia, 1875–1922* (Princeton, 1993), especially 3–37, 73–76 and 114–136. For Carlson's useful summary, see her "Fashionable Occultism: Spiritualism, Theosophy, Freemasonry and Hermeticism in Fin-de-Siècle Russia," in Bernice Glatzer Rosenthal, ed., *The Occult in Russian and Soviet Culture* (Ithaca, 1997), 135–152. For an even broader context in the history of religion, see Bruce F. Campbell, *Ancient Wisdom Revived: A History of the Theosophical Movement* (Berkeley, 1980). Both Ouspensky and Bragdon contributed ideas to such Russian artists as Kazimir Malevich as well; see Robert C. Williams, *Artists in Revolution: Portraits of the Russian Avant-Garde, 1905–1925* (Bloomington, Ind., 1977), 117–123.

12. Bragdon, *More Lives*, 260ff. Bragdon, *Four-Dimensional Vistas*, introduction to the second edition; unsigned forward to P. D. Ouspensky, *Tertium Organum* (New York, 1981).

13. Bragdon, *Tertium Organum*, 33, 37; the passage is too long to quote usefully here, but for a relatively lucid summary of core ideas, see 226–227. The pre-eminent guide to all this literature remains Henderson, *Fourth Dimension*. For the context in religious history, see Robert S. Ellwood, *Religious and Spiritual Groups in Modern America* (Englewood Cliffs, N.J., 1973), has helpful sections, 74ff., 88ff., 159ff.

14. Bragdon, See *More Lives*, 195, for a list of plays Bragdon designed.

15. Ibid., 321ff.

16. Blanche Matthias to CB, February 1926, as printed in Sarah Whittaker Peters, *Becoming O'Keeffe* (New York, 1991); see 72–79, passim. There is a substantial Bragdon/Stieglitz correspondence for the 1930s, with copies at both Rochester and Yale; and Bragdon's letters to Dorothy Brett, also at Yale, have numerous references to the couple as well.

SIXTEEN

1. Ezra Pound (hereafter EP) to Harriet Monroe, 5 August, 1914, *Poetry* Papers, University of Chicago; EP to Margaret Anderson (hereafter MA), 29 November, 1916, 26 January and 8 February, 1917, in Thomas L. Scott et al., eds., *Pound/*The Little Review: *The Letters of Ezra Pound to Margaret Anderson:* The Little Review *Correspondence* (New York, 1988), 3–18 (hereafter cited as *Pound/*LR). The best history of the journal is still Jackson R. Bryer, "'A Trial Track for Racers': Margaret Anderson and The Little Review" (Ph.D. diss., University of Wisconsin, 1965). Once rare, the magazine became readily available in 1967 when Kraus Reprints reproduced it in toto. Citations will be to this edition. Note that some issues of the original had incorrect volume numbers.

2. Margaret Anderson, *My Thirty Years' War* (New York, 1969), 174–175 (hereafter cited as MA, *30 Years*); Jane Heap, "James Joyce," most readily available in Margaret Anderson, ed., *The* Little Review *Anthology* (New York, 1953), 129–131.

3. John Quinn to EP, 2 June and 31 October, 1917, as quoted in B. L. Reid, *The Man from New York: John Quinn and his Friends* (New York, 1968), 287–289; EP to MA, ascribed to ? May 1917 in D. D. Paige, ed., *The Selected Letters of Ezra Pound 1907–1941* (New York, 1971), 111–112.

4. Quinn to EP, 24 September and 16 October, 1920, in Reid, *Quinn*, 344–346, 442ff.; see also 291. For other details, see Jackson R. Bryer, "Joyce, *Ulysses*, and the *Little Review*," *South Atlantic Quarterly* 66 (Spring, 1967), 148–164.

5. MA, *30 Years*, is often chronologically unreliable or just vague, but see 206ff. especially 230–231.

6. MA, *30 Years*, 130–132 and passim; *The Fiery Fountains* (New York, 1969), 5–7 (hereafter cited as MA, *Fiery Fountains*). For a brief sketch of Anderson's life, see Mathilda M. Hills, "Margaret Carolyn Anderson," in Barbara Sicherman and Carol Hurd Green, eds., *Notable American Women: The Modern Period* (Cambridge, Mass., 1980), 21–23. For a larger portrait, see Hugh Ford, *Four Lives in Paris* (San Francisco, 1987).

7. Georgette Leblanc, *Souvenirs: My Life with Maeterlinck* (New York, 1932), deals with French musical material only; *La Machine à courage* (Paris, 1947), 61–66, 80–81, 87–90, portrays MA, George Antheil, and Bernardsville. MA, *Fiery Fountains*, 6–9, 57, gives MA's version.

8. MA, *30 Years*, 243ff.; Little Review *Anthology*, 339, 344–346.

9. Virtually all of MA's writings after *30 Years* are devoted to a series of meditative rambles over this material: see *Fiery Fountains; The Strange Necessity* (New York, 1969); and *The Unknowable Gurdjieff* (London, 1991).

10. MA, *Fiery Fountains*, 108ff.; Gorham Munson, *The Awakening Twenties* (Baton Rouge, 1985), ch. 15. See also: Louise Welch, *Orage with Gurdjieff in America* (London, 1982), ch. 1; Susan Jenkins Brown, *Robber Rocks: Letters and Memories of Hart Crane, 1923–1932* (Middletown, Conn., 1969), 25; Cynthia Earl Kerman and Richard Eldredge, *The Lives of Jean Toomer* (Baton Rouge, 1987), 126ff.; Thomas S. W. Lewis, ed., *Letters of Hart Crane and his Family* (New York, 1974), 367, apparently misdates this as 1924; the letter itself has only a guess of 9–24 November.

11. MA, *Fiery Fountains*, 110ff.

12. Louise Welch, *Orage with Gurdjieff*, ch. 1; William Seabrook, *Witchcraft: Its Power in the World Today* (London, 1970), pt. 3, ch. 3. Colin Wilson, *The Occult* (London, 1971), 385–412, bases much of his account on Seabrook; see especially 393–394.

13. Munson, *Awakening Twenties*, 255, 258–261. T. S. Matthews, *Name and Address* (New York, 1960), 204–207, has a sardonic recollection of Gurdjieff very different in tone. Edmund Wilson recalled Matthews without naming him in an even more caustic account: see "The Consequences of the Crash," *The Shores of Light* (New York, 1952), 494–497. As Wilson points out, Croly was much more involved, contrary to his image in conventional academic writing. See David W. Levy, *Herbert Croly of* the New Republic (Princeton, 1985), 295–299.

14. MA, *Fiery Fountains*, 114; Leblanc, *Machine*, 198–200; Glenda Dawn Goss, *Music and the Moderns: The Life and Works of Carol Robinson* (Metuchen, N.J., 1993), 40 and passim; Welch, *Orage with Gurdjieff*, 40–41.

15. My chief source for material on Gurdjieff and the life at Prieuré is James Webb, *The Harmonious Circle;* although unfootnoted, it has an extensive bibliographical apparatus. For Mansfield, see Cherry A. Hankin, ed., *Letters Between Katherine Mansfield and John Middleton Murry* (New York, 1988), 373, 377–381, 385–388.

16. Webb, *Harmonious Circle*, 140–146, is probably the most lucid brief overview, although the memoir literature leaves the distinct impression that no two believers agreed fully about any definable idea. See also MA, *Gurdjieff*, 23 and passim; and Colin Wilson, *Occult*, 394–412. For primary material, see Ouspensky's *In Search of the Miraculous* (New York, 1949) and Gurdjieff's *Meetings with Remarkable Men* (New York, 1963). The very hardy should turn to Walter Driscoll, et al., *Gurdjieff: An Annotated Bibliography* (New York, 1985).

17. Thomas de Hartmann, *Our Life with Mr. Gurdjieff*, revised and enlarged from memoirs of Olga de Hartmann (San Francisco, 1983). For a useful summary

of relevant memoir literature, see Roger Lipsey, "Gurdjieff Observed," in Jacob Needleman and George Baker, eds., *Gurdjieff* (Paris, 1992; New York, 1996), 324–350.

18. MA, *Fiery Fountains*, 116–128.

19. MA, *Gurdjieff*, 28–29; Kathryn C. Hulme, *Undiscovered Country* (Boston, 1966), chs. 4–6, quote from 73. See also Brenda Wineapple, *Genêt* (New York, 1989), passim, and Irving Drutman, ed., *Janet Flanner's World: Uncollected Writings 1932–1975* (New York, 1979), 319–332.

20. Goss, *Robinson*, xviii, 25, 43; Robert C. Twombly, *Frank Lloyd Wright* (New York, 1973), 147, 172, 175–176.

21. See Peter Blake, *The Master Builders* (New York, 1976), 393.

22. Lincoln Kirstein, *Mosaic: Memoirs* (New York, 1994), 126–155. See also Nicholas Jenkins, ed., *By With To & From: A Lincoln Kirstein Reader* (New York, 1991), 63–67. For a recent example in British theatrical circles, see Peter Brook, *Threads of Time* (Washington, 1998).

CODA

1. For students interested chiefly in literature, the most useful memoir remains the revised edition of Malcolm Cowley, *Exile's Return* (New York, 1951). Close behind it are the Robert McAlmon/Kay Boyle revision of *Being Geniuses Together* (New York, 1968) and the Canadian Morley Callaghan's carefully crafted and focused memoir of 1929, *That Summer in Paris* (New York, 1963). Matthew Josephson, *Life Among the Surrealists* (New York, 1962) and Gorham Munson, *The Awakening Twenties* (Baton Rouge, 1985), were still feuding into the grave.

Many memoirists were only on the fringes of both Paris life and/or modernism. Harold Stearns, *Confessions of a Harvard Man* (Santa Barbara, 1984; orig. *The Street I Know* [New York, 1935]), devoted much of his time to alcohol and gambling. Samuel Putnam, *Paris was our Mistress* (Carbondale, 1970), survived chiefly as a translator. However famous he has become, William Carlos Williams was chiefly a family doctor in a New Jersey suburb of New York. *The Autobiography of William Carlos Williams* (New York, 1951) suffers not only from his geographical marginality, but from health problems during the writing of the book. Another Canadian, John Glassco, in *Memoirs of Montparnasse* (Toronto, 1970), offers the most atmospheric account of the years around 1930. There are numerous other volumes, most notably those of Stein, Hemingway, and Margaret Anderson, that supply information and anecdotes but are less reliable even by the relaxed standards of the genre.

In the classical music area, the two best memoirs are Virgil Thomson, *Virgil Thomson* (New York, 1967), although it carefully avoids the central issue of homosexuality; and George Antheil, *Bad Boy of Music* (New York, 1945). Jazz works are almost always filtered publicly through collaborators. The best relevant to this early phase are Mezz Mezzrow and Bernard Wolfe, *Really the Blues* (New York, 1946); Ethel Waters with Charles Samuels, *His Eye Is on the Sparrow* (New York, 1951); Pops Foster, *The Autobiography of a New Orleans Jazzman*, as told to

Tom Stoddard (Berkeley, 1971); Sidney Bechet, *Treat It Gentle* (New York, 1960); and Alan Lomax, *Mister Jelly Roll* (Berkeley, 1973).

In the visual arts, Man Ray, *Self Portrait* (Boston, 1963), stands virtually alone.

2. Malcolm Cowley, *Exile's Return*, esp. 6, 9, 16–20, 38, 60–63, 214, 218, 224–226, 240–241, 287.

LIST OF ABBREVIATIONS
USED IN NOTES

NAMES

AAK: Alfred A. Knopf
HC: Hart Crane
AC: Aaron Copland
HPR: Henri-Pierre Roché
AD: Arthur Dove
HS: Herbert Seligman
AKM: Arthur K. McComb
JDP: John Dos Passos
AP: Anita Pollitzer
JHL: John Howard Lawson
AS: Alfred Stieglitz
JJ: James Joyce
AT: Allen Tate
JT: Jean Toomer
BK: Blanche Knopf
KB: Kenneth Burke
BS: Barbara Sessions
CB: Claude Bragdon
CR: Carl Ruggles
LH: Langston Hughes
CS: Charles Sheeler
MA: Margaret Anderson
CVV: Carl Van Vechten
MB: Mary Louise Bok
EB: Ernest Bloch
MD: Marcel Duchamp

EEC: E. E. Cummings
MP: Maxwell Perkins
EH: Ernest Hemingway
PR: Paul Rosenfeld
EO'N: Eugene O'Neill
PS: Paul Strand
EP: Ezra Pound
EW: Edmund Wilson
RS: Roger Sessions
FHW: Florence H.
   Williams
SA: Sherwood Anderson
FSF: F. Scott Fitzgerald
ST: Scofield Thayer
GA: George Antheil
VT: Virgil Thomson
GM: Gorham Munson
WA: Walter Arensberg
GO'K: Georgia O'Keeffe
WCW: William Carlos
   Williams
GS: Gertrude Stein
WF: Waldo Frank
WRM: Walter Rumsey
   Marvin
WS: Wallace Stevens

ARCHIVAL COLLECTIONS

AAK-UT: Alfred A. Knopf Papers, Harry Ransom Humanities Research Center, University of Texas, Austin

AGD-AAA: Arthur G. Dove Papers, Archives of American Art

AS-YU: Alfred Stieglitz Papers, Beinecke Library, Yale University

CR-YU: Carl Ruggles Papers, School of Music Library, Yale University

CS-AAA: Charles Sheeler Papers, Archives of American Art

EP-YU: Ezra Pound Papers, Beinecke Library, Yale University

GA-LC: George Antheil Correspondence, Library of Congress

HPR-UT: Henri-Pierre Roché Papers, Carlton Lake Collection, Harry Ransom Humanities Research Center, University of Texas, Austin

KB-PSU: Kenneth Burke Papers, Pennsylvania State University Library

KDSA-YU: Katherine Dreier Société Anonyme Papers, Beinecke Library, Yale University

JHL-SIU: John Howard Lawson Papers, Southern Illinois University Library, Carbondale

PR-YU: Paul Rosenfeld Papers, Beinecke Library, Yale University

PS-CCP: Paul Strand Archive, Center for Creative Photography, Tucson

SA-NL: Sherwood Anderson Papers, Newberry Library, Chicago

ST-YU: Scofield Thayer Papers, Beinecke Library, Yale University

WA-PMA: Walter Arensberg Papers, Philadelphia Museum of Art

WCW-YU: William Carlos Williams Papers, Beinecke Library, Yale University

OTHER ABBREVIATIONS

BGT: *Being Geniuses Together,* by Robert McAlmon and Kay Boyle

CEP: *Collected Earlier Poems of William Carlos Williams*

JOHP: Jazz Oral History Project, Institute of Jazz Studies, Rutgers University, Newark

NAACP: National Association for the Advancement of Colored People

NORK: New Orleans Rhythm Kings

ODJB: Original Dixieland Jazz Band

SSO: Southern Syncopated Orchestra

WCWR: *William Carlos Williams Review*

ABOUT THE AUTHOR

Robert Crunden was Professor of American Studies at the University of Texas, Austin. His previous books include *A Brief History of American Culture* (1990, 1994), *American Salons: Encounters with European Modernism, 1885–1917* (1992), and *Ministers of Reform: The Progressives' Achievement in American Civilization, 1889–1920* (1982). He died in March 1999 at the age of 58.

A NOTE ON THE TYPE

This book is set in Caslon type. Around 1720, after some years as an engraver of guns, William Caslon opened a type foundry in London. Caslon's types were immediately recognized for their natural elegance, simplicity and legibility. His work established England as a primary source of type and printing, which broke its dependence on Europe.

As an example of Caslon's wide appeal, Benjamin Franklin caused the first authenticated copies of the Declaration of Independence to be printed using Caslon types. This typeface was the choice of the late 18th century literati and today *The New Yorker* magazine continues to print in Caslon.

Excepting a brief fall from favor in the early 19th century, Caslon's design continues to have a remarkable life. Dozens of foundries and designers have issued variants bearing Caslon's name but rarely his sophistication.

INDEX